2021: A Musical Odyssey

By Adam Colton

To Buy Or Not To Buy:
A Uniquely Personal Guide To Classic Rock
Albums

"It is amazing that evolution has produced creatures that can communicate emotions through music, yet these same creatures try to solve most of their problems by killing each other"

– Adam Colton

Contents

Prologue – Simply The Best

Let's start at the top.

This is primarily a book of music reviews and there are more genres of music than there are stars in the universe. Well, not quite, but it must be close.

For you to know whether or not it is worth picking up this book and taking it to the till you need to know the kind of music we will be reviewing, so I will present to you what at the age of 45 are my top ten favourite songs of all time. I guess these could be categorised as 'classic rock,' and as we get into the nitty-gritty of this book other more diverse artists and genres will appear, but this is the bread and butter I guess. If none of the songs appeal, you probably listen to Radio 1! And that's not an insult, by the way; it means you are young.

I should state that this is a book of opinions and I don't expect everybody to agree with everything I write. Any comments that indicate otherwise are intended as humorous, as music is such a subjective topic but one that arouses such strong passions that we often believe that our own taste is definitive. So let's cut the waffle and get to the 'crux of the biscuit' to paraphrase Frank Zappa. If you wish, you can use your imagination a bit and think of legendary DJ Alan Freeman doing the countdown. Not 'arf!

10) Kings of Leon – Slow Night So Long (2004)

This was the first Kings of Leon song I ever heard, a little behind the times in 2007, while 'sitting on a railway station, with a ticket to my destination' and a personal CD player. Having pretty much given up on modern music I wasn't expecting much, but by the time I got to the full blown chaos at the end of the first verse with its stubbornly unusual drum rhythm I knew this band was something different. The track contains a hidden tune at the end which shows the Kings in a much more laid back frame of mind. All these years later the band are a regular soundtrack to the many camping trips I have with friends and I can even understand Caleb Followill's vocals.

9) Oasis – The Masterplan (1995)

Originally just a B-side to the Wonderwall single, I would declare this to be a far superior song that gets only a fraction of the airplay. Noel Gallagher handles the vocal of this ballad which begins in a minor key expressing confusion and alternates with a major key chorus stating 'All we know is that we don't know.' The backwards guitar solo is no doubt a nod to their Liverpudlian heroes, the Beatles, as is the reference to Ringo Starr's 'Octopus's Garden' recited in a slightly silly voice at the end.

8) Dire Straits – Private Investigations (1982)

I first heard this brooding classic on the BBC Radio 1 top 40 chart run-down when I was seven years old. Mark Knopfler's lyrics and vocal delivery are slightly menacing sounding with some succulent Spanish style guitar runs. Once the words 'private investigations' are uttered half way through, the mysterious ambience is unleashed for several more tense minutes.

7) The Beatles – While My Guitar Gently Weeps (1968)

George Harrison's finest song in my opinion, although I cannot claim to having heard all of his solo work. This 'White Album' track includes Eric Clapton as a guest for the weeping guitar solo to augment George's lyrics expressing the frustration that any thinking person will have about humanity's behaviour. This seems to be a message that is more urgent than ever today, yet I have a sneaking suspicion that George was channelling his frustration about his bandmates at this time as much as anything.

6) Queen – The Show Must Go On (1991)

It is surprising that the lyrics were as much Brian May's creation as Freddie Mercury's at a time when Freddie was literally staring death in the face. Here he gives the 'life is all a show' theme all he can muster, perhaps knowing that it is virtually his final chance, while Brian May whips off one of his most evocative guitar solos. It doesn't get much more dramatic.

5) Lynyrd Skynyrd – Free Bird (1973)

The guitar hero's favourite. This nine-minute track begins as a ballad with some gentle slide guitar and lyrics about a wish to keep moving on. Upon reaching the conclusion of being unable to change, the duelling guitar solos illustrate the metaphor of the bird breaking free. The whole band then go full tilt for almost six minutes of frenetic soloing. Each time you think it can't get any more intense the string-bends move up the fretboard a little further.

4) The Beatles – A Day In The Life (1967)

I remember listening to this as a teenager on a Walkman in my grandparents' bedroom and thinking 'This is scary sounding. I'm never taking drugs!' This, the closing track to 'Sgt. Pepper,' sees John Lennon pitying those whose lives he views as dull and unenlightened, before an orchestral riot leads to McCartney's jaunty bridge, a little like the hurricane taking Dorothy to the Land of Oz. Lennon's lugubriousness has the final say before the orchestral chaos leads to one of the longest notes in rock music, hammered out on five pianos simultaneously if I remember rightly. Even the Beatles couldn't really top this for ingenuity.

3) Queen – Bohemian Rhapsody (1975)

A superbly crafted classic that never grows stale. The first time I heard this was on the bus going to school. I thought 'What a depressing song!' How things change. 'Bo Rhap' opens with feelings of regret, gradually building into a whirlpool of despair with Brian May's solo leading into the operatic middle section which perhaps represents madness taking over or even fear of Hell. Then the rocking finale breaks out as if to say that the music is even bigger than all of that. Yet, Freddie Mercury's melancholic vocal has the final word, before the gong at the end seals his character's fate.

2) Pink Floyd – Comfortably Numb (1979)

A rare writing collaboration between David Gilmour and Roger Waters. The verse and chorus are a vocal duel between Waters, who is trying to coax the central character out of his apathy, and Gilmour declaring that all is fine in his fantasy world. The first guitar solo sets the tone before David Gilmour lets rip properly for the dramatic conclusion. Nick Mason's cymbals hammer out the devastation just for good measure at the end. The track fades just a bit too early in my opinion, but maybe it's best to leave us wanting more.

1) Led Zeppelin – Stairway To Heaven (1971)

A song so good that I even walked down the aisle to its opening strains. This begins in a quiet folky style and gradually picks up the pace and volume. John Bonham picks up his drumsticks about half way through and eventually Jimmy Page's guitar solo takes it into another dimension. Then, just when you think there's no way they are going to top that, Robert Plant gives it the full power vocal treatment as a crescendo. The lyrics are ambiguous enough that you can make it about anything you want. For me it seems to be about making choices in life, so it seemed perfectly fitting as a wedding song.

And here are a few tracks that nearly made the top ten:

The Animals - House Of The Rising Sun (1964) An impassioned lament for a wasted life. This was a much older song recorded by Woody Guthrie among others, which appeared with this tune on Bob Dylan's debut album before the

Animals took it to number one in the UK.

Procol Harum – A Whiter Shade Of Pale (1967) A gibberish classic which reinvents Bach. The Beatles might have consciously tried to top this with 'I Am The Walrus.'

Gerry Rafferty – Baker Street (1978) Irascibly, I include this song not just for the much-loved saxophone part but for the impassioned guitar solo which seems to hack into your central nervous system every time. I think that's what people call 'goose bumps!'

Rolling Stones – Gimme Shelter (1969) This moody sounding track opens the 'Let It Bleed' album and only narrowly pips 'You Can't Always Get What You Want' for me, which is the track that closes it.

The Kinks - Waterloo Sunset (1967) Ray Davies' wistful song is evocative of gazing out over the Thames. This was one of the first songs that I really took notice of when playing taped 'hand me down' records as a child.

And for a couple by female vocalists I would choose the following:

Peggy Lee – Is That All There Is (1969) A dark song about the futility of all things, delivered theatrically. When I first heard it as a child I thought the lyrics were heinous, now I view it as a bitter-sweet classic.

Bobbie Gentry – Ode To Billy Joe (1967) A story song set to a lone acoustic guitar with haunting strings. Did Billy Joe commit suicide? One of the darkest things to hit the pop charts in the sixties.

If you want a second Pink Floyd choice I'd go for 'The Great Gig In The Sky.' If you want a second Led Zeppelin choice I'd go for 'Since I've Been Loving You.' For Oasis try 'Champagne Supernova.' For Kings of Leon maybe 'Arizona.' For the Beatles just buy all their albums and listen to the whole lot!

Chapter 1 – Musical Youth

I do not claim to have had a life that readers will want to pour over, such as those of many of the rock stars who feature in this book, but I include personal memories to illustrate how music can colour even the most ordinary of lives. I was born in 1975 in the town of Ashford in Kent, a town that is now spreading almost as fast as coronavirus. We lived in a nearby village for the first four months of my life, before moving to a larger village four miles down the road. Needless to say I don't remember my first home.

I remember hearing the 1979 number one 'Video Killed The Radio Star' by Buggles emanating from a transistor radio in my grandparents' kitchen, which would make me four, but my first real experience of music was through 'hand me down' records received from older relatives. I had a portable record player that operated at four speeds – 16 2/3, 33 1/3, 45 and 78. I have still not seen a 16 rpm record to this day, concluding that they are as rare as the ejectamenta of the proverbial rocking horse. Among the 45s that were tossed my way were Chuck Berry's novelty single 'My Ding-A-Ling,' the Carpenters version of 'Jambalaya' backed with 'Mr. Guder,' and the theme music to Van der Valk, namely 'Eye Level' by the Simon Park Orchestra. This had the theme to TV's 'Crown Court' on the flip side.

Albums began to be flung my way from various aunts and uncles, and I particularly remember the Marble Arch compilations of hits from the sixties which introduced me to such classics as 'A Whiter Shade Of Pale' by Procol Harum and 'Waterloo Sunset' by the Kinks, both of which would still be on any 'favourites' list of mine today.

I had a friend called Mark who was a year older than me and lived across the road, and it always seemed mysterious that his parents' vinyl record of the greatest hits of the Kinks should also contain the very same track, 'Waterloo Sunset,' as my 'various artists' record of the hits of 1967. Two different pieces of vinyl; one song, Thus I was introduced to the concept of the compilation album. And I didn't feel a thing! I was also introduced to the concept of vulgarity as humour as Mark regularly postulated that cassette tape was something extremely nasty sandwiched between two pieces of Sellotape. While some music could be likened to the brown stuff, I don't think there was a lot of credence to his theory.

My parents still watched 'Top Of The Pops' on TV in those days but bedtime for me was at 7pm. My mother used to pacify me by saying that I could still hear it from upstairs, which was true, but what about the 'vision' part of 'television?' Particularly memorable were the Shakin' Stevens hits which always seemed to end the show, seemingly holding their place at number one week after week. Let's not forget, the Welsh rock and roller was the UK's biggest selling singles artist of the eighties.

I found records fascinating as a child, and when I wasn't spinning the black circles I used to cut out discs of paper and draw the grooves on them between the songs, pretending to be playing them as I rambled my way through self-composed gibberish, even amusing one of my primary school teachers by singing a bizarre ditty that I'd made up and thought was the cleverest thing since the Kinks. My father used to record me singing this 'material' on a reel to reel tape recorder, and when he upgraded to a radio cassette player I immediately wanted one of my own. This I duly received as my fifth birthday present and I rewarded my parents by repeatedly playing a tape recording of my mother asking my father if he'd left the kettle on before going out to which he responded 'Bugger the kettle!' Classic 'fly on the wall' stuff!

From then on for the next ten years I would tape my vinyl records onto cassettes. I have no idea why I did this. Walkmans had yet to catch on, so I only played music at home, negating any real need to copy the vinyl. Albums I received as 'hand me downs' included Suzi Quatro's 'Your Mamma Won't Like Me,' a three-LP box set by the Wombles (alias Mike Batt) and '20 Golden Greats' by the Shadows. I also had 45s of Rod Stewart's 'Sailing' and 'Fanfare For The Common Man' by Emerson, Lake & Palmer. Looking back, it really wasn't a bad start in life musically at all!

Of course the other children at school had very different tastes, preferring the bands of the eighties such as Wham! - the exclamation mark is part of the name, not a sign of my excitement. The girls unilaterally adored George Michael and detested Andrew Ridgeley, as though the pair were a perfect balance of yin and yang, but I never understood this. Maybe it was something to do with female hormones. I do remember a girl being surprised to hear me singing the Thompson Twins hit 'Doctor! Doctor!' making a comment along the lines of 'I didn't know you liked pop music.' I didn't.

I seemed to prefer the company of my grandparents to other children at this age; at least their musical tastes made more sense to me. My paternal grandmother was always singing, and I consequently absorbed a range of songs from a span of around sixty years. Favourites of hers included 'Blueberry Hill' by Fats Domino, Abba's 'I Have A Dream' which she was convinced was by Doris Day, Lena Martell's 'One Day At A Time' and Donald Peers' signature tune 'In A Shady Nook By A Babbling Brook.' As I only had a couple of young friends, including one with unsavoury ideas about cassette tape, it seemed inevitable that these tastes would rub off.

At the same time I used to spend every Friday night with my maternal grandparents. Breakfast TV was a new thing, and there used to be a children's show called 'Data Run' on every Saturday morning, presented by Lulu's sister Edwina Lawrie. Apart from liking Edwina in an innocent schoolboy's way, there were always pop videos on this show and I recall seeing Tears For Fears singing their classic 'Shout' on a clifftop. This was a rare thing – a song I actually liked from the eighties. There was also David Bowie belting out 'Let's Dance' standing against a tiled wall – another ripper!

Every Sunday morning I used to listen to Barbara Sturgeon's Sunday request programme on BBC Radio Kent. Here I discovered a bit of Beatles stuff, although very old fashioned requests for artists such as Billy Cotton were still being made at this time. I even sent in a couple of requests by letter myself, these being for my grandmother who also listened religiously to the show. Meanwhile, my mother was fan of country artists such as Billy Jo Spears and George Hamilton IV, so I also found myself listening to Wally Whyton's Country Club on BBC Radio 2 on Thursday nights.

One unusual excursion musically was a penchant I had for taping the music from the test card on TV. There were only three channels at the time, and these often ran out of programmes, so for long periods during the daytime we were treated to a static image of a girl with a blackboard and a doll, surrounded by various shaded squares that were designed to help you to correctly tune in your TV. Indeed, you had to tune in the channels by twiddling a knob in those days. This televisual equivalent of wallpaper was accompanied by what I would describe as Musak, but I had tapes and tapes of the stuff! Later, technology pepped things up a bit and the test card was replaced with pages from teletext – basically a screen filled with printed news and information, accompanied by the same perfunctory music.

The BBC teletext service was called Ceefax, and when Channel Four came along showing pages from a rival service called Oracle, I discovered that these 'new kids on the block' had better tunes. There was country, jazz, orchestral bits, you name it, and I filled a pack of four brightly coloured cassettes I had been given as a Christmas present in no time.

During secondary school, the tastes of my fellow pupils began to change. They would regularly talk of bands such as Pink Floyd and Black Sabbath, which I now regard as 'classic,' but at the time I just wanted to hear stuff that my grandmother liked – she seemed to be the ultimate arbiter of taste as far as I was concerned. I did watch 'The Chart Show' on TV before going off to Friday night Scout meetings though, but more as research into modern tastes than anything, finding the variety of genres quite interesting. There was a dance chart, a heavy metal chart and an indie chart. I had no idea that 'indie' just meant music released on independent labels, but I noticed that the indie chart invariably contained the most unusual music, such as 'Birthday' by the Sugarcubes, the Icelandic band with Björk as the vocalist. I also used to record the songs I liked from BBC Radio 1's top forty rundown on Sunday evenings. I had been doing this on and off since 1982, when I first encountered the mysterious Dire Straits track 'Private Investigations' as well as the Animals classic 'House Of The Rising Sun' (which re-entered the chart that year). By the late eighties, the chart songs that I actually liked were definitely in the minority, with Stock, Aitken and Waterman's hit machine all too prominent for my liking. I still thought the sixties wiped the floor when it came to music.

My grandmother died in January 1990, so I was then attempting to formulate my own tastes with no octogenarian guide. I had heard music from 'Wet Wet Wet' to

13

the Beach Boys during Scout camps and I used to bring along my own compilations of sixties stuff that I thought my peers could tolerate.

At the time my home town of Ashford had a market in the town centre, before it was flung out into the suburbs like a disgraced schoolboy. Later everyone scratched their heads as to why the town centre was dying. Once at college, I used to catch the train into the town from my village, with an extra trip on Saturdays to visit the library, eat a McDonald's burger and frequent the market to buy tapes. This was the height of hedonism at the age of sixteen! The first tapes that I bought were of the Beach Boys and the Hollies. Or so I thought. I'd actually been duped into buying two tapes of covers by tribute bands, one of which was called the Surf Men. It was some serious feat of lateral thinking to come up with that name, right?

Not satisfied with this, I then purchased the genuine albums from the shops instead. However, not every shop in every town stocked the same albums, so I began to spend my hard earned paper round wages, not just on the cassettes themselves, but on train fares to get to other towns where the selection in Woolworths, Boots, John Menzies, WHSmith and Our Price was slightly different. I was branching out into the uncharted territory of Maidstone, Canterbury, Folkestone and Hastings. And I guess this is where we come to the reviews.

The entire premise of this book is that music and memories go hand in hand, and as you probably don't know me, a book of my memories isn't going to cut the mustard, but how about a book of reviews of the albums that lit life's path like streetlights on a winter's night? Well, that's a different kettle of fish. So, without further ado, I thank you for reading this preamble and let's launch ourselves into the material that I listened to in the second half of my teenage years with gusto. No, I don't know who 'Gusto' is either.

Chapter 2 – Teenage Kicks

Please beware, the chapter titles refer to songs or artists that are often not featured in this book, so if you're a huge fan of the Undertones, I'm afraid nearly all of the music in this chapter predates punk considerably.

As I suspect is the case for many, my teenage years were not a time of wild abandon or punk rebellion, they were really quite introspective. I didn't have a group of friends as such but established a peer group through attending weekly meetings. School came to an end, Scouts led to Venture Scouts and I remember feeling the sting of depressive thoughts for the first time when on a coach coming home from my final summer camp. This had been located at the top of Fairlight Cliffs near Hastings in Sussex, conveniently situated above a naturist colony – a literal 'eye opener' for youngsters like ourselves!

I wasn't someone who formed friendships easily, so during my first year of college my best friends were often songs, some of them still are, but at an age that seems perilously young now, one is still learning, and what was comfortable for me at the time was to explore the music of the past. My mother had always stated that the music of the sixties was the best, so it seemed a logical place to start. Uncool, though it may have been, my interest in music began with compilations of greatest hits, and thus our ship begins its voyage upon the soundwaves and sinewaves of the latter part of the twentieth century.

2.1) 20 Golden Greats – The Beach Boys (1976)

EMI's '20 Golden Greats' series was a great way for youngsters like myself to discover more about the classic bands of the past. Inevitably they contained all the well known hits, and occasionally an artist such as Cliff Richard, who'd had myriad dalliances with the top ten, was treated to a double album of '40 Golden Greats.' This particular Beach Boys album did exactly what it said on the tin, with 'Surfin' USA,' 'Help Me Rhonda,' 'I Get Around,' etc. included, as well as the full-length version of 'Barbara Ann' which I always enjoyed due to hearing the Beach Boys larking around after the radio edit would have faded. This track was actually from their 1965 album 'Beach Boys' Party!' where they faked a party atmosphere for an entire album.

The other track that struck a chord with me was 'Heroes And Villains.' Whilst 'Good Vibrations' dabbled with psychedelia, 'Heroes And Villains' dived headlong into the pool. The peculiar backing vocals and Halloween-organ intrigued me, as well as Van Dyke Parks' 'stream of consciousness' lyrics. Also included on '20 Golden Greats' were some of the boys' lesser known hits from the late sixties, such as 'I Can Hear Music' and 'Break Away.' It seemed that just as their popularity was fading in the USA, the British were lapping them up.

I'm not going to focus too heavily on compilations in this book, but upon borrowing 'Summer Dreams' (1990) from my auntie, I decided to purchase this later 32-track collection myself in order to gain a further twelve tracks by the band. After that it was surely time for some albums. It used to irritate me that compilations by sixties artists often included one minor hit from more recent times which tended to stick out like a sore thumb stylistically from all the others. In the case of 'Summer Dreams' it was the band's jangly cover of the classic 1965 song by the Mamas & the Papas, *California Dreamin'*.

2.2) Pet Sounds – The Beach Boys (1966)

This album regularly appears in top ten charts of the best albums of all time, and at sixteen I expected the contents to be more lively like the hits it produced, 'Wouldn't It Be Nice,' 'Sloop John B' and 'God Only Knows.' The rest of the package is a more dreamlike affair with introspective lyrics and arrangements performed by the Wrecking Crew that seem to pre-empt psychedelia. It seems that Brian Wilson was off on a tangent with Tony Asher while the other Beach Boys had to just twiddle their thumbs. 'Caroline No' exemplifies the moody feel and is followed by the sound of a passing train. Two of the tracks are dreamy instrumentals (three if you have the bonus track version of the album). My favourite song here is 'I Just Wasn't Made For These Times' which sums up how I felt as a teenager listening to this, reassured that there was at least one other person who felt completely detached from what his peers were doing, his name being Brian Wilson. This was heady stuff from the band that gave us 'Fun Fun Fun.'

2.3) 20 Golden Greats – The Hollies (1978)

The 'Golden Greats' series never included a photo of the artist(s) on the cover, but an image that was intended to represent them. The Beach Boys image was of course a surfer; the Hollies one was of the towering chimneys of a power station in Northern England.

Of course I was familiar with 'I'm Alive,' 'He Ain't Heavy (He's My Brother),' 'The Air That I Breathe,' 'I Can't Let Go,' etc., but there was also the bluesy 'Long Cool Woman In A Black Dress' which was a much bigger hit in the USA than in their homeland, sounding like Dire Straits before Dire Straits existed. When I eventually bought 'The Air That I Breathe' (1993), which was a more comprehensive compilation, I discovered a couple more tracks in this style, namely 'The Day That Curly Billy Shot Down Crazy Sam McGee' and 'Hey Willy.' Personally I always wished that the Hollies had churned out a few more of these rocky guitar tracks in the early seventies. Mike Batt's 'Soldier' is the glaring omission in the selection however, being a superb symphonic creation written by the creative force behind the Wombles. The 'eighties sore thumb' on 'The Air That I Breathe' was a cover of Nick Kershaw's 'The Woman I Love.' In hindsight, I now quite like the song.

2.4) 20 Golden Greats – The Shadows (1977)

Having been given this album on vinyl as a child I decided that a cassette upgrade was in order. At the time, I had still to learn to play the guitar, quite possibly the best single decision I made in my entire life, but Hank Marvin is of course one of the pioneers of the instrument and sadly not celebrated as often as he should be these days. In these modern times of short attention spans it has been said that if no lyrics appear within seven seconds listeners merely move on to another track, but instrumental hits were once hugely popular, and the Shadows had no less than five UK number ones. Among the more unusual tracks that I liked were 'The Rise And Fall Of Fingal Blunt' and 'The Warlord' which was heavy rock before heavy rock was a *thing*. If anybody knows who Fingal Blunt was, please enlighten me.

2.5) 40 Golden Greats – Cliff Richard (1977)

Harry Webb, alias Cliff, has had a poor press at times, often being viewed as uncool and 'middle of the road.' Whilst some of the material may sound twee to modern ears, this collection of early hits should at least provide some kind of counter-argument. Opening with 'Move It,' Cliff started out as the 'English Elvis.' It's a shame we aren't treated to more early rockers here. As the sixties dawned, ballads were en vogue and Cliff jumped on board at once. Elvis did the same, so you can put those claws away. The mid-sixties produced a run of interesting songs from 'In The Country,' to a cover of the Rolling Stones song 'Blue Turns To Grey' and the moody track 'The Day I Met Marie.' Eschewing psychedelia, Cliff could still rock. 'Devil Woman' deserves an airing every Halloween, and my favourite is 'Throw Down A Line,' where Cliff reunites with Hank Marvin from the Shadows for an almost grungy rock song. It's all a bit out of fashion now, but if you think about it, when these artists that were rooted in the fifties changed with the times it was really as radical as when David Bowie threw himself into drum and bass in the nineties.

2.6) The Very Best Of Jim Reeves – Jim Reeves (1990)

I can hear the complaints already. It's all a bit 'easy listening' so far, right? Well, this twenty-track RCA cassette firmly belongs in the 'music my grandparents liked' genre, although my father was a big Jim Reeves fan in his younger days. The deep-voiced country balladeer achieved his only UK number one posthumously, this being 'Distant Drums' in 1966. Songs such as 'Moonlight & Roses (Bring Mem'ries Of You),' 'He'll Have To Go' and 'Welcome To My World' were all regular requests on the radio when I was a teenager in spite of already being over twenty years out of fashion. Lush strings adorn the gentle instrumentation, and there are some less often heard tracks here such as 'Snowflake' and 'The Blizzard,' another wintry tale which almost ditches the 'love and romance' theme as the central character stays with his pony and pays the ultimate price when he was 'Just a hundred yards from Mary Ann.'

I had a tape of Pat Boone's greatest hits too, but I'll move on before I get lassoed by the 'anti easy listening' brigade!

2.7) The Very Best Of The Everly Brothers, Vols 1&2– The Everly Brothers (1988 and 1990)

I knew all the big hits from my father's home-taped cassette which I listened to as a child. When I was old enough to buy music, this pair of Pickwick Music compilations were really all I needed, with the first volume covering the late fifties and the second volume covering the early sixties. The Everly Brothers' distinctive harmonies were a big influence on Simon & Garfunkel, who famously covered 'Bye Bye Love.' Teenage dilemmas are the main subject matter, so I was the target audience, although I was about thirty years late. Some tracks are amusing like 'Bird Dog' and 'Poor Jenny,' while the plane crash drama of 'Ebony Eyes' is pretty harrowing. The Everlies could really rock too. Check out 'Temptation' (1961) and 'The Price Of Love' (1965); both are underrated classics.

2.8) The Best Of Buddy Holly / The Legendary Buddy Holly – Buddy Holly (1986 and 1988)

As we have just seen, retro artists were often given a budget release of two cassettes at the time, and this pair of Pickwick tapes (the first of which was released on the Hallmark label) covered the essentials by this extremely influential artist from Lubbock, Texas who tragically lost his life in a plane crash at the age of 22. Buddy topped the UK hit parade with the Crickets in 1957 with 'That'll Be The Day' and did it again solo in 1959 with 'It Doesn't Matter Any More.' If you don't know hits like 'Peggy Sue,' its sequel 'Peggy Sue Got Married,' 'Oh Boy!' and 'Raining In My Heart' you are clearly from another planet. His real name was Charles Hardin Holley and his rock and roll was country influenced and often relatively gentle compared to the other big names of the era. A few of the ballads were overlaid with sumptuous strings, such as 'True Love Ways.'

The second volume delves deeper into the catalogue and my favourite here is the wistful 'Learnin' The Game.' 'Words Of Love' was covered by the Beatles, 'Not Fade Away' was covered by the Rolling Stones, and 'Love Is Strange' (which Buddy didn't actually write) was covered by Wings. Are you convinced yet or do I need to continue?

2.9) The Very Best Of The Mamas & The Papas – The Mamas & The Papas (1988)

The Mamas were Cass Elliot and Michelle Phillips, the Papas were her husband John Phillips and Denny Doherty, the band were from LA, the sound could be categorised as 'hippie folk pop' and the hits are all here on this Pickwick compilation - you know, 'Monday, Monday,' 'California Dreamin' and the dreamy 'Dedicated To The One I Love,' which was my favourite at the time with its wistful observation that 'Life can never be / Exactly like we want it to be.' I think these days my favourite is the autobiographical twelve-bar ditty 'Creeque Alley' which tells the story of the early years of the band. There are plenty of covers too, including 'I Call Your Name' by the Beatles. Remarkably it was the M&Ps version of this song that I heard first. Think 'strummed acoustic guitar and nice harmonies' similar to the Australian sixties group, the Seekers. Mama Cass became a household name but sadly joined the 'choir invisible' at the age of 32. Rock and roll is a dangerous game.

2.10) Golden Days: The Collection Of 20 All-Time Greats – Roy Orbison (1981)

'Golden Days' takes its name from a line in the song 'It's Over,' an archetypal ballad that soars to a crescendo, just like 'Crying' and 'In Dreams,' which together represent my three favourite Roy Orbison tracks. Another tune that I remembered hearing as a child was 'Only The Lonely.' Even then it was a 'golden oldie,' as I first heard it on a chart rundown from 1960 on Jimmy Savile's 'Old Record Club.' The less said about Savile the better.

All that, and you've still got 'Oh, Pretty Woman' to go. Roy Orbison, of course enjoyed a resurgence with his hit 'You Got It' in 1989. I was still at school at the time and I remember waking up early most mornings to listen to Ray Moore's show on BBC Radio 2. This song was popular at the time, but I've yet to find an Orbison compilation with all the studio tracks from 'Golden Days' as well as the hits from his comeback period. Let's start a wish list...

2.11) Joseph And The Amazing Technicolor Dreamcoat – Original Cast Recording (1974)

Jason Donovan had had a number one hit with 'Any Dream Will Do' in 1991, but this was a cast recording with not a single celebrity in sight, leaving one to concentrate purely on Andrew Lloyd Webber and Tim Rice's songs. I had been in a performance of the musical at primary school so it was also a bit of nostalgia for me. 'Joseph's Coat' is a basically a list of colours, one of a number of 'list songs' I'd encounter over the years, 'Potiphar' is a 1920s pastiche and Pharoah does a pretty good impression of Elvis. It's good fun and the instrumentation is quite rocky at times. Nobody else did so much to make bible stories 'cool' and 'Jesus Christ Superstar' is almost as good.

2.12) The Simon & Garfunkel Collection: 17 Of Their All-Time Greatest Hits – Simon & Garfunkel (1981)

When I was a child my dad had bought a vinyl LP in the pretty Sussex town of Rye containing the greatest hits of Simon & Garfunkel, but performed by Sefton & Bartholomew. 'Who?' I hear you ask. Had he made the same mistake as I would do a decade later with my Beach Boys and Hollies 'tribute' tapes? Who knows?

Anyway, I always quite liked the songs, and when I borrowed this particular slab of vinyl from my auntie another lifelong avenue of pleasure was opened. To a teenager, the lyrics and sophisticated production were enigmatic. Particularly striking was the dissonant orchestral section of 'Old Friends,' which seemed to represent the turmoil of loneliness in old age. Perhaps the Beatles song 'A Day In The Life' had been the catalyst for the idea of using classical instruments in such an unorthodox way. The other monster track for me was 'The Boxer,' being a largely acoustic story of loneliness that builds to a massive orchestral crescendo, complete with a thrashing drum which I understand was played in an empty lift shaft to create the desired reverberation.

2.13) The Hit Singles Album – Gerry And The Pacemakers (1986)

Until fellow Liverpudlians 'Frankie Goes To Hollywood' repeated the feat in the eighties, Gerry and co. were the only act to have their first three singles reach number one in the UK chart. They were even ahead of the Beatles when it came to hitting the top spot. This compilation is presented chronologically as a series of A and B-sides, which I think is how compilations should be presented. I am not a fan of the 'chop and change' approach that mishmashes together songs from unconnected eras - now de rigueur when it comes to assembling such selections.

A lot of this album is uptempo rocking, and there's nothing wrong with that at all, but it's the ballads that really steal the show. These are 'Don't Let The Sun Catch You Crying,' 'Ferry Cross The Mersey' and of course 'You'll Never Walk Alone,' which Gerry no doubt helped manoeuvre from its genesis in the musical 'Carousel' to its apotheosis as the anthem of Liverpool Football Club.

2.14) 20 Greatest Hits – The Beatles (1982)

I always like the moment where BBC TV's comedy character Alan Partridge is asked what his favourite Beatles album is and he reveals his lack of musical knowledge by replying 'I think I'd have to say "The Best Of The Beatles,"' but in truth isn't that where we all started? Yes, this was the first Beatles tape that I owned, and apart from the opening track of 'Love Me Do' every other track on the album was a UK number one hit – seventeen of them to be exact, with two being double A-sides. For youngsters, that meant you flipped the bit of plastic over and there was an equally good song on the back of it!

As a result, the group's early years are perhaps better represented here, as the main focus of the Beatles was on producing albums in the latter half of their career. Criminally, the double A-side of 'Penny Lane' and 'Strawberry Fields Forever' did not reach number one and therefore neither of the songs appear on this album. 'Please Please Me,' 'Magical Mystery Tour' and 'Let It Be' stalled at number two too and 'Something / Come Together' peaked at number four. The addition of these seven massive songs would have added extra colour to this compilation and hastened my inevitable exploration of the Beatles work.

What I did like here was the way the ominous final piano note of 'Lady Madonna' seemed to set the scene for the epic 'Hey Jude,' which took the crown of 'longest UK number one single' from the Animals and held onto it until Oasis grabbed it in 1997. At the time I thought McCartney's manic vocals during the 'na na na' refrain were a bit over the top and I wished they'd faded the coda about three minutes before they did. Looking back, I would now tell my younger self not to be so serious / silly! The two things are often the same.

2.15) The Red Album / 1962-1966 – The Beatles (1973)

In the early nineties Beatlemania was just beginning for me, as I decided to expand my Beatles collection from the twenty tracks of the previous compilation to 'a whole lot more.' I began to raid my Auntie Cally's collection of tapes. Well, not exactly 'raid' them; I was invited to borrow whatever I liked, but raiding them sounds more rock and roll, right? The Beatles' 'Red Album' illustrates the steady rate of development in their songwriting and arranging skills, from the simplicity of 'Love Me Do' through to the sophistication of 'Eleanor Rigby' and the wackiness of 'Yellow Submarine.' A new track for me at the time that I particularly liked was McCartney's song, 'All My Loving.' I was also hearing 'Eight Days A Week' and 'Drive My Car' for the first time. However, I did wonder, 'Why no *Twist And Shout*?' The answer of course, is that the Beatles didn't write it.

2.16) The Blue Album / 1967-1970 – The Beatles (1973)

This was the album that finally launched me into a lifelong love of the Liverpudlian quartet. I was listening to my auntie's tape on a generic 'Walkman' in bed at my grandparents' house in what they always described as 'the blue room.' Coincidence or what? My parents were at one of my father's company Christmas meals and I was experiencing some of my favourite music for the first time. From the opening of 'Strawberry Fields Forever' to the closing of 'The Long And Winding Road,' the 'Blue Album' is a true musical odyssey.

Hearing 'A Day In The Life' for the first time was something of a revelation. Lennon's sleepy sounding vocal delivery, the orchestral chaos and McCartney's jaunty middle section were an exercise in light and shade, akin to classical compositions. Then after the brief respite of 'All You Need Is Love' comes 'I Am

The Walrus.' I'd never heard anything like it before lyrically, as Lennon's kaleidoscope of bizarre images bursts forth like an overflowing dam. There were further surprises after 'Hey Jude,' with the full blown rock of 'Back In The USSR,' 'Revolution' and 'While My Guitar Gently Weeps,' which in my opinion is George Harrison's finest song. As a footnote, it is only after many years that I realised that perhaps 'The Ballad Of John And Yoko' is a reference to the Georgie Fame hit 'The Ballad Of Bonnie And Clyde,' in that the pair viewed themselves as outlaws.

I don't think the impact that this compilation album had on me can be underestimated really. It contains two of my all-time top ten favourite songs, and at the time I'd never heard either of them before. The only glaring omission to my youthful mind was 'When I'm 64,' but perhaps this would have lightened the overall feel a bit too much, although this didn't stop the compiler from including 'Ob-La-Di, Ob-La-Da!'

2.17) Bob Dylan's Greatest Hits [UK Version]– Bob Dylan (1967)

Another 'biggie' for me was Bob Dylan. I was friendly with a pair of twin brothers at the time. Both of them liked Simon & Garfunkel, but one liked Bob Dylan and the other preferred Boyz II Men. In truth you couldn't get further apart stylistically. Boyz II Men were a Motown band that were popular in the early nineties, singing harmonies that the Beach Boys would have been proud of, augmented with the occasional burst of mostly palatable rap, while Bob Dylan was a raucous troubadour with what David Bowie described in one of his songs as 'a voice like sand and glue.' I guess Simon & Garfunkel were the natural mid-point between these two brothers' tastes, with blissful vocals delivering poetic and thought provoking lyrics. It was just out of curiosity that I bought this particular greatest hits tape. Simon & Garfunkel had once covered *The Times They Are A-Changin'*, so I deduced that there clearly must be some merit in Mr. Zimmerman's output. I was not wrong.

The UK version of this compilation was arranged in much the same way that Dylan's classic album 'Bringing It All Back Home' was, with one side consisting of more acoustic sounding material and another side with the instruments firmly plugged in. The acoustic tracks are 'bread and butter' classics such as 'Blowin' In The Wind' and 'Mr. Tambourine Man,' while the electric stuff included the lyrical deluge of 'Subterranean Homesick Blues,' as well as the six-minute epic, 'Like A Rolling Stone.' Apart from the odd track on an album of classical music from TV adverts and the aforementioned 'Hey Jude,' this would have been the only track in my collection to break the six-minute mark at the time. So you see, for me in the nineties, this was just as groundbreaking as it was for listeners hearing it for the first time in the sixties.

I had finished college by now and I was earning a bit of money window cleaning. A tall young man who I worked with used to take the Mick out of my liking for Bob Dylan, declaring Robert Palmer to be the epitome of great music. I've nothing against Robert Palmer. He was good. But come on...

2.18) More Bob Dylan Greatest Hits – Bob Dylan (1971)

Just as Bob Dylan sang that he 'started out on Burgundy but soon hit the harder stuff,' one listen to Bob's greatest hits inevitably leads to a lifetime of addiction. Early on in this second volume of 'hits' we experience Bob Dylan's 'new' smooth voice on 'Lay Lady Lay,' which is perhaps the most famous song from his country crooning period. Thus, when the opening harmonica wail of 'Stuck Inside Of Mobile With The Memphis Blues Again' kicks in one tends to breathe a sign of relief; 'Thank God, it's still the same old Bob!' However, this track is also a bit of a challenge upon first hearing, being over seven minutes long with no chorus and just the same melody repeated with every new verse.

A favourite from this selection that I first heard at a Venture Scout booze up in a barn is 'Just Like Tom Thumb's Blues.' Venture Scouts seemed to be mostly about drinking, but anyway, I digress. My friend, whose brother liked Boyz II Men, had put 'More Bob Dylan Greatest Hits' on as we imbibed, and it seemed to be a fitting soundtrack to such hedonistic pursuits as downing cheap wine from the local shop on our Scout leader's farm. It may have even been this moment when I first decided to give Mr. Dylan's music a try. Anyway, this second volume of 'hits' includes more essentials like 'Maggie's Farm,' 'I'll Be Your Baby Tonight' (which my window-buffing colleague's hero Robert Palmer would later cover), 'All I Really Want To Do' and 'The Mighty Quinn' (Quinn The Eskimo).' Many of these were bigger hits for other artists.

2.19) Back To Front – Lionel Ritchie (1992)

This may seem something of a misfit, being a completely different genre to my early music dabblings, but Lionel's hits 'Do It To Me One More Time' and 'You Are My Destiny' represented a rare thing at the time - something that I actually liked in the pop charts. 'Three Times A Lady' is of course a gem from his days with the Commodores and the zippy electric guitar solo on 'Easy Like Sunday Morning' was always a highlight too. There used to be a 'love hour' on Southern Sound which was a Sussex radio station that later became Southern FM, so I guess this softened me up for balladry of this kind. The party anthems like 'Dancing On The Ceiling' did less for me however. Who wants to party when you're a teenager?

2.20) The All Time Greatest Hits – Elvis Presley (1987)

In the early nineties I would religiously tune in to Alan Freeman's weekly 'Pick Of The Pops' programme on BBC Radio 2 to enjoy chart rundowns from years gone by. It was then that I first thought 'Maybe this *Presley* guy is worth a listen,' and I duly purchased this double cassette compilation. Although I've never been hugely into Elvis, he clearly did evolve over the few decades that he lived through, and at the time my favourite period of his was not the rock and roll of the fifties but the relaxed style of hits like 'She's Not You' and 'Good Luck Charm' from the early sixties. I especially like the Shakespearean touch to 'Are You Lonesome Tonight?' The seventies hit 'Way Down' sees Elvis having a somewhat belated go at glam rock, but the standout tracks for me now are both from 1969 – 'Suspicious Minds' and 'In The Ghetto.' It's a shame Elvis didn't pursue this introspective route further. It may have even saved his life.

2.21) Blast From Your Past - Ringo Starr (1975)

Lennon, McCartney and Harrison are quite rightly viewed as composers of epic stature, but poor Ringo often seems to get overlooked, yet in terms of the singles chart he was arguably the most successful of all the former Beatles in the early seventies. This is a great compilation with no filler. Ringo was always a fan of country music so 'Beaucoups Of Blues' allows him to indulge himself, while the two covers from the rock and roll era, 'You're Sixteen' and 'Only You,' predate Lennon's 'Rock 'N' Roll' album. Mr. Starr gives the drums a good old thrash in 'Back Off Boogaloo' and satirises his own dalliance with drugs in the 'No No Song.' The Lennon-penned song 'I'm The Greatest' is another fun reappraisal of the past ('Yes, my name is Billy Shears') and Ringo seems to answer this with his own composition, 'Early 1970.' All this, and you've still got the hits 'Photograph' and 'It Don't Come Easy' to go. Not to be underestimated.

2.22) Relics - Pink Floyd (1971)

Pink Floyd were a slightly later discovery for me than all of the above, but as my interest in them was launched by a pair of compilations, I'll include both in this chapter. I'd first heard 'Relics' at my friend Simon's house which was in the village where I slept and drooled as a baby. At the age of about thirteen I dismissed it as 'drug music,' as did my friend who had borrowed the tape, but then when one of the first tracks you hear is 'Interstellar Overdrive,' what do you expect?

It was time to reappraise this collection, which covers the years from 1967 to 1969. There is a mixture of oddities and album tracks here, and I was pleased with the variety contained within this budget cassette. Included are the two Syd Barrett-penned chart hits, 'Arnold Lane' and 'See Emily Play,' as well as the hypnotic 'Cirrus Minor' which is adorned with birdsong. Styles vary dramatically with the bluesy 'Biding My Time' and the full blown heavy metal of 'The Nile Song.' Syd has the final word with the quirky 'Bike.' The compilation is also mostly chronological, which you'll remember is what I like.

2.23) A Collection Of Great Dance Songs - Pink Floyd (1981)

The title is ironic. Before the band released any of the compilations that are available these days, this was the companion volume to 'Relics,' with an interesting cover more akin to the style of the regular Floyd albums, which I would soon be purchasing. A whole world of music was opened up to me when on a dull bank holiday afternoon I listened to a run-down on Radio 1 of what listeners had voted as the best albums of all time. Naturally Pink Floyd featured prominently in this programme, so 'Shine On You Crazy Diamond' and 'Money' were already familiar to me. The version of 'Money' included here is actually a re-recording, but barely noticeable are its differences to the 1973 track from the absolute pinnacle of musical achievement known as 'The Dark Side Of The Moon.'

'Another Brick In The Wall, Part 2' is of course included, being the band's only number one hit and the last number one of the seventies. The other classics here are the Doctor Who-esque instrumental 'One Of These Days,' the poignant acoustic song 'Wish You Were Here' and the bombastic 'Sheep,' where Roger Waters vents his anger at unquestioning followers of organised religion. At the time I viewed it as controversial, but having seen the 'sheep' depicted in the lyrics elect a narcissist like Donald Trump to the most powerful position in the world, I think it's fair comment now! What would Jesus do? I don't think 'Vote for Trump' would be the top answer on TV's 'Family Fortunes.'

2.24) All The Best – Paul McCartney (1987)

I remember listening to this a lot while at college, and with the exceptions of 'Live And Let Die' and 'Jet,' I recall finding it all somewhat 'easy listening' compared to the Beatles albums that I was working my way through at the time. I would get into Paul's albums more thoroughly later on in life, but in hindsight Paul's early experimentations like the reggae pastiche 'C Moon' are good fun. Out of interest, 'L7' meant 'square' at the time so 'C Moon' was supposed to mean the opposite, being circular! Meanwhile, 'No More Lonely Nights' has a superb guitar solo at the end courtesy of Pink Floyd legend David Gilmour.

'Another Day' is a favourite of mine, a story song encapsulating that feeling of 'going through the motions' that we all know too well. Perhaps this compilation suffered a bit from slamming together songs from very different eras, (I've told you about that, haven't I?), so McCartney's collaborations with Stevie Wonder and Michael Jackson nestle uncomfortably beside the earlier tracks. Oh yeah, and there's 'We All Stand Together' too. Even Paul McCartney doesn't strike gold every time!

2.25) Just The Two Of Us – Various Artists (1990)

Perhaps under the influence of Southern Sound's 'love hour,' some of the girls had put this compilation on during a community coach trip from my village to

Winchester, and as I liked 'some of the girls' I thought it was also appropriate to like 'some of the music.' In hindsight, the eighties was probably *the* classic era for romantic pop music, although a few of the tracks here are from the seventies. Bill Medley, of 'Righteous Brothers' fame, and Joe Cocker both add a bit of 'gravel' to the vocals of Jennifer Warnes, while Diana Ross and Lionel Ritchie do a duet, and in case it all seems a bit uncool, Billy Preston duets with Syreeta. Yes, *that* Billy Preston who played the keys on the Beatles' 'Get Back.' Meanwhile George Michael and Aretha Franklin prove that you can pull off a romantic duet even when you're from completely different generations. Gladys Knight performs 'The Wind Beneath My Wings,' and Tammy Wynette duets with Mark Gray on 'Sometimes When We Touch.' With apologies to said artists I still prefer Dan Hill's version.

2.26) Don't Stop... Doo Wop! – Various Artists (1991)

Doo-wop music struck me as tremendous fun when I was a teenager, with the scat backing vocals often outshining the lead. It was something of a party trick for us teenagers to try to emulate the backing vocals from songs like the Marcells version of 'Blue Moon' (included here) and Johnny Cymbal's 'Mr. Bassman' (not included here). The roll call of forgotten classics includes 'What Do You Want To Make Those Eyes At Me For?' by Emile Ford and the Checkmates, which was the first number one of the sixties in the UK. Just for the record, the last number one of the sixties was 'Two Little Boys' by Rolf Harris, but again, the least said about him the better. Hmm, déjà vu.

Some of the tracks on this compilation date from way before music was even considered 'pop,' such as 'Earth Angel' which appears in the '1955' section of one of my favourite films, 'Back to the Future.' These tracks from the early fifties have a jazzier feel, and this compilation takes us almost up to the mid-sixties, with 'Crying In The Chapel' by the Dixie Cups being one of the later offerings. Curtis Lee's 'Pretty Little Angel Eyes' is good fun too.

2.27) 60 Number Ones Of The Sixties – Various Artists (1990)

Eventually I would compile a complete collection of number ones from the inception of the chart in 1952 until 1992, after which I would only collect the ones that I could at least tolerate, finally throwing in the towel at the end of 2008. I'm not going to mention the classics by artists we will cover in this book, but this album includes essential stuff like Scott McKenzie's 'San Francisco (Be Sure To Weat Flowers In Your Hair),' and 'A World Without Love,' a Paul McCartney composition (officially Lennon-McCartney) recorded by Peter & Gordon. This is also a great demonstration of just how versatile the pop charts were in those days, with jazzy contributions from the Temperance Seven and Georgie Fame nestling alongside reggae-tinted hits by the Equals and Desmond Dekker.

There's Motown courtesy of the Diana Ross & the Supremes and Marvin Gaye, a fun mix of rock and roll and Tchaikovsky from B Bumble & the Stingers, raunchiness from Serge Gainsbourg & Jane Birkin, drama from Dusty Springfield, wistfulness from Bobbie Gentry and two songs which truly sum up the feel of the sixties for me, Procol Harum's 'A Whiter Shade Of Pale' and Thunderclap Newman's 'Something In The Air.'

Chapter 3 – The Four Tops

The chapters of this book will of course overlap a little. Nobody completely exhausts the repertoire of one artist and then moves on to the next thing with clean, clinical precision. That would be like those weird people who eat a meal by consuming each foodstuff in turn. You know – meat first, then potatoes, then carrots, then peas. Oddballs!

So, as my acquaintances from weekly meetings were tentatively developing into friendships, it became possible to pick out my four top artists – a gold standard that I would return to throughout my life, regardless of what new and exciting genres I would discover. These artists were Paul Simon, the Beatles, Bob Dylan and Pink Floyd.

I'd begun having guitar lessons, a pivotal decision which I've always maintained was one of my best. I was taught by a lady called Suzanne who encouraged both myself and my sister, who was five years younger than me, to perform in a folk club in the country town of Tenterden in Kent. Thus the first three of these artists provided me with plenty of music that I could play acoustically. I had a few attempts at writing songs myself, but generally I locked these away in a case designed for cassettes as I wasn't sure they were up to any standard where I could perform them. Looking back, it seems strange that music cassettes would be viewed as something you would feel a need to lock away in the first place!

By the time we reach Pink Floyd I will have turned eighteen, and would be making what disapprovers viewed as the 'grave mistake' of eschewing university for 'cash in the pocket' from a window cleaning job, eventually destroying a patio door with scratch marks and walking off the job when my uninsured boss tried to hand me the bill. Next up was a stab at accounts, but alas this wasn't for me either, and I would have stabbed *myself* if I'd done much more of it! Once again, music came to the rescue, providing a consistent backdrop to all those ups and downs of early working life, when confidence and experience are both at rock bottom, but you're paradoxically expected to sell yourself like a pro, in both senses of the word!

Something I view as being somewhat embarrassing now, was being cajoled into filling out what I thought was a questionnaire for a personality test when cycling through the seaside town of Eastbourne with a friend. Later I went to Brighton to collect the results, which was a seriously long train journey from my home. I had no idea that the self-help being offered was part of a religion (you can guess which one I'm sure), and I even presented some of the ideas to the Venture Scout group I belonged to and mentioned them in a job interview I had at a local prison. Needless to say I didn't get the job. Seriously though, it's tough sifting the wheat from the chaff when you're only eighteen and looking for easy answers, but there were actually some great second-hand music shops in The Lanes in Brighton, so at least visiting this den of indoctrination did provide me with some musical sustenance.

Indeed, the psychedelia of the later Beatles records and early Pink Floyd perhaps provided a kind of escape route from the mundanity and existential angst of what weren't easy years. So no, it wasn't just crazy lyrics about a bloke who 'keeps a ten-bob note up his nose' or 'had a wooden leg [and] won it in the war, in 1944!'

So, we're done with dabbling a toe into the musical water; it's time to dive into the lake of classic rock and pop with our old friend Gusto again.

3.1) Wednesday Morning 3 A.M. – Simon & Garfunkel (1964)

We'll deal with the S&G albums chronologically, as this is pretty much how I encountered them. I found this album a little disappointing when I first got the cassette home, as it was all acoustic. Apart from a bit of banjo on 'The Strangest Dream' and the cellos on 'Benedictus,' which is even more sparse sounding, Paul Simon's lone guitar is left to hold the fort. It was a far cry from the big production pieces I was used to from the greatest hits album. Even 'The Sound Of Silence' is the basic track before the band were overdubbed.

Once you've got your head around that you can begin to enjoy it. 'The Strangest Dream' is a cover, but a great anti-war song. 'Go Tell It On The Mountain' is also a lively rendition that is surprisingly absent from radio airwaves at Christmas. Some of the lyrics are pretty dark, such as the final verse of 'The Sun Is Burning.' My favourite song here is 'Bleeker Street,' which is an early example of the duo's sublime harmonies.

3.2) Sounds Of Silence – Simon & Garfunkel (1966)

It was in winter 1991 that I went into Woolworths (now defunct) and bought the remaining albums of the entire S&G collection on tapes (now also defunct). I think this came to £27, which would have been about five weeks of my paper round money.

Anyway, on this one we get the 'plugged in' version of the title track that we know and love. The story of 'Wednesday Morning 3 A.M.' is given a reboot in 'Somewhere They Can't Find Me,' and Paul Simon adeptly manoeuvres his fingers around the Davy Graham instrumental 'Anji' which uses the same descending pattern of notes. The dark themes continue with two songs about suicide on side two. One is 'Richard Cory,' and the other is 'A Most Peculiar Man,' one was successful, the other a recluse, so I guess the point was that nobody is exempt when it comes to depression.

In truth at the age when I listened to Simon & Garfunkel more than anything else I was at college and found it hard to make friends. The lyrics of songs such as 'I Am A Rock' seemed to strike a chord as I wandered the winter residential streets of

Ashford with my headphones on. I think the three-hour gap in my day was intended for study. Well, nobody said the study couldn't include classic albums and local geography!

3.3) Parsley, Sage, Rosemary And Thyme – Simon & Garfunkel (1966)

More pure gold from the transatlantic duo. This one has the atmospheric song 'The Dangling Conversation' and some thought provoking lyrics in 'Patterns' and 'Flowers Never Bend With The Rainfall.' Paul Simon was clearly contemplating the brevity and apparent meaninglessness of life in his early years. On my original set of tapes, 'Homeward Bound' was on 'Sounds Of Silence' rather than this album, so the running orders of my CD versions always seem slightly alien to me.

Nobody has ever sang so poetically about somebody daubing a swearword on an Underground wall and nobody has ever been brave enough to juxtapose one of our favourite Christmas carols with a news report reflecting the truly dismal state of the world ('7 O'Clock News / Silent Night'). Top notch stuff. S&G forever!

3.4) Bookends – Simon & Garfunkel (1968)

I always viewed this album as the 'weird one' in the duo's catalogue, but it was also the most compelling, from the snippet of 'The Sound Of Silence' woven into 'Save The Life Of My Child' to the dissonant orchestral backing on 'Old Friends.' The first half is a journey from childhood to old age with the tempo gradually slowing with each track. I tend to think of the ages of the four main songs as the speeds on my old record player – 16, 33, 45 and 78 (although the line 'How terribly strange to be seventy' in 'Old Friends' indicates otherwise).

I'm convinced that there are two homages to the Beatles song 'I Am The Walrus' here too, with the reference to a Kellogg's cornflake in 'Punky's Dilemma' (*a la* 'Sitting on a cornflake...') and the 'coo coo ca-choo' in 'Mrs. Robinson.' 'Fakin' It' is just a great song, full stop, as is 'Hazy Shade Of Winter,' which really should be played among the seasonal wintry songs every Christmas. I may be in the minority but I even like 'Voices Of Old People.'

As a footnote, there is also a soundtrack album to 'The Graduate.' This features a different version of 'Mrs. Robinson,' which was used in the film, and some alternative takes of other S&G songs, but half of the album is incidental music composed by Dave Gruisin. This could be your next step after purchasing the album that follows...

3.5) Bridge Over Troubled Water – Simon & Garfunkel (1970)

And so we reach the duo's zenith, ironically created at a time when they were already pursuing their own individual interests. The opener is a gentle ballad sung by Garfunkel until the production team decided to thrown in everything except the kitchen sink on the last verse. 'El Condor Pasa' perhaps presaged Simon's later interest in world music, in spite of its downbeat lyric that 'A man gets tied up to the ground / He gives the world its saddest sound.' 'The Only Living Boy In New York' is blissful, and the almost choral feel is captured by multi-tracking the vocals. 'So Long, Frank Lloyd Wright' was Paul Simon's lyrical joke, as Art Garfunkel had been an architecture student and Frank Lloyd Wright was an... Sorry, I'll switch 'patronising' mode off again. Garfunkel sings the track earnestly in spite of this, and the wintry arrangement is evocative. And then there's 'The Boxer.' Need I say more?

3.6) Paul Simon – Paul Simon (1972)

Let's keep it chronological for the mo. With the double-act dissolved, Paul Simon produced this downbeat offering. Again, think of me wandering the Victorian terraces of South Ashford beneath overcast skies, trying to hear this on my generic Walkman over the howling wind, occasionally popping into a shop to purchase some chocolate, the height of hedonism during my college years.

The biggest hits aren't necessarily representative of the general feel of the album, being 'Mother And Child Reunion' and 'Me And Julio Down By The Schoolyard,' which both flirt with reggae. 'Everything Put Together Falls Apart' encapsulates the feel more with lines like 'It's plain to see you're on your own.' Armistice Day has a nice surprise when the funky guitar kicks in just as you think it's fading out, and the second half of this album is exquisitely sequenced, with 'Papa Hobo' leading into 'Hobo's Blues,' an instrumental with Stéphane Grappelli on violin, followed by 'Paranoia Blues,' which has some great slide guitar work. For me the line that sums up the album is 'It's just after breakfast, I'm in the road, and the weatherman lied.' It was normally late morning when I experienced this feeling over twenty years later. The weatherman was still getting it wrong even then!

3.7) There Goes Rhymin' Simon – Paul Simon (1973)

This album was more relaxed stylistically than its predecessor and had some gospel style vocal backing from the Jessie Dixon Singers. I remember at the time cycling a sixteen-mile round trip to the town of Tenterden to post a Valentine's card to a girl who lived about a mile from me while listening to this album on my personal stereo. The idea was that it would have a different postmark adding mystery and intrigue as to who sent it. Whilst this was ultimately an exercise in futility, the album was not. 'Tenderness' has some great backing vocals, 'Take Me To The Mardi Gras' has some terrific New Orleans style brass during the fade out and the whole album has a generally sunny outlook. My favourite line of the album could apply to any politician, 'Everybody got the runs for glory / Nobody stop and scrutinise the plan.' 'Something So Right.' I agree, Paul.

3.8) Still Crazy After All These Years – Paul Simon (1975)

The lyrics of one of the songs, 'Yesterday it was my birthday / I hung one more year on the line,' pop into my head at least once a year, if you see what I mean. This track, called 'Have A Good Time,' ends with an improvised saxophone coda. It would be a good 25 years before I really appreciated jazz riffing like this. The album seems to pick through the bones of marriage, sometimes humorously *a la* 'You're Kind' and sometimes wistfully as in the case of the title track, which harks back to 'Old Friends' with its slightly dissonant instrumental section. Meanwhile, Paul Simon's approach to religion is a bit ambiguous on this album. He talks of pledging allegiance to the wall in 'My Little Town,' a duet with Garfunkel which appeared on the solo albums of both artists, while in 'Silent Eyes' he sounds genuinely pious, and the epic note he holds is impressive. Steve Gadd's drumming on '50 Ways To Leave Your Lover' must be one of the most emulated drum patterns in history, and I learned a load of basketball terms I'd never heard before from the downbeat 'Night Game' too.

3.9) One Trick Pony – Paul Simon (1980)

A soundtrack to a film starring Mr. Simon himself, and an album that often gets overlooked. There are some live tracks like the title track and 'Ace In The Hole,' while 'Late In the Evening' pretty much serves the same function as this book, in documenting the singer's relationship with music from childhood to middle age, albeit with more brevity! The album has a tired feel to it, but not in a negative way. 'Jonah' and 'Long, Long Day' are both enjoyable in their low-energy way. 'God Bless The Absentee' has a great piano riff too. 'Some people say music is the ace in the hole.' I guess I'm one of them, Paul.

3.10) Hearts And Bones – Paul Simon (1983)

One of Paul Simon's best and most underrated albums. Paul pours over his life and stirs the ashes of marriage in songs like 'Train In The Distance' and the title track, which I always think form a trilogy of story songs with the 1977 single 'Slip Slidin' Away.' There are two versions of 'Think Too Much,' in which Paul looks back over his youth, trying to find the point at which his brain was switched into overdrive. His attempt at a Northern English accent on the funky 'Cars Are Cars' is funny and I always wonder if Gary Numan's 'Cars' inspired him to write this. Meanwhile, 'Song About The Moon' is very melodic, and the album's closer is a tribute to 'The Late Great Johnny Ace' as well as John Lennon, who was tragically shot in 1980. The cold orchestral strings at the end say it all.

3.11) Graceland – Paul Simon (1986)

At the time of this album's release I was eleven and even then I couldn't get my head around the fact that this was 'Simon' of 'Simon & Garfunkel' playing such 'modern sounding' music, which was actually pretty ancient being traditional South African in style. It was a good five years later that I finally appreciated the album.

'Graceland' is a superb song with lyrics that seem to essentially continue the 'marriage break up' theme of 'Hearts And Bones.' In 'Under African Skies' Tucson in Arizona gets a mention in song for the first time since the Beatles encouraged us to 'Get Back.' This was purely because Paul Simon wrote a verse for Linda Ronstadt who sang on the record and was born in... OK, you're already there. If you want to hear the South African vocalists on their own there's 'Homeless,' and once you've heard the album a few times you realise that there are actually quite a variety of different sounds and feelings within the oeuvre. And before anybody says it, yes I know, the virtuoso bass fill towards the end of 'You Can Call Me Al' is a high point. Happy now?

3.12) Rhythm Of The Saints – Paul Simon (1990)

The 'rhythms' in question this time were Latin American. 'Can't Run But' is possibly my favourite track here, having an almost ambient vibe to it. 'Is it about Chernobyl?' I wonder when I hear the line 'A cooling system burns out in the Ukraine.' The only 'hit' this time around was 'The Obvious Child' which only reached number 15 in the UK. Needless to say, the album topped the charts. In spite of its upbeat title, this is really quite a laid back affair, and the observant will notice that the opening horn motif at the start of 'The Obvious Child' seems to be a direct lift from the fadeout of 'Get A Job' by the Silhouettes (1957), which was featured on a doo-wop album I've already reviewed. 'Further To Fly' perhaps encapsulates Paul Simon's approach to music, never staying in one place, and in hindsight he was clearly ahead of the game with his lyric 'The planet groans every time it registers another birth.' It's still groaning now and there are almost eight billion of us.

3.13) A Hard Day's Night – The Beatles (1964)

This is going to frustrate the hell out of many, but I am going to review the Beatles albums roughly in the order that I first heard them. So we begin with a visit to my auntie's house in the Ashford suburb of Willesborough during one of those extended wanders during breaks intended for study at college, which were used for downing a cup of tea while rummaging through drawers of magnetic tapes encased in plastic, designed to pass through a playback head at 1 7/8 inches per second. Sorry, I might have overdone the detail a bit there.

Here we have an album from the earlier years of the Beatles. Young and innocent days? Well, not really, and I get the impression that John Lennon in particular hated the 'clean cut' image. Anyway, the music holds up. My favourites are not the big hits but the more introspective songs, particularly 'If I Fell' and 'Things We Said Today.' That said, the rock and roll of 'You Can't Do That' is tremendous, with Ringo pushing the cowbell into overtime. When you think that this was rushed out as a soundtrack, you realise that the Beatles could just churn out quality at the drop of a hat!

3.14) Help – The Beatles (1965)

Another tape from my auntie's legendary drawer, and a similar structure to 'A Hard Day's Night' with one side of songs from the film and a second side of extra songs. 'Ticket To Ride' was the first Beatles track to exceed three minutes in length ('Strawberry Fields Forever' was first to break the four-minute barrier, two tracks on 'Sgt. Pepper' topped five minutes and of course 'Hey Jude' finally faded out after a little over seven minutes).

I think the album would have been better arranged with 'Yesterday' as the closing track, but the aim was not to leave the punters on a low, so the rock and roll cover of 'Dizzy Miss Lizzy' was bolted onto the end. Ringo indulges his country side with 'Act Naturally' and George is allowed to pen not just one but two songs, which is how things would be done from now on. 'You're Going To Lose That Girl' is a favourite of mine with John in 'angry' mode as well as some serious bongo bashing.

3.15) Rubber Soul – The Beatles (1965)

Another tape from my auntie's... Oh yes, you've guessed that bit. Don't worry, I did have to shell out and buy some albums for myself after this one, 'Abbey Road' and 'Let It Be.' The distorted photo on the cover perhaps hints at the mind-bending direction the band would eventually take, but on this album, folk is as big an influence as anything, 'Norwegian Wood (This Bird Has Flown)' being the obvious example. 'The Word' is a favourite of mine with its early attempt at a funk rhythm, Paul dabbles with French in 'Michelle,' Ringo gets a bit of country music out of his system on 'What Goes On' and the fuzzed guitar tone on 'Think For Yourself' is a new sound for the group. However, the crown goes to John Lennon on this album for the wonderfully thoughtful track, 'In My Life.' George Martin's speeded up piano solo is to be credited too.

3.16) Abbey Road – The Beatles (1969)

There is something legendary about the combination of the 'Fab Four' with George Martin, the only contender for the epithet 'fifth Beatle' in my opinion, as he literally made the impossible possible. Perhaps the appeal is partly the way these working class lads conquered the world and then promoted the 'love and peace' ethos, which has been sadly lost in the era of Trumpism and hate masquerading as political views. However, if you visit the Cavern Club in Liverpool you'll find that it's still very much alive. Anyway, 'Abbey Road,' what can I say? Classic follows classic, and there is Paul's symphonic finish which even Elbow couldn't touch with their rendition of 'Golden Slumbers' a little while back.

George gets his first A-side on a single with 'Something,' Ringo gets his second self-penned song onto a Beatles album with 'Octopus's Garden,' and one of my favourites is John's 'I Want You (She's So Heavy)' which sees the foursome simultaneously dabbling in jazz, lyrical minimalism and heavy rock. Apart from the 'Revolution 9' sound collage, this is the only track the group released in the sixties to top 'Hey Jude' for length.

3.17) Let It Be – The Beatles (1970)

The liner notes announce 'This is a new phase Beatles album.' Sadly for us it wasn't a very long phase, in fact it was just a solitary album! Even though Paul McCartney was disappointed with the way Phil Spector had overdubbed, mixed and compiled this album, it's still a pretty fine swansong. We open with the folky number, 'Two Of Us,' and we are treated to a mix of studio and live recordings from the famous rooftop concert which had all eyes facing upward from the streets of London. The sequencing of John's surrealist humour before Paul's songs may have been somewhat cheeky, but then George had no objection to the statement of 'Queen says no to pot-smoking FBI member' before his quirky ditty 'For You Blue.' The album version of 'Let It Be' features a brilliant overdriven guitar solo and runs for an extra chorus than the single. 'One After 909' sees one of the group's earliest songs given a reboot, and McCartney almost gets the last word with the classic track, 'Get Back.' John's closing remark of 'I think we passed the audition' seems most fitting.

It's interesting to note that the album was originally going to be called 'Get Back' with the Beatles replicating the cover of their debut album 'Please Please Me,' but this concept was dropped and the photo was eventually used for the 'Blue Album / 1967-1970.' Historians should also note that 'Abbey Road' was recorded after 'Let It Be,' but released first.

3.18) Please Please Me – The Beatles (1963)

Having exhausted my auntie's Beatles collection, I now had to part with some money. This one was a yellow tape which I purchased from Ashford Market, where you could buy everything from a Biro pen to a cow. It's true! Rewinding right to the beginning of the Fab Four's career, the boys exploded into our hearts and minds with the famous count-in of 'I Saw Her Standing There.' I can only think of three other songs of their career which were preceded by a count-in on the records, namely 'Taxman,' 'Yer Blues' and 'Dig A Pony.' I particularly like the Lennon-McCartney song 'Misery,' but the album's highlights for me are not 'Twist

And Shout' or the title track, but two covers where John Lennon's vocal drips with pathos, these being 'Anna (Go To Him)' and 'Baby It's You.' Debut albums don't get much better than this.

3.19) Revolver – The Beatles (1966)

The album that preceded 'Sgt. Pepper' often eclipses it in charts of 'best ever albums,' and it is perhaps more stylistically varied if I'm honest. The album opens with one of George's best songs, 'Taxman,' a track so good that the Jam pretty much copied it for their 1980 hit, 'Start.' There are nice harmonies on 'Here, There And Everywhere' and Ringo gets a vocal on a Beatles double A-side with 'Yellow Submarine,' three years before George did, although I don't think Mr. Harrison would have been too disappointed, getting an unprecedented three compositions onto an album here, including his first song with entirely Indian instrumentation, 'Love You To.' Paul's 'Eleanor Rigby' is the first Beatles track with purely orchestral backing (the second would be 'She's Leaving Home' and the third 'Good Night') and just when you think it's all over, John blows our socks off with the hypnotic psychedelia of 'Tomorrow Never Knows.'

3.20) Sgt. Pepper's Lonely Heart's Club Band – The Beatles (1967)

Obviously this was a 'must have' album for me, often cited as the greatest album of all time. The problem was, I'd heard most of the best bits courtesy of the 'Blue Album / 1967-1970.' Initially I found what was George's second song backed entirely by Indian instruments, 'Within You, Without You,' a bit on the long side, preferring Paul's vaudevillian tendencies in 'When I'm 64.' The second half of the album gradually picks up pace via 'Good Morning Good Morning' into 'Sgt. Pepper's Lonely Hearts Club Band (Reprise),' via a series of inspired segues, before exploding into Lennon's downbeat and brilliantly cynical 'A Day In The Life.' And just when you think it's all over there's a dog whistle and a loop of gibberish. McCartney's 'She's Leaving Home' is also a highlight, laying on the drama in spades.

3.21) Magical Mystery Tour – The Beatles (1967)

Another yellow cassette tape for me, but not really another *bona fide* album as such. This was initially a USA-only release comprising the 'Magical Mystery Tour' EP and the remaining A and B-sides from 1967 - often described as the Beatles psychedelic peak. Paul's whimsical 'Your Mother Should Know' makes the perfect counterpoint to both John's venomous 'I Am The Walrus' which follows it and George's soporific 'Blue Jay Way' which precedes it. Seriously, I don't have to advocate this album's place in rock history, it's got 'Hello Goodbye,' 'Strawberry Fields Forever' and 'Penny Lane.' What more could anybody want?

3.22) The Beatles (aka The White Album) – The Beatles (1968)

You still find me wandering around the streets of Ashford disconsolately in my study breaks, and this was another soundtrack to my perambulations. I first experienced the eponymous 'White Album' at a sleepover event for Venture Scouts in our sparsely decorated hall. Basically, this was a booze up with music and sleeping bags. I had been lent the album by our leader and decided that it was time to play it once everybody's drinks were beginning to kick in. An astute move, even if I say so myself, for this was the Beatles at their most eclectic and avant-garde. I would listen to it more studiously during my walks of course.

On this album, the foursome did whatever they felt like with no constraints of commercialism. Styles vary from folk to Charleston to 'country and western' to heavy metal, and 'Revolution 9' simulates the effect of waking up during a series of bizarre dreams, before Ringo lulls us back to sleep with 'Good Night.' George as ever got to write and sing one track per LP side while Ringo got to sing one track per LP. Here, he presents his first foray into songwriting with 'Don't Pass Me By.' However, the high point of the whole album for me is the segue from 'The Continuing Story Of Bungalow Bill' into 'While My Guitar Gently Weeps.' Segues are a lost art. The world need more segues!

Just for the record, acoustic demos of virtually the entire album, as well as epic-length versions of 'Revolution' and 'Helter Skelter,' which top ten and twelve minutes respectively, would eventually surface on the reissued 'White Album 50th Anniversary' box set (2018). Go on. Treat yourself!

3.23) Yellow Submarine – The Beatles (1969)

Like Simon & Garfunkel's soundtrack to 'The Graduate,' this is one of those 'be careful' albums, as the second half comprises solely of George Martin's orchestral compositions for the feature-length cartoon. Good though these are, there are only four 'new' Beatles tracks here, of which the best is 'Hey Bulldog' which uses a piano riff similar to the one in 'Money (That's What I Want).'

George gets two of his hypnotic compositions onto this album, both being in a similar dreamy vein to 'Blue Jay Way' from 'Magical Mystery Tour.' This leaves McCartney's 'All Together Now,' a childlike bit of fun, but entertaining nonetheless, right down to the honking horn at the end. One senses that he was generally trying to lighten the mood. This album always reminds me of taking part in an organised ramble at the foot of Wye Downs in Kent. I had music wherever I went in those days you see. 'Why?' No – Wye!

3.24) With The Beatles – The Beatles (1963)

And so we come to two early Beatles albums that seemed slightly less essential to me, hence them entering the hallowed gates of my collection after all the others.

Perhaps I took this view because of the lack of UK hit singles on both, but really you can't call anything 'Beatles' non-essential. There was a great shop in our town centre called Sam Goody at the time, with the strapline 'Goody. Got it.' Well, this was pretty true, and the opening of this particular store put a stop to me gallivanting all over Kent in search of music. Thus, I completed my Beatles collection with ease.

This album is now a favourite of mine. John reprises the emotion-filled vocal style of 'Baby It's You' on 'You Really Got A Hold On Me,' and he goes for some 'Twist And Shout' style voice box laceration on 'Money (That's What I Want).' Paul's cover of 'Till There Was You' is my mother's favourite Beatles track and she got to play it herself when I eventually walked down the aisle in 2015. Songs that seem simple like 'Hold Me Tight' and 'All My Loving' brim with atmosphere, and if you want to experience this vibe in its purest form I suggest you visit Liverpool's Cavern Club where you can hear such tunes night after night. Unless there's a coronavirus lockdown, that is.

3.25) Beatles For Sale – The Beatles (1964)

After 'A Hard Days Night,' which was composed entirely of Lennon-McCartney originals, the inclusion of covers on this album may have seemed a step backward, but this is still a very satisfying album, opening with the archetypal Beatles track 'No Reply.' There are further introspective / downbeat classics like 'Baby's In Black' and 'I'm A Loser' to follow, but in my opinion Paul's composition 'I'll Follow The Sun' tops the lot. Contrastingly, as 'Kansas City / Hey Hey Hey Hey' fades he treats us to the crazed vocal style that he would later use in the codas of 'I'm Down' and 'Hey Jude.'

3.26) Past Masters Volume 1 / Past Masters Volume 2 – The Beatles (1988)

Phew! We made it. Once you have all the above albums this double release will complete your Beatles collection. At least it did until they released those 'Anthology' things in the nineties. 'Past Masters' is all essential stuff, from the 'Long Tall Sally' EP to B-sides like 'She's A Woman' and 'Rain,' which was the first Beatles track to feature backwards vocals when released in 1966. I remember feeling genuine excitement when I first played this compilation in the nineties, knowing that there was still music of this calibre that I had not heard before. Even 'You Know My Name (Look Up The Number),' the wacky B-side to 'Let It Be,' has its place!

Two curios are the German-lyric versions of 'She Loves You' and 'I Want To Hold Your Hand.' Not included on this album is a similar attempt at singing 'Get Back' in German, although one gets a sense that they were just larking around by then. High points for me include the melancholic ballads 'This Boy' and 'Yes It Is,' where John gives his own material the same pathos that he did with 'Anna (Go

With Him)' and 'Baby It's You.' And there's plenty of rock and roll too.

3.27) Bob Dylan – Bob Dylan (1962)

It seems strange now that I would buy Mr. Zimmerman's debut album, which consists largely of covers, so early on, but perhaps at the time I was trying to establish where he came from and how I could become a folk music superstar myself. Hmm, high hopes. His voice is pretty raw at times, yes, even more raw than on his better known works. 'Talkin' New York' and 'Song For Woody' are his own compositions, but perhaps it was 'House Of The Rising Sun' that had the most impact, as following this album, British group, the Animals took the song to number one with this tune. Frenetic tracks like 'Gospel Plow' and 'Freight Train Blues' have a great sense of fun, belying the fact that most of Bob's choices here are fixated with death.

3.28) The Freewheelin' Bob Dylan (1963)

Bob Dylan's second album was his first to consist entirely of self-composed material. The Beatles would follow suit with their third album in 1964, so at the time this was pretty radical. 'Blowin' In The Wind' is an all-time anti-war anthem, with simple lyrics that never lose their impact sadly, because the world never learns. 'Masters Of War' takes the same message and dials up the anger to 'eleven.' 'Honey, Just Allow Me One More Chance' is the only track with the 'hillbilly' feel of the first album. 'A Hard Rain's A-Gonna Fall' is an apocalyptic track, with what was probably Dylan's first stab at surrealism. My favourite though is 'Don't Think Twice, It's Alright,' with its satisfying guitar pick, bitter-sweet lyrics and a harmonica solo where Bob seems to blow his soul out.

3.29) Bringing It All Back Home – Bob Dylan (1965)

Lyrically I think this is Dylan's masterpiece. You've got 'Mr. Tambourine Man' and 'Subterranean Homesick Blues', but for me the highlight is the verbal deluge of 'It's Alright Ma, I'm Only Bleeding,' where the guitar riff he used on 'Highway 51 Blues' is employed to punctuate the lava-flow of imagery. Phrases like 'Money doesn't talk, it swears' seem to stick in the mind, and he summarises it all at the end with the line 'It's life and life only.'

This album is half folk and half rock, both sides of Mr. Zimmerman's oeuvre, but in truth the rock tracks were merely acoustic tracks overdubbed by producer Tom Wilson, so people got their knickers in a twist for no reason whatsoever really. For this reason some of the tracks sound quite similar, notably 'Subterranean Homesick Blues,' 'Maggie's Farm' and 'Bob Dylan's 115th Dream,' which is a very amusing story in the same vein as 'Motorpsycho Nightmare' from 'Another Side Of Bob Dylan.' 'It's All Over Now Baby Blue' is yet another dollop of fabulousness, but seriously, is there anything not to like here?

3.30) Blonde On Blonde – Bob Dylan (1966)

I've often cited 'Bringing It All Back Home' as my favourite Bob Dylan album, although in reality it is so hard to choose one with so much quality. This one was arguably the first double album released by a rock act, the other one being 'Freak Out' by Frank Zappa & The Mothers Of Invention released a week later. Either way the contents are terrific, with bluesy tracks such as 'Pledging My Time' and 'Leopard-Skin Pill-Box Hat' interspersed with folky classics like 'Just Like A Woman.' There's a humorous poke at the Beatles' 'Norwegian Wood' with 'Fourth Time Around,' although in truth the flow of influence was mutual. 'Visions Of Johanna' builds tremendously to the bizarre line 'On the back of the fish truck that loads / While my conscience explodes,' and finally there's 'Sad Eyed Lady Of The Lowlands' – an eleven-minute epic with Dylan at his most poetic.

3.31) The Times They Are A-Changin' – Bob Dylan (1964)

So having duly purchased what I regarded as the pivotal Dylan albums of the sixties I went back to 1964 to pick up the ones that slipped through the sieve the first time. This is pretty much how I explore the work of any artist, so hopefully you'll get used to the format of 'essentials first' by the time you finish this book. The anthem this time around is the title track, which is about the generation gap. I find it pretty soul destroying that many of the youths he was singing about looking for a fairer world have turned into today's 'me, me, me' fat cats. 'With God On Our Side' is another anti-war anthem which never loses its power; 'If God's on our side, he'll stop the next war.' There are some pretty grim tales on this album from Hollis Brown's suicide to 'The Lonesome Death Of Hattie Caroll.' At the time nobody realised that Bob's 'Restless Farewell' was literally saying 'goodbye' to the protest genre, at least until 1971's 'George Jackson.'

3.32) Another Side Of Bob Dylan – Bob Dylan (1964)

Although still acoustic, this album was a departure from the earlier Woody Guthrie-inspired works. The famous tracks are 'All I Really Wanna Do' and 'It Ain't Me Babe,' but the pivotal track seems to be 'My Back Pages,' where Dylan proclaims 'I was so much older then, I'm younger than that now,' reflecting upon his former 'troubadour' status ('A self-proclaimed professor's tongue / Too serious to fool'). Here, he lays his cards on the table for what was to come. The eight-minute closer, 'Ballad In Plain D,' is a weary tale of personal angst, concluding with another one of those harmonica solos where Bob blows his guts out.

3.33) Highway 61 Revisited – Bob Dylan (1965)

Initially I was disappointed with this album. It didn't have the same vibe as 'Blonde On Blonde' which followed it, or the seriousness of 'Bringing It All Back Home' which preceded it. The poetry is more surreal and playful, 'Tombstone Blues' and 'Ballad Of A Thin Man' being prime examples. Obviously 'Like A Rolling Stone' is an instant classic, and 'Desolation Row' right at the end should keep the die-hard folkies happy, giving us eleven sublime minutes without an electric guitar or drumkit in sight. 'Just Like Tom Thumb's Blues' is a favourite of mine, and the brash irreverence of the line 'God said to Abraham "Kill me a son"' on the title track is always striking. This album always reminds me of a house party I went to where the front room flooded. I guess that was one way my friends at the time found to get out of listening to Bob Dylan!

3.34) The Basement Tapes – Bob Dylan (1975)

Glimpsing the year '1975' I hear you say 'Oh no, he's gone off on one again!' Well actually, while 'The Basement Tapes' weren't released until 1975, they were recorded in the interregnum between 'Blonde On Blonde' and 'John Welsley Harding.' So there!

What we have here are some of Dylan's finest songs which could have been forever left in the vault. 'Tears Of Rage' seems to express disappointment at the direction America has taken, while 'This Wheel's On Fire' has a brooding ambience, building to the punchline 'This wheel shall explode!' There are funny songs like 'Clothes Line Saga,' which seems like a humorous riposte to Bobbie Gentry's hit 'Ode To Billy Joe,' and the whole album has a feeling of Bob and the Band getting drunk and having fun. For example, 'Going To Acapulco' sounds heartfelt in spite of its bawdy humour. Dylan isn't the only vocalist on the album, although he sings the lion's share of the songs.

3.35) John Wesley Harding – Bob Dylan (1967)

This was the first of four consecutive UK number one albums for Mr. Dylan. The lyrics seem more philosophical here, compared to the surrealism of his preceding albums. 'As I Went Out One Morning' seems to express disappointment that the ideals of Thomas Paine and the founders of the USA have sadly not been met, summarised in the line 'I'm sorry for what she's done.' And Trump was only a young whippersnapper then! 'The Ballad Of Frankie Lee And Judas Priest' is a story song, which is encapsulated in the maxim 'be careful what you wish for,' while 'All Along The Watchtower' achieved fame as a Jimi Hendrix song. Meanwhile the final track, 'I'll Be Your Baby Tonight' sets the stage for Dylan's next album – a full blown stab at country music.

3.36) Nashville Skyline – Bob Dylan (1969)

'Bob goes country,' and he begins by teaming up with the legend that is Johnny Cash to reprise his own song 'Girl From The North Country.' Bob's new 'mellow voice' does sound a bit feeble alongside Cash's to be honest. His own voice has more depth on 'Lay Lady Lay,' the album's biggest hit. 'I Threw It All Away' is perhaps my favourite track from this album, while 'Nashville Skyline Rag' is a pleasant instrumental. Overall it sounds like Bob is having fun here. And why not?

3.37) Self Portrait – Bob Dylan (1970)

This double album often gets slated, not least because many of the songs are covers and the laid back style is often interpreted as 'can't be bothered.' There is a companion volume in the form of 1973's 'Dylan' album. Perhaps controversially, I actually do enjoy 'Self Portrait' regularly. The opening ditty, 'All The Tired Horses' doesn't feature any Dylan vocals at all. Instead it lets the female vocalists set the scene with an endlessly circling melody. 'Days Of '49' is a story song about of the US gold rush, and 'Little Sadie,' which appears in two versions, is about murdering your partner (as you do). Bob also presents his own version of 'The Mighty Quinn (Quinn The Eskimo)' following the hit that the British group Manfred Mann had with his song. I also like the laid back version of 'Like A Rolling Stone' where he stuffs up the words, and what an honour for Paul Simon and Gordon Lightfoot to have their songs covered by someone of Zimmerman's stature. This is a fun Bob Dylan album and shouldn't be viewed as anything more.

3.38) New Morning – Bob Dylan (1970)

One encounters an eclectic mixture of styles here. 'If Not For You' was a hit for Olivia Newton-John and 'Winterlude' is a country classic which I always think should be aired at Christmas. Bob toys with jazz on 'If Dogs Run Free,' with its female scat vocal looping around Dylan's dry delivery. 'One More Weekend' is a nice uptempo rocker, similar to 'Watching The River Flow,' which you'll need 'More Bob Dylan Greatest Hits' to hear. The gospel organ of 'Three Angels' and the lyrics of 'Father Of Night' perhaps hint at the religious zeal that Bob would discover by the end of the decade. Let's skip a couple of albums and fast forward to the year I was born now, as this was when Bob had a creative resurgence.

3.39) Blood On The Tracks – Bob Dylan (1975)

Who invented the 'break-up' album? Well, that's an interesting question, but this was Bob's emphatic contribution to the subgenre. This always reminds me of driving to the Isle of Grain in the Thames Estuary with my cassette of this album for accompaniment to buy a second hand reel to reel tape recorder. 'Keeping it reel' (groan) is certainly what Bob was up to here, as most of the songs are stories which seem to echo his real life, albeit given a twist and some artistic licence. 'Simple Twist Of Fate' is told in the third person, and 'You're Gonna Make Me Lonesome When You Go' is in the first person, but it's all from the same hymn sheet for sure. The standout track is 'Idiot Wind' which alternates between nostalgia and rage, sometimes even at the same time. Dylan characterises himself as the 'Jack of Hearts' in one of the songs and the whole album is one you will play again, and again, and... You get the idea!

3.40) Hard Rain – Bob Dylan (1976)

Whilst 'At Budokan' has my favourite live performance of Bob's ('Forever Young'), this live album is on the whole more satisfying, as he beefs up material from 'Blood On The Tracks' and older songs alike. 'You're A Big Girl Now,' 'One Too Many Mornings 'and 'I Threw It All Away' are particularly engaging, and there's some great violin work from Scarlet Riviera. 'Maggie's Farm' is given a new tune, but the ultimate cut is 'Idiot Wind,' an epic performance where Bob vents his spleen at his marriage breakdown via a kaleidoscope of images. Another all-time epic track from the master!

3.41) Desire – Bob Dylan (1976)

And so to yet another top notch album from what many regard as a 'classic' period in the man's long and varied career. It must get boring being so good! The sound is very different to the last studio album, 'Blood On The Tracks,' with some seriously souped-up drums and plenty of violin from Scarlet Riviera. Jacques Levy helped to write some of the songs and we get the first protest material since 1971's 'George Jackson' single in the form of 'Hurricane,' a tale of injustice concerning a black boxer. The piano-led 'Isis' uses the same chord sequence as the Small Faces track 'Call It Something Nice' as the setting for a wacky tale of misadventure. We are treated to the third eleven-minute song of Bob's career in the form of 'Joey,' which seems to plead innocence for a gangster. 'Black Diamond Bay' expresses the detachment one feels from real life events while watching the news, a theme Bob would return to in 'T.V. Talking Song' from 1990's 'Under The Red Sky.' There's still a lament for his first wife in the form of 'Sara.' Perhaps a radical conversion to Christianity a few years later would help Bob to move on?

3.42) Bob Dylan At Budokan – Bob Dylan (1979)

This is a double live album where Dylan experiments with the arrangements of his own songs. We open with a folk rock rendition of 'Mr. Tambourine Man.' 'All I Really Want To Do' gets similar treatment and is consequently very pleasant. I've always wondered if the audience are expecting Eric Clapton's 'Wonderful Tonight' when they applaud at the start of 'I Shall Be Released' before it's possible to tell what it's going to be. 'It's All Right, Ma' gets heavied up, and it works, but the show-stopper is 'Forever Young,' which completely eclipses the version on 'Planet Waves,' especially when the pounding bass kicks in for the last chorus. The encore of *The Times They Are A-Changin'* is also excellent.

3.43) Under The Red Sky – Bob Dylan (1990)

This was an album that one of the twins I knew used to taunt me with, using words along the lines of 'You only listen to *old* Dylan; I listen to *any* Dylan.' Well, I did listen to it, but I guess when you open an album with something like 'Wiggle Wiggle' it's going to be an uphill struggle. 'Under The Red Sky' sounds like a nursery rhyme and '2X2' sounds like a counting exercise for kids. However, just because Dylan takes a different approach, we shouldn't dismiss it. 'T.V. Talking Song' explores the relationship between television and reality, and 'Cat's In The Well' has a 'fun folk feel,' which is something you shouldn't try to say after a few drinks. So, let's be fair, it's frivolous, it's pretty catchy, and after two acoustic folk 'covers' albums Dylan's next studio album of original material was the mighty 'Time Out Of Mind.' With Mr. Zimmerman, you're never more than a decade away from a masterpiece.

3.44) The Gaslight Tapes – Bob Dylan (1985)

Who wants to rewind? Here we go right back to 1962 before anyone had heard of Mr. Zimmerman. This is a fabulous glimpse of Dylan at the height of his 'folk' era. Some tracks were released as 'Live At The Gaslight' and there are just four tracks that would eventually appear on his regular albums. There is a sense of melancholy about his renditions of folk staples such as 'Barbara Allen.' 'Hezekiah Jones (Black Cross)' highlights racism, 'Rocks And Gravel' and 'Motherless Children' have a great bluesy feel, and best of all is 'John Brown,' a Bob Dylan original that really hammers home the senselessness of war with the same starkness of 'Masters Of War.' A 'nearly lost' Dylan classic for sure.

3.45) The Dark Side Of The Moon – Pink Floyd (1973)

As with the Beatles and Dylan, I'm going to review the Pink Floyd albums in roughly the sequence that I bought them. For many years I've viewed this as my favourite album of all time. Yet when I picked up a tape copy from the Ashford branch of Boots in the early nineties I was somewhat underwhelmed. Hype is like that. You have to listen for yourself, and a lot of the best albums take many listens to work their magic. This album spent roughly six years on the UK album chart and all human life is explained in the lyrics, from madness to war. All your favourite things!

'Breathe' is sublime with its slide guitar oozing resignation, while 'Money' is about the only song on this album which receives regular airplay (often edited because of the rude word). Once you get over the shock of the chiming clocks, the lyrics of 'Time' seem particularly apt, and if you feel nothing upon hearing Clare Torry's impassioned vocal on 'The Great Gig In The Sky' we may as well throw in the towel now. To me, the track seems to represent the struggles of life and the irony of finally finding peace when slipping away. Be rest assured, like the cover, the outlook is not pink, it's black.

3.46) Wish You Were Here – Pink Floyd (1975)

Although I've just nailed my colours to the mast in declaring 'The Dark Side Of The Moon' to be my favourite album of all time, this is the one I tend to go to for instant Floydian gratification. 'Shine On You Crazy Diamond' is a symphony dedicated to the band's original lyricist Syd Barrett, which comes in two halves with some of David Gilmour's bluesiest soloing. The whole album reflects on fame being something of a poison chalice, e.g. 'Welcome To The Machine' and 'Have A Cigar.' The keyboard work by Richard Wright reminds me a bit of Procol Harum at times and every song on the album is an out and out classic. This is one to return to again, and again, and... Enough said.

3.47) Meddle – Pink Floyd (1971)

This album consists of the epic track 'Echoes,' which fills side two, and five very pleasant tracks on side one (anyone remember 'sides?'). This is Pink Floyd at the nearest they ever got to *easy listening*. 'A Pillow Of Winds' is a dreamy affair, 'Fearless' has an added surprise for Liverpool fans, there's the vaudevillian 'San Tropez' and finally 'Seamus' where the band let a canine handle the vocals. If you don't believe it's a dog watch 'Live In Pompeii.' There's also the Doctor-Who-like 'One Of These Days (I'm Going To Cut You Into Little Pieces).' As a footnote, I have a hazy memory of this album as a 'hand me down' vinyl record as a child, although it would have been a bit tough for a ten-year-old to appreciate admittedly.

3.48) Piper At The Gates Of Dawn – Pink Floyd (1967)

As with the Beatles, once I was familiar with the classics, I returned to the beginning for a more thorough rumble through the artifacts. Pink Floyd burst onto the album charts in 1967 with this offering, named after a line from Kenneth Graham's book, 'The Wind In The Willows,' which is fitting as Syd Barrett's childlike imagery and nursery rhyme poetry are very much to the fore. That said, we open with a slab of space rock in the form of 'Astronomy Domine.' 'Lucifer Sam' has a great riff and there are some nice harmonies in the first half of the album too. Once our minds have been blasted into outer space with 'Interstellar Overdrive,' the material seems to thin out with 'The Gnome,' 'Chapter 24' and 'The Scarecrow,' all of which seem to have relatively sparse arrangements. Roger

Waters' cynicism is already evident in the sneering 'Take Up Thy Stethoscope And Walk.'

3.49) A Saucerful Of Secrets – Pink Floyd (1968)

My first encounter with this was on a double-length tape where the songs were interspersed with those from the band's first album. It was cheekily called 'A Nice Pair,' but the tracks didn't gel at all as 'Saucerful' is a very different album to 'Piper.' With Syd's brain more or less turned to mush, he only contributed one song to this album, which is the closing track. David Gilmour gives us his first guitar solo in 'Let There Be More Light,' and 'Set The Controls For The Heart Of The Sun' is ambient music before anybody knew what ambient music was. 'Corporal Clegg' lifts the mood a bit, seeming to be a comedy song, but equally a comment on the futility of war. The key track is 'A Saucerful Of Secrets' itself, which is a kind of sound collage, and a scary one if you are still a teenager and listening with the lights out.

3.50) More – Pink Floyd (1969)

I remember buying this soundtrack album on cassette from a second hand music shop in a basement in Folkestone, which is now buried beneath Bouverie Place shopping centre. There you go, a bit of Kent history for you! I would say that this is the band's most 'sixties' sounding album, taking in styles from ambient soundscapes to folk. Roger Waters' basslines are like a template holding it all together on tracks like 'Main Theme.' There are a few comedic moments and a couple of attempts at heavy rock, which is most unusual for Pink Floyd. My favourite moment is when the fade of 'Cirrus Minor' almost lulls us to sleep with its birdsong, before the grunge guitar of 'The Nile Song' blows us all to kingdom come.

3.51) Ummagumma – Pink Floyd (1969)

This is the band's most bizarre album. For a start it is a double album, but my cassette didn't present it as it was supposed to be heard, as one studio album and one live album, but instead it mixed all the tracks up together. Ugh, why do they do this?

Birdsong is used once again, this time on two tracks. One is Roger Waters' acoustic ditty 'Grantchester Meadows,' named after an area they were familiar with in Cambridge, while the other is Richard Wright's hybrid of classical piano playing and avant-garde soundscapes known as 'Sysyphus.' There's a similar moment to the one I mentioned on 'More,' where we are virtually lulled to sleep before jarring awake, this time with a startling organ and mellotron chord which sounds like it has been lifted straight out of a horror film. Gilmour's own drumming is superb on part three of his contribution, 'The Narrow Way,' and Nick Mason puts together seven minutes of drum solos and doodling himself in the form of 'The Grand Vizier's Garden Party.'

The live album is very 'out there' and contains my favourite version of 'A Saucerful Of Secrets.' Gilmour was very brave to attempt the vocal alone, as it is more 'choral' in the album version of the track. I love the way the melody circles, each time coming back around with more vigour, and just as you think it can't get any more full on, it does. This rendition was a high point of the band's entire career in my opinion. Controversial, hey?

3.52) Atom Heart Mother – Pink Floyd (1970)

'What the hell is this?' would have been my reaction when initially picking up the cassette case in Sam Goody's music shop and seeing song titles like 'Breast Milky' and 'Funky Dung.' In spite of the 'heavy metal sounding' title, the contents are surprisingly easygoing. The first side, 'Atom Heart Mother' itself, is a symphonic piece with orchestrations and choral additions by Ron Geesin, a musical maverick whose works I would explore a good twenty years later. 'If' is a very nice ballad combining love and insanity, and 'Alan's Psychedelic Breakfast' comprises three instrumentals while the band's roadie literally makes his breakfast. It evokes sunlight streaming in through a window, with Richard Wright's piano sounding as though it's being played on a Sunday morning in a church hall. Although this album has often been dismissed, it was the band's first UK number one album and I find myself listening to it a lot.

3.53) Obscured By Clouds – Pink Floyd (1972)

Like 'More,' this was a soundtrack the band produced to a film directed by Barbet Schroeder. I thought that 'More' was quite a good film, depicting the dehumanising effect of drugs, whereas 'La Vallée' really didn't cut the mustard for me. The album however, is great. High points include 'Free Four,' which is an almost humorous Roger Waters song about old age and death, the latter being a subject he would explore much more seriously on 'The Dark Side Of The Moon.' Meanwhile 'Stay' is a remarkably rare thing – a Pink Floyd love song, 'The Gold It's In The...' is a great rocker where Gilmour gets a chance to shine on the guitar, and my favourite of all is the melancholic 'Wots... Uh The Deal,' which deals with the transition from vibrant youth to middle age. I'm sure they could have come up with some better titles however.

3.54) Animals – Pink Floyd (1977)

This was the album where Roger Waters first bared his teeth at the world. I recall cycling a 45-mile round trip from my home to Kent's county town of Maidstone to add this cassette to my collection. It was worth it, and Sutton Valence Hill is a killer on a bike! With the loose theme of dogs, pigs and sheep inspired by George Orwell's 'Animal Farm,' the venom is pointed at business, control / censorship by the elite, and religion in equal measure. At the time I found the corrupted version of the Lord's Prayer somewhat distasteful, but 'Sheep' *is* a great song, with some nice electric piano tinkling at the start building to a rocking finish. The steady cowbell in 'Pigs (Three Different Ones)' is also fab, but the dramatic chord at the end of the penultimate line of 'Dogs' is the *piece de resistance*. As for 'Pigs On The Wing,' worth checking out is the version where the two halves are joined together with a solo by Snowy White. Seriously, look it up...

Chapter 4 – Men At Work

The nineties represented the last golden age of pop as far as I am concerned. During my childhood and teenage years the music of the past seemed to be of higher quality than virtually everything in the pop charts. I learned to play the guitar at the age of seventeen and you couldn't exactly play 'No Limit' by 2 Unlimited or 'Pump Up The Volume' by M/A/R/R/S on an acoustic Spanish guitar, although I'd have the greatest respect for anyone who pulled either of these examples off. However, there was a bit of a folk rock revival at the time and one such band that I had a couple of albums by was the Irish group, the Saw Doctors.

I used to do a regular gig singing and playing acoustic guitar at a local pub for a while, but it turned out that the locals merely wanted some backing for their dirty rugby songs. I recall a night when somebody asked if he could play a song on my guitar. He then launched into a captivating rendition of the song 'Soldier' by Harvey Andrews. This was a mixed blessing, as it pretty much blew what I was doing out of the water, but it did introduce me to a great track which I still love.

Well, being a folk rock superstar wasn't to be, and after five months working in a call centre taking bookings for cross-Channel ferries, I gravitated to the company that I would work for for 25 years. Initially I tried accounts again, but as with the first time, watching paint go from a liquid state to a solid state seemed more exciting. It was when I was moved to the post-room that I found a new social group and discovered some 'current' music that I actually liked!

Oasis. Yes, the clue was in the name. Their music was a pool of thirst-quenching water in a barren landscape of synthesised blips and beats. I recall popping into Our Price Records one lunchtime, egged on by a colleague, and buying around eight Oasis CD singles, which were extraordinary value for money, possessing some great B-sides which were often even better than the A-side. But it wasn't just Oasis who donned guitars at that stage in time. There was Blur, R.E.M., Radiohead, and myriad others, all bands that will be popping up from time to time for the remainder of this book.

The glaring omission, you will note, is Nirvana. For some reason I had dismissed the likes of Cobain and pals, along with Guns 'N Roses, Red Hot Chili Peppers, etc. as 'noisy gits' at the time of their peak popularity. It would take another fifteen years for me to fully appreciate that I'd actually grown up in a pretty good era for music, where staggering musicianship just happened to be overdriven. In fact, I even came to Led Zeppelin somewhat tentatively, having wrongly assumed them to be 'heavy metal,' which was not a genre but an insult to me in those days. Perhaps it was memories of those testosterone-fuelled boys at school who used to sing the praises of the likes of Iron Maiden, Anthrax and Megadeth that put me off - this coupled with the, perhaps unfair, reputation that such bands had for being fixated on trying raise the dark one from the pits of Hell. Parents needn't have worried. The clowns they voted for did a far better job at raising Hades than any rock band ever could!

Anyway, with 'brass in pocket' I would spend my lunch breaks perusing the second hand music shops of the seaside town of Folkestone in Kent, when my colleagues and I weren't in the pub, that was. It was the nineties and you could do that then. I remember pressuring my boss at the time to sign me up for some courses that I thought might further my chances of career progression, to which he replied something like 'I think what's more important to you is just having some money in your pocket to buy music.' He was of course right, but it was still a bit of a lame excuse for not teaching me essential computer skills.

It was around this time that I joined a youth band, although I wasn't exactly a youth by then, and my sister, who *was* still a youth, named us 'The Flood,' inspired by an episode of the BBC comedy 'The Young Ones.' One of the members of our band eventually became an astrophysicist, and that's the nearest any of us got to mingling with the stars. Boom boom.

But what goes up must come down, and the popularity of guitar bands started to wane towards the end of the nineties. I remember a friend who I used to call 'Death Metal Dan' coming into the pub and announcing, 'At last, there's something decent in the charts – the Spice Girls.' Was he being sarcastic? Or did he really think that 'Wannabe' was up there with his favourite bands like Pantera and Cradle Of Filth? See what I mean? Even the names sound scary!

Without further ado, let's get on with the reviews of the albums I bought in this pivotal era of early adulthood. For ease of browsing I've split these into four sections, the first covering the albums of predominantly acoustic artists that I bought on tape, the second covering other vintage tapes, particularly from the 'prog rock' era, thirdly we'll look at CDs from vintage artists, and fourth and finally we'll contemplate what were 'modern' albums at the time. You can file most of this fourth section under 'indie rock.' To keep some kind of structure I'll try to put the artists we've encountered already on our journey at the start of each section. However, I just couldn't do this with the albums by Bob Dylan, Paul Simon and Paul McCartney in section four. It just seemed wrong to usurp Oasis as the flag-bearers of 'my generation.'

I remember for a while I used to wander seven doors along my road so that a friend could copy purchases that I could only get on CD onto tapes for me. Often I would travel sixty miles by train to London to purchase said discs, conveniently forgetting that at the time I didn't have a CD player. As they say, where there's a will there's a way. His name wasn't Will by the way, it was 'Ian!'

i) Unplugged

4.1) American Pie – Don McLean (1971)

This was an album introduced to me by my friends who were twin brothers in possession of impeccable taste in music. Everybody knows the eight-minute history of popular music known as 'American Pie' and the poignant tribute to Van Gogh, 'Vincent,' but this whole album is full of atmospheric tracks, such as the anti-war song 'The Grave' and the tongue in cheek egoism of 'Everybody Loves Me, Baby.' The acoustic guitar has a succulent warmth to it at times, yet it would be a good twenty years before I checked out the album that preceded this one, 'Tapestry,' which is also well worth a listen.

4.2) What's Bin Hid And What's Bin Did – Donovan (1965)

For a young man learning to play guitar, Donovan was a natural 'second' to Dylan. Indeed the Scottish songwriter started off very much in the Zimmerman mould with this album, containing the classic 'Catch The Wind.' Other well known tracks include 'Josie' and 'Why Do You Treat Me Like You Do.' The American influence is obvious with 'Remember The Alamo' and the Woody Guthrie song 'Car Car (Riding In My Car),' and there's even a couple of tracks that are augmented with drums and bass guitar. However Bob Dylan had beaten Donovan to it with his half-electric album 'Bringing It All Back Home' released a couple of months before this one.

Although I eventually bought this collection on a CD release called 'Josie' I'm including it here as I had most of the songs on cassette first. No bickering please.

4.3) Fairytale – Donovan (1965)

This album sees Donovan finding his own feet as a songwriter. The classic here is 'Colours' and the rendition of 'Candy Man' is also a high point for me. 'To Try For The Sun' is another evocative track which will make almost everyone feel old with the line 'Our years put together counted thirty.' The jazzy 'Sunny Goodge Street' indicates the direction Donovan would go next, with its allusion to the swinging London of the sixties. Songs like 'The Ballad Of Geraldine' seem to show where Donovan was headed, with more poetic and surreal subject matter.

4.4) The Greatest Hits... And More – Donovan (1989)

It would be many years before I discovered what Mr. Leitch did next, as I was content with a couple of greatest hits compilations for many years. This one is superb. Due to contractual reasons the original versions of 'Catch The Wind' and 'Colours' could not be used, so Donovan re-recorded them in 1968 and these versions are even more atmospheric in my opinion. 'Sunshine Superman' was hailed as the first psychedelic hit, 'Mellow Yellow' mixes jazz and psychedelia, and 'Atlantis' shows Donovan clearly influenced by the Beatles song, 'Hey Jude.' There are some quieter tracks here too like 'Laléna.' 'Season of the Witch' is also a *bona fide* classic which deserves to be on everyone's Halloween playlist.

4.5) The Collection – Donovan (1990)

This Castle Communications collection augments 'The Greatest Hits... And More' nicely, remaining comprehensive but with minimal duplication. Here we get to see how Donovan progressed into the seventies with the sleepily evocative tracks, 'Lord Of The Reedy River' and 'The Ocean,' as well as rockier material like 'Cosmic Wheels' and 'Song For John.' 'Turquoise' also illustrates the precise transition point between folk and psychedelia. I would eventually acquire virtually all the albums from which these tracks were taken. Those who dismissed Donovan as 'Dylan light' will have missed out on a lot of very good music.

4.6) The Very Best Of Woody Guthrie (Legend Of American Folk Blues) - Woody Guthrie (1992)

Bob Dylan was something of a hero to me in my early twenties, and Woody was his biggest influence, so naturally I wanted to investigate further. The famous songs are of course 'This Land Is Your Land' and 'So Long, It's Been Good To Know You,' which depicts the poverty of the American Dust Bowl, as do many of Guthrie's songs. There is an interview on this compilation and he comes across as a very modest man, whose talent massively eclipsed his ego – pretty much the opposite of many of today's stars. 'A Picture From Life's Other Side' is thought provoking, but my favourite here is the song 'Jesus Christ,' which implies that it was the message that the rich should give to the poor that got JC killed. In truth I wouldn't be surprised. To paraphrase the popular coffee cup motif, 'Same s***, different millennium!'

4.7) King Of Skiffle - Lonnie Donegan (1994)

Just as Woody Guthrie was the seed from which Dylan's tree of knowledge grew, Lonnie Donegan was the catalyst for the Beatles. Skiffle music, which often used home-made instruments such as a washboard for percussion, meant that anyone from any background could now play. Lonnie was a huge star, bagging three UK number one singles, concluding with the ubiquitous 'My Old Man's A Dustman.' The vocal delivery is often frenetic, such as on 'Gamblin' Man.' Blues and gospel influences abound, and Lonnie's version of 'Michael Row The Boat Ashore' tops the more popular version by the Highwaymen in my opinion. Many of the songs have spoken introductions; the subject matter was important, you see? 'Nobody's Child' is particularly poignant, being a song about an orphan, while 'Puttin' On The Style' was a favourite of my paternal grandmother, so I knew it well from childhood days. This Castle Communications release is not just a quaint artifact, this is one of the roots of most of the music we know and love.

4.8) Spiral Staircase – Ralph McTell (1969)

This is a 'must have' for anyone exploring the folk music of the sixties. As a child I remember Ralph McTell being on a children's programme called 'Tickle On The Tum' so I had no idea that he could write such serious songs. My copy of this album was a re-release called 'Streets Of London,' with the label obviously wanting to boost sales by naming McTell's biggest hit. Some tracks are mellow and atmospheric, like 'Mrs. Adnam's Angels' and 'Bright And Beautiful Things,' while 'Last Train And Ride' is a vaudevillian affair with the amusing line 'You've got 57 ways of being mean to me / 57 varieties like Heinz.' Surprisingly this was Ralph McTell's second album and the title track does make a serious point about homelessness while we whine about our cushy lives.

4.9) Acoustic To Electric Blues – Various Artists (1992)

Picked up while cycling through Brighton with a friend who was heavily into jazz, this Deja2 compilation provided an overview of a genre that I would later come to love. I had recently learned to play the guitar and the twelve-bar blues sequence is of course pivotal to so much music. The recordings by Mississippi John Hurt are quite rough in quality, although 'Stack Olee Blues' still sticks in my mind today. There are three classic songs from Leadbelly and another three rippers from Robert Johnson, the guy who supposedly sold his soul to the dark one. Woody Guthrie performs 'House Of The Rising Sun' to an unfamiliar tune and he presents a stinging satire with 'Mean Talking Blues.' As we move into the electric blues era we meet John Lee Hooker, Elmore James, B.B. King and others. This album is a good place to start for sure, but blues is a 'long and winding road.'

ii) Reel 2 Reel

4.10) Motown's Greatest Hits – The Temptations (1992)

It was the song 'Ball of Confusion' that prompted me to investigate the Temptations. Obviously I knew them for their typical Motown fare of 'My Girl' and 'Get Ready,' but this lyrical deluge about the chaotic planet of the late sixties sung over semi-psychedelic backing intrigued me greatly. 'Cloud Nine' is another good track from the band's 'psychedelic soul' period, and 'Papa Was A Rolling Stone' has a vibe of timelessness; the band take a full six minutes to let the story unfold, with the strings adding a sense of mystery. There are even a couple of later tracks on this compilation like 'Treat Her Like A Lady' and *The Jones'* which proved that the band continued to adapt to the times but not in an unpleasant way.

4.11) Unplugged – Eric Clapton (1992)

Clappers gets back to his blues roots in what was one of the most popular releases from the 'Unplugged' series in which big names in rock treated us to live acoustic renditions of their biggest hits and more. 'Before You Accuse Me' and 'Nobody Knows You When You're Down And Out' stand out, but he also gives us a laid back version of 'Layla' as well as 'Tears In Heaven' which was written for his son who he tragically lost. 'San Francisco Bay Blues' lightens the tone with that rarest of things – a kazoo solo.

4.12) The Best Of Status Quo 1968-1971 – Status Quo (1989)

If you think of Status Quo as a three-chord 'one-trick pony,' think again. This overview of the early years mixes their initial lightly psychedelic sound on 'Josie' and 'Hey Little Woman' with the gritty blues of 'Down The Dustpipe' and 'In My Chair.' 'Daughter' has a great riff, 'Railroad' is a blues song with three distinct rhythms, and '(April) Spring, Summer & Wednesdays' is another riff-based high point. I once witnessed 'Gerdundula' being passed off as a traditional song at a folk club. Naturally I was delighted by this piece of deception by the performers.

4.13) Rocking All Over The Years – Status Quo (1990)

Of course, once you've realised what a good band the Quo were, you're going to want all the hits, and this album fits the bill perfectly. After 'Pictures Of Matchstick Men' and 'Ice In The Sun,' they crank up the guitars and boogie right on to the end of the album. All the hits are here, and I recall the DJ at our local Scout and Guide discos just whacking on a load of these tracks when I was a teenager, and quite frankly they always succeeded as floor-fillers, so why not? The

Quo clearly mastered the art of intros with 'Whatever You Want' and the brief piano doodle at the start of 'Rockin' All Over The World.' 'Wild Side Of Life' is a great rendition of a country classic and later on we get a change in style with 'In The Army Now' and 'Burning Bridges,' which was later adopted as an anthem for Manchester United Football Squad, giving the Quo their second UK number one in 1994 (the first was 'Down Down' in January 1975).

If you want to scale up on your Status Quo collection, the 2008 compilation 'The Status Quo Story' has all the essential tracks, sometimes in longer 'album' formats, and adds a few rip-roarers like 'Again And Again.'

4.14) Led Zeppelin (1969)

In truth I bought the 'Remasters' (1990) double cassette before I bought any 'regular' Led Zeppelin albums, again inspired by that Radio 1 documentary on the 100 greatest albums that I might have mentioned once before. However, as we are covering all of the pivotal albums the foursome released, I'm going to cut straight to the chase. Opening with the anthemic 'Good Times, Bad Times,' the band soon immerse themselves in the 'drop A minor' acoustic folk sequence of 'Baby I'm Gonna Leave You' which relaxes you before exploding. Led Zep started off as a blues band and this is evident on 'You Shook Me' and 'I Can't Quit You Baby.' 'Your Time Is Gonna Come' perhaps harks back to the earlier styles of the sixties, but for an angst-ridden sonic assault it has to be 'Dazed And Confused,' with lines like 'Soul of a woman was created below.' Now don't be sexist, boys!

4.15) Led Zeppelin II (1969)

How's this for productivity – a second Led Zeppelin album maintaining the high quality of the first in spite of being released in the same year? 'Whole Lotta Love' is an anthem that was even re-recorded as the theme for BBC TV's 'Top Of The Pops,' and 'Heartbreaker' is another rip-roarer with Jimmy Page left to indulge himself solo on the guitar in the middle. But it's not all full on. 'Ramble On' is folky, while Robert Plant sounds like an old blues vocalist at the beginning and end of 'Bring It On Home and John Bonham shows what he can do on the drums in 'Moby Dick.' 'Thank You' sounds more 'sixties' in style, while 'The Lemon Song' is just plain naughty!

4.16) Led Zeppelin III – Led Zeppelin (1970)

'III' is an album of two halves. The first half opens with the archetypal Zeppelin of 'Immigrant Song' and includes the seven-minute blues epic 'Since I've been Loving You,' which I remember putting on the jukebox in a pub that my father ran for two weeks, with his reaction being along the lines of 'What the hell is this?' There's also 'Out On The Tiles' (which is very similar to 'Good Times, Bad Times' from the first album), but it is the relaxed folky second half of the album that impresses the most, particularly 'Tangerine' and 'That's The Way,' which are both great for sitting round a campfire! Jimmy Page gives us some great slide guitar on 'Hats Off To Roy Harper' and John Paul Jones holds the three massive egos together on bass as always.

4.17) Led Zeppelin IV (1971)

'IV' is not strictly the name of this album which showed four symbols as its title, but I like Roman numerals so I'm sticking to it. This was the first Led Zeppelin album I bought and what a start! This is the album that contains the best song of all time ('Stairway To Heaven') and that statement is non-negotiable, but 'Stairway' isn't even the finisher. For that we get the anthemic blues of 'When The Levee Breaks' with one of the most sampled drumbeats of all time. 'Misty Mountain Hop' seems to echo back to a more 'sixties' sound and there are a couple of folky tracks too, one with Fairport Convention's Sandy Denny as a guest vocalist. And I haven't even mentioned the full blown rock and roll of 'Black Dog' (a metaphor for depression) or the track 'Rock And Roll,' with its self-reviewing title!

4.18) Houses Of The Holy – Led Zeppelin (1973)

Oh, shucks, they stopped doing the Roman numeral thing on this one. What was wrong with calling it 'Led Zeppelin V?' Those who purchased the greatest hits collection will be surprised that the song 'Houses Of The Holy' isn't actually on this album, but the content is vary varied. We have the melancholic 'Rain Song' which I'm sure consciously lifts a chord sequence from Buddy Holly's track 'Raining In My Heart.' There's folk in the form of 'Over The Hills And Far Away,' there's a 'James Brown' style funk pastiche called 'The Crunge' and the finishing track 'The Ocean' shifts gear near the end, but don't rush it – it contains one of the best guitar riffs of all time. Oh yes, and 'No Quarter' is sublime with a middle instrumental that always makes me think of a grand piano in an empty room in a mansion.

4.19) Physical Graffiti – Led Zeppelin (1975)

'Led Zeppelin VI?' No, it looks like we're firmly into the 'names' thing now. This double album opens with a CD that runs almost like a 'greatest hits,' with 'Custard Pie,' 'Houses Of The Holy,' 'Trampled Underfoot' and 'Kashmir' being four of its six tracks. 'Kashmir' was probably one of the first Led Zep songs I appreciated, once again from that seminal Radio 1 countdown of the greatest albums. The Eastern orchestrations and John Bonham's epic drum fills create one hell of an ambience. Even longer than this track is 'In My Time Of Dying,' which is a remarkably different beast to the acoustic version on Bob Dylan's first album. This is an instrumental workout for the entire band. The second disc presents a greater variety of styles. 'Down By The Seaside' shows a gentle side to the mighty Zeppelin, as do 'Boogie With Stu' and 'Black Country Woman,' which still surprises me with its syncopated rhythm at the point that the bass drum starts pounding.

4.20) A Night At The Opera – Queen (1975)

Queen's 'Greatest Hits' is the biggest selling album of all time in the UK and it was my starting place with Mercury and pals, but I'm not going to review it simply because all the band's albums would eventually find their way into my collection. Casting my mind back to my school days, there was one particular wooden desk where a pupil had carved the entire track listing of Queen's 'Greatest Hits' into the wood, presumably with the end of a compass, such was the zeal this band could produce. And no, it wasn't me!

The first two *bona fide* Queen albums that I owned were a pair of tapes, both named after Marx Brothers films and both picked up in Brighton if my memory serves me well. Opening with the scathing rock of 'Death On Two Legs,' which teases with the bracketed addition '(Dedicated To...)', we are in for a ride through musical styles including folk (*'39*) and vaudeville ('Lazing On A Sunday Afternoon' and 'Seaside Rendezvous'). And it isn't just 'Bohemian Rhapsody' that steals the show. Longer and just as bold is 'The Prophet's Song,' which strips down to a vocal collage before Brian May slams in some enormously satisfying guitar chords. If you want to bawl your eyes out there's 'Love Of My Life' too!

4.21) A Day At The Races – Queen (1976)

Repeating the formula of 'A Night At The Opera,' we again begin with a rocker in the form of 'Tie Your Mother Down.' 'You Take My Breath Away' subs for 'Love Of My Life' and I always enjoy 'Good Old-Fashioned Lover Boy' as Freddie sounds genuinely happy here. Instead of 'Bo Rhap,' the symphonic leanings are satiated with 'Somebody To Love.' 'White Man' is a fabulous rocker against colonialist bigotry, and the album closes with one of those sound illusions where the notes seem to rise interminably *a la* the end of Pink Floyd's 'Echoes.'

4.22) Opel – Syd Barrett (1988)

If you need reminding that taking drugs is not a good idea, this is the album for you. By 1968 poor old Syd could barely function and was consequently replaced by David Gilmour in Pink Floyd's line up. He even says it himself in one of the lyrics; 'I've tattooed my brain!' This album comprises the best of what was left in the vaults after Syd's two solo albums were released. 'Opel' has a truly harrowing feel to the vocal, while 'Clowns And Jugglers (Octopus)' sounds like he is reverting to childhood in a crazed vision. Some tracks like 'Milky Way' are quite endearing and some are very sad, such as 'Wouldn't You Miss Me.' Others are just 'off the wall,' like 'Word Song,' which consists of, well, words, I mean a literal list of unconnected words! Much of the material is acoustic and the bonus tracks lift the mood of the album somewhat. One glaring omission, 'Bob Dylan Blues,' which wasn't released at the time of this compilation, shows that Syd's sense of humour had at least remained intact. It can be found on the compilation 'An Introduction To Syd Barrett' (2010) which also includes the twenty-minute jam 'Rhamadan.'

4.23) The Very Best Of Elton John – Elton John (1990)

The first Elton John compilation I had was a single cassette and I duly upgraded to this double album, before later progressing onto the double CD set 'Greatest Hits 1970-2002.' The problem with Elton is that he's never released a completely comprehensive hits collection. Modern compilations tend to miss off 'Passenger' which was a big hit in the eighties, as well as 'Candle In The Wind '97' (the 'Princess Diana tribute' version) and numerous other essentials. For many years, this was by far the best compilation.

The track listing is literally hit after hit, and the chronological ordering shows Elton's progress from the shyness of 'Your Song' to the flamboyance of his covers of 'Pinball Wizard' and 'Lucy In The Sky With Diamonds.' The standout tracks for me are all ballads; the original 'Marilyn Monroe' version of 'Candle In The Wind,' 'Rocket Man,' 'Don't Let The Sun Go Down On Me' and 'Someone Saved My Life Tonight' – all 'bread and butter' stuff that should be in every collection. Hats off to lyricist Bernie Taupin too. One track I always enjoy that doesn't often get mentioned is 'Honky Cat,' which reflects on growing up in the countryside. I doubt you'll stop with just this collection to be honest. For a start you're going to want the classic early-noughties hit 'This Train Don't Stop There Any More' which to my mind harks back to Reginald Dwight's glory days.

4.24) Deepest Purple (The Very Best Of Deep Purple) – Deep Purple (1980)

Are you ready to rock? 'Black Night' and 'Smoke On The Water' are of course included and the energy level doesn't drop once during the opening three tracks. 'Fireball' is a candidate for 'best ever intro' with John Lord's organ lulling you into a false sense of security before Ritchie Blackmore's guitar and Ian Gillan's voice box explode. There's a ten-minute epic in the form of 'Child In Time,' and 'Highway Star' is another surge of energy. It's a cliché, but this album really is 'all thriller, no filler.'

4.25) Pilgrimage – Wishbone Ash (1971)

In my early twenties I established a lifelong penchant of looking for something different, and this album certainly provided it, with the jazzy prog openers 'Vas

Dis' and 'The Pilgrim' leading the way with no lyrics whatsoever. 'Jail Bait' is a stomper that Status Quo would have been proud of, and the ten-minute closer, 'Where Were You Tomorrow,' is a blues workout with a minimalist middle section. Did they invent drum and bass? There are also some very nice harmonies on 'Valediction.' Later I would purchase 'Argus' (1972), which was the album that followed this. It is a more vocal affair and the opening track, 'Time Was,' is melodic, harmonic, rocky and wistful all at once. And not a lot of bands can pull that off!

4.26) The Zombies / The Singles A's and B's [sic] – The Zombies (1984)

This was a 'See For Miles' release, and at the time I only knew 'She's Not There,' as the Zombies pretty much never reached the upper echelons of the British singles charts again – a travesty. The material is all very high quality and extremely melodic, with Colin Blunstone's vocals always sounding sweet. 'I Love You' is short and to the point in particular and 'Tell Her No' made the US top ten.

Eventually I would progress to the double album release of the same name minus the stray apostrophes (2002) by Repertoire Records, which additionally includes some great tracks from the band's acclaimed album 'Odyssey And Oracle,' such as the haunting psychedelic anti-war track 'Butcher's Tale (Western Front 1914),' the evocative 'Beechwood Park' and the extremely catchy 'Friends Of Mine.' There's even a third stab at US chart success with 'Time Of The Season.' Keyboard player Rod Argent went on to form the band 'Argent' (now that's not egotistical, is it?) which produced two rock classics, 'Hold Your Head Up' and 'God Gave Rock And Roll To You.'

4.27) Framed – The Sensational Alex Harvey Band (1972)

Another second hand tape that opened up new vistas. Alex Harvey was one of Scotland's finest and he died too young, but his distinct and eccentric vocal style meant that his legacy was safe. The title track is a rip-roaring rock and roll rendition – just wait for Zal Cleminson's guitar solo. 'Hammer Song' expresses the plight of the working man, and just as you think it's faded out Alex screams justified anger in your face. With apologies to Etta James, Harvey's version of 'I Just Want To Make Love To You' is the definitive version for me, with the horns rising up through the melee at the end. 'Hole In Her Stocking' has some crazy saxophone, and the album also contains the only Christmas song I know that includes an electric chair in the lyrics. And this was only the group's first album.

4.28) Next – The Sensational Alex Harvey Band (1973)

Alex Harvey tones up the risqué lyrics on this 1973 release, with 'Gang Bang' being the obvious example. I guess no one worried about STDs in this era! 'The Faith Healer' has a brooding atmospheric quality which contrasts with the rock and roll material. 'Next' is the most controversial song that Alex *didn't* write, although it perhaps has a serious point about abuse in the army. This leads perfectly into 'Vambo Marble Eye' (almost a segue). The closing epic, 'The Last Of The Teenage Idols,' has a wonderfully deranged vocal and consists of three distinct parts which get increasingly 'tongue in cheek' stylistically.

4.29) The Impossible Dream – The Sensational Alex Harvey Band (1974)

What did the ever-eccentric Alex do next? He reprised the 'Vambo' theme as 'Part 1' of his 'Hot City Symphony' and gave us a 'film noir' style monologue for 'Part 2.' 'Long Hair Music' has a great 'feedback and drums' opening (could that be a genre?) and I used to put the forty-second jazz joke, 'Hey,' on repeat when my friend Simon used to visit me for boozy sleepovers, just for the sheer devilment of it. The closing track, 'Anthem,' is a nod to Harvey's Scottish heritage and builds slowly to the bagpiped conclusion. You canna beat it, man!

4.30) The Penthouse Tapes - The Sensational Alex Harvey Band (1976)

This album is worth it alone for the crazed version of Leadbelly's 'Goodnight Irene.' 'Gamblin' Bar Room Blues' evokes the feel of a whisky joint in the American Wild West and there are a couple of full on rock assaults with covers of Alice Cooper's 'School's Out' and 'Crazy Horses' by the Osmonds. The album ends with a live rendition of the old standard 'Cheek To Cheek.' I've no idea what was going on on that stage but the audience clearly enjoyed it. Oh yes, and Alex dispenses handy advice against the perils of urinating in the water supply at one point too. Charming.

4.31) The Great British Psychedelic Trip 1966-1969 – Various Artists (1986)

A fabulous release from See For Miles Records, but beware, the tape version is much better than the CD version which was released later and has a different track listing. We open with 'The Tales Of Flossie Fillet' which sees a band called Turquoise sounding like the Kinks. 'Created By Clive' is a great pastiche on sixties fashion, 'Baked Jam Roll In Your Eye' is just bonkers and 'Ice Man' has a touch of the early Pink Floyd about it. It's the album's finale that really excels though, with 'Father's Name Was Dad' by the Fire being a long lost rock classic. The Flies also infuse 'I'm Not Your Stepping Stone' with menace that was only hinted at in the Monkees' more famous version.

4.32) Fontana - The Sixties Album – Various Artists (1992)

This was a great sampler cassette of artists from that legendary decade who were signed to the Fontana label, taking us from the straight up beat material of the early sixties to the New Vaudeville Band's homage to Winchester Cathedral, the Herd's psychedelic hit 'From The Underworld' and the minimalist 1970 'stomp' of 'Neanderthal Man' by Hotlegs, an early incarnation of 10cc. Also included are the Merseybeats, the Pretty Things, the Troggs, Dave Dee, Dozy, Beaky, Mick And Tich – in fact it's pretty much a musical encyclopedia of the sixties, and the longer CD version gives us even more fun, including one of my favourite party hits from the era, 'Bend It.'

iii) Gold

4.33) Smiley Smile – The Beach Boys (1967)

Here I transitioned into a new age where you could get a whacking eighty minutes of music on a little silver circle. To begin with I didn't possess a CD player and I would travel to Tower Records in London to buy all manner of obscurity that I couldn't get in Kent and then politely ask my friend Ian from seven doors along my road if he could copy them to tape for me. This was one such example.

I enjoyed the two semi-psychedelic tracks, 'Good Vibrations' and 'Heroes And Villains,' so I was curious to purchase this, but it isn't the much-heralded 'Smile' album but the ashes of the product which were left when the mind of the creative genius Brian Wilson imploded. Some of the best tracks, such as 'Surf's Up,' would surface later in the Beach Boys career, but what we have here is a bizarre mix of psychedelia and comedy. 'She's Going Bald' is both eerie and daft, while 'Wind Chimes' is just spooky. 'With You Tonight' is really just the backing vocals to an uncompleted song, but they are very nice and the organ sounds creepy. 'Vegetables' includes band members chomping on said foodstuffs as percussion, while 'Wonderful' includes what seems like a ghostly version of the party atmosphere of 'Barbara Ann.' Really this should be viewed as a Halloween album, and the bonus tracks actually outshine the main material for polish.

4.34) Wild Honey – The Beach Boys (1967)

My CD copy of 'Smiley Smile' was one of a number of 'two for one' CDs that packed together two Beach Boys albums. As I said, you could get eighty minutes of music onto a disc and USA album releases were particularly short in the sixties. So as a bonus I got to hear this album which has a sense of 'ground zero' after Brian Wilson stepped back from creative control. The title track and the cover of *Darlin'* were both hits for the band, and the mood is not psychedelic although it still has a slightly mysterious feel. 'I'd Love Just Once To See You' has a cheeky punchline, while 'Let The Wind Blow' sounds like a leftover from 'Smiley Smile.' 'Mama Says' was precisely that, and this closes the album, as though the ghost of the abandoned 'Smile' project was still watching over everything the Beach Boys did.

4.35) Sweetest Apples / More Sweet Apples – The Beatles (1994)

When I bought this pair of illegal CDs compiled by the dubious 'Julia Taxman' and released on 'Robber Soul Records,' it was great to get my hands on some 'new' Beatles material, and there really are some gems here from the years 1966-1970. George's 'White Album' outtake 'Not Guilty' would get an official release two years later as part of the 'Anthology' project. Take 26 of 'Strawberry Fields Forever,' which continues relentlessly where the record fades out and back in, would eventually surface on the fiftieth anniversary edition of Sgt. Pepper. The long versions of 'Hey Majesty' and 'Dig It' presented here are both interesting and have never seen the official light of day. Outtakes from the 'Get Back / Let It Be' sessions that you'll only find here include 'The Walk' and a drunk sounding rendition of 'Save The Last Dance For Me.'

Don't be fooled by the three Harry Nilsson tracks from the album 'Pussy Cats,' which the compiler tries to pass off as John Lennon recordings, or the 'outfake' of 'Glass Onion' which has a non-Beatles guitar effect whacked onto it. 'I Lost My Little Girl' is interesting because it was the first song written by Paul McCartney. The version of 'Get Back' in pidgin German and French is funny, while the version entitled 'No Pakistanis' perhaps shows how the song began, as a satire on racist attitudes. If you need confirmation that the Beatles were on the progressive side of the debate, listen to 'Commonwealth' which lambasts Tory MP Enoch Powell and his speech about 'rivers of blood.'

4.36) Anthology 1-3 – The Beatles (1995-1996)

Imagine my excitement when the Beatles released a single within my own lifetime, even if it did sound more like ELO. Jeff Lynne as co-producer had clearly left his mark on the track 'Free As A Bird,' which used an old piano demo of Lennon's and overdubbed instruments and vocals by the three remaining Beatles. It's a shame they didn't score their eighteenth UK number one hit with this, as it would have pushed their tally of original chart-toppers ahead of Elvis. Instead it was the band's fifth 'number two.' A second track, 'Real Love,' was given the same treatment, but George Harrison pulled out of a third 'new' song, which is believed to have been a track called 'Now And Then.' Someone on the Internet has had a go at this anyway and the results are very good indeed.

'Anthology 1' is at its best in documenting the Fabs' pre-fame years, with humorous material like 'Three Cool Cats' and early recordings of rocked up standards, such as 'My Bonnie' with Tony Sheridan and 'Ain't She Sweet.' If you want to explore the early years more, 'The Decca Audition' is well worth a listen and much easier to digest, but is it legal? Ahem.

'Anthology 2' shows that even the songs the Beatles binned were pretty good. Good examples are 'That Means A Lot' and the Ringo-fronted song 'If You've Got Trouble.' '12-Bar Original ' is an atmospheric instrumental (you can imagine the cigarette smoke swirling around them). Meanwhile 'I'm Looking Through You' has a bolt-on twelve-bar section here, and there's a dreamy version of 'Tomorrow Never Knows.'

'Anthology 3' gives us acoustic demos, although the fiftieth anniversary edition of the 'White Album' presents virtually the whole work acoustically as a bonus disc. 'What's The New Mary Jane' is a six-minute mind-blast and the demo of 'Come

And Get It,' which was a hit for Badfinger, is very nice too.

To summarise, there was clearly more gold in the vaults, but like the curate's egg, you have to pick your way through some quite uninspiring stuff to get to it. Ditto for all the anniversary reissues of the Beatles' albums which I would have organised completely differently myself. Why? Well, for a start I don't need fifteen different takes of the same track. A couple of radically different versions will do nicely, but thanks for offering. No, I'd rather see some braver inclusions worthy of the pioneers that the band were in the sixties, such as the spooky 'Jessie's Dream' from the 'Magical Mystery Tour' film or the long version of 'Flying' with its coda of ambient mellotron doodling (both can be heard on YouTube at the time of writing). And while we're at it, let's have a listen to 'Carnival Of Light,' Paul's sound collage from January 1967 which predated John's 'Revolution 9' (1968). There are only 'fakes' on YouTube of this one so don't be fooled. The wish list goes on, but I've other albums to review...

4.37) The Wall – Pink Floyd (1979)

I took a long time adding this 'essential' to my Pink Floyd collection, possibly because of my childhood mistrust of synthesisers. However, Richard Wright keeps it pretty subtle really. This is a true rock opera, documenting the loneliness of a musician from childhood to rock excess, before his mind finally collapses into a nightmare vision where he is the leader of some kind of fascist party. It's seriously dark stuff and we are treated to not just 'Part 2' of 'Another Brick In The Wall,' which provided the band with their only UK number one single, but 'Part 1' and 'Part 3' as well. The awesomeness of David Gilmour's solo on 'Comfortably Numb' goes without saying, and another highlight is the melancholy 'Nobody Home.' Some of the tracks on the second disc are augmented with orchestrations, paving the way for the phantasmagorical finish where the central character, Pink, is subjected to a court assessing his whole life before tearing down the metaphorical wall he has built between himself and reality. The film has an even darker feel, although the movie version of 'Outside The Wall' has a brassy uplift at the end, like a single ray of sunshine breaking through the gloom.

4.38) The Final Cut – Pink Floyd (1983)

Declaring itself 'A requiem for the post-war dream,' it's pretty clear this isn't an album for revellers or dancing queens. Roger Waters leads his bandmates through the darker recesses of his mind, relating to losing his father in World War II and the frustration of seeing Britain go to war once again. This time, it was the Falklands conflict. You can't deny that this is stirring stuff, with tracks like 'Your Possible Pasts' and the feeling of laying awake at night ruminating encapsulated in 'One Of The Few.' David Gilmour gets to let rip on the guitar occasionally, which is always nice. Thankfully 'When The Tigers Break Free' has been added into the re-released album, being only available as a single for many years. Oh yes, and mind your language on 'Not Now John.' It's a '15' certificate from me, Rog.

4.39) A Momentary Lapse Of Reason – Pink Floyd (1987)

Bassist and chief songwriter Roger Waters left the band but was rather disgruntled when Gilmour and Mason continued to use the name. Keyboardist Richard Wright, having been booted out of the band before 'The Final Cut,' was welcomed back as a guest musician. Top tracks for me are 'Dogs Of War' and 'Sorrow,' which opens with a monumental brooding solo from Gilmour. 'A New Machine,' presented in two parts, is pretty minimalist, consisting largely of just a processed vocal track. Waters famously called the album 'a pretty fair forgery.' It's a forgery I listen to quite often however.

4.40) The Division Bell – Pink Floyd (1994)

The band were clearly back in business with this album which hit number one in the UK charts, a feat previously only achieved by 'Atom Heart Mother,' 'Wish You Were Here' and 'The Final Cut.' After some ambient doodling, we launch into 'What Do You Want From Me' with some searing guitar from David Gilmour which is up with his best work in my opinion. 'Keep Talking' uses the computerised voice made famous by legendary physicist Stephen Hawking, and 'High Hopes' is 'classic Floyd' without a doubt, with its ominous piano motif and church bell representing the single threads that run through life from childhood to old age.

4.41) Music From The Body – Roger Waters & Ron Geesin (1970)

Put this in the pigeonhole marked 'wacky.' You may recall my friend Simon who used to visit my converted garage room at my parents' house for nights of beer and indulgence. Well, this album was often the soundtrack to these nights, with us positively cracking up at the track 'Body Transport,' which we referred to as 'the breathing song.' This consists of somebody snoring loudly while two voices titter around trying not to wake the sleeper. It's actually very funny after a few beers, and it's typical of Ron Geesin's bizarre creativity, which included using body sounds as instruments. The tracks performed by Pink Floyd's Roger Waters are sparse with just an acoustic guitar for backing. Lyrically these are wistful musings about the journey of life, and I like the early environmentalism of the line 'Spidery fingers of industry reach for the sky.' Each of these acoustic tracks feels like waking up after a series of bizarre dreams, before the subconscious takes over again and lures us into the labyrinth of Geesin's avant-garde instrumentals. The concluding track, 'Give Birth To A Smile,' features all the members of Pink Floyd, and if you've seen the accompanying film the feeling is triumphant after you've watched the real-time birth of what was then the planet's youngest inhabitant.

4.42) Tomorrow Belongs To Me – The Sensational Alex Harvey Band (1975)

I had to get my local branch of *Richard's Records* to order this CD from continental Europe. It's all so easy these days. Who else misses the era when you had to scale mountains and swim across shark infested waters just to get a CD?!! Anyway, highlights this time include 'Soul In Chains' which is one of those songs that builds up from a cool electric piano opening into a frenzy. 'The Tale Of The Giant Stone Eater' is a monologue set to music with an environmental message. 'Tomorrow Belongs To Me' reworks a tune from the musical 'Cabaret,' perhaps reclaiming its sentiment from the Nazis for more innocent purposes.

4.43) Hunky Dory – David Bowie (1971)

In the nineties BBC Radio 1 was not just an outlet for the latest music but had documentaries about the heroes of the past. There was a particularly interesting one on David Bowie, and I was intrigued by the way his music morphed from the 'Anthony Newley' style vaudeville songs of his first album to the full blown rock of the 'Ziggy Stardust' era. The 'in between' period when this album was produced fascinated me the most, and I picked this gem up from one of the many music shops that used to be in The Lanes in Brighton. I did buy 'Changesonebowie' (1976) on tape early on, but as we will eventually look at all of the albums covered by this compilation we'll crash straight in.

'Changes' pretty much sums up Bowie's entire output in a word, while 'Oh! You Pretty Things' again uses Rick Wakeman's piano to great effect. 'Life On Mars' started out as a parody of the Paul Anka-penned classic 'My Way,' but takes on a life of its own with its series of surreal images summing up life on this crazy planet called Earth. Bowie questions the heroes of the day in 'Song For Bob Dylan' and 'Andy Warhol,' and leaves us thinking 'What on earth was that about?' at the end of 'The Bewlay Brothers.' I wonder if he ever did get his gravy!

4.44) The Gospel According To David Bowie – David Bowie (1993)

This was a Spectrum Music compilation of early recordings from the pre-Space Oddity sixties, when Bowie sounded more like Anthony Newley than Ziggy Stardust. The tracks are quirky and fun but have often been overlooked. 'The Laughing Gnome' even became a top ten hit when it was re-released in 1973. David Bowie cracks dodgy 'gnome' puns in a speeded up high-pitched voice and this is one of the few songs I know that mention the Sussex town of Eastbourne. 'The Gospel According To Tony Day' has a great rhythm and amusing lyrics about (presumably) imaginary friends. 'Love You Till Tuesday' concludes with the punchline 'I might be able to stretch it till Wednesday.' The quirkiness was still apparent in some of the 'Hunky Dory' tracks, and later I would purchase 'The Deram Anthology 1966-1968' (1997) to complete my collection of Mr. Jones's early output, David Jones being his original name, changed to 'Bowie' to avoid confusion with that bloke from the Monkees.

4.45) The Man Who Sold The World – David Bowie (1970)

So, with 'Space Oddity' under his belt as a UK top ten hit in 1969, what did the young Bowie do next? Of course, he put on a pretty dress for the cover of his next album and launched himself into heavy rock. In my opinion, this album really doesn't get the recognition it deserves and it's certainly in my 'Bowie top three.' The title track has been covered by artists as diverse as Lulu and Nirvana, and David tries on the persona of a psychopath in 'Running Gun Blues.' 'After All' presages the ending of 'The Bewlay Brothers' with its peculiar vocals, and best of all there's 'All The Madmen' which blends folk and heavy rock while David muses 'I'd rather stay here / With all the madmen / Than perish with the sad men roaming free' in a lyric which seems to be set in an asylum. All the while humans view torture and war as 'normal' I'm inclined to agree with this sentiment. It's better to be a bit bonkers at least.

4.46) The Rise And Fall Of Ziggy Stardust And The Spiders From Mars – David Bowie (1972)

In my younger days, I was a bigger fan of this album's predecessor, 'Hunky Dory.' However, for pure escapism, 'Ziggy' is a masterpiece and now one of my all-time favourites. The first three tracks run together like a trilogy, as do the final three. The tracks in between don't exactly drop the baton either. Bowie starts out theatrically with 'Five Years,' observing ordinary life through an apocalyptic lens. Mick Ronson's soaring guitar solos excel throughout, for example on 'Moonage Daydream.' This is the album with 'Starman' on it too. The use of strings on what became known as 'glam rock' was perhaps pioneered by T. Rex, but the style surely reached its zenith on Bowie's 'Rock And Roll Suicide.' It's a bold statement, but this album provides a rare glimpse of something beyond the mundane.

4.47) Heroes – David Bowie (1977)

I remember being somewhat underwhelmed when I first listened to this on cassette. The title track is of course an instant classic but the rest of the album is a challenge for the uninitiated, which meant *me* at the time. Following 'Low,' this was the second album of what became known as Bowie's 'Berlin trilogy' and the format is similar, with a side of actual 'songs' and a side of German-inspired ambient instrumentals. The only difference this time is that he wakes us up at the end with 'The Secret Life Of Arabia.'

4.48) Alice's Restaurant – Arlo Guthrie (1967)

Monologues were once popular in the folk tradition and Woody's son perhaps came up with the most famous monologue of all time in the form of the 'Alice's Restaurant Massacree.' The basic anti-war punchline is that he was banned from killing people in the army because of a littering offence but the way he tells it, bookending it with a catchy refrain, makes its eighteen minutes highly entertaining. Of the remaining tracks 'The Motorcycle Song' is the most memorable. I first became aware of this album via my friend, near-neighbour and CD copier, Ian.

4.49) The History Of Fairport Convention – Fairport Convention (1972)

Another folk masterpiece from 'Ian's music introduction service.' Fairport were perhaps the embodiment of folk-rock and vocalist Sandy Denny is always a pleasure to hear. 'Meet On The Ledge' and 'Who Knows Where The Time Goes' are fine examples of her brief tenure with the band. 'Sloth' and 'Matty Groves' run to epic lengths, the latter being a traditional folk song which I encountered when learning guitar from a lady called Suzanne. The version in her book had no less than 22 verses. When Denny departed, the band moved towards a more traditional sound and both eras are well represented here. There's even a version of the Dylan-penned song 'If You've Gotta Go, Go Now' sung in French. C'est tres bien.

4.50) The Hangman's Beautiful Daughter – The Incredible String Band (1968)

Who's ever heard of psychedelic folk music? No, I didn't think so. Well, this duo were actually quite influential in the late sixties. 'Koeeoaddi There' sets the mysterious scene perfectly with some sitar added into the mix, 'The Minotaur's Song' sounds amusingly like a precursor of Monty Python's 'Lumberjack Song' and my favourite is 'Mercy I Cry City' which is an early environmental song with the bizarre line 'Your slowly killing fumes now squeeze the lemon in my head.' 'A Very Cellular Song' is just that – a song constructed from separately recorded 'cells,' a technique that Brian Wilson used for 'Good Vibrations' and his 'Smile' project with the Beach Boys.

4.51) Collectors Items: The First Three EPs - Country Joe And The Fish / Peter Krug / Country Joe McDonald & Grootna (1980)

Country Joe McDonald was perhaps more famous for his 'call and response' sequence with the crowd at the Woodstock festival rather than his music. You know, 'Give me an F, give me a U...' etc. Anyway, the music contained here is great, beginning with two versions of 'I Feel Like I'm Fixin' To Die Rag,' a darkly comedic anti-war song with lines like 'You can be the first person on your block /

To have your boy come home in a box.' Country Joe dabbles with a psychedelic sound for the next four tracks, and after a couple of acoustic protest songs by Peter Krug, Country Joe comes back even more fired up about the war and Nixon with some infectiously catchy tracks like 'Kiss My Ass' and 'Tricky Dicky.'

I think at the time I was keen to try out virtually any music from the late sixties, including buying a 'greatest hits' package by Jefferson Airplane. Sadly this one didn't grab me, perhaps because nothing seemed to match the splendidness of 'White Rabbit' which builds up to Grace Slick's astounding vocal urging you to 'feed your head.' My next 'brain food' was to be a healthy slab of voodoo jazz...

4.52) The Very Best Of Dr. John – Dr. John (1995)

I'm not sure how I stumbled across Dr. John. It might possibly have been the fact that a Johnny Jenkins cover of Dr. John's 'Walk On Guilded Splinters' was sampled by Beck for his nineties hit 'Loser.' The original version on this Rhino release sounds nothing like the Beck track, being a brooding voodoo-inspired mantra. Most of the album has a feeling that seems to sum up New Orleans, 'Iko Iko' being a song most will recognise. The album eventually wanders into jazz territory with 'Accentuate The Positive' and 'Makin' Whoopee!'

4.53) My Generation: The Very Best Of The Who - The Who (1996)

At the time I bought this I was a bit of a sixties purist when it came to The Who, and it was hits like 'Pictures Of Lily,' 'I'm A Boy,' 'Substitute' and the title track that I appreciated the most, with Keith Moon's frenetic drumming ever to the fore. Over the years I've come to appreciate what followed this era more and more. 'Won't Get Fooled Again' is a whopper of a song, with Roger Daltry providing one of the best screams in the entire history of rock while seeming to express disappointment at the implosion of the hippie dream. 'Baba O'Riley,' also from 1971, is similarly iconic, and even later tracks like 'Who Are You?' and 'You Better You Bet' now hold their own against the classics of the more ancient past.

4.54) Tommy – The Who (1969)

With the greatest hits in the bag, the next album for me to get by the instrument-smashing wild men was their first rock opera, 'Tommy.' Everybody knows 'Pinball Wizard,' but the compositional approach to the whole project is almost classical with an 'Overture' containing snippets of many of the songs that follow, as well as an 'Underture,' which is a dark instrumental where Keith Moon gets to give the drums a good thrashing. The country-tinted 'Sally Simpson' is a favourite of mine and the 'See me, feel me' refrain is never far away on this album. The principal subject matter is a deaf, dumb and blind boy who is repeatedly abused but becomes a kind of celebrity with fanatical followers. Ken Russell's film tried to lighten the mood, most memorably with actress Ann Margaret writhing in baked beans. Yuck!

4.55) Live At Leeds – The Who (1970)

This is often cited as the best live album of all time and it's easy to see why. There are rock and roll covers of 'Summertime Blues' and 'Shakin' All Over,' which almost eclipse the originals by Eddie Cochran and Johnny Kidd And The Pirates respectively. 'My Generation' is turned into an epic with inserts from 'Tommy.' Pete Townsend truly excels with his guitar solos on this album and the sound is not a million miles away from their contemporaries, Led Zeppelin. An extended version of 'Magic Bus' provides a rocking finish.

4.56) The Best Of The Tremeloes – The Tremeloes (1998)

This group's only number one was a cover of 'Silence Is Golden' by the Four Seasons. However, the band shouldn't be written off. There's a party atmosphere to hits like 'Here Comes My Baby' and 'Even The Bad Times Are Good.' Meanwhile, '(Call Me) Number One' and 'Me And My Life' are great prog rock hits, and there's a virtually identical cover of 'Yellow River,' a song the band passed over as a single release, allowing Christie to take it to number one. Doh! And to close this Crimson release there's a couple of hits from the Brian Poole days including another number one in the form of 'Do You Love Me?'

4.57) The Early Years – The Move (1992)

This Birmingham band spawned two monster groups, namely the Electric Light Orchestra and Wizzard. They had a UK number one hit in early 1969 with 'Blackberry Way' and their 1967 song 'Flowers In The Rain' was the first track to be played on BBC Radio 1. There is much more besides. Classical influences can be seen in 'Night Of Fear' and the lengthy coda to 'Cherry Blossom Clinic.' There are some great rock tracks such as 'Brontosaurus,' and the conclusion to 'Disturbance' is genuinely scary sounding. Insanity was clearly a popular subject in the band's lyrics. 'What?' which concludes the album, is a mini-epic, pointing the way towards the sound of ELO.

4.58) The Early Years – Humble Pie (1992)

The band was hailed as a 'supergroup' featuring Steve Marriott from the Small Faces and Peter Frampton of the Herd. The band only had one hit though. This was 'Natural Born Bugie' (aka 'Natural Born Woman') which was misspelled upon its release as you can see. Sounding like a cross between 'Get Back' and 'Revolution' by the Beatles, this is a superb track. The rest of the album is different though still enjoyable. They even sound like an American country blues band on 'Alabama 69.' Dojo's 'The Early Years' was actually a great set of compilation CDs and it would be roughly twenty years before I got my hands on the T. Rex edition which is also very good.

4.59) Planet Gong: Live Floating Anarchy 1977 – Planet Gong (1978)

I was working in a post-room and my supervisor, who was into prog rock, mentioned a band called Gong that he used to listen to, so when I spotted this in a local music shop called 'Suite 16' it was an instant purchase. The content took a bit of getting used to however. The cover art implies 'psychedelia,' but this is mixed with a heavy dollop of punk and eccentric humour. 'Floating Anarchy' and 'Opium For The People' express the punk ethos, for example the lyric 'Violence is caused by governments, armies, police force.' 'Stoned Innocent Frankenstein' has a great riff, and there are two lengthy psychedelic jams. The 'surreal' knob is turned up to 'eleven.'

4.60) Masters Of The Universe – Hawkwind (1977)

Many years later I would download this band's first four albums as a digital 'box set' - surely a misnomer if ever there was one – how do you box up a bunch of zeros and ones? As I've decided not to review each album individually I am going to review two compilations that I bought in the nineties which were almost identically named. So for kick off, this album has got nothing to do with He-Man, Skeletor and all that lot. You'll soon get used to Lemmy's chugging bass which really comes to the fore in the ten-minute juggernaut 'Orgone Accumulator.' 'Brainstorm' is another lengthy jam and 'Sonic Attack' seems like a completely deranged take on government information broadcasts. It seems peculiar that the band's biggest hit, 'Silver Machine,' was omitted from this album.

4.61) Master Of The Universe – Hawkwind (1997)

This Pulse / Castle compilation feels less 'official' than the EMI album with the additional 'S,' but the live version of the title track has a furious energy which almost segues into the high-octane riff of 'Angels Of Death.' Included is the re-recorded version of 'Motorhead,' which is more rocky than the original, and 'Hash Cake '77,' which sounds like it could have been Pink Floyd in '69. This is largely an album of alternate versions of Hawkwind's biggest songs. 'Hurry On Sundown' is a rough recording compared to the smoothness of the version on 'Epocheclipse: 30 Year Anthology' (1999), but the guitar solo that closes 'Who's Gonna Win The War' is great, and the intro to 'Silver Machine' is one of the best openings I've ever heard, literally feeling like it is launching off into space. The nutty side of Hawkwind is also well represented with tracks like 'Ghost Dance.' And just in case it's all a bit wacky and scary for you, there's some good old fashioned blues in the shape of 'Dealing With The Devil' which dates from way back in 1967.

4.62) The Best Of Canned Heat – Canned Heat (1997)

The American band Canned Heat seemed to reflect back the British blues boom of the late sixties, which spawned everything from Led Zeppelin to Fleetwood Mac. The big hits are 'On The Road Again' which has an Eastern vibe, the quirky 'Going Up The Country,' and the anthemic 'Let's Work Together,' famously recorded as 'Let's Stick Together' by Brian Ferry. This Disky compilation contains covers of blues classics like 'Dust My Broom' and two very long tracks, including the twenty-minute 'Parthenogenesis,' which serves as a sampler for all the band's eclectic styles.

4.63) In The Court Of The Crimson King – King Crimson (1969)

The track opens with the 'sonic attack' of 'Twenty-First Century Schizoid Man' with its distorted vocal, rapid-fire instrumental, stop-start rhythm and completely chaotic ending. If this is your first experience of Robert Fripp's unusual guitar style, it's an induction by fire. The rest of the album is very mellow, with lots of mellotron and flutes on 'I Talk To The Wind.' Woodwind instruments were popular in rock songs around this time, and it's a shame that this innovation, utilised by everyone from Jethro Tull to Focus, has never been revisited. 'Moonchild' descends into tinkling sounds that remind me of bubbles on a lake at night, and many years later my wife and I would have an argument when I put on the title track on a pub jukebox one Christmas Eve, because it was viewed as 'inappropriate' for the festive season! My view? King Crimson is *never* inappropriate.

4.64) Larks' Tongues In Aspic – King Crimson (1973)

Intrigued by the wacky title, the wacky contents take a bit of work to get into. The title track comes in two parts and 'Part One' relaxes you with ethereal tinkling before blasting you with one of the most aggressive guitar passages ever recorded. 'Easy Money' is the nearest track to conventional rock and 'The Talking Drum' builds from strange reverberations floating on the wind into a violin crescendo. 'Part Two' of the title track uses a rising chord sequence which would also appear in tracks on the band's next two albums, which it goes without saying are brilliant. Worth noting is that the drums were augmented with extra percussion in the form of household objects. Imagine someone thrashing a baking tray and you get the idea!

4.65) Face To Face – The Kinks (1966)

Although I started off with a greatest hits package of the Kinks, we all know rock classics like 'You Really Got Me' and 'All The Day And All Of The Night,' so I'm going to steam in with their 'proper' albums. The first three Kinks albums, 'The Kinks' (1964), 'Kinda Kinks' (1965) and 'The Kink Kontroversy' (1965) are all good, but this is where we start, as this was the album when Ray Davies' songwriting really began to flourish. 'House in The Country' predates Blur's 'Country House' by 29 years and has some great lines like 'He got his job when drunken daddy tumbled down the stairs.' I find 'Session Man' somewhat insulting to the unknown yet skilled musicians who often made bands seem more adept than they were, but Ray redeemed himself with 'Sunny Afternoon' which is an out and out 'ripper.' Make sure you get the version with bonus tracks as the quality just keeps on coming; 'Mister Pleasant' and the stark 'I'm Not Like Everybody Else' are both indispensable.

4.66) Something Else By The Kinks – The Kinks (1967)

While most bands were singing about purple mushrooms and pink elephants floating on orange clouds, the Kinks adopted the 'keep calm and carry on' approach, with 'Lazy Old Sun' perhaps being their only concession to psychedelia. It has a great lyric by the way; 'When I was young / My world was three foot seven inch tall.' 'David Watts' is a bass-driven uptempo song about every school's 'golden boy.' This album contains the masterpiece 'Waterloo Sunset' and ends with the vaudevillian 'End Of The Season,' with humour that seems like the sun briefly coming out on an overcast day. Younger brother Dave is even allowed to pen a track or two, although strangely when released as a single 'Death Of A Clown' was issued under his own name and not the band's name. Make sure you get the version with bonus tracks again. 'Autumn Almanac' was a favourite from my childhood and like a fine wine, it gets even better with age.

4.67) The Kinks Are The Village Green Preservation Society – The Kinks (1968)

No bonus tracks needed, as this is a complete entity, an early concept album from start to finish which sees Ray Davies longing for the simplicity of village life in calmer times. Dave Davies' distorted guitar on 'Wicked Annabella' seems to pre-empt Blur's Graham Coxon stylistically. 'Picture Book' seems to be part of a pair with 'People Take Pictures Of Each Other,' similar to 'The Village Green Preservation Society' having a companion piece in the form of 'Village Green.' My favourite is the dreamy 'Sitting By The Riverside.' It is nothing short of a travesty that the Kinks weren't respected as an album band like the Beatles and Rolling Stones, because these London boys produced some of the best concept albums ever made.

4.68) Arthur (Or The Decline And Fall Of The British Empire) – The Kinks (1969)

I remember buying this CD while visiting the shopping Mecca of Bluewater in Kent with my friend Simon, copying it onto tape for reasons I cannot now remember while we continued the party in my bedroom, which was a converted garage at my parents' house. I remember liking the track 'Driving' so much that I put it on 'repeat' for about half an hour. Following the more famous 'Village Green Preservation Society' album, the concept this time is of an old man looking back over his life and assessing the worth of it, from the Victorian era ('when the rich were so mean' to quote the lyrics), to the world wars, to his family emigrating to Australia, and finally the sad repeated refrain of 'Arthur, we love you and want to help you' at the end. Here the Kinks gave us longer instrumental jams like 'Australia,' which actually feels like a journey nearing its completion with the addition of a wobble board. There are some nice guitar solos and tasteful brass additions on this album too.

4.69) Lola Versus Powerman And The Moneygoround, Part One – The Kinks (1970)

The quality just kept on coming from the Davies brothers with their loyal bandmates Mick Avory and Pete Quaife. The opening to 'Lola' seems to replicate the clanging guitar sound at the start of 'Dedicated Follower Of Fashion,' recorded four years earlier. 'Apeman' is a great track expressing the desire to escape from the modern world ('I don't want to die in a nuclear war'), a theme that Ray Davies would explore more on the excellent 'Muswell Hillbillies' album. He actually sings 'The air pollution is a-fogging up my eyes,' but it's fun to think that he's saying something else! The opening and closing tracks both have the same intro, with 'I've Got To Be Free' making a great finish to a great album which would have no 'Part Two.' It's a shame people didn't appreciate this enough to put it up there with the Beatles' 'Let It Be' or the Stones' 'Let It Bleed' in the charts. Still, the band had their final 'number two' single success with 'Lola,' so there was some solace at least.

4.70) Percy – The Kinks (1971)

We are going to leave the Kinks temporarily after this one, for I would discover their seventies material later in my existence. 'Percy' was the soundtrack to a truly dismal film in which a man has a delicate organ transplanted from somebody else. You'd never guess this from the album though, which has some wistful vocals on 'Friends' and wise advice for arrogant humanity on 'All God's Children.' There's an Elvis pastiche in the form of 'Willesden Green' and a quirky instrumental version of 'Lola.' Not one of their masterworks, but you can put this in the pigeonhole marked 'pleasant.' You know where to file the movie!

4.71) Ogden's Nut Gone Flake – The Small Faces (1968)

Designed to look like a tobacco tin, the front cover to this album is round. Being square was out in the late sixties, you see. The first track is an instrumental, complete with psychedelic phasing effect and 'Afterglow' is a full blown rocker. 'Rene' and 'Lazy Sunday' both start off with Steve Marriott singing in an almost comedic Cockney accent and end as pop-rock classics; the droning guitar solo at the end of 'Rene' is a high point. The second half of the album is a wacky concept held together by Stanley Unwin's equally 'off the wall' monologue. I understand that he carefully listened to how members of the band spoke to one another so that he could incorporate the colloquialisms of the day into the nonsense tale. As the lyrics of the final track declare, 'Life is just a bowl of All Bran.'

I would later purchase this CD again as part of 'The Immediate Record Collection' which includes the 1967 album 'Small Faces' and 'The Autumn Stone,' which was a kind of 'greatest hits' with added live material. Just to confuse things, the group's 1966 debut album is also called 'Small Faces.' The fashion for Roman numerals to denote eponymous albums had yet to take off at the time.

4.72) Live Peace In Toronto – John Lennon / Plastic Ono Band (1969)

After three pretty much unlistenable albums recorded with Yoko Ono, John gets back to basics here. The first six tracks show that this could have been a live album to rival The Who's 'Live At Leeds,' with John Lennon returning to his rock and roll roots while fronting a supergroup with Eric Clapton on lead guitar. John's version of 'Blue Suede Shoes' tops Elvis for me (sorry!) and he turbo-charges the Beatles tracks 'Money (That's What I Want),' 'Dizzy Miss Lizzy' and 'Yer Blues,' but hold on what's that wailing going on in the background? After 'Cold Turkey' and a 'laid back to the point of horizontal' version of 'Give Peace A Chance' John hands over centre stage to Yoko Ono to 'do something all over you' as he puts it. Uh-oh! 'Don't Worry Kyoko' actually has a great riff, reminiscent of Bob Dylan's 'It's Alright Ma (I'm Only Bleeding)' and 'John John (Let's Hope For Peace)' would almost have an ambient feel, were it not for the screeching vocals. I don't think I'm being harsh, as Yoko *could* turn out a nice vocal when she wanted to. Listen to her singing 'Remember Love' on the flip side of 'Give Peace A Chance' if you are in any doubt. But I guess this was 'art' and she wasn't trying to sound 'nice,' unlike this reviewer who is trying to *be* 'nice.' As always.

4.73) John Lennon / Plastic Ono Band – John Lennon (1970)

Before we got the 'John as a saint' persona (which he never encouraged), we had this – a raging diatribe against all society's norms. This would have been something of a shock for those who remembered the Beatles as lovable clowns from their early years. 'Working Class Hero' is a classic, although I would advise a '12' certificate if you have kids. Was this the first F-word on a successful album?

And more to the point, did the world end? 'Look at Me' is a very nice introspective acoustic track, and in case anybody was hoping for a continuation of the Beatles' career, John laments 'The dream is over' on the penultimate track. After some activism, John would settle into family life before his tragic demise, and comparing the relaxed feel of his final songs with this album is like comparing chalk and cheese. There's a companion 'Yoko Ono / Plastic Ono Band' album too. Try it if you dare.

4.74) Imagine – John Lennon (1971)

Total classic. No debate required.

Oh, you want me to write something? OK, well you've got John at his most apologetic and poignant with 'Jealous Guy,' as well as the bluesy 'Crippled Inside.' He gets political on the ranting 'Give Me Some Truth,' as well as 'I Don't Wanna Be A Soldier.' 'How?' is a nice track, while 'How Do You Sleep?' is just plain nasty, with a series of vitriolic digs at his old bandmate McCartney ('The only thing you done was yesterday / And since you've gone you're just another day'). In fairness Lennon thought McCartney had been digging at him with tracks like 'Too Many People' on an album I'll review much later in this book. There is a longer, more bluesy bootleg version of 'How Do You Sleep?' on a release called 'The Sweetest Apples' (1994) which blows the released version into a copped hat by the way. Here the Beatles minus McCartney are all involved. No wonder Paul got pretty depressed at this time. Friends will be friends...

4.75) Mind Games – John Lennon (1973)

'Some Time In New York City' was Lennon's next album and we'll review that later, but the 'Imagine' album now cast a long shadow over all his latter works; audience expectation was through the roof. John shows his softer side on 'Mind Games,' with tracks like 'Aisumasen (I'm Sorry)' and my favourite, 'You Are Here.' He also rocks with tracks like 'Meat City' and 'Tight A$.' 'Nutopian International Anthem' is just a few seconds of silence which was a protest at his own immigration issues in the USA. Put it on repeat if you really love silence that much!

4.76) Lennon Box Set CD4 – John Lennon (1990)

Apologies to Yoko Ono, who I am not a hater of, but I am not going to review 'Double Fantasy' (1980) or 'Milk And Honey' (1984), which were evenly split between the couple, *per se*. All of Lennon's tracks from these two albums, both of which I had on tape in the nineties, were collated onto this final disc from a now-obscure box set. Bearing in mind that the six tracks from the 'Milk And Honey' album were put together after his death, you'll realise that the quality of John's songwriting never dropped.

From 'Double Fantasy,' I like the lyrics of 'Watching The Wheels' where John uses similar alternating piano chords to 'Imagine' while promoting his new 'chilled out' approach to things, which I think was more wishful thinking than anything. I also like the rock aggression of 'I'm Losing You' (the version John did with Cheap Trick is worth seeking out too). However my favourite Lennon lyric of all is from 'Beautiful Boy,' this being 'Life is what happens while you're busy making other plans.'

From the album 'Milk And Honey,' 'Grow Old With Me' is very sad, considering how John's life was cut short, and I remember hearing 'Nobody Told Me' on the radio as a child and concluding that I preferred rock to pop, based on this one track. It's fun to hear John larking about at the end of the reggae-influenced 'Borrowed Time' too.

4.77) All Things Must Pass – George Harrison (1970)

A triple album is as rare as a snake's foot but here's one that worked, now conveniently packaged as a double CD. Seeming somewhat repressed while in the Beatles, George had a back catalogue of his own compositions that he was eager to record. 'My Sweet Lord' was the obvious big hit, topping the charts a second time in 2002 when George had sadly left the planet. This album also contained 'What Is Life' which provided Olivia Newton-John with an early hit. George also performs Dylan's 'If Not For You,' which also provided Olivia Newton-John with an early hit. She had good taste for sure. The styles are quite varied, for example compare 'Apple Scruffs' and the stately 'Let It Down.' The seventies 'wall of sound' is quite dominant, but following 'It's Johnny's Birthday,' which blatantly rips off the Cliff Richard hit 'Congratulations,' we enter a series of instrumental blues jams with Eric Clapton and pals. Clappers eventually married Harrison's first wife. And they remained friends.

4.78) Beggars Banquet – Rolling Stones (1968)

There are many ways to get your hands on the Rolling Stones' classic hits of the sixties. I went for the compilations 'Big Hits (High Tide And Green Grass)' and 'Through The Past Darkly (Big Hits Vol. 2),' and if the greatest hits are all you want, this pair and 'Jump Back: The Best Of The Rolling Stones ' pretty much hit the mark. However, I'm not going to review any of these as I would eventually get most of their albums, picking up the missing early tracks on 'The Singles Collection: The London Years.'

'Beggars Banquet' is a great place to start, with the band emerging from dabbling in psychedelia, with 'Sympathy For The Devil.' Quite why people find this controversial I've no idea. Mick Jagger sings the song as Lucifer himself, so unless you believe that the greatest thing to come out of Kent since the A259 is the actual devil incarnate it's not really that serious, right? Keith Richards does a brilliantly economical guitar solo on this track too. Similarly 'Stray Cat Blues' contains the controversial line 'I can see that you're fifteen years old / But I don't want your I.D.' Let's hope Sir Mick was taking on the character of a similarly-aged boy here. 'Parachute Woman' is a good rocker and 'Dear Doctor' has a great country feel. The anthems here are 'Street Fighting Man' and 'Salt Of The Earth.'

4.79) Let It Bleed – Rolling Stones (1969)

The Stones were on a roll, opening this album with the sublime 'Gimme Shelter.' 'Love In Vain' is a great blues song and the title track is 'proper naughty' but a brilliant piece of country rock. 'Country Honk' is a stripped back version of their hit 'Honky Tonk Women,' and best of all is the epic closing track, 'You Can't Always Get What You Want,' starting quietly and ending with a full choir. I still wish Mick had sang 'I went down to the Chelsea drugstore / To get your prescription *beer*,' which is how I've always misheard the lyric.

4.80) Sticky Fingers – Rolling Stones (1971)

When an album opens with 'Brown Sugar' it's not going to go far wrong, although it does surprise me that the track still gets radio airplay in these more politically correct times. 'Wild Horses' heralded further seventies ballads, but it is the extended jam of 'Can You Hear Me Knocking?' which really highlights the band's musicality. The final four tracks show that the flamboyant Stones could also be amazingly mellow. The album's conclusion, 'Moonlight Mile,' is a little-known classic that deserves regular airplay. Great for sitting round a campfire!

4.81) Exile On Main Street – Rolling Stones (1972)

Perhaps because this is a double album I've always found it a challenge to take in. It ranks among the best in pretty much every survey, but for me the last three albums all top it. I'm perhaps in the minority here. 'Rocks Off' is a great track, while 'Tumbling Dice' is quintessential 'seventies' Stones and 'Sweet Virginia' is great and melodic, with some nice harmonica and a hook-line that ensures it never gets radio airplay. 'Sweet Black Angel' is acoustic with some nice percussive effects. American blues styles pervade throughout. It's more 'Delta' than 'Dartford.'

4.82) The Best Of 1968-1973 - Steve Miller Band (1990)

'The Joker' provided this group with a UK number one in 1990, almost seventeen years after its release. The two songs it references lyrically, 'Space Cowboy' and 'Gangster Of Love,' are both on this compilation too. Paul McCartney provides a guest vocal on 'My Dark Hour,' and 'Evil' is a tremendous heartfelt piece of blues.

If you want something that sounds like 'The Joker,' there's 'Little Girl.' Great stuff.

4.83) Greatest Hits - Steve Miller Band (1998)

Effectively this is 'volume two' of Mr. Miller's greatest hits, carrying on where the last compilation left off, but due to a change in record companies the title implies that everything that went before was irrelevant. That said, this is more quality from Steve and his band, and there's even room for a segue going from the ethereal 'Space Intro' into 'Fly Like An Eagle.' 'Take The Money And Run' is essential stuff, and unlike many old rockers Steve even adapted pretty well in the eighties with the catchy hit, 'Abracadabra.' Country, blues, rock and pop all converge in this selection.

4.84) A Salty Dog – Procol Harum (1969)

The title track is an atmospheric piece with seagull cries and strings, yet maintaining the Procol Harum feel we know and love. 'Juicy John Pink' is pure blues and sounds like something straight out of Chicago in the fifties. 'Wreck Of The Hesperus' has a memorable piano riff with orchestral additions pre-empting Barclay James Harvest, and 'Pilgrim's Progress' sounds like a clearer thinking version of 'A Whiter Shade Of Pale.' Gary Brooker and pals led the way for many bands, but sadly they are mostly only remembered for a single chart-topping hit.

4.85) The Most Of The Animals – The Animals (1971)

This compilation opens with two absolute whoppers, 'House Of The Rising Sun,' which needs no introduction, and 'We Gotta Get Out Of This Place,' which I used to sing a lot when I was working in a post-room. Eric Burden's vocal at two minutes 12 is surely one of the earliest examples of the 'rock scream.' Much of the album is in the 'rhythm and blues' vein, although 'Bring It On Home To Me' leans towards soul. 'Don't Let Me Be Misunderstood' is another top track, but 'Road Runner' (not on the original 1966 release) never fails to remind me of the similar closing music to Rik Mayall and Adrian Edmondson's TV comedy 'Bottom.'

4.86) The Best Of Traffic – Traffic (1969)

Steve Winwood, who had been a pivotal member of the Spencer Davis Group, took a more psychedelic turn with the band Traffic, and this Island Records collection presents a fair overview. There's the Indian-flavoured hit 'Paper Sun' and the even more 'far out' 'Hole In My Shoe,' which is complete with a child going on about flying on an albatross. It's all archetypal 'sixties' fare, but the addition of saxophone to their sound puts Traffic in a different lane to the rest. The closing track, 'Dear Mr. Fantasy,' concludes the album with superlative drumming from Jim Capaldi and a great guitar solo too. Lyrically it seems to be proposing music as an anti-depressant. If they keep churning out rock classics like this they've got my prescription.

4.87) The Velvet Underground And Nico – The Velvet Underground (1967)

Remember my friend from our youth band, the astrophysicist? I think it's fair to say that he single-handedly introduced me to the legend that was Lou Reed. This was the album where Mr. Reed, John Cale, Sterling Morrison and that rarity, a female drummer, Maureen (Mo) Tucker, first burst onto the music scene. It was often said that not a lot of people bought the famous 'Andy Warhol / banana' album, but everyone who did went out and formed a band. I wish I could draw the same consolation that the select audience who bought my books all went out and wrote their own. Well, I can loosely claim this about two of my readers anyway, so there!

The album opens with the peaceful 'Sunday Morning,' but this lulls you into a false sense of security before the pounding rhythm of 'Waiting For The Man' launches itself. 'Run Run Run' has a Dylan-esque feel and 'Venus In Furs' deals with masochism and sadism while John Cale grinds his viola. 'There She Goes' quite deliberately copies the main riff of 'Hitch Hike' (I know the Rolling Stones version best), and 'European Son' assaults the ears for almost eight minutes, almost seeming to copy and paste the jangly guitar solo from 'Run Run Run' into the mix. Nico was a German songstress who sings on three of the tracks.

4.88) White Light / White Heat – The Velvet Underground (1968)

This has to be one of the most indulgent records ever released. The title track starts off as a infectious rocker before seeming to get stuck in the groove. John Cale recites 'The Gift' in his fine Welsh accent over instrumental backing, predating Will Self's monologue on the Bomb The Bass album 'Clear' by almost three decades. 'Lady Godiva's Operation' is creepy but enjoyable and the guitar solo on 'I Heard Her Call My Name' is utterly bonkers, but the leviathan is 'Sister Ray,' which clocks in at over seventeen minutes and mostly consists of band members trying to outdo each other by turning their instruments up to ear-splitting levels. On this occasion John Cale wins the battle with his keyboard. Easy listening it ain't!

4.89) The Velvet Underground – The Velvet Underground (1969)

Guitarist Sterling Morrison remained with Lou and Mo, while John Cale was replaced with Doug Yule who seemed to be a calming influence on the group whose sound became remarkably laid back on this eponymous third album. Lou Reed sounds genuinely in need of divine inspiration in 'Jesus' and he sounds triumphant on 'Beginning To See The Light.' 'Pale Blue Eyes' is a strikingly poignant song about an affair ('The fact that you are married / Only proves you're my best friend'). The organ is simple but effective on 'What Goes On?' and drummer Maureen Tucker closes the album with her quaint sounding vocal on 'After Hours.' But just in case you thought the band had lost the ability to blow human minds, there's 'The Murder Mystery' which bombards us with two sets of confusing spoken words simultaneously. No drugs were involved I'm sure.

4.90) Loaded – The Velvet Underground (1970)

The VU's final album with Lou Reed was slicker than your average, opening with 'Who Loves The Sun' which you can almost imagine being a 'hit parade smash' with its 'ba ba-ba baaa' backing vocals. Two Lou Reed classics follow in the form of 'Sweet Jane' and 'Rock & Roll' but Doug Yule gets the glory, taking the vocals on 'Oh! Sweet Nuthin' – a superbly empathetic song in a similar vein to Ralph McTell's 'Streets Of London,' but building to an instrumental frenzy, perhaps following the template of 'The Boxer' by Simon & Garfunkel, and certainly leading the way towards Lynyrd Skynyrd's 'Free Bird.' Little known, but legendary.

One more studio album was released under the 'VU' name, this being 1973's 'Squeeze.' With only Doug Yule from the original band it failed to set the world on fire, but a certain group containing Jools Holland decided to name themselves after it.

4.91) Transformer – Lou Reed (1972)

I first heard this album coming over the speakers when browsing through a second hand music shop in Kent's county town of Maidstone. The shop is long gone, but the music lives on, although I never was a fan of the controversial 'banana in the pocket' album reverse. Lou's two best known songs are here, in the form of 'Perfect Day' and 'Walk On The Wild Side' which recounts memories of characters from his days among Andy Warhol's entourage. It also has some nice saxophone playing which I always thought was by David Bowie but is actually by Ronnie Ross. Bowie actually produced the album with Mick Ronson. You have to overlook the fact that Lou rhymes 'head' with 'head' in one of his famously provocative couplets. The verse about hairy bears in 'Andy's Chest' is just hilarious, as is the 'spoke, spoke' backing in 'Wagon Wheel.' 'Hangin' Round' is a nice dollop of rock and roll, and I love the drunken vocal style of the vaudeville finisher 'Goodnight Ladies.' This is Lou at his most fun.

4.92) Berlin – Lou Reed (1973)

Fresh from the commercial success of his quirky album 'Transformer,' what did

Lou follow it up with? How about a dark tale of drugs, domestic abuse and suicide, complete with the harrowing sound of screaming children being prised from their mother? Good old Lou, you have to love him! My friend Barney, a future astrophysicist, bought this first, listening to it while his mother gave me a piano lesson. Upon asking him if the concept album was more depressing than Pink Floyd's 'The Wall,' he was affirmative. That said, I love it. We begin with a deranged version of 'Happy Birthday' which sounds like the end of a party, dwindling away to just a lonely piano and Lou's lethargic vocal, 'In Berlin / By the wall / You were five foot ten inches tall.' As the tale progresses he piles on the misery, culminating in 'The Kids' with the aforementioned distressed minors. But no, that's still not dark enough. How about a suicide in the next track? Then right at the end, almost sarcastically, we have 'Sad Song' which gives the central character's violent partner the last word. Jesus wept Lou, what are you doing to us?

4.93) Metal Machine Music – Lou Reed (1975)

Lou's next studio album was 'Sally Can't Dance' (1974) which seemed more commercial in style, yet again lulling us into a false sense of security. No one will ever know if Lou Reed really thought he'd created a new concept in music with this, or if he was just having a laugh at the critics' expense. Described on the cover as 'a dextrorotatory components synthesis of sympathomimetic musics' this album is literally an hour of squealing feedback. The concept was loosely to bung a load of equipment in a room, whack the volume up to the max, record what happens and break it up into four movements. This album provided me with much humour when playing it to bewildered friends, especially the time I turned the lights out with my friend Simon and accompanied this cacophony with a strobe light. Psychedelic, man. Actually, on second thoughts it was just torture!

4.94) Street Hassle – Lou Reed (1978)

After two more albums, we were treated to one of Lou's better works in my opinion. He paraphrases his own 'Sweet Jane' on 'Gimme Some Good Times,' gives us a gritty and hypnotic tale of street life in the lengthy title track, tempts controversy with 'I Wanna Be Black' and tells us all emphatically to bog off in 'Leave Me Alone.' It's a mixture of studio and live tracks and it shows Lou at the bombastic peak of his 'don't give a monkeys' persona. If you want to hear him verbally abuse his own audience, the live album 'Take No Prisoners' verges on being comedic, although the musical content is not up to the standard of 'Street Hassle.'

4.95) Lou Reed – Lou Reed (1972)

Chronologically this was the first album Lou Reed released after leaving the Velvet Underground, but remember, I tend to go for the essentials first and then rewind to the beginning? This wasn't a big seller but you can see the opening vistas of many avenues that he would explore, including an early version of 'Berlin' which even has a chorus. The songs are actually very good, but it would take Bowie's production on 'Transformer' to elevate the sound. 'Lisa Says,' 'Walk And Talk It' and 'I Can't Stand It' wouldn't be out of place on any greatest hits collection, and with its crashing cymbals 'Ocean' provides us with an ethereal conclusion.

4.96) New York – Lou Reed (1989)

Lou's comeback began with this 'tales from NYC' album. 'Xmas In February' is an anti-war song for the eighties and the monologue-like 'Last Great American Whale' lambasts stereotypical American attitudes towards nature. 'Sick Of You' is an unusual country-style anti-love song which also expresses tiredness at the daily catalogue of horrors that is the news. Lou scales up the same theme on what I view as the album's *piece de resistance*, 'Straw Man' – 'Does anybody need yet another politician / Caught with his pants down and money sticking in his hole?' I think you know the answer to that one, Lou!

4.97) Magic And Loss – Lou Reed (1992)

Fresh from the commercial success of his gritty album of urban tales, 'New York,' what did Lou follow it up with? How about an entire album devoted to the theme of cancer? Good old Lou, you have to love him. Again! This is very tastefully done, however, and you can tell that Lou generally meant it as a fitting tribute to his departed friends. It's all pretty mellow until we get to 'Gassed And Stoked' and 'Power & Glory, Part 2.' 'Harry's Circumcision' is not as gross as you might expect, but a bizarre monologue about an attempted suicide, stylistically reminiscent of 'Lady Godiva's Operation' from his Velvet Underground days, but the weeping guitar adds a certain reverence to the stark material.

4.98) Never Mind The Bollocks, Here's The Sex Pistols – Sex Pistols (1977)

This was another loan from my astrophysicist friend, being flung my way with words along the lines of, 'Seriously, it's actually not bad.' I was never a big punk fan, but the raw energy of Johnny Rotten spitting out political anger certainly sets this album above the rest of the 'shock and safety pins' milieu. The only full on swearing is during the track 'Bodies,' and it seems almost as though this was tacked on to create controversy. 'New York' borrows the chord structure from 'All The Day And All Of The Night' by the Kinks, but whereas the Doors were challenged for using the riff in 'Hello, I Love You,' the Kinks left the Pistols well alone. There is always a debate as to whether or not 'God Save The Queen' got to number one in the UK, the conspiracy theory being that the chart was rigged to keep it at number two so they wouldn't have to play it on the radio. It all seems rather amusing these days that there was such a bleeding fuss!

4.99) The Great Rock And Roll Swindle – Sex Pistols (1979)

Arguably, without Glen Matlock's contribution to the writing, it seemed that the Pistols were reduced to a rock and roll circus. I originally had a twelve-track tape of this album which concentrated on the more professional sounding tracks. The sprawling full-length issue is sequenced bizarrely, with the Black Arabs reggae medley appearing before one of the songs that it satirises, this being 'No One Is Innocent,' which is performed by Ronnie Biggs of 'great train robber' fame. He also has a bash at 'Belsen Was A Gas,' but whereas Johnny Rotten sings the song with genuine disgust at Nazi atrocities, it seems that Mr. Biggs was having way too much fun with it. There's a dirty rugby song given a 'punk' kick up the derrière and even a French accordion cover called 'Anarchie Pour Le UK.' Syd Vicious handles some of the rock and roll covers, as well as a corrupted version of Paul Anka's 'My Way,' while Ed Tudor-Pole, of later 'Crystal Maze' TV fame, generally comes across as a bit of nutter. The turbo-charged version of 'Anarchy In The UK' is pure comedy too.

4.100) Hotel California – The Eagles (1977)

Who's ready for a whopper? Look no further. The title track with its tales of decadence and its coda of duelling guitar solos will be set in stone forever as a rock classic, so much that I used to put £1 into the jukebox at our local Woolpack Inn and select the track four times. DJs should be physically punished for talking over it or fading it, but there's much more besides 'Hotel Cal.' 'Life In The Fast Lane' is a brilliant rocker, and the segue from the orchestral reprise of 'Wasted Time' into the dramatic chords of 'Victim Of Love' is sequencing at its best. And just when you think they've burnt themselves out they give us the anthem 'The Last Resort.'

4.101) Their Greatest Hits 1971-1975 – The Eagles (1976)

If you're not going any deeper into the Eagles' discography this is the perfect companion volume to 'Hotel California.' 'Take It To The Limit' is an all-time great love song, 'One Of These Nights' has a memorable bass opening and 'Lyin' Eyes' has deliciously smooth vocals and a sad country vibe. 'Take It Easy,' 'Desperado,' come on, this is 'lesson one' stuff, you know it and love it...

4.102) The Best Of Emerson, Lake & Palmer - Emerson, Lake & Palmer (1980)

I remember picking this up from a boot fair, another source of cheap second hand music that I used to frequent. The version of Aaron Copland's 'Fanfare For The Common Man' is just the radio edit. For the full nine minutes you'll need an album called 'Works Volume 1' (1977) which shows off the skills of each individual band member, with a complete piano concerto being Keith Emerson's contribution. Anyway, it's the 'Best Of' album that we're reviewing here. Parry's 'Jerusalem' also gets the ELP treatment, as does Henry Mancini's 'Peter Gunn Theme.' 'Karn Evil 9' was even used as the theme to 'The Generation Game' on TV during Jim Davidson's tenure as presenter. If you prefer the more acoustic end of the rock spectrum you'll particularly enjoy 'Lucky Man.'

4.103) The Best Of – Jeff Beck Featuring Rod Stewart (1995)

Everybody knows 'Hi-Ho Silver Lining' but this poppy hit was perhaps not representative of the majority of the music Mr. Beck turned out. 'Beck's Bolero' is a nice instrumental and there's a blissful acoustic rendition of 'Greensleeves.' The legend goes that Henry VIII wrote it for Ann Boleyn, who eventually became his second wife as well as his first spouse to grace the chopping block. So much for romance! Rod Stewart provided vocals to a lot of the blues / rock and roll on this album, while 'Rice Pudding' is a seven-minute jam, but why the savage edit at the end? Did Henry VIII chop the tape too?

4.104) The Sensational 70s Oh Boy! CD3 – Roy Wood & Wizzard (1998)

This was part of a Reader's Digest box set with companion CDs by Mud and 10cc. The disc gathers together work from Wizzard, the last days of the Move and Roy Wood solo. We open with Wizzard's two UK number one singles, 'Angel Fingers (A Teen Ballad)' and 'See My Baby Jive.' The sound is very much influenced by Phil Spector's production of many sixties records and this has come to be a sound that we associate with Christmas. It goes without saying that Wizzard's monster Christmas hit is included here, although I now associate it with a man being stuck eternally in a snow globe in TV's dystopian anthology series 'Black Mirror.' Much of Wood's output is very melodic, such as 'Dear Elaine,' while other songs are pastiches, like 'Premium Bond Theme' and 'When Gran'ma Plays The Banjo.' Best of all is the joyful 'Goin' Down The Road' which starts off folky and ends with bagpipes.

4.105) Jeff Wayne's Musical Version Of War Of The Worlds – Jeff Wayne / Various Artists (1978)

A huge undertaking, and if only H.G. Wells had been around to hear his story adapted in this way. Like Mick Jagger and the A259, Wells was one of the best things to ever come out of Kent! Richard Burton proves that he has the ultimate narrative voice, and with stars like David Essex, Phil Lynott and Julie Covington involved, how could this album really fail? The opening track, 'The Eve Of The War,' sets the scene with its mix of rock, disco and orchestral styles, while 'Forever Autumn' provided a hit for Justin Hayward of 'Moody Blues' fame. Brooding and slightly psychedelic at times, you just have to let this double album do its thing and take in the story. Prog rock pretty much came to an end after this. Nobody was going to top it for scale after all.

4.106) Autobahn – Kraftwerk (1974)

In the late nineties I had an unusual hobby of videoing road journeys around my local area for posterity. In this era of YouTube, some of them are now proving extremely popular. It was surprising that I never used the road-inspired title track on this album to accompany any of them. 'Autobahn' takes up the whole of one side, a bit like a vehicle on a two-way road. It is very relaxing and brings to mind cruising along a traffic-free European highway rather than doing battle on the M25. The synthesiser rhythm chugs along and the piece diverts into different themes, before returning safely to the main melody, like changing lanes to overtake and then drifting back. The second half of the album consists of four experimental pieces. By the way, it's 'fahren, fahren, fahren' and not 'fun, fun, fun.' There's definitely no Beach Boys influence here.

The group went on to have a UK number one hit in early 1982 with 'The Model,' a double A-sided single with 'Computer Love,' but for me 'Autobahn' was always A1.

4.107) Great Balls Of Fire: 16 Original Greatest Hits – Jerry Lee Lewis (1998)

Jerry Lee was one of the rock and roll pioneers, some of whom we'll encounter when we look at blues music. His 'plonk plonk' piano style was derided by 'serious' pianists, but you can't deny the energy of these classic tracks, epitomised in 'Great Balls Of Fire' and 'Whole Lotta Shakin' Goin' On.' However, there is some versatility here too, with a cover of country star Hank Williams' 'You Win Again' and a revved up version of 'In The Mood' which you will probably know as a Glenn Miller ditty. This is another budget collection from Hallmark.

4.108) King Of Ragtime – Scott Joplin (1990)

It's great to have something in your collection that was actually recorded in the nineteenth century and the oldest track by the ragtime pianist here is 'Original Rags' from 1898. If you can handle the scratchy sound and 'savage edit' endings which often chop off the final note, this 'Giants Of Jazz' collection is a lot of fun, bringing to mind the silent films of Charlie Chaplin and his ilk, although twenty tracks is a lot to listen to in one go. Scott had more or less disappeared into obscurity until 'The Entertainer' was used in the film 'The Sting' in 1973. You may also recognise 'Maple Leaf Rag.' 'Reflection Rag' is the most modern recording here, being bang up to date from 1917.

4.109) Duelling Banjos From The Original Soundtrack Deliverance – Eric Weissberg & Steve Mandell (1973)

Like the Scott Joplin collection, this was an album loaded with tracks of unvarying style, but fun it is nevertheless. The title track is slightly misleading as there is one banjo and one guitar, and this pair of musicians achieved fame when the instrumental ditty was used in the film 'Deliverance' (1972). However the original composer, Arthur 'Guitar Boogie' Smith, wasn't credited so the lawyers had some work to do. Like the title, the track misleads by beginning as though the two musicians can barely play, until the pace picks up and resembles a bluegrass hoedown. The melody is reprised as 'End Of A Dream,' occasionally there's the welcome addition of a fiddle and many tracks, such as 'Buffalo Gals,' start off slowly and then repeat at double-speed.

I remember picking this up in the seaside town of Ramsgate in Kent one snowy Saturday and later satirising boy racers with their booming stereos by driving around Ashford town centre with the album blasting out. It was the kind of thing my friend Simon encouraged me to do in those days. I guess we hadn't learned that clowning around can sometimes backfire, as I'd previously managed to hit a fence post and flip my parents' Skoda onto its roof. Strangely enough the cassette that was in the rolled car's player was 'Jump Back' by the Rolling Stones and when I went back to the car to retrieve it my friend's advice was to do precisely that. I didn't jump back, as I'd only just bought the tape. If the car had blown up that would have been a huge sacrifice for a Rolling Stones cassette, but I guess, like my driving, I wasn't thinking straight.

4.110) Mouldy Old Dough - Lieutenant Pigeon (1998)

Until Adam Colton & Teresa Colton (who?), Lieutenant Pigeon were the only musical combo I could name that featured a mother and son. Hilda Woodward's piano playing is the central feature of most of this band's largely instrumental output, which includes the title track, a UK number one single in 1972. Being young men from the country, pubs were few and far between, so my friends and I would regularly go for nights out, with a designated driver not only getting free soft drinks but also getting the privilege of blasting the others with his choice of music. 'Mouldy Old Dough' was often my choice, initially taped from a vinyl 45. It seemed a fittingly bonkers start for a night out somehow. There are even vocals on some tracks on this Emporio collection, such as 'Auntie May,' 'I'm A Window Cleaner' and 'Dirty Old Man' with its bawdy lyrics that seem somewhat inappropriate to sing in front of one's mother!

I would later acquire 'The Best Of Lieutenant Pigeon' which presents all the A-sides and B-sides from the band's singles, with some more experimental offerings in the form of 'Opus 300' and 'The Villain,' which was literally 'drum and bass' before 'drum and bass' was an actual thing! Good fun, and who said fun is not allowed in music? Lighten up!

4.111) Greatest Hits - Chas & Dave (1984)

Keeping things humorous, Chas & Dave were a London duo who sang about down to earth subjects like going to the pub. I'd eventually purchase many of their albums, but for a general overview this was a great compilation. 'Ain't No Pleasin' You' is a rare serious song by the duo that got to number two in the UK singles chart. 'The Sideboard Song' is almost rap-like in its delivery and once prompted my father to eject my tape from the car stereo on a family holiday to Dorset because it was doing his head in! 'Stars Over 45' is a medley of old music hall songs, something Chas & Dave would specialise in with the 'Jamboree Bag' albums. Everything you want to hear is here, from 'Rabbit' to 'London Girls' to 'Margate' to 'Harry Was A Champion.' They even have a go at being poignant on 'Wish That I Could Write A Love Song,' but for me the 'top trump' is 'Turn That Noise Down' for its complete hilarity.

4.112) The Wurzels & Adge Cutler & The Wurzels - The Wurzels (1991)

British regional accents are so diverse and brilliant for comedy material. So we go from Chas & Dave's London to 'Good Old Somerset.' The hits are here, from the number one 'The Combine Harvester,' based on Melanie's hit 'Brand New Key,' to 'I Am A Cider Drinker,' based on Jonathan King's hit 'Una Paloma Blanca,' and the less we say about him the better. Hmm, déjà vu. Again. 'The Blackbird' and 'I Got Me Beady Little Eye On Thee' are essential Wurzels, and the second half of the album is assembled from older, folkier, live recordings made when Adge Cutler fronted the band. 'The Wurple-Diddle-I-Doo Song' is just ridiculous and really it all just makes you want to move to a farm in the West County and down a bucket-load of cider. You'll struggle to find anything more rousing than 'Drink Up Thy Zider.' There's also a moment I always found mysterious at the end of the song 'Twice Daily' where the audience laughter sounds remarkably similar to that at the end of the Beatles track 'Within You Without You.' The full conspiracy theory is explained in my book 'England And Wales In A Flash.' and if that won't inspire you to buy a book on lighthouse visits I don't know what will!

In truth, I had always liked the Wurzels since I acquired a childhood tape of their 1977 album 'Golden Delicious' from my Uncle Graham, who coming from

Portsmouth seemed half way there in terms of accent. Another item for the wish list is a CD release of this. 'School Days Young Days,' even shows a serious side to the band and a rare female vocal, while 'Pheasant Plucker's Son,' 'Morning Glory' and 'Rock Around The A38' are more of the band that we know and love. Yes, 'love.' So there!

4.113) The Ultimate Monty Python Rip Off – Monty Python (1994)

I promise we will get serious again in a bit, but if you wanted to get the best of the comedy troupe's songs as well as the cream of their sketches, this was a must. Nothing ever made crucifixion sound as jolly as 'Always Look On The Bright Side Of Life,' and 'The Galaxy Song' blinds us with science and then delivers its punchline. It was Eric Idle who composed most of the group's musical offerings, but there are clips from the films here too. My favourite sketches included here are 'Argument' and 'Travel Agent' which both work very well as audio pieces. I'm going to slap a '15' certificate on this though, as John Cleese in particular peps up some of the language when freed from the constraints of TV. I'd eventually purchase 'Monty Python Sings' (1989) which is all music.

4.114) Back To The Future Soundtrack – Various Artists (1985)

The trilogy of films directed by Robert Zemeckis has always been a favourite of mine and the musical choices that capture the essence of both the fifties and the eighties in the first film meld well with the two orchestral pieces from the film's score. The version of 'Johnny B. Goode' on the album doesn't contain the frenetic guitar solo that Marty McFly does in the film however, and 'Mr. Sandman,' a pivotal track in the movie, is strangely absent. There are two songs by Huey Lewis And The News, of which the obvious one is 'The Power Of Love.' Although a similar mixture of styles could have been put together as a soundtrack album for the second film, the sequel disc is entirely orchestral, as is the one for 'Part 3,' except for one short 'hoedown' instrumental. I never knew that ZZ Top were around in 1885!

4.115) Pulp Fiction Soundtrack – Various Artists (1994)

Whatever you think of Tarantino's films, his soundtracks were very enjoyable. The furious instrumental, 'Misirlou,' by Dick Dale And The Del-Tones sets the stage for this mixture of surf instrumentals and old hits, which included Dusty Springfield's 'Son Of A Preacher Man' and Chuck Berry's 'You Never Can Tell.' For the uninitiated, surf music was generally based around the twelve-bar blues sequence and led by a jangly guitar. There are a couple of soul tracks courtesy of Al Green and Kool & The Gang, but be warned, there's some child-unfriendly dialogue sprinkled between the tracks too. 'Flowers On The Wall' has a great country feel and I'd advise getting the collector's edition that includes 'Rumble' by

Link Way & The Wraymen, a pivotal track from the film. I can do without sixteen minutes of Tarantino chatting however.

4.116) Reservoir Dogs Soundtrack – Various Artists (1992)

Tarantino's first soundtrack album was held together by a low-energy radio DJ, who sounds almost comatose while introducing some of the songs. There's also some dialogue from the movie, again not for kids. 'Little Green Bag' by the George Baker Selection has a infectious seventies bassline, 'Hooked On A Feeling' by 'Blue Swede' opens with what sounds like an attempt at a native American Indian chant, and 'Stuck In The Middle With You' is a sweet song which was used for one of the film's nastiest scenes. 'Coconut' was my first realisation that Harry Nilsson was much more than just an interpreter of ballads like 'Without You.' Listen to how this eccentric, almost throwaway song circles to a frenzy as Harry's vocal rises across the octaves.

4.117) Crescendo Records Sampler Volume Four – Various Artists (1994)

'What on earth is this?' I hear you say. Well, I spotted this CD in the 'Suite 16' music shop in Folkestone one lunch break, and lured by its promise of 'Action / adventure, surf, sci-fi [and] new age' I parted with a minimal sum and enjoyed a smorgasbord of instrumental music which opened new horizons. The surf instrumentals reminded me of the 'Pulp Fiction' soundtrack, and I like the way the album morphs into the spacey style known as new age, before Neil Norman takes it away with a clutch of tracks no doubt inspired by films like 'Star Wars.' These have a great seventies feel each time the melodies emerge from the primordial ambient soup of sound.

4.118) Raised On Rock: 70's Rock UK – Various Artists (1989)

Knight Records released UK and USA discs for the sixties, seventies and eighties, but this CD seems like the *piece de resistance*, opening with the Boomtown Rats' tale of mass murder, 'I Don't Like Mondays.' Argent's 'Hold Your Head Up' and the rhythm-shifting 'Question' by the Moody Blues are high points, as is the 'talking guitar' effect on Peter Frampton's 'Show Me The Way,' but really there are no lows here. Juicy Lucy's 'Who Do You Love?' has a hillbilly feel, Scottish rockers Nazareth make an appearance, and the Strawbs hit 'Part Of The Union' provides a folky finish. I used to think the lyrics were sarcastic, but in fact the song was written in praise of unions. Power to the people!

4.119) Hits From The 70's, Volume 2 [sic] – Various Artists (1994)

Usually released as a three-disc box set, I was prompted to buy 'Volume 2' of this collection from the 'Music For Pleasure' label, based on the quality of the material. From Hot Chocolate's disco funk on 'Every 1's A Winner' to the Knack's catchy punk riff on 'My Sharona,' this is all good stuff. There's folk from The Band (who I'm sure you know started off backing Bob Dylan) as well as McGuinness Flint, there's pop from the Fortunes and Maxine Nightingale, and to top the lot, there's 'Peaches' by the Stranglers, which I remember being used as the theme music for Keith Floyd's cookery programmes way back when.

iv) My Generation

4.120) Definitely Maybe – Oasis (1994)

Often the first album released by an artist has a vibrancy that the other albums don't quite possess. I sometimes put this down to not having the comforts of money and fame. A friend of mine who I knew as 'Death Metal Dan' was the first person to show me this album while on a non-landing ferry trip / waterborne booze up. Guitars were back in and I let out a silent 'Hallelujah.' Favourites of mine are the psychedelic blues of 'Shakermaker,' the moody mantra-like 'Columbia' and the epic 'Slide Away,' announced by its memorable opening guitar note. There's even room for a bit of comedy with 'Digsy's Dinner' and 'Married With Children.' People said they were the new Beatles at the time, although the influence wasn't blatantly obvious until the release of the 'Whatever' single.

To really appreciate the quality Oasis were churning out you need the deluxe editions of these early albums which contain all the B-sides from the singles. Here you'll get the band's phantasmagorical cover of the Beatles' 'I Am The Walrus' as well as some acoustic gold like 'Talk Tonight.'

4.121) (What's The Story) Morning Glory? – Oasis (1995)

This was huge. The Manchester boys scored their first UK number one with 'Some Might Say' which has my favourite Gallagher line; 'Some might say they don't believe in Heaven / Go and tell it to the man who lives in Hell.' The Beatles homage is clear at the end of 'She's Electric' which paraphrases the closing melody from 'With A Little Help From My Friends.' 'Wonderwall' and 'Don't Look Back In Anger' are the two tracks that still get radio airplay these days, but 'Champagne Supernova' blasts them all out of the water in my opinion, with its high point being the dramatic guitar chord just before the first chorus.

I recall walking to a Christmas meal at a pub with my colleagues one lunchtime in December 1995 and popping into Our Price Records to purchase all the CD singles the band had released so far. To get the brilliant B-sides too numerous to list I'd again encourage anybody to get the deluxe version of the album. Top of the pile is 'The Masterplan.'

4.122) Be Here Now – Oasis (1997)

With typical bravado the band included this album's release date on its cover, signalling that this was going to be 'an event.' The songs got longer and the band even knocked their heroes, the Beatles, off of the pedestal for the longest ever UK number one. Indeed, 'D'Ya Know What I Mean' (which lyrically is virtually a list of Beatles songs) even eclipsed the mighty 'Hey Jude' for length. Oasis would soon top their own record, when 'All Around The World' hit the top spot, with its similarity to 'Hey Jude' somewhat obvious with all those 'na na nas.' The title track has an instrument that sounds reminiscent of Johnny And The Hurricanes. Meanwhile, 'Fade In-Out' is broody and bluesy, while 'Stand By Me' is anthemic. Again there are plenty of fabulous B-sides, the best of which is 'Flashbax' in my inhumble opinion. That Gallagher spirit is rubbing off!

4.123) Out Of Time – R.E.M. (1991)

It's strange how songs always evoke memories, and I bought this album when most people had filed it away in the cupboard. I remember being totally bored one night, wondering Kinks-style 'Where have all the good times gone?' and consequently driving 35 miles to Margate with 'Out Of Time' on my car stereo. I am more aware of the impact of unnecessary driving on the climate these days of course. Anyway, a couple of tracks have additional vocals by Kate Pierson from the B52s (remember 'Love Shack?'). The music is pretty varied, with the instrumental 'Endgame,' the brooding 'Low' (possibly my favourite track), the Elvis-esque vocal on 'Belong' and of course the classics, 'Shiny Happy People' and 'Losing My Religion.' The next two albums the band did were similarly top notch, but there are many others that are well worth listening to as well.

4.124) Automatic For The People – R.E.M. (1992)

This was the Georgia band's most highly acclaimed album, containing the weepy ballad 'Everybody Hurts' which was adorned with strings for extra impact. 'Drive,' which opens the album, has a moody feel with the release coming when the electric guitar kicks in. 'The Sidewinder Sleeps Tonight' taught us Brits that a sidewinder is a snake and 'Man On The Moon' is of course a legendary track with another Elvis impersonation. Like 'Out Of Time' this collection has a folky feel, and the closing track is wonderfully melodic. The drummer, Bill Berry, felt a bit under-utilised, so the next album was to be a return to amplified rock.

4.125) Monster – R.E.M. (1994)

'What's The Frequency Kenneth?' was the lead single, but it was 'Crush With Eyeliner' that struck a chord with me. The surreal lyrics and wacky appearance on BBC TV's 'Top Of The Pops' prompted my sister to ask the question 'What's happened to R.E.M.?' but in truth, this song has one of the best openings of any rock track, with an epic guitar chord being allowed to reverberate just long enough for maximum effect before the tapping drumsticks usher the rest of the band to kick in. 'Strange Currencies' was like an amplified version of 'Everybody Hurts.' It's all very grungy and it's all very good. Just wait for those dissonant vocal notes at the end of 'You.'

4.126) New Adventures In Hi-Fi – R.E.M. (1996)

The title may sound pompous, but R.E.M. really were cutting edge in the nineties, and as with Blur and Radiohead, it was always exciting to discover where they would push the boundaries of music next. 'How The West Was Won And Where It Got Us' is a great opener with some edgy piano playing reminiscent of David Bowie's 'Aladdin Sane.' 'The Wake-Up Bomb' (we all need one of those sometimes) is a great rocker, and 'Leave' introduces the melody acoustically before rocking out with what sounds like an incessant car alarm. R.E.M. were good enough musicians to include instrumentals on their albums and here we get 'Zither.' It is my, perhaps unfair, opinion that concentration spans are too paltry for modern albums to punctuate the attention grabbers with ethereal tracks like this. As Blur declared 'Modern life is rubbish.'

4.127) Up – R.E.M. (1998)

At the time we all wondered what R.E.M. without drummer Bill Berry would sound like. There was no major need for concern though as the drum machines give the contents a pleasant ambient feel, apart from the song 'Lotus' which is more like the R.E.M. of yore. 'At My Most Beautiful' sounds like 'Pet Sounds' era Beach Boys, while 'Daysleeper' was a notable single from this album. And we all like a kip in the day, don't we? 'The Apologist' seems to touch on the aspect of confession within religion, and 'Why Not Smile' has a sweetly optimistic sentiment. For me, this was the last great R.E.M. album. Stipe, Buck and Mills passed the audition.

4.128) The Presidents Of The USA – The Presidents Of The USA (1995)

Although I didn't acquire this, or any Presidents albums until at least ten years later I did buy the singles 'Lump,' 'Peaches' and 'Dune Buggy,' which included many of this album's tracks as B-sides, albeit often with live versions. Therefore, I think the album qualifies for inclusion at this point. PUSA were a grunge band from Seattle who didn't take themselves too seriously, well, not very seriously at all to be truthful. Most of the tracks seem to be humorous ditties about animals, and the use of expletives in 'Kitty' is actually quite unusual for the band. They even take the Mick out of their own abilities in 'We Are Not Going To Make It.' 'Naked And Famous' perhaps satirises the tendency for celebrities to strip off as soon as they make it big. Perhaps their skin becomes intolerant to fabric as wealth increases, and I cringe when I think that an all-time rock hero like John Lennon was one of the first to do this. Conversely it's quite funny when the vocalist urges a stripper to 'put some clothes on and call me' in the song 'Stranger.'

I'd later get my hands on the PUSA albums 'II' (1996), 'Pure Frosting' (1998) and 'Love Everybody' (2004), which are all entertaining but in the same vein, hence no review. As a footnote the slightly smutty B-side to 'Lump,' 'Carolyn's Bootie,' was something that my friend Simon and I used to leap about to on those legendary nights of booze and grub in my converted garage bedroom, so my memories of PUSA will always be slightly silly.

4.129) Parklife – Blur (1994)

I remember my sister wanting this album on in the car on a family holiday to Lancashire in the nineties and finding it irritating. Like Liam Gallagher, who compared Blur to Chas & Dave (who I actually like), I had dismissed the band prematurely based on Damon Albarn's accent. Schoolboy error. This album contains far more than the singalong anthems of 'Girls And Boys' and 'Parklife,' which features a guest vocal from Phil Daniels who famously played the central character in the film version of The Who's 'Quadrophenia.' There's some punky stuff in the form of 'Bank Holiday,' a Syd Barrett pastiche called 'Far Out,' and the album's highlight in my opinion, 'This Is A Low,' an anthem that the Oasis boys would have surely been proud of.

4.130) Blur – Blur (1997)

This was the album when I finally recognised the Essex boys as a creative force. I had a friend called John who I used to spend my lunch breaks with at work and this album, as well as R.E.M.'s 'New Adventures In Hi-Fi,' were the daily soundtrack. 'Beetlebum' scored the band their second UK number one (the first being 'Country House' in 1995) and 'Song 2' is two minutes long and reached number two in the charts. It's easy to remember stuff like that! 'M.O.R.' more than borrows from David Bowie's 'Boys Keep Swinging,' and Graham Coxon's guitar at the end of 'Country Sad Ballad Man' is satisfying in a similar way to David Gilmour's riff at the end of Pink Floyd's 'Sheep.' I once came into work with my hand cut from an anger outburst. Noticing this, John declared 'You've been listening to too much *Chinese Bombs*!' You'll see what he meant when you hear the track. 'Death Of A Party' and 'I'm Just A Killer For Your Love' are lo-fi classics, and there's more Bowie influence in 'Strange News From Another Star.' The closing track, 'Essex Dogs,' is a brain-melt with a dentist's drill doubling as an instrument.

4.131) 13 – Blur (1999)

Blur are usually remembered for the Cockney sounding singalongs from the 'Parklife' era, but on this album they pushed the envelope, with everything from a seven-minute folk anthem ('Tender') to several all-out sonic assaults worthy of Hawkwind. I think Damon Albarn was trying to illustrate how his head felt at the time following a break-up, and he did a pretty good job. This was one of the last times that I really thought a band were pushing what constitutes music beyond previous limits (Radiohead's 'Kid A' is the other example that springs to mind).

There was a genuine excitement for me about purchasing this album with its eerie ambience pervading. The final track 'Optigan' reminds me of Stanley Kubrick's film 'The Shining,' seeming like something creepy from the 1920s filtering across the decades.

4.132) Leisure – Blur (1991)

I remember popping out to buy this album while staying in a hotel in Bude in Cornwall with my father during our first lighthouse visiting trip, attempting to fulfill a challenge which inspired our book 'England And Wales In A Flash.' When I got back to the room with the CD my dad remarked 'You've gone downmarket!' I still disagree. In spite of being 'Essex dogs,' Blur's debut very much emulated the Manchester indie rock style popular at the time. 'Sing' is a moody and experimental piece with minimal lyrics, while 'She's So High' is a memorable early hit. And all this was several years before anybody had heard of Oasis. 'Come Together' and 'Birthday' are not to be confused with the Beatles classics, the latter of these is a downbeat piece with nice harmonies.

4.133) Trainspotting Soundtrack – Various Artists (1996)

I was never a fan of the film which was a bit too 'gross' for my liking, but the soundtrack album is superb. We open with Iggy Pop's 'Lust For Life' before Brian Eno's 'Deep Blue Day' takes us into ambient territory. The title track by Primal Scream is a hypnotic tune based around a blues sequence. There's 'Mile End' by Pulp, and of the course the 'lager lager lager' chant of 'Born Slippy,' presented here in its full nine minutes. Damon Albarn also shows off his knowledge of Bond films, but only the Sean Connery ones, in 'Closet Romantic.' All in all, this is pretty much a musical encyclopedia of the nineties.

4.134) Vanishing Point – Primal Scream (1997)

Primal Scream were another band introduced to me by my astrophysicist friend, Barney. Well, he wasn't an astrophysicist then, he was still at school. The pair of us liked all things 'sixties' and I remember he'd bought the three CD singles from this band's sixties-influenced album, 'Vanishing Point.' 'Burning Wheel' emulated the psychedelic sound adeptly, with plenty of mellotron *a la* '2000 Light Years From Home' by the Rolling Stones. We have the aforementioned 'Trainspotting,' and the keyboard sounds like a harmonica again on 'Star.' There's an intense cover of Hawkwind's 'Motorhead,' and 'Stuka' is perhaps the oddest track of all, being a masterclass in 'dub,' a genre that grew out of ska with heavy use of studio effects such as reverb being applied. The vocal here sounds like Stephen Hawking's voice box on LSD.

4.135) Screamadelica – Primal Scream (1991)

This was the band's third album but it was their first major hit, being viewed by many as a perfect synthesis of the nineties dance and rock cultures. 'Movin' On Up' could have graced a Rolling Stones album, while 'Loaded' uses the chords of the 'na na' refrain from the Beatles' 'Hey Jude' in a more dance oriented context. 'Damaged' seems like a misfit on this album being almost acoustic, but it neatly precedes the second half which was designed for chilling out after the rave up, in a similar vein to music by acts such as the Orb.

4.136) Give Up But Don't Give Out – Primal Scream (1994)

...Or how to out-Stones the Rolling Stones. 'Jailbird' leads straight into 'Rocks' which I actually thought was a new track by Jagger and pals at the time. Lead singer Bobby Gillespie seems to have a voice that can adapt itself to any style. 'Funky Jam' does what it says on the tin, with the title track following suit stylistically. Denise Johnson provides vocals on these two tracks, as well as on 'Free,' a piano ballad with some smooth saxophone. Funk legend George Clinton is also vocalising on 'Funky Jam' and the title track. You can't say this album isn't diverse.

4.137) Odelay – Beck (1996)

Yet another new artist for me from 'Barney's music introduction service.' Beck was a purveyor of the 'copy and paste' approach to music, assembling songs from samples of often quite old records. Some of the tracks on this album have very prominent vinyl crackling sounds and one could argue as to whether or not these were on Beck Hanson's samples or if they were added to create a certain feel. The big hit here was 'Devil's Haircut' and Beck's often rapped lyrics are very reminiscent of Bob Dylan's surreal mid-sixties output. 'Minus' is the only heavy rock track, and the acoustic guitar dominated 'Ramshackle' has a resigned sadness to it, before Beck blasts us to smithereens with the hidden track 'Discobox.'

For youngsters, hidden or secret tracks were particularly popular in the nineties, with a song not listed on the cover artwork programmed as a surprise at the end of the album. Irritatingly, these often followed a lengthy pause, so once you knew of the existence of a track you would have to fast forward though ten minutes of silence to find it. One of the worst examples I can think of is the twenty-minute gap before the secret track on Nirvana's 'In Utero.'

4.138) Mellow Gold – Beck (1994)

This was the album that went with the song 'Loser,' which is what launched Beck out of complete obscurity. 'Loser' contains one of those surreal raps that became Beck's staple. My mother also had a serious dislike of the line 'I'm a loser baby /

So why don't you kill me?' Elsewhere you can find some downbeat folk and even obscenity-filled heavy metal. Beck employs some weird vocal techniques at times, such as on 'Truck Driving Neighbors Downstairs,' the intro of which sounds like 'trash reality TV' before the genre even existed. 'Blackhole,' which closes the album, sounds like a long lost Leadbelly track, but be warned, lyrically Beck has never minced his words so be prepared for some colourful lingo. Mostly blue.

4.139) One Foot In The Grave – Beck (1994)

The albums that Beck Hanson recorded before he was famous are a challenge to say the least, but this is one of the more consistently enjoyable offerings, with just the odd rock blast punctuating a set of acoustic material, often evoking the style of Woody Guthrie. 'I Have Seen The Land Beyond' shows this influence most clearly, while 'He's A Mighty Good Leader' is a rewrite of a song by bluesman Skip James. My favourite Beck lyric is on this album; 'Got a funny feeling they've got plastic in the afterlife.' Brill!

4.140) Mutations – Beck (1998)

So with Beck's reputation as the ultimate cross-genre *enfant terrible*, what did he do next? He went all country on us of course. Whereas Bob Dylan changed genres every three or four albums, Beck started alternating styles with every release. This is a very enjoyable album and you'll be pleased to know that the creative lyrics are still there. 'Bottle Of Blues' has a bluesy feel (obviously) while 'Tropicalia' leans towards bossa nova, and 'Sing It Again' is a sleepy country song. The penultimate track on the UK edition is the only truly frenetic offering here (listen to those drums) with 'Runners Dial Zero' ending the album, sounding like somebody picking through the radioactive scraps of a post-apocalyptic world.

4.141) Midnite Vultures – Beck (1999)

The most eclectic lone wolf since Bob Dylan marches relentlessly on, but can the fans keep up? With 'Mutations,' we thought Mr. Hansen was mellowing into a folk artist, so then he gives us 'Midnite Vultures' which is unashamed in paying homage to the multi-named multi-instrumentalist, Prince. The spelling of 'Sexx Laws' is surely a reference to Prince's track 'Gett Off' if ever I saw one, and Beck delivers a falsetto vocal over the seventies style wash of 'Debra.' In between, he gets a bit saucy with his raps, seems to have a go at an 'A Day In The Life' style orchestral crescendo in 'Nicotine & Gravy,' and there is some succulent steel guitar on 'Beautiful Way.'

4.142) Different Class – Pulp (1995)

'Barney's music introduction service' cranks into action again, although this album took me much longer to fully appreciate. 'Common People' was an instant classic with some real pent up anger coming out in Jarvis Cocker's vocal delivery of lyrics that seemed to sum up the era. 'Disco 2000' was another big hit, although the sentiment is a little dated now that the turn of the millennium is ancient history; the girl in the song is probably not just a mother but a grandmother now. 'Mis-Shapes' expresses frustration that the rich don't seem to give a flying whatsit for the working class majority, and 'Sorted For E's And Wizz' [sic] is more about the unity of festivals than drugs. Honest! Some of the lyrics seemed a little *risqué* at the time, although the humour shines through on 'Underwear' – 'If fashion is your trade / Then when you're naked / I guess you must be unemployed.' Boom boom.

4.143) The Bends – Radiohead (1995)

Pretty much every song on here is a nineties anthem. The band from Abingdon seemed to sum up the mood with the line 'I wish it was the sixties / I wish I could be happy / I wish, I wish / I wish that something would happen.' The nineties were the nearest thing we will get to a rerun of the sixties in my lifetime I'm sure, but while many were out raving, this group from Oxfordshire presented the stark reality of things. 'Fake Plastic Trees,' 'Nice Dream' and 'Bullet Proof... I Wish I Was' are all devastatingly sad. 'Just' is simply a great rock song, and vocalist Thom Yorke gets angry on 'My Iron Lung.' The album leaves us with the haunting 'Street Spirit (Fade Out).'

4.144) OK Computer – Radiohead (1997)

Radiohead went beyond rock here, with experimentation hinting at what would come on later albums, whilst retaining some very memorable songs such as 'Paranoid Android' and 'Karma Police,' which both present a rather cynical look at life (*a la* Pink Floyd's 'The Dark Side Of The Moon'). 'No Alarms And No Surprises' gazes at provincial life through a bleak lens ('A job that slowly kills you'), while summing up the apathy many felt, and still do feel, about the government. 'Exit Music (For A Film)' was famously the music playing in the TV comedy 'Father Ted,' when a suicidal priest that Ted and Dougal had spent the whole episode trying to cheer up decides that launching himself off a cliff is perhaps the best option after all! Radiohead was never party music, that's for sure.

4.145) Pablo Honey – Radiohead (1993)

Having bought the two most essential albums it was time to rewind to the band's debut. Whilst it does contain 'Creep,' which needed to have one word substituted for radio airplay, this collection is less distinctive in style than its monster successors. The second best track is 'Anyone Can Play Guitar' which does the same 'quiet / loud' thing that 'Creep' and many Nirvana songs do. Thom sings that he wants to be Jim Morrison. At the time he probably had no idea that his band would be up there with rock aristocracy like the Doors by the end of the decade.

4.146) Time Out Of Mind – Bob Dylan (1997)

Just when everyone thought that Bob Dylan's best work was all two decades behind him, he comes up with this absolute whopper of an album. I would say that this marked the start of the late stage of his career, with a voice and style that seemed to indicate his status as a classic blues singer, up there with the greats such as B.B. King or John Lee Hooker. We open with 'Love Sick,' which expresses a rarely heard sentiment that everyone feels at some point; 'I'm sick of love / I'm so sick of it!' We have a song that provided British singer Adele with a huge hit early in her career, 'Make You Feel My Love,' and there is a supremely dark feel to many of the lyrics elsewhere. I have no idea what Bob was going through at this point in his life, but if you listen to 'Not Dark Yet' and 'Cold Irons Bound' you'll see what I mean. We conclude with 'Highlands,' which at the time was Bob's longest ever track at sixteen minutes. The tale eventually opens out into a funny story about an exchange with a waitress in a restaurant before returning to the theme of longing to be in, one would assume, Scotland.

'Love And Theft' (2001), which followed this, varies the styles a bit more but lacks the boldness and verbal punch of this album. After 'Modern Times' and 'Together Through Life' Bob would give us a Christmas album. Then just as people had begun to write him off again he treats us to another masterwork in the form of 'Tempest.' We will return to Bob later. Or should I say, Bob would return to us.

4.147) Song From The Capeman – Paul Simon (1997)

After a break of seven years Paul Simon came back with a work that was bewildering to many. 'Songs From The Capeman' was ravaged by the media upon its release. No doubt they were expecting him to explore a third genre of world music, but Paul had other ideas. How about a musical about a notorious gangster, with a doo-wop feel to the songs and language that seemed most uncustomary for Mr. Simon? That should send the critics packing, ha! Those of us who were left to listen discovered the true stature of Paul Simon's narrative vocal style in the opening song 'Adios Hermanos.' 'Vampires' has a Cuban feel and more 'certificate 18' language, and 'Satin Summer Nights' has some extremely evocative female harmonies that might make the hairs on your neck stand on end. If not, it's back to 'Graceland' with ya!

This is the last of the Paul Simon albums I am going to review. He has turned out consistently good material since, but the songs that are written in *my* 'heart and bones' are mostly the ones up to and including this album. Yes, *including* it!

4.148) Flaming Pie – Paul McCartney (1997)

Paul was out of fashion for about a decade (I blame 'the frog song'), but with Oasis leading the way for guitar bands, and the release of oodles of 'new' Beatles material via the 'Anthology' project, this album was perfectly timed. And very good it is too. 'The World Tonight' has an 'ELO' feel with its steady drumbeat, while the title track references John Lennon's quote that the name 'The Beatles' came to him in a dream of a man on a flaming pie. There are acoustic moments like 'Little Willow' and an anthem in the form of 'Beautiful Night.' McCartney was far from finished.

Chapter 5 – Millennium

It is interesting to note that when I was younger I always imagined that at some point my CD collection would be complete, just as I imagined having life entirely sussed out and never feeling down or angry after the age of 32. Some hope.

Music and life are both essentially like science. The more you discover, the more there is to discover.

I spent New Year's Eve on what was regarded as the dawn of the millennium in bed with flu. Why get excited about a bunch of zeros on a date anyway? I guess you could say this heralded a more settled era for me, at least to begin with, and I think my musical tastes were pretty settled too. I knew what I liked and I liked what I knew. 'No alarms and no surprises please,' to quote Radiohead.

The critical among you will probably observe that the list hasn't been hugely diverse so far, although few would fail to acknowledge the musical heritage of bands like the Beatles as going back to the blues via rock and roll and Motown groups. Well, hold your horses, during this time as well as expanding my collection of classic rock, I was simultaneously buying up every CD I could find from the Orbis partworks series, 'The Blues Collection,' which was released between 1993 and 1997. I think my interest in blues music began from nights with friends at a semi-rural pub called the Hooden Horse, which at the time was dimly lit, with candles dripping wax all over the tables as the smoke from a thousand cigarettes wafted around. The blues music in the background was ever-present.

The smoking ban in pubs would prolong lives, but it would also make such atmospheric venues a thing of the past. I decided that I wanted some of this music and began with Sonny Boy Williamson II and Otis Rush. The series covered a few rock and roll pioneers too. We'll look at a selection of these CDs in the section called 'Blue.' Whether the title brings to mind a Joni Mitchell album or a British boy band is up to you.

A genre not explored in these pages is that of jungle / drum and bass. If you remember my first experience of Pink Floyd at my friend Simon's house as a teenager, we now find him driving around in a brown Vauxhall Nova with a constant background of tapes recorded from raves with names like 'Hysteria,' 'Helter Skelter' and 'Dreamscape.' At the time I hated this music and wished that he'd play something with 'proper instruments' in, but in truth the entire genre *is* based on proper instruments, consisting of recorded loops of drum breaks from much older records played at high speed. The most famous of these is known as the 'Amen break,' which originated from a song called 'Amen, Brother' by the Winstons, dating right back to 1969.

Apart from Blur's '13' album (from the last chapter) and Radiohead's 'Kid A' (included in this chapter), jungle was perhaps the last time I can say that I heard something truly original that had never been done before, so on the merit of this I feel that the genre at least deserves a mention. Even David Bowie had a go at drum and bass in the nineties with his 'Earthling' album, and that's good enough for me.

I'm afraid rap has never been a genre that I've truly appreciated, although I did purchase the Beastie Boys album 'Licensed To Ill' (1986), as much for their use of Led Zeppelin's guitar riffs and nostalgia from the old school bus as anything.

Now during this time I decided that life on the road was for me. Sadly this didn't mean gigging with a successful rock band but merely swapping postal deliveries around an office for van and lorry deliveries for the same company which operated cruise ships. During long journeys from Kent to the cruise terminal at Southampton I would uniformly listen to Radio 2, but I can't say that a lot of 'current' music from the noughties grabbed me. Musical styles had changed.

I also realised that I had not explored female artists very thoroughly at all. My sister was a fan of Sheryl Crow, who I quite liked, but Joni Mitchell was probably the first female songwriter that I came to appreciate, and female vocalists featured prominently in the band, the Beautiful South, which like Simon & Garfunkel, I discovered from borrowing albums from my Auntie Cally. I guess this is partly the point of this book, to illustrate how appreciating music is a journey that is never over, and a collection is never complete. And thank goodness for that.

For several years I had been touring the coastline of England and Wales, lighthouse-spotting with my father, and in 2003 the pair of us released 'England And Wales In A Flash,' a book which documented our adventures. Yet, as far as finding a girlfriend went, these were barren times. As friends began to settle down and my book sales didn't take off like the 'supersonic rocket ship' I'd imagined, I began to experience yearly 'downers' in the twilight months of the year. And herein lies another point of this book. I think to appreciate music and lyrics at a core level it may even be beneficial to have experienced what lies in the darker recesses of the mind; the music seems to cut deeper for some reason.

Towards the end of this period I would reignite my passion for camping, which had been dormant since my Scouting days, by hiking from Kent to Somerset with a friend called Tom, an adventure which became the subject of my second book, 'Mud, Sweat And Beers' (2006). I imagined returning from this trip full of new confidence, like Moses coming down from the mountain, but whilst it did sow the seed for many later camping trips, sometimes with added cycling, life was still much the same, and a brief tenure on the local parish council proved to be a most unpleasant experience. Almost a decade later the Stereophonics released an album called 'Keep The Village Alive,' but I discovered that the local establishment figures didn't share my ideas of what 'alive' means.

So, it's on with the show, and just in case the non-chronological order of these albums is becoming frustrating, there is an index at the end of this book to tie it all together. Come on, what's not to like? As McCartney once sang 'Step on the gas and wipe that tear away!'

i) Disco 2000

5.1) Planet Waves – Bob Dylan (1974)

Let's start by filling in the early seventies gap in my Bob Dylan collection. Apart from the 'covers' album 'Dylan' (1973), he also released a soundtrack album to the film 'Pat Garrett & Billy The Kid' which is mostly instrumental, but it does contain several versions of a nice song called 'Billy' and the all-time classic 'Knocking On Heaven's Door.' 'Planet Waves' was the next traditional studio album and it's a transitional one. Bob has moved on from the laid back country approach but hasn't quite found his stride which we would see with 'Blood On The Tracks' and 'Desire.' The standout track is 'Forever Young' which comes in two completely different versions. 'Going Going Gone' is also very nice and has some guitar licks which could easily come from a seventies Rolling Stones record. I always wonder if the title was inspired by Donovan's 1973 album 'Cosmic Wheels,' or even Van Morrison's 1968 album 'Astral Weeks.'

5.2) Street-Legal – Bob Dylan (1978)

This was the final studio album before Bob 'got religion.' My friend Mark, who had some seriously warped ideas about cassette tape as a child, found a bag of tapes thrown down a railway track while walking the line, Johnny Cash style, for his job. One of those tapes was this one which he was more than glad to toss my way. The instrumentation is a similar 'band' set up to 'Live At Budokan' with saxophones, etc. 'Changing Of The Guard' is probably the most well known song here, but 'Is Your Love In Vain?' actually made it into the UK singles chart, with its appeal for space within a relationship. Other top tracks include the bluesy 'New Pony,' although it's generally best not to compare your partner to a horse. The spirited finisher, 'Journey Through Dark Heat,' seems like an attempt at writing something akin to 'Like A Rolling Stone' for the seventies.

5.3) Slow Train Coming – Bob Dylan (1979)

It is often incorrectly assumed that when Bob Dylan 'got religion' he lost his compositional edge. I disagree. 'Gotta Serve Somebody' opens the album with a mellow bluesy feel and interesting lyrics in spite of its simple point (John Lennon responded musically to this with 'Serve Yourself'). Some of the tracks have a great groove to them, such as 'Slow Train' itself and 'Gonna Change My Way Of Thinking.' These songs are both impassioned invectives about the state of the world viewed through the idealistic lens of his new faith. The closing track is a highlight, with Bob singing to just a lone piano. There's also 'Man Gave Names To The Animals' which leaves its punchline hanging in the...

5.4) Shot Of Love – Bob Dylan (1981)

Bob's next album, 'Saved' (1980), is a full blown gospel affair and better suited to a church service than a book reviewing rock albums. On 'Shot Of Love' he seemed to recover just enough 'Dylanescence' to make something I'd listen to more than a handful of times. 'Lenny Bruce' is a genuinely touching song that honours the American comedian as a fighter for free speech and justice. 'The Groom's Still Waiting At The Altar' is Bob's best song of the eighties in my opinion. He's back in 'verbal deluge' mode and it really rocks. We love it when he's angry. 'In The Summertime' even has a retro sound with some harmonica, and it is nothing to do with Mungo Jerry. The final track, 'Every Grain Of Sand,' is also sublime. If he's trying to convert anybody, this is the way to do it.

'Infidels' (1983) isn't bad, although 'Empire Burlesque' (1985) has percussion sounds that you would expect to hear on a Pet Shop Boys record, which isn't a bad thing, but come on, horses for courses.

5.5) The Bootleg Series Volumes 1-3: Rare And Unreleased 1961-1991 – Bob Dylan (1991)

For a man who has released so much material, you'd expect this to be barrel-scrapings. Au contraire! Disc one is from Bob's folky period and includes the poignant 'He Was A Friend Of Mine' and the melodic 'Only A Hobo,' which is very much in the 'Guthrie homage' vein, as well as a spoken word tribute to the man himself.

The second disc charts his mid-sixties transition to rock and is indispensable, with Bob's own version of 'If You Gotta Go, Go Now,' which became a hit for Manfred Mann, and 'She's Your Lover Now,' a viciously sarcastic 'end of love' song from the 'Blonde On Blonde' era. He shows his country side on 'Santa Fe,' and 'Call Letter Blues' sounds like a more upbeat twin of the 'Blood On The Tracks' tune 'Meet Me In The Morning.'

The third CD surprises even further, with majestic sounding gems like 'Angelina,' 'Foot Of Pride,' 'Blind Willie McTell' and 'Series Of Dreams.' With Bob's eighties albums being significantly less than awe-inspiring, you can't help but wonder what on earth he was thinking of, leaving quality material like this unreleased at the time.

5.6) Amused To Death – Roger Waters (1992)

Since leaving Pink Floyd Roger Waters has specialised in concept albums, but whereas the concepts for 'The Pros And Cons Of Hitch-Hiking' (1984) and 'Radio K.A.O.S.' (1987) were quite convoluted, on 'Amused To Death' it was clear, and the result was one of Roger's masterworks, which should be considered in the same league as 'The Wall' and 'The Dark Side Of The Moon.' Here we look at the futile behaviour of humans, particularly their keenness for war, from an outsider's perspective. 'Perfect Sense' sums up the fact that it's all about money, 'Watching TV' calls to mind the 1989 massacre in Tiananmen Square in Beijing, and the rest is a kind of requiem for humanity, which it concludes was given enough rope to hang itself and consequently 'amused itself to death.' As an aside, many years later my Russian father-in-law put this on at a birthday celebration in Moscow. I think I was the only one who noticed the irony.

5.7) The Madcap Laughs – Syd Barrett (1970)

Exiled from Pink Floyd, Syd's 'would have been' bandmates David Gilmour and Roger Waters produced some of the tracks on his debut solo album. Tracks like 'Terrapin' and 'Love You' have a childlike innocence about them. The version of 'Octopus' here is more punchy than the outtake on 'Opel,' and there are echoes of psychedelic instrumentation, but towards the end of the album Syd is left alone with his acoustic guitar. I'm not sure if Dave and Rog were trying to demonstrate Syd's mental state by leaving in the fumbles and confusion at the start of 'If It's In You' but it's really not comfortable listening and the album would have been more enjoyable for those who bought it with some tasteful editing. The 'steel rail' Syd sings about would be referenced in Pink Floyd's tribute to him, 'Wish You Were Here.'

5.8) Barrett – Syd Barrett (1970)

Syd's second album always seemed more cohesive, with more sympathetic 'band' overdubs to his sparse and eccentric tracks. The hazy childlike lyrics and vocals were just Syd's style at this time, and the track 'Dominoes' is my favourite, being both whimsical and sad. The vocal on 'Maisie' plumbs the depths as Syd sings from his guts about the 'bride of a bull.' The steady organ chords throughout this album seem like something solid to hang Syd's fractured audio sketches upon. 'Effervescing Elephant' is a fun jungle story to conclude, demonstrating that despite his troubles Syd still had a sense of humour. Nobody knew at the time that this would be his final album of new material.

5.9) December's Children (And Everbody's) – Rolling Stones (1965)

Up until around 1967 it was common practice for UK groups to release a separate set of albums in the USA. Whilst the definitive set of early Beatles albums remains the UK set, the Rolling Stones seem to show more affinity with their transatlantic early releases, so the definitive CD set seems to comprise the USA releases up to and including 'December's Children (And Everybody's),' swapping to the UK releases for 'Aftermath' and 'Between The Buttons.' Seriously gents, you're British, what are you doing? And let's make Dartford the 'Liverpool' of Kent for your fans while we're at it!

Half of the songs here weren't penned by Jagger and Richards, and surprisingly 'You Better Move On' is one of the covers. Mick and Keith got their revenue though; 'Blue Turns To Grey' provided Cliff Richard with a UK hit, and the lonely ballad 'As Tears Go By' did the same for Marianne Faithful. This is the album with 'Get Off My Cloud' too.

5.10) Aftermath – Rolling Stones (1966)

At the time, this was viewed as a bold step for the Stones. 'Mother's Little Helper' opens with the same Eastern sound as 'Paint It Black.' Mick also belts out the song that gave Chris Farlowe his only UK number one, 'Out of Time,' while there's a quiet moment with 'Lady Jane.' 'Stupid Girl' and 'Under My Thumb' express nasty sentiments indeed, while 'High And Dry' is memorable and not to be confused with the Radiohead track of the same name. The quintet also pushed the time boundaries in a way that only Bob Dylan and Frank Zappa had done before with the eleven-minute 'Goin' Home.' Personally, I think it drags on a bit and they should have gone home five minutes earlier!

5.11) Between The Buttons – Rolling Stones (1967)

This is a pleasant album, beginning with the gentle but scathing 'Yesterday's Papers.' 'Back Street Girl' is similarly cruel in attitude, with its 'use and discard' approach to an extra-marital affair. The tune seemed to have heavily influenced the nineties indie band Shed Seven when they put out 'By Your Side.' The Stones were not immune to influence too though, as 'Who's Been Sleeping Here?' has strong stylistic echoes of Bob Dylan. 'Miss Amanda Jones' seems thrown in just in case anybody thought the band were getting too mellow, and you can imagine Mick decked out in a Union flag for the vaudevillian 'Something Happened To Me Yesterday.' I am trying to second-guess the pedants here, who will point out that it's only a Union 'Jack' when it's displayed on a ship.

5.12) Epocheclipse: 30 Year Anthology – Hawkwind (1999)

This triple-CD set is a great way to dive a bit deeper into the work of Hawkwind from the launch board of the two compilations I reviewed earlier. The tracks are often linked together and there is a marked change in style between the first and second discs, with Lemmy leaving the band to form Motörhead (named after the last Hawkwind track he played on) and Bob Calvert writing some very creative lyrics, 'Spirit Of The Age' and 'High Rise' in particular. 'Steppenwolf' is an epic and nothing to do with the band that produced 'Born To Be Wild.' 'Back On The Street' is a refreshing 'short and sweet' rocker, like a nice cleansing sorbet after the main course. The third disc is less essential, although the tracks from 'Levitation,' which gets its own review later, are very good. 'Black Elk Speaks' seems to epitomise the style of their later years for me.

5.13) Aladdin Sane – David Bowie (1973)

Bowie only really used the 'Ziggy Stardust' persona for two albums, of which this is the less widely appreciated second. The crazed piano solos on the title track and 'Lady Grinning Soul' give this a different sound to its predecessor however. If you're looking for a big hit there's 'The Jean Genie,' with a riff that also appears on the Sweet's number one hit 'Blockbuster.' Highlights for me are the driving rhythm of 'Panic In Detroit' and best of all the theatrical 'Time,' where Bowie delivers the lines about 'having so many breakthroughs' with a mix of contradictory emotions. And if all that wasn't enough, there's a furious rendition of the Rolling Stones hit 'Let's Spend The Night Together' tossed in for good measure. Just accept it, 'A Lad Insane' is a classic.

5.14) Scary Monsters And Super Creeps – David Bowie (1980)

When I moved a whopping 400 yards from my childhood home in 2000, there was a bunch of vinyl records abandoned in the shed, inclduing this gem. I hadn't played any plastic for years, so the records, and the player, were dusted off and new vistas were opened up. The first track 'It's No Game' literally assaults the senses with King Crimson's Robert Fripp playing the edgiest lead guitar lines you're ever likely to hear. The lyrics are helpfully also voiced up in Japanese, and best of all is Bowie's deranged shout on the line 'Three steps to Heaven.' He literally sounds tortured. 'Ashes To Ashes' brings Major Tom back down to earth by revealing what was really going on with the character in 'Space Oddity.' Meanwhile 'Fashion' was used to accompany virtually every TV feature about said topic for decades. The more laid back rendition of 'It's No Game' that closes the album echoes Bowie's double-use of a single melody on the album that preceded this one, 1979's 'Lodger.'

5.15) Let's Dance – David Bowie (1983)

Another vinyl treat from the shed. It's hard not to like a collection of songs when it opens with three massive hits. These are 'Modern Love,' 'China Girl,' which was actually written by Iggy Pop, and best of all 'Let's Dance.' From its triumphant rising chord sequence at the beginning to the guitar solo and meandering sax solos that you only get to hear on the full eight-minute version, this song is one of the highlights of the eighties. 'Shake It' is typical of the style popular at the time, but is very catchy nonetheless.

5.16) Earthling – David Bowie (1997)

'Bowie does drum and bass.' Now you'd imagine that this was going to end in tears of embarrassment, but it really doesn't. 'Little Wonder' was even a chart hit, with David employing his London accent to great effect. Contrary to popular belief, there are only really a handful of tracks that are full blown drum and bass. 'I'm Afraid Of Americans' is particularly entertaining, professing that 'God is an American.' He clearly wasn't *that* afraid of them as he chose to spend much of his life in the USA.

5.17) Band On The Run – Paul McCartney / Wings (1973)

This was the album when people realised that Paul McCartney was still a force to be reckoned with, even without his original three bandmates. In truth, they probably didn't understand what he was doing with his first four post-Beatles releases. The title track consists of three parts and Paul declares 'All I need is a pint a day.' So much for rock and roll lifestyles! 'Let Me Roll It' is another top track, with some very bluesy electric guitar, and 'Picasso's Last Words (Drink To Me)' reprises some of the themes from other tracks on the album. 'Bluebird' is also a very nice song which evokes feelings of contentment.

5.18) London Town – Paul McCartney / Wings (1978)

With the group trimmed back to Paul, Linda and Denny Laine, who had been the original vocalist with sixties group the Moody Blues, this is quite a folky affair at times. Paul rocks out a bit on 'I've Had Enough' and clowns a little on 'Famous Groupies,' a song with character lyrics similar to some of John Lennon's parts of the Abbey Road medley. 'With A Little Luck' sounds as though the band have just discovered a new synth sound and want to utilise it to the max. Although not a masterwork, I do think this album was a step up from 'Venus And Mars' (1975) and particularly 'Wings At The Speed Of Sound' (1976).

5.19) McCartney II – Paul McCartney (1980)

After one more album, 1979's 'Back To The Egg,' Wings were done and dusted, so this was the sequel to 'McCartney' which was Paul's debut solo album after the Beatles imploded. Both are experimental affairs where Paul plays all the instruments, and there is now an album called 'McCartney III' too. He's got the right idea; Roman numerals are brill! The tracks are pretty 'out there' at times, with 'Temporary Secretary' and 'Coming Up' being the most well known. 'On The Way' has a more traditional blues sound while 'Bogey Music' satirises it. There are a lot of synthesiser doodles, but they are fun to listen to, and McCartney leaves us with 'One Of These Days,' accompanied only by his acoustic guitar, as if to prove that he can still do this. Indeed he can - with his eyes closed. An underrated album.

5.20) Some Time In New York City – John Lennon & Yoko Ono (1972)

'Sprawling' is how I would describe this release, although the first disc of the pair is very satisfying. First up is 'Woman Is The N***** Of The World' where John compares misogyny to racism. You don't need me to tell you that both are bad. Actually, looking at the state of world politics, maybe some people do. Both are bad!

Yoko fronts three out of ten songs on the first disc and her vocals are much easier to digest than on 'Live Peace In Toronto.' The songs are very political with 'Sunday Bloody Sunday' and 'The Luck Of The Irish' relating to the troubles of Erin. McCartney was of a similar frame of mind with his single 'Give Ireland Back To The Irish' at this point, and it's worth remembering that at the time the IRA had yet to enter its terrorist phase. John Sinclair is about a man given ten years in jail for possessing two cannabis joints ('They gave him ten for two') and the diary-like 'New York City' is almost 'The Ballad Of John And Yoko, Part 2.'

It's on the live second disc where things start to unravel. The cover of 'Well (Baby Please Don't Go)' is the best track here, not least because of one of Frank Zappa's signature guitar solos. The rest of it is quite frankly (no pun intended) a mess, with Lennon chanting 'Scumbag' repeatedly and Yoko doing that wailing thing again. Put a sock in it the pair of you!

5.21) Walls And Bridges – John Lennon (1974)

Another good effort from JL, overlooked yet again by an audience expecting 'Imagine, Part 2.' 'Whatever Gets You Thru The Night' gave John his first USA number one single and '#9 Dream' is an atmospheric track that perhaps references the 'number nine, number nine' bingo caller in the Beatles sound collage 'Revolution 9.' It always seemed to me that John had regretted his bitter stab at McCartney in 'How Do You Sleep?' and had written 'Steel And Glass' to subject himself to the same harsh treatment. 'What You Got' is very funky, 'Old Dirt Road' was co-written by the genius that is Harry Nilsson and 'Ya Ya' was an excuse for John to get his son Julian's childhood drumming onto record. Whilst the Lennons seemed to present themselves as living in domestic bliss, various biographies postulate that this was far from the truth. Consequently, this album could represent John's last truly open songwriting. His next album, 'Rock 'N' Roll' (1975), would be all covers.

5.22) The Who Sell Out – The Who (1967)

The band's first two albums were 'My Generation' (1965) and 'A Quick One' (1966), which showed their eccentric side with 'Boris The Spider,' the wacky instrumental 'Cobwebs And Strange,' and the 'cut and paste' mini-musical of the title track. However, their third release was a big step forward being an album presented like a pirate radio show, complete with adverts. For younger readers, until the creation of Radio 1 in 1967 the BBC did not play pop music, so fans had to tune in to illegal stations that were, er, stationed, offshore beyond British jurisdiction.

OK, we open with 'Armenia City In The Sky,' a psychedelic barnstormer with a speeded up vocal. Just in case it all sounds a bit serious we then get an advert for Heinz baked beans! 'Tattoo' is a thoughtful song given its subject matter. Meanwhile, 'I Can See For Miles' is a megalithic track right from its opening chord. 'Rael 1,' which closed the original album is a mini-musical, more serious than 'A Quick One While He's Away' had been on the band's previous album, indicating the direction the band would go with 'Tommy,' particularly when the second theme kicks in at 3.40. Make sure you get the version with the bonus tracks. 'Melancholia' is supremely dark and the rock rendition of Grieg's 'In The Hall Of The Mountain King' is just 'fab,' as they said in the sixties.

5.23) The Who – Quadrophenia (1973)

Following Tommy, The Who put out 'Who's Next?' (1971) and then banged out a second rock opera, and I couldn't believe my luck in finding this double album on vinyl gathering dust in the shed. This time the story was a look back at the era of the mods and rockers in the sixties. Here they create atmosphere with synthesised string effects, and John Entwistle augments the sound by playing the French horn. 'Bell Boy' is one of the quirkier tracks where the central character, Jimmy, sees a mod that he used to idolise seemingly 'sold out' and working in said occupation. '5.15' is my favourite track here, where Jimmy tries to get 'out of his brain on the train,' but the deep-seated sadness inevitably takes over with the evocative piano theme stealing his thunder. 'Love Reign On Me' gives the album the monster finish it needed. Adam's board of classification gives this album a '12' certificate if you have kids.

5.24) Sunflower – Beach Boys (1970)

After the 'Wild Honey' album that we looked at earlier, the Californian group gave us the albums 'Friends' and '20/20,' both of which we'll look at later. 1970's 'Sunflower' album was seen as a return to form by some and it was no doubt helped by the inclusion of a track from the aborted 'Smile' project in the form of the atmospheric 'Cool Cool Water,' which contains the lyric 'In an ocean / Or in a glass / Cool water is such a gas!' Tracks like 'Got To Know The Woman' will satiate rockers, while 'At My Window' may be slightly twee in admiring a visit from a sparrow, but then if appreciating nature is 'twee,' bring on the tweeness. A love song called 'Deirdre' may seem dated now because of the name, but at the time who would have known that this name would age while 'Michelle' would have been timeless? I guess Paul McCartney had the better crystal ball.

5.25) Surf's Up – Beach Boys (1971)

This album is packaged together with 'Sunflower' as a 'two for one' CD. This time around the long lost 'Smile' track that closes the album is the title track with its surreal 'stream of consciousness' lyrics being typical of the Brian Wilson / Van Dyke Parks collaboration. How could they have left such quality in the vault for four years? This album could be subtitled 'The Beach Boys Go Political,' with 'Don't Go Near The Water' being an environmental plea and 'Student Demonstration Time' being about...er... Yes, you've got it! 'A Day In The Life Of A Tree' reminds me of 'Butcher's Tale (Western Front 1914)' by the Zombies, with a lone organ accompanying the haunting vocal.

We'll fill in some gaps in the Beach Boys discography later, but if you wish to venture further into the seventies 'Holland' (1973) even contained a chart hit ('Sail On Sailor'), while 'L.A. (Light Album)' (1979) saw the boys adapt a Bach melody for chart success with 'Lady Lynda,' and transform 'Here Comes The Night' into a ten-minute disco epic.

5.26) Brian Wilson Presents Smile – Brian Wilson (2004)

I'm going to slot Brian in here, as the Beach Boys' lost album from 1967 finally appeared in the early noughties as a re-recorded solo effort (but still sounding like the surfing group). More like a concert-piece of linked songs, the lyrics are fun and random (such as a song about vegetables), but with a sense of triumph that the composer, who pretty much lost his mind making this the first time around, had finally pulled the album together. It includes 'Heroes And Villains' as it was supposed to be heard, and 'Good Vibrations,' which is often voted as the best single of all time. Brian's sense of humour is still intact with experiments like 'I Wanna Be Around/Workshop,' and you'll also hear the saddest sounding rendition of 'You Are My Sunshine' that you're ever likely to hear.

A few years later someone took the time to plough through the Beach Boys recordings made for the abandoned original and assembled them as 'The Smile Sessions' (2011). This album is so good, you won't mind having two different versions in your collection.

5.27) Presence – Led Zeppelin (1976)

The first six Zeppelin albums were a tough act to follow and with the dawn of punk they were perhaps seen as an anachronism at the time, just like the airships the band were named after. 'Presence' opens with the ten-minute rock workout of 'Achilles Last Stand,' but my money is on the rock / blues of 'Nobody's Fault But Mine,' which treats us to a searing harmonica solo amid the stop-start rhythm. The album is not hugely diverse in styles, but 'Tea For One' is a treat, reworking the slow blues style of 'Since I've Been Loving You' with a feeling of twilight about it. Go on, pour yourself a cuppa.

5.28) In Through The Out Door – Led Zeppelin (1979)

Unless you count the outtakes album 'Coda' (the twelve-track 1993 version is best), this was the legendary band's final studio album and the styles are as varied as 'Houses Of The Holy' had been. Fans may have been shocked at the use of synthesisers at the time, most prominently on the ten-minute 'Carouselambra'. However 'Late In The Evening' still rocks and 'Hot Dog' is a fabulously fun country pastiche. 'I'm Gonna Crawl' is a strangely self-deprecating closer to a glittering career. Jimmy Page plays his socks off nevertheless.

5.29) Coney Island Baby – Lou Reed (1975) [UK: 1976]

After the madness of 'Metal Machine Music' 'Coney island Baby' seems like a return to form, with the cowbell rhythm of 'Charley's Girl' disguising its dark lyrics, and the tongue-in-cheek humour on 'The Gift' where he declares 'Like a good wine I'm better as I get older.' 'Kicks' is hilarious, being needlessly violent, while the title track is sublimely relaxed as Lou looks back on younger days at school, with the mood rising to one of triumph at being able to see the wood from the trees for a moment. But wait a minute, the fun's not over if you get the version with the bonus tracks. 'Downtown Dirt' has a jazzier vibe than 'Uptown Dirt' which appeared on his 1978 album 'Street Hassle,' and 'Leave Me Alone' is even more punchy than the version on that album.

Next we got 'Rock And Roll Heart' (1976), which isn't bad and concludes with the genuinely menacing 'Temporary Thing,' before his next high point, the brilliant 'Street Hassle.'

5.30) Modern Life Is Rubbish – Blur (1993)

This was the first of what came to be known as the band's Britpop trilogy, although I don't think 'Britpop' was even a word when this was released. 'Chemical World' perhaps presaged 'Brothers And Sisters' from the band's album 'Think Tank' thematically, and 'Sunday Sunday' is melodic Britpop at its best and great for carving up your roast beef to. There are a couple of the kind of quirky instrumentals that would later become a bit of a trademark tacked onto the end of 'Chemical World' and 'Resigned.' Meanwhile 'Miss America' creates an ambience with its 'not quite tuned in' guitars, a sound that the Red Hot Chili Peppers seemed to emulate with 'Porcelain' on 'Californication' (1999).

5.31) Think Tank – Blur (2003)

After '13' it seemed that Blur could venture no deeper into dark experimental territory, especially with guitarist Graham Coxon no longer a member proving just how crucial he was to creating that sound. 'Crazy Beat' is the token gesture 'Song 2' this time around, and 'Out Of Time' is a downbeat track with a resigned feel to it. 'Brothers And Sisters' is a list of drugs, some legal, others not, recited over a bluesy guitar motif with gospel-style backing vocals. The 'list song' is a favourite subgenre of mine, and if you cast your mind back to the 'Trainspotting' soundtrack Damon Albarn had already had a go at this with Bond film titles. 'Battery In Your Leg' gives the album a mysterious conclusion. And no, I don't know what it means.

5.32) Murmur – R.E.M. (1983)

This was the American band's debut album and stylistically I find it slightly similar to the Cure, which is a compliment ('A Forest' is a great track). 'Moral Kiosk,' 'Radio Free Europe,' it's all good, and R.E.M. clearly had a keen ear for melody right from the start, listen to 'We Walk' for example. At times the lyrics aren't particularly clear. I guess they were still formulating what they wanted to say at this stage.

5.33) Document – R.E.M. (1987)

I recall hearing 'The One I Love' on 'The Chart Show' when I was eleven and not really taking much notice of it. Little did I know that I'd just been introduced to what would become one of my favourite bands. This album contains that track and much of the material really rocks. 'It's The End Of The World As We Know It (And I Feel Fine)' is one of those 'lyrical deluge' songs, in the same vein as Dylan's 'Subterranean Homesick Blues.' 'Oddfellows Local 151' closes the album with some slight discordance adding to the atmosphere.

5.34) Kid A – Radiohead (2000)

Having caught up with Radiohead just in time to buy this when it was released, I was somewhat excited by what I might find within. 'Everything In Its Right Place' lulls us with electric piano and Thom Yorke's almost mechanical sounding vocals. The title track mangles his voice so much that the words are indecipherable and 'The National Anthem' builds from a bass riff into an insane brass frenzy. The segue from 'Optimistic' into 'In Limbo' is a high point, and 'Idioteque' could even be a climate change awareness anthem. Best of all, 'How To Disappear Completely' expresses a despairing disbelief before Thom seems to be carried away by the discordant string section. Majestic stuff.

5.35) Amnesiac – Radiohead (2001)

This was essentially 'part two' of 'Kid A' – 'Kid B' if you like! 'Pyramid Song' even made the UK top ten – something like that getting into the chart these days is simply unimaginable. 'Pulk/Pull Revolving Doors' is like a hybrid of 'Kid A' (the song) and 'Idioteque.' The whole album is all very 'under the weather' in terms of mood and drafting in bandleader Humphrey Lyttelton for the final track was something of a coup.

5.36) Hail To The Thief – Radiohead (2003)

'Hail To The Thief' was regarded as a cross-breed of the previous two albums and 'OK Computer,' retaining the experimentation but with more guitars. 'There There' reminds me of Simon & Garfunkel's 'Bridge Over Troubled Water' in the way it holds back until the final verse when Philip Selway's drums burst forth. I love the way Thom Yorke bends the long note around the three-minute mark too. '2+2=5' seems to express disbelief at the Bush / Blair 'War on Terror,' 'I Will' is the album's gentlest song and the finale is one of those 'lyrical deluge' songs. Thom Yorke would appear to find some solace mentally for the albums that followed, which don't get a review in this book but are still worth a listen. However, if you're expecting a return to the indie rock style they began with you'll need to rewind to 'Pablo Honey.'

5.37) The Man Who – Travis (1999)

I fist encountered this album when a colleague at work lent me the CD, and after cycling sixteen miles home I laid on the bed and put it on, suddenly realising that Travis had progressed tremendously from when I saw them open for Fleetwood Mac's Peter Green at a gig in Folkestone. 'Turn' is possibly my favourite Travis song of all time, as vocalist Fran Healy intones 'I want to live in a world where I belong.' 'As You Are' is a close second, beginning with Fran musing 'Everyday I wake up alone because I'm not like all the other boys' and building up to a cathartic shout. I hardly need to state that 'Driftwood' and 'Why Does It Always Rain On Me?' are classics, and don't forget to wait for the bonus track at the end which would be the band's last flirtation with fully blown rock for many years.

5.38) Good Feeling – Travis (1997)

I saw the band of Scotsmen perform as a warm-up band before they were famous and dismissed them as 'Oasis wannabes.' I was wrong. 'The Man Who' gets all the plaudits, but this was the group's raw debut which I believe I picked up while on holiday in Toronto with my mum. Like so many on this list, it's an album of two halves. 'All I Want To Do Is Rock' is a simple yet rousing opener, and 'Tied to the Nineties' sums up how we may have felt at the time about what now seems to have been a 'classic' decade. The love songs come thick and fast at the end. Travis have never seemed so impassioned since, although once they unplugged the guitars and found a formula, they would achieve stardom.

5.39) The Joshua Tree – U2 (1987)

This was the Irish band's monster album and it opens with three *bona fide* 'whoppers.' The Edge's jangly guitar on 'Where The Streets Have No Name' is quintessential U2, and 'I Still Haven't Found What I'm Looking For' seems to acknowledge that even with a strong Christian faith there is still much searching for contentment in life. The hypnotic feel of 'Bullet The Blue Sky' is a high point for me with Bono's monologue at the end seeming to be about the connection of war with money. If only governments had listened, but do they ever?

5.40) Rattle And Hum – U2 (1988)

I was never a big fan of this lengthy album which combined live and studio material. There are some great tracks on it, but I do wonder if a shorter album of ten or so tracks would have been easier to digest. It did give the band their first UK number one single however ('Desire'). There are duets with both B.B. King and Bob Dylan, and 'Angel Of Harlem' is very melodic with its trumpets hinting at soul. 'God Part II' is a top track as well, with its litany of things that Bono doesn't believe in before he concludes 'I believe in love.' This is perhaps the only hint of the band's next direction. There are also a couple of covers too, including the Beatles' 'Helter Skelter' but for me you'll never top McCartney's screaming original.

5.41) Achtung Baby – U2 (1991)

Perhaps this is controversial to some, but this my favourite U2 album, with a seemingly perfect blend of rock and experimentation. The pulsating 'Zoo Station' sets the tone, but there were hits galore here, of which 'One' is the most audience friendly, even being covered by country legend Johnny Cash. 'The Fly' gave the band their second UK number one, something that would become a bit of a habit for them.

5.42) Zooropa – U2 (1993)

At the time people questioned whether or not U2 had lost the plot. They hadn't; this album is superb. 'Stay (Faraway, So Close!)' has a haunting feel to it, and to this day I remember the angel in the video which seemed very Lynchian. 'Numb' sees Bono experiment with an unusual robotic vocal style and Johnny Cash joins the band for 'The Wanderer.' Well, if Tammy Wynette can join the KLF, why not?

5.43) Experience Hendrix – Jimi Hendrix (1997)

Er... how do I introduce this? This is just 'bread and butter' stuff that everybody should know and love. From the opening guitar twang of 'Hey Joe,' Jimi embarked upon a short but legendary career. 'If Six Was Nine' always reminds me of the classic hippie film 'Easy Rider,' and 'Voodoo Child (Slight Return),' sometimes misspelled 'chile,' demonstrates the guitar gymnastics that Jimi excelled at. It was also a UK number one hit in 1970. Some of the more mellow tracks on this album may surprise; 'Angel' and 'Night Bird Flying' are simply succulent.

5.44) The Cream Of Clapton – Eric Clapton (1995)

From one guitar hero to another. Gosh, people were spoiled in the sixties. This album gives us a healthy dollop of Eric's material with Cream, of with 'I Feel Free' and 'Sunshine Of Your Love' are perhaps the best known. We get the full-length version of 'Layla,' complete with it mellow piano-driven second half, and there's also a representative selection of Eric's solo material, of which 'Let It Grow' is an underrated pleasure. If you really need proof of Clapton's guitar playing prowess the blistering cover of Robert Johnson's 'Crossroads' should convince even the hardest sceptic. Note, this should not be confused with the 'similar but different' compilation 'The Cream Of Eric Clapton' from 1987.

5.45) The Best Of The Doors – The Doors (1985)

Yet more late sixties musical gold. 'Light My Fire' takes the jazz aesthetic of long improvised instrumentals and gives it a rock twist, 'Spanish Caravan' similarly adapts the flamenco style and 'Alabama Song' riffs on the American honky tonk style with a bleakly hedonistic sentiment. The Doors could pretty much do anything. 'Riders On The Storm' is a smouldering bluesy piece with a constant backdrop of falling rain, but best of all is 'The End,' presented here in its definitive eleven-minute form and feeling like a free-associating requiem for civilisation. Civilisation is still here, sadly Jim Morrison is not.

5.46) 25 Thumping Great Hits – Dave Clark Five (1978)

While my father and I were hawking our travel book 'England And Wales In A Flash' around bookshops, our 'tour of desperation' took us to the historic town of Faversham in Kent, where I picked up this 'historic' cassette second hand for a quid. The band were one of the few that were named after the drummer, and it's pretty much 'drums to the fore' from the outset, with their two number one hits and other stompers like 'Over And Over.' As the hippie years dawned the group's style mellowed with the ballad 'Everybody Knows' and the semi-psychedelic track 'Red Balloon.' The album ends with the anthemic tracks 'Sha-na-na' and 'Put A Little Love In Your Heart,' but rock and roll was always king for the quintet, and it is the medley of tracks called 'Good Old Fashioned Rock 'N' Roll' that takes the tally of tunes to 25.

5.47) (Here They Come) The Greatest Hits Of The Monkees – The Monkees (1997)

Although I had a tape of Monkees hits in the nineties, it was this 25-track collection that provided me with the best overview of the band that were manufactured to replicate the charm of the early Beatles at the time that they were busy 'blowing their minds.' And ours! Neil Diamond wrote their early hits 'I'm A Believer' and 'A Little Bit Me, A Little Bit You.' However, the Monkees proved that they could hold their own with 'Randy Scouse Git,' which was deemed too provocative a title for Britain, where it was released as 'Alternate Title.' 'Pleasant Valley Sunday' sums up the naïve optimism of late sixties suburbia, and the band consciously tried to change their style with 'Porpoise Song (Theme From "Head"),' which is getting into Procol Harum territory with its prominent organ sound. The film 'Head' is a superb piece of comic psychedelia which few ever truly appreciated. They were no match for the Beatles, but they shouldn't be dismissed.

5.48) Barclay James Harvest – Barclay James Harvest (1970)

In truth BJH were bigger in Germany than in their native England and I first encountered them on a compilation album called 'Early Morning Onwards' which I'd picked up in a second hand shop in Folkestone in Kent. The natural next step was to upgrade to the double album 'The Harvest Years' and then to get the four albums that these compilations covered, of which this was the first. BJH were the only band I know that had their own touring orchestra, right from this, their debut album. The release takes in a variety of styles from the rock of 'Taking Some Time On' and 'Good Love Child' to the balladry of 'Mother Dear.' I particularly like the orchestrations and plodding bass of 'When The World Was Woken,' and the closing track, 'Dark Now My Sky,' is a symphonic masterpiece. Eccentric, yes, but superb!

5.49) Once Again – Barclay James Harvest (1971)

This was the band's second album and another *bona fide* classic, although lyrically pretty dark with a slightly unhealthy fixation on shuffling off this mortal coil, 'Happy Old World' being the most obvious example. It always seems a bit excessive to use a mellotron when you have an orchestra, as a mellotron was a keyboard instrument playing recorded loops of orchestra notes, but that's exactly what BJH did here to excellent effect. To break up the drama there is the lighter 'Vanessa Simmons' and the rock blast of 'Ball And Chain.' There's even a Jew's harp on the final track, but the show-stopper is 'Mocking Bird' which builds from a quiet ballad into frenetic rock before exploding into two of the most dramatic orchestral chords you'll ever hear in a rock song. If You like Pink Floyd, you'll like BJH.

5.50) Barclay James Harvest And Other Short Stories – Barclay James Harvest (1971)

Personally, I like BJH's early albums the best, of which this was the third. Lighter in feel than the first two albums, this one still has some great moments. 'Little Lapwing' reminds me of Simon & Garfunkel's 'Song For The Asking' with a 'Boxer-esque' crescendo bolted on the end, complete with thrashing drum sound. 'Medicine Man' similarly has an orchestral bolt-on coda and 'Blue John's Blues' builds to a frenzy, reminding me of the Beatles' 'Hey Jude' a bit. 'Harry's Song' is a favourite of mine, but the high point for me, as is so often the case, is a segue – this time between the gentle song 'The Poet' and the dramatic chords at the beginning of 'After The Day.' The segue is a lost art now that most people just download individual tracks. A pity.

5.51) Baby James Harvest – Barclay James Harvest (1972)

There are only six tracks on this album, but don't think you're being hard done by as two of them are 'longuns.' However, I do think that the album is not lyrically or musically as strong as the first three. 'Delph Town Morn' has some brassy bits and 'One Hundred Thousand Smiles Out' is very melodic, but it seems that the band only remembered that they had an orchestra at their disposal for the final track, 'Moonwater.' This is BJH at their symphonic best and for the first time the instrumentation is entirely orchestral. As one would expect the track builds from a whimper into sounding like something from 'Scott Of The Antarctic.' The other 'longun' is 'Summer Soldier' which is really two songs preceded by a sound collage. Such vehemently anti-war material is rarely produced these days. Either everybody has got used to needless death on a daily basis or the money men in charge of everything won't let anybody sing about it.

The band switched labels after this album and ditched the orchestra. The 1975 album 'Time Honoured Ghosts' is very good, and the track 'Titles' has lyrics that try to cram in the names of as many Beatles songs as is humanly possible. You may also hear the BJH track 'Hymn' (1977) on the radio at Christmas.

5.52) Sex Machine: The Best Of James Brown – James Brown (1991)

This compilation is arranged chronologically, which is brilliant as you can see how James Brown evolved from the gospel style of 'Please, Please, Please' into the more rhythmic tracks like 'Papa's Got A Brand New Bag' and 'I Got You (I Feel Good),' eventually developing into the full blown funk of the title track. There are a few tracks from the eighties before we backtrack to the electrifying live version of 'Soul Power.'

5.53) What's Going On – Marvin Gaye (1971)

A pivotal album from the time that Motown artists of the sixties were producing 'serious' albums that were much more than just a collection of songs. Stevie Wonder's works explored many styles, while 'What's Going On' has a consistent hypnotic feel. The 'street voices' throughout the album add atmosphere and the theme is of longing for justice. 'What's Going On' is an anti-war anthem, while 'Mercy Mercy Me (The Ecology)' is an early environmental song. It's a shame politicians are only just waking up to the threat of global warming fifty years later. Trust your musicians; they're normally ahead of the curve by several decades.

5.54) Songs In The Key Of Life – Stevie Wonder (1975)

I picked this double album up on cassette in a second hand shop in the Old Town in Hastings, which was a Mecca for music collectors at the time. Several of the songs had been sampled / copied for contemporary hits at the time. Will Smith played around with 'I Wish,' and 'Pasttime Paradise' became 'Gangsta's Paradise' in the hands of Coolio. The jazzy 'Sir Duke' looks back to the jazz legends of the past, in particular Duke Ellington. The songs are often epic in length, from 'Isn't She Lovely' to 'Another Star.' 'Ordinary Pain' is a high point for me, starting off as an introspective sad song before morphing into funk as if to consciously snap the song's character out of it. 'Ebony Eyes' is incredibly catchy and 'Black Man' is an eight-minute history lesson that promotes appreciation of all races.

5.55) Hits – Joni Mitchell (1996)

Interestingly, Joni released a companion volume called 'Misses.' All the hits are here, from the environmentalism of 'Big Yellow Taxi' (see my comment at the end of 'What's Going On'), to an electric piano-led rendition of her song 'Woodstock' which became a UK number one single in the hands of Matthews Southern Comfort. 'Both Sides Now' is my personal favourite of her songs, philosophically looking at clouds, love and life from both the light side and the dark side, although 'The Circle Game' comes a close second with its musing on the passing of time. 'River' is one of the saddest Christmas songs you're likely to hear too. Like Leonard Cohen, who I had yet to discover, Joni is proof that Canada was a serious hotbed of songwriting talent at the time.

5.56) Welcome To The Beautiful South – The Beautiful South (1989)

My aunt who lent me myriad Simon & Garfunkel albums as a teenager was always saying how good the Beautiful South were, but it took a long time for me to give them a bash. Since then I've never looked back. Formed from the ashes of the Housemartins (also worth checking out), Paul Heaton and Dave Hemmingway teamed up with Dave Rotheray for hits like 'Song For Whoever,' 'I'll Sail This Ship

Alone' and 'You Keep It All In' which featured vocalist Briana Corrigan. 'Have You Ever Been Away?' points the finger at flag-wavers who keep banging on about the war with no knowledge of the hell that war is. 'Woman In The Wall ' is a dark tale about a murder and 'I Love You (But You're Boring)' is an enigmatic closer. This album set the stage for the intriguing mix of dark themes and a soft sound that became the group's bread and butter.

5.57) Choke – The Beautiful South (1990)

The second BS album introduced female vocalist Briana Corrigan as a permanent member of the band, a decision that paid off with the band's only UK number one, 'A Little Time,' which could be described as a spiky duet. 'I Think The Answer's Yes' is a highlight, analysing how injustice breeds terrorism with a haunting refrain of 'rope or gas.' 'I Hate You (But You're Interesting)' has a much darker feel than its companion track from the first album and almost presaged some of Radiohead's work. And just so the album doesn't end on a low, there's the jazzy instrumental 'The Rising Of Grafton Street' to finish.

5.58) 0898 – The Beautiful South (1992)

The BS's third offering is far from 'BS!' It has a poppier feel than the first two albums with more prominent use of keyboards, not just as backing to the guitars, but driving some of the songs. The songwriting remains superlative. 'Old Red Eyes Is Back' looks at alcoholism, which would become one of Heaton and Rotheray's consistent themes, and '36D' was ahead of the curve in expressing disapproval at the superficiality perhaps exemplified with the Sun newspaper's page three which used to feature a topless woman, 'We Are Each Other' expresses the mundanity of a relationship that has grown old, while 'When I'm 84' defiantly celebrates rebellion in old age. The album's title comes from the dialing code that often presaged salacious chat lines in the UK.

5.59) Miaow – The Beautiful South (1994)

With some artists the lyrics matter less than the music, but the Beautiful South were always firmly in the same camp as Dylan and Paul Simon with varied and often controversial subject matter. 'Hold On To What?' is a brilliant opener, with sorrow turning to anger towards the end. 'Especially For You' should not to be confused with Kylie and Jason's January 1989 number one; it couldn't be more different. There's a cover of *Everybody's Talkin'* as well as a track mixed by former Housemartin, Norman Cook, who would later be known as Fatboy Slim. 'Mini-Correct' is a condemnation of misogyny that doesn't mince its words, while 'Poppy' illustrates dissociation from the horrors of war, comparing the experience of watching events unfold on TV to a popular prank show at the time called 'Beadle's About.' The album's lyrics seemed to be a step too far for vocalist Briana

Corrigan who surrendered her place in the band for Jacqui Abbott here. The songwriting was only going in one direction as we would soon find out.

5.60) Blue Is The Colour – The Beautiful South (1996)

This album does indeed have a bluesy feel and certainly opens with some blue language on 'Don't Marry Her.' A 'clean' version was recorded for the radio, but it's clear that the F-word intensive version is the definitive take from its inclusion on several 'greatest hits' packages. 'Rotterdam (Or Anywhere)' was the album's other big hit. 'Blackbird On The Wire' is a dark and evocative piano ballad, 'Liar's Bar' is another 'drink' song, and the album's closing track, 'Alone,' is wonderfully despondent; 'We only smoke when bored / So we do two packs a day.' Reminds me of my father!

5.61) Quench – The Beautiful South (1998)

The BS were on a roll, banging out classic after classic. Here the 'Fatboy' was drafted in again to give 'Perfect 10' its pop aesthetic that propelled it to number two in the charts. 'Dumb' was a lesser hit being more downbeat in feel. As ever, it's all incredibly melodic, with some lovely harmonies. 'I May Be Ugly' is an unusual track, being a series of self-directed insults as well as an ironic celebration of alcoholism. And finally 'Your Father And I' addresses the fact that there is nothing romantic at all about many conceptions, but it gives the theme a twist in addressing it directly to the offspring.

5.62) Painting It Red – The Beautiful South (2000)

It's almost a rite of passage for an artist to produce at least one double album and this was the Beautiful South's, although a single disc version which omits several key tracks was also available. 'Who's Gonna Tell?' is a catchy acoustic track about fading glory, while 'Closer Than Most' was the key single this time around. The melodies are top notch as usual, e.g. 'Baby Please Go,' while the lyrics don't mess about, e.g. 'Property Quiz'. The Beautiful South touched all bases and I recall walking around Totonto with my mother with the tunes etched in our minds, particularly when wandering down to view Lake Ontario.

I would also recommend the band's covers album 'Golddiggers, Headnodders & Pholk Songs' (2004) if you're curious to hear what everything from S Club 7 to the Ramones sounds like performed 'Beautiful South' style. If you'd rather delve back further into the history of Heaton and Hemingway, I recommend the Housemartins compilation 'Now That's What I Call Quite Good.' A self-reviewing title which saves me time and effort!

5.63) The Best Of The Seekers – The Seekers (1997)

My mother had been given several cases of cassettes from an old lady in the village. She kept the country ones while I got to select any that I wanted from the others. This was one such album and the Seekers were a perfect embodiment of the folk rock movement of the mid sixties. This is a bumper EMI collection of 23 songs, beginning (of course) with the acoustic twelve-string guitar riff of 'I'll Never Find Another You.' 'The Carnival Is Over' was the band's other UK number one single but my favourite was always 'Morningtown Ride,' as I remember the lullaby-like song from one of my dad's reel to reel tapes as a child. 'Georgy Girl' and 'A World Of Our Own' were also big hits. Judith Durham leads the vocals for the Australian group. By this time my mum had learned to play guitar and 'When Will The Good Apples Fall?' was one of the songs that we used to play together in folk clubs. I might even sneak in a review of one or two of our own albums before this book is over, but don't tell anyone.

5.64) Live At The Palladium – The Carpenters (1976)

Another tape from the batch of freebies from Mrs. King. This was a great album if you didn't have a 'greatest hits' by the brother and sister act comprising Karen and Richard Carpenter, as side two opened with a medley of their biggest songs, my favourite of which has always been 'Goodbye To Love,' with its despondent lyric uplifted by a truly sensational guitar solo at the end. There's also a Gershwin medley here. Karen was a talented drummer as well as a unique vocalist, as she demonstrates. It was really very sad when the complications of anorexia ended her life at the age of 32.

5.65) King Cotton – Fivepenny Piece (1976)

This was a folky freebie for me by a band from Lancashire that were discovered on the TV talent show 'New Faces.' The fivesome included two pairs of siblings and they are proud of their northern heritage with songs like 'Where There's Muck There's Brass.' There actually *is* brass on this album, as many songs are linked by a slightly melancholy sounding brass band. Linda Jane Meeks provides many of the vocals including 'Mi Gronny,' which celebrates grandmothers, and 'T.V. Addict,' which demonstrates the group's gentle humour. The harmonies are nice and occasionally they sound a bit like Rod, Jane and Freddy from the children's TV series 'Rainbow.' I could even imagine 'Watercolour Morning' being performed on a show of this kind.

5.66) The Best Of The Ink Spots – The Ink Spots (1974)

This MCA collection was the final tape I picked from Mrs. King's selection. The Ink Spots were at their peak in the 1940s and their harmonies were an influence on the doo-wop music that came later. The songs here nearly all follow a pattern, beginning with their trademark opening chord sequence on the guitar and piano and including an obligatory spoken-word verse towards the end. This may even have influenced the band Boyz II Men all those decades later with their 1992 number one hit 'End Of The Road.' The vibe is nearly always melancholic, but there are two exceptions – 'Java Jive,' with its 'I love coffee, I love tea' theme, and 'Your Feet's Too Big.'

5.67) Freak Out! – Frank Zappa / Mothers Of Invention (1966)

Right, here we encounter what would become a major artist for me, but my initial reaction to Zappa's rule-breaking and satirical approach was more along the lines of 'What the hell is this?' Right from the outset Zappa and his band, the Mothers Of Invention, didn't compromise an inch. 'Any Way The Wind Blows' is the only track that could be considered remotely commercial on what was generally regarded as one of two contenders as the first ever rock double album. For the record, the other contender was Bob Dylan's 'Blonde On Blonde.'

The album opens with a broadside at the superficiality of American life, and 'Who Are The Brain Police?' sounds like something from a horror film. Even tracks that hark back to the doo-wop era of the fifties are performed in a way that borders on parody. The whole affair steps up a gear with 'Trouble Every Day,' a lyrical deluge reflecting on racism and civil unrest. This track may indicate that Zappa wanted to be a crusader like the early Bob Dylan but soon realised how ineffectual such well-meaning sentiments are, consequently seeking solace in a particularly dark form of comedy. The final three tracks are avant-garde compositions. Listen to the wacky vocals on 'It Can't Happen Here' for example. Zappa didn't just push the boundaries, he fired them at the moon!

5.68) Absolutely Free – Frank Zappa / Mothers Of Invention (1967)

The second Mothers Of Invention album was emphatically in the 'satirical' camp. I wonder if the track 'Call Any Vegetable' inspired the Beach Boys track 'Vegetables' or if Zappa had already got wind of such psychedelic whimsy and decided to lambast it. At the end of the track there's a quote from Holst's 'Jupiter' from 'The Planets' before Zappa lets rip on the first of his epic solos in 'Invocation And Ritual Dance Of The Young Pumpkin.' Before the second half commences, the CD reissue inserts two stabs at pop done Zappa-style which are both enjoyable. The scale of composition is raised with 'Brown Shoes Don't Make It,' which seems to imply that the awful predatory behaviour that we know went on at the time was perhaps more widespread than anyone imagined. This composition also seems to utilise the cellular style of assembling tracks, beloved of Brian Wilson from the Beach Boys. In hindsight the pair were remarkably similar in their genius, with Brian on the light side and Zappa firmly in the shadows.

5.69) We're Only In It For The Money – Frank Zappa / Mothers Of Invention (1968)

The cover is a pastiche of the Beatles' 'Sgt. Pepper' album, so it's ironic that the Liverpool boys were actually fans of Zappa and John Lennon even ended up performing with him, although the result would lead to considerable acrimony. Zappa literally tears everybody a new you-know-what with this album, attacking the brutality of the police and the naivety of the hippies in one fell swoop. Stylistically there is some vaudeville in the form of 'Bow Tie Daddy,' and psychedelic ambience with 'The Chrome Plated Megaphone Of Destiny.' Zappa mastered the art of the segue with 'Absolutely Free' and took it one stage further here, mixing 'proper' songs with all manner of tape manipulation.

5.70) Hot Rats – Frank Zappa (1969)

Zappa's only top ten album in the UK is a largely instrumental affair where he demonstrated that he could give Hendrix, Clapton and others a serious run for their money when it comes to grinding the guitar. The album's only vocal is performed by Captain Beefheart on 'Willie The Pimp' which gives the collection its title, and let's not elaborate on what that means. Zappa's trademark tape manipulation is in evidence too with the fast brass interjection on 'Peaches En Regalia.' The alternating chords on 'Son Of Mr. Green Genes' remind me of Pink Floyd's 'Breathe,' which was four years away in the pipeline at the time. There's some epic violin improvisation on this album from Don 'Sugarcane' Harris too.

5.71) Waka/Jawaka – Frank Zappa (1972)

Don't panic, or maybe do panic - we'll look at many of Frank's albums that I've omitted later in this book. The reason for this format is that I bought these albums as two box sets, the first exploring the satirical works of the early Mothers Of Invention and the second delving into the largely instrumental offerings, 'Hot Rats,' this album and 'The Grand Wazoo.'

This is a more jazz oriented offering, which could be described as 'fusion,' a genre combining elements of jazz and rock perhaps most finely disseminated by trumpeter Miles Davis. Being Zappa, this is no straight fusion album however. 'Your Mouth' displays the usual comedic approach to lyrics ('Your mouth is your religion / You put your faith in a hole like that?') and there is a brilliant steel guitar solo on 'It Just Might Be A One-Shot Deal.' Not as accessible as 'Hot Rats,' but let's face it, all of Frank's albums require some work and dedication from us listeners, an approach that very few artists these days would dare to take for fear of languishing in the commercial doldrums. Frankly, my dear, Zappa didn't give a damn – there's a pun in there somewhere.

5.72) The Grand Wazoo – Frank Zappa / Mothers Of Invention (1972)

Here, the 'fusion' template from 'Waka/Jawaka' seems to have been scaled up with a fuller brass section (or is that just my perception?). During this period Zappa rarely handled the vocals himself, and only one track contains any lyrics at all this time around. 'Cleetus Awreetus-Awrightus' begins in a jazzy vein and morphs into rock and roll with a honky tonk piano. 'Eat That Question' has a mellow electric piano opening before one of the most memorable riffs bursts forth. The title track eventually settles into a pleasing trumpet solo, but with the feel of other instruments invading until it all breaks down into chaos. In this way, you could view many of Zappa's works like little films or stories in music.

5.73) Overnite Sensation – Frank Zappa / Mothers Of Invention (1973)

How did I acquire this album? Oh yes, a work colleague brought in a bag of tapes to play in the company van and this was one of them; 'Zappa goes rock.' We are treated to Frank's deep narrative style perhaps for the first time with 'I'm The Slime,' which highlights the amorality of television. There's a crazy organ solo and an even crazier vocal courtesy of Ricky Lancelotti in 'Fifty-Fifty.' 'Dinah-Moe Humm' is bawdy to say the least, with Zappa sounding incredibly sleazy, and on 'Montana' he sings about raising a crop of dental floss! It's actually surprising to learn that Zappa had a staunch anti-drugs policy. Clearly he didn't need them.

The next Mothers Of Invention albums would be 'Roxy & Elsewhere,' a live album from 1974, and 'Bongo Fury,' a 1975 release which features Captain Beefheart, another 'off the wall' kind of guy! In truth I did once try to get my head around his 1969 album 'Trout Mask Replica' but found the irregular rhythms, growled vocals and 'grit and gravel' sound a step too far.

5.74) Apostrophe (') – Frank Zappa (1974)

And so to Zappa's only US top ten album. I'm surprised that a third box set exploring Zappa's early rock dabblings wasn't compiled from 'Overnite Sensation,' this album and 'One Size Fits All,' which we'll look at later. It's rare that record companies miss a marketing opportunity like that. 'Don't Eat The Yellow Snow' might indicate that we're in for more scatology, but he actually tones it down a bit on this album. The instrumental title track is a satisfying slab of rock and soloing, and at the end of 'Stink-Foot' Frank explains the function of an apostrophe in his deep satirical voice, as though it were some great hidden mystery. He also references 'conceptual continuity,' the concept of continual reference to previous works throughout his whole career. I try to employ a similar approach with my books. As the liner notes on 'Freak Out!' declare 'You don't care.' Let's fast forward to 1979 for now...

5.75) Joe's Garage, Acts I-III – Frank Zappa (1979)

When I first purchased this album it amazed me that somebody as skilled as Zappa could become so 'filth infatuated' (to paraphrase the Prodigy). I had similar feelings when I first encountered the early Red Hot Chili Peppers albums. This is a double album with a concept about music being made illegal and 'Joe's Garage' was where an illegal band practised their illegal songs. The title track also contains a brief summary of the various trends that came and went in popular music. 'Act I' is eclectic and accessible in style if you can handle tracks like 'Fembot In A Wet T-Shirt' and 'Why Does It Hurt When I Pee?' which is actually very funny in the way it combines trite lyrics with dramatic production. It's when we get to 'Act II' that it seems to go one step beyond good taste. 'Act III' picks up the pieces nicely though, with just four lengthy tracks which put Frank's relentless guitar soling to the fore. 'Watermelon In The Easter Hay' is sublime, but it's as though he realises that we almost caught him being serious, so he launches into the silly voice of 'Little Green Rosetta' immediately afterwards.

Ever-inventive, this album utilises 'xenochrony' which involved taking guitar solos, often performed live, and 'pasting' them over new tracks, which often had completely different rhythms. Apologies to hardcore fans but I'm skipping the album 'Tinsel Town Rebellion.'

5.76) You Are What You Is – Frank Zappa (1981)

Controversial in places but far less smutty than 'Joe's Garage,' the tracks nearly all segue here which you'll remember is good. I especially like the way 'Doreen' changes into something chaotic the moment the vocal 'woooh' launches the coda. 'Society Pages' lambasts small-town small-mindedness, but this is merely Zappa sharpening up his tongue for a trilogy of songs aimed at the hypocrisy of religious TV preachers getting rich in the name of belief. 'Dumb All Over' features his now-familiar monologue-like style albeit heavily processed. Here he lambasts the whole of humanity; 'Whoever we are / Wherever we're from / We shoulda noticed by now / Our behaviour is dumb.' It's hard to disagree really. Then just when you think it can't get any more surreal he finishes with 'Drafted Again' and more wacky vocals.

Zappa released an album almost every week in the eighties. OK, I'm exaggerating, and we will look at the best of these later in this book, but for now let's fast forward to 1989...

5.77) Broadway The Hard Way – Frank Zappa (1989)

I often wish that Frank Zappa had been alive during the Trump era. This seventeen-track CD shows him at his most political, and the humour only thinly disguises his anger at the hypocrisy of politicians from both USA parties, as well as TV preachers who indulge themselves. As ever, the lyrics are uncompromising and even Elvis and Michael Jackson are sent up, but this was the point – there should be no 'holy cows' if speech is truly free. Those purely in it for the music will lap up the guitar solo in 'Outside Now' and should enjoy the jazzy feel of 'Murder By Numbers' sung by Sting. The references may be dated but the issues are more prominent than ever. Behind the madness FZ seemed to always be on the side of tolerance and diversity and this mix of live and studio tracks goes to both ends of the Zappa spectrum. There's even a brief rap on this one.

5.78) Lumpy Gravy – Frank Zappa (1967)

We now rewind to the sixties for some serious wackiness. This album consists of just two fifteen-minute tracks which are both collages of quirky instrumentals mixed with Zappa's first attempts at composing for an orchestra and bizarre conversations. The opening sounds comfortably like a speeded up Shadows song and the first appearance of the orchestra is pretty melodic, playing 'Oh No!' which would appear with lyrics on the delightfully named 'Weasels Ripped My Flesh' album. After this it gets difficult, with the compositions sounding increasingly like the music from a horror film until we reach the quirky closing theme of 'Take Your Clothes Off When You Dance.' Living in a drum, pigs and ponies, dreaming is hard, a bit of nostalgia for the old folks... If you know this album you'll know what I'm on about. If not, a safer bet would be the Mothers Of Invention's doo-wop album 'Cruising With Ruben & The Jets' (1968), but be warned the CD version has been tweaked. To hear the original mix you need a download called 'Greasy Love Songs.' Got that?

5.79) Uncle Meat – Frank Zappa / Mothers Of Invention (1969)

This is like 'Lumpy Gravy' but minus the orchestra and more accessible. The conversational snippets are generally of the band itself with the voice of a fictional groupie called Suzy Creamcheese. There are very few lyrics on this album and they are normally little more than jokes that only make sense to the Mothers. The music is mostly like jazz chamber music but the styles do vary, with the fusion monster track 'King Kong' as a closer. 'The Uncle Meat Variations' is enjoyable as it whips itself up towards the end. However, Zappa has taken the revisionist approach to the CD reissue again and has bunged in some material on disc two which is clearly not from 1969, breaking the continuity of what is quite a good album.

5.80) Tubular Bells – Mike Oldfield (1973)

When Richard Branson signed up the young Mike Oldfield I don't think either of them knew what a huge seller this album would be. Its use in the horror film 'The Exorcist' was of course instrumental in this, but as Oldfield plays almost every instrument you hear, this definitely lives up to the hype. Everybody knows the opening section and most people are familiar with the sequence where Mike names all the instruments he is playing, sounding like an eccentric country gent rattling around in a stately home. 'Part 2' of the opus builds up to the section known as 'Piltdown Man' which a friend informs me is the sound that came out of his mouth when he once took part in a ouija board experiment. It's definitely Halloween stuff, resplendent with werewolf howls. This then gives way to a section which reminds me of watching the sun coming up when you've been up all night camping, as the shimmering guitar lines rise out of the organ chords. After all this, it does seem as if Mike just thought 'cobblers to it' at the end, suddenly launching into a sailor's hornpipe. Who said he didn't have a sense of humour?

5.81) Hergest Ridge – Mike Oldfield (1974)

Most people's exploration of Oldfield began and ended with 'Tubular Bells.' Its sequel also hit the top spot in the UK album chart however, and it follows the same format, with two very long pieces on which Mike plays most of the instruments. The mostly relaxing style, inspired by rural walks on the aforementioned ridge, makes the intense sonic assault a third of the way into side two even more striking. Did Mike invent 'techno' here?

5.82) Ommadawn – Mike Oldfield (1975)

Mr. Oldfield stuck with the 'long form' structure of dividing an album into two on this, his third release. After a moody introduction he treats us to a variety of folk instrumentals. The uilleann pipes are particularly nice to hear and the album contains that rare treat of Mike Oldfield singing, closing the album with the ditty 'On Horseback.' He even drafts in a few kids to boost the vocal sound!

5.83) Platinum – Mike Oldfield (1979)

After 'Incantations' (review coming later), Mike finally ditched the 'long form' approach with this album and embraced a poppier sound. There's no drop in quality however. 'Charleston' has some brassy synth and honky tonk piano, while the love song 'Into Wonderland' segues superbly into 'Punk A Diddle' which was written in response to the popularity of... Yes, you've got it! 'Woodhenge' is all atmosphere, and there's even a sad sounding version of Gershwin's 'I Got Rhythm.' The vocalist is Wendy Roberts.

If you want to explore later albums without getting lost in wishy-washy synth sounds I recommend 'Five Miles Out' (1982), 'Crises' (1983), 'Guitars' (1999) and 'Amarok' (1990) which nearly gave Richard Branson a heart attack, being a single hour-long track, with no individual theme lasting long enough to be promoted as a single and an impersonation of Margaret Thatcher tossed in for good measure.

5.84) Oxygène – Jean-Michel Jarre (1976)

A synthesiser symphony in six parts. The French keyboardist lulls us with ambient soundscapes until you get that 'Aah yes' moment during 'Part IV,' for this tune graced many a TV feature when I was a child. If the bulletin was anything to do with technology you could bet your life that Jarre's melodic little piece would be drafted in. Mike Oldfield's 'Portsmouth' was used in a similar way for more traditional features. I did try Jarre's follow-up album 'Equinoxe,' but it didn't grab me in the quite the same way, so unlike his legions of fans I said *au revoir.*

5.85) Play – Moby (1999)

I was very sceptical of the 'dance music' genre in the nineties, but this was the gateway. Moby chopped up old blues records and infused new life into them. 'Find My Baby' samples an impassioned blues vocal and 'Why Does My Heart Feel So Bad?' translates the world weariness of the past for a new generation. The styles are wide ranging, with more intense tracks like 'Bodyrock' and some spoken vocals and ambience in the second half. Rapper, Eminem quipped '[Moby], nobody listens to techno' in his 2002 hit, 'Without Me.' Perhaps he should have listened more closely; techno is '2 Unlimited!'

5.86) Songs From The Big Chair – Tears For Fears (1985)

Rummaging through a bundle of vinyl albums that I found in the shed after moving a whopping 400 yards down the road opened up a lot of new avenues for me musically. 'Songs From The Big Chair' found its way into my collection rather than onto the jumble sale pile purely because 'Shout' was such a good song. The other two hits 'Everybody Wants To Rule The World' and 'Head Over Heels' appeal next, but then one gets into the more ethereal stuff and you soon realise that Tears For Fears were not really an eighties pop band like Duran Duran at all, but more akin to bands like Pink Floyd in what they were trying to achieve.

5.87) Dire Straits – Making Movies (1980)

Like Pink Floyd in the seventies, Dire Straits just seemed to churn out classic after classic in the eighties and this was the first of their big hitters. From the ghostly organ intro of Tunnel Of Love to the light and jokey 'Les Boys' at the end, 'Making Movies' is a pleasure to listen to. 'Romeo & Juliet' overshadows the rest though, with its subtle picked guitar opening to its lyric documenting a relationship from the initial hope to the conclusion that 'It was just that the time was wrong.' Mr. Shakespeare would have surely approved.

5.88) Love Over Gold – Dire Straits (1982)

I remember hearing 'Private Investigations' on the top forty rundown at the age of seven, and being impressed even then by the ambient coda to the track. A Spanish guitar has never sounded so menacing either, but the goodies don't stop there. This album includes the fourteen-minute 'Telegraph Road' (which seems like a brief history of civilisation) and the amusing 'Industrial Disease' in which Mark Knopfler impersonates a doctor!

5.89) Dire Straits – Brothers In Arms (1985)

I remember somebody playing this album in the changing room when I was performing in a Scout gang show as a teenager. To be brutally frank I found it depressing. Tastes change though, and it is clearly one of the most acclaimed albums of all time for a reason. The upbeat tracks were the two big hits. 'Money For Nothing' had an intriguing cartoon video and I remember a lad once trying to blast out my eardrums with its opening sequence on a personal stereo. School years were such fun, weren't they? 'Walk Of Life' is a jolly rocker, but it is the mellower tracks that leave more of an impact. 'Your Latest Trick' has a saxophone motif that is almost as well known as the one from Gerry Rafferty's 'Baker Street,' and Mark Knopfler's guitar seems to drip late night ambience here. Then there's the title track, the eight minutes of which seem to pass in about three. Not only did Dire Straits create a masterpiece, but theirs were tracks so good they could even distort space and time!

5.90) The Specials – Specials (1979)

Yet another classic from the shed. 'Classics From The Shed' is actually a great album title. Somebody should use it. The Specials were a Coventry band that started out with ska music, which was originally a precursor to reggae. The whole album is extremely catchy from 'A Message To Rudy' all the way to the low-energy vocal delivery of 'You're Wondering Now.' The long version of 'Too Much Too Young' is included here. It was a shorter live version that topped the charts as the key track from an EP. There's a punky feel to tracks like 'Little Bitch,' and 'Doesn't Make It Alright' addresses issues of prejudice and racism.

5.91) More Specials – Specials (1980)

This is my favourite Specials album. The opening rendition of 'Enjoy Yourself' is a joy to listen to, but the album mixes dub-style manipulation of sounds on tracks like 'Man At C&A' with the pure ska of 'Sock It To 'Em J.B.' J.B. is James Bond and C&A was a high street store in the UK at the time. 'International Jet Set' is a fun song with a scary finish, 'Stereotypes' repeats the 'long form' inclusion of 'Too Much Too Young' on the first album and 'Pearl's Cafe' ends with a 'certificate 12' chorus that everybody feels like singing at times! Go on, you're intrigued...

5.92) In The Studio – The Special AKA (1984)

With the band's initial vocalists having jumped ship, this album was a reboot with both male and female vocals. It also showed a change in style with a more loungey feel. The big hit was '(Free) Nelson Mandela.' 'Alcohol' has the feel of spy movie and 'Racist Friend' continues the plea for tolerance. 'War Crimes' is the long track this time, and following the COVID-19 lockdowns of 2020 / 2021 we can all empathise with 'House Bound,' being 'caught in a housetrap.'

5.93) The Singles Collection – The Specials (1991)

Having got the above three albums you'd think there wouldn't be a lot left in the vault from the band's pivotal years. Think again. This collection gives us essentials like the band's second number one 'Ghost Town,' which was memorably the only record owned by a DJ in the Irish comedy 'Father Ted.' 'Nite Klub' is more essential listening, although I certainly don't fancy that beer they're singing about. 'Friday Night, Saturday Morning' is also a compelling track and it was clearly an influence on Blur. They're not really selling this 'going out drinking' lark once again! It's just 'PG' this time. I'm having fun dishing out these ratings.

5.94) Out Of The Blue - Electric Light Orchestra (1977)

There are only a handful of people for whom endlessly creating great melodies is natural. Paul McCartney and Harry Nilsson, who we'll encounter later in this book, spring to mind. Jeff Lynne is another master. This double LP was another 'gift from the shed' and from the opening of 'Turn To Stone' to the closing of 'Wild West Hero' the quality never drops. I even like 'Birmingham Blues,' where Jeff demonstrates a genuine affection for Britain's second largest city. The joyous 'Across The Border' has a Mexican feel to it with trumpets, and there's plenty of bittersweet melancholy in the form of 'Steppin' Out' and my personal favourite 'Big Wheels.' Three words: what a song.

5.95) Discovery – Electric Light Orchestra (1979)

ELO started off as a prog rock act which I'd bracket along with the early Barclay James Harvest albums. In 1979 they briefly embraced the disco sound without sacrificing their ever-melodic approach, a prime example is 'Last Train To London.' 'The Diary Of Horace Wimp' seems to borrow the strings from the Beatles' 'I Am The Walrus' and surprises us with its happy ending. You are constantly waiting for something to go wrong in Horace's romance. 'Midnight Blue' has a blissful melody, and the full blown rock of 'Don't Bring Me Down' offers a change in style at the end, a sound they would repeat with 'Hold On Tight' and 'Four Little Diamonds' – all under-appreciated 'rippers.'

The next album the band released was a joint effort with Olivia Newton-John, being a soundtrack to 'Xanadu' (1980), so the next *bona fide* album was 'Time.'

5.96) Time - Electric Light Orchestra (1981)

In the nineties the Irish band the Divine Comedy intoned 'There's something in the wood shed.' Well, here's yet another gem that I acquired on vinyl for the effort of a simple walk across the backyard. And what an album – did Jeff Lynne have a crystal ball when he wrote this? This is ELO's futuristic concept piece where the future could be the time we are living in now, and he muses 'I wish I was back in good old 1981.' 'The Way Life's Meant To Be' sounds stylistically like it could have been written by Dave Edmunds, while expressing nostalgia for more prosperous times, predicting the decay of our town centres and communities adeptly. '21st Century Man' indicates that all the technology in the world cannot provide happiness, a lesson we are still learning. And just to cheer us up at the end, the band rock out with 'Hold On Tight.' The strings are less prominent on this album, often having been replaced by synthesiser, but it's played tastefully so that you barely notice this change. Oh yes, and they can sing in French too.

5.97) Semi-Detached Suburban (20 Great Hits Of The Sixties) – Manfred Mann (1979)

Manfred Mann was the keyboard player and the band that took his name had a sixties career that can be divided neatly into two halves. When Paul Jones was lead vocalist, the band had a primarily 'rhythm and blues' sound, name-checking themselves in the lyrics of '5-4-3-2-1' and hitting the top of the UK hit parade with 'Do Wah Diddy Diddy.' As time went on the influence of Bob Dylan was felt, and they achieved a second number one with 'Pretty Flamingo' with alternating chords which seem just a little bit similar to 'Like A Rolling Stone' in spite of the song's positive theme. During the second half of the sixties Mike d'Abo became the front man and the band's sound incorporated light psychedelia on tracks like 'Ha Ha Said The Clown,' while Dylan's 'Mighty Quinn' netted them a third spell at the top spot. 'Mr. James' in the title track reminds me of one of Ray Davies' characters, and indeed Manfred Mann were no pioneers but they certainly reflected back all the major influences of the time, and as 'the time' was the sixties that can only be a good thing.

5.98) The Very Best Of Cat Stevens – Cat Stevens (1990)

This man must have had as many name changes as Prince. In between being Steven Demetre Georgiou and Yusuf Islam he had a hugely successful music career which saw him mentioned in the same breath as artists like Leonard Cohen. You'll be familiar with many of the songs, from 'Moonshadow' to 'Father And Son' which was covered by Boyzone, but we won't hold it against him, hey? All the way from 'I Love My Dog' in 1966 to '(Remember The Days Of The) Old Schoolyard' in 1977, Stevens was never far from writing a hit. My favourite song of his is the philosophical 'Wild World,' which muses 'A lot of nice things turn bad out there.' The melody of the verse seemed to form the basis of the Pet Shop Boys 1987 hit, 'It's A Sin,' which is their best song after 'West End Girls' in my opinion, but I am digressing.

If you wish to investigate Cat Stevens further, 'Tea For The Tillerman' (1970) and 'Teaser And The Firecat' (1971) have quirky titles and quirky covers, but 'Foreigner' (1973) has a superb eighteen-minute title track and some soul influenced tunes which show that Stevens really was the cat's whiskers. Groan!

5.99) The By-Pass Syndrome – Vin Garbutt (1991)

Vin Garbutt was a folk singer from Teesside who I had the pleasure of watching in Kent several times. He specialised in songs with a social conscience interspersed with rambling humorous banter and it was my friend Ian, CD copier extraordinaire, who introduced me to him. This is my favourite album of Vin's, with its title track being about a topic that has always been close to my heart – roads. The pivotal line is 'The bypass that bypassed the bypass already fouled up.' The song postulated that we have gone too far down a road (pun intended) that we can't just build our way out of. Vin's anti-abortion songs are definitely an acquired taste however. He sings about coal mining here too, from two opposing viewpoints, and he deals with exploitation in 'Page Three Girl.' 'The November Wedding' even channels a bit of Bach into the mix. This is a good album to start with as many of the tracks have drums and a 'band' feel, so it's certainly not just one for folk purists.

5.100) Bandalised – Vin Garbutt (1994)

This album intersperses instrumental tracks performed by Vin's folk band with more of his poignant songwriting. 'England My England' laments the rich / poor divide, 'Be As Children' touches on how helping a child can be viewed as suspicious, while 'Philippino Maid' [sic] praises the integrity of those who do the jobs that English people don't seem to want. Vin Garbutt is also a master whistle player and there is plenty of it here during the instrumental tracks.

5.101) Word Of Mouth – Vin Garbutt (1999)

Vin could evoke a huge amount of pathos with his renditions of not just his own songs, but those of others too. 'City Of Angels' and 'Dark Side Of The Moon' (nothing to do with Pink Floyd) are both examples. Those who like a bit of a rhythm are catered for with 'Beyond The Pale' and 'The Truth Is Irresistible,' although he does shoehorn a line or two about abortion into this one. Ah, that old chestnut again! 'The Troubles Of Erin' deals intelligently with the Northern Ireland conflict and longs for peace. Thankfully this wish came true. Don't mess it up boys!

If you're still with me and you want to hear some of Vin's banter, 'The Young Tin Whistle Pest' (1975) and 'Shy Tot Pommy' (1985) are fine examples of his live act but only available on vinyl. Sadly Mr. Garbutt is no longer with us, but his back catalogue lives on. There's much gold in this vein.

5.102) Tossin' A Wobber – Vin Garbutt (1978)

The title merely means losing your temper, and here we are digging back to a period when Vin's music was all acoustic. Don't panic though; the song quality is seriously good. 'Man Of The Earth' ponders retirement spent on an allotment, and 'Photographic Memory' is another early environmental song, about familiar landscapes being changed forever by industry. 'They Don't Write 'Em Like That Any More' brings to mind working class life of old in the North and 'One-Legged Beggar' is augmented by a cello and brings attitudes about homelessness out into the light.

Vin released three albums on the Trailer label which can only be purchased on vinyl. However, you can download this album, as well as 'Eston California' (1977) which includes the legend of 'The Hartlepool Monkey,' 'Little Innocents' (1983) which shows the peak of Vin's anti-abortion fervour as well as his first dabblings with a 'band' sound including drums, and 'When The Tide Turns' (1989) which has a title track that seems to postulate that over-population isn't going to be a problem. Against my own intuition I hope he's right as I can't see humans slowing down the baby making machine any time soon.

5.103) The Vin Garbutt Songbook Vol 1 – Vin Garbutt (2003)

Although I have most of Vin's albums I realise that you may not be familiar enough with the legend to require a complete discography, so I'll just review this 'greatest hits' package and move on. This collection was a mixture of favourites from the albums I've reviewed above and older material, some of which had to be re-recorded acoustically due to the ramifications of having albums with different record companies. 'The Valley Of Tees' celebrates Vin's local area, while making the error of assuming that salmon is pink when it's still in the river. This doesn't mar the enjoyment of the song at all however. 'The Land Of Three Rivers (John North)' is another celebration of the Northeast and 'Old Cissy Lee' is a tale of an old lady's incredulity at human behaviour as encountered on the news, such as the dumping of food in the sea. We need more songwriters like Vin. In fact, we need more *people* like Vin.

5.104) By Request – Eric Bogle (2001)

Eric Bogle's accent is located somewhere between Scotland and Australia, and he alternates between 'poignant' and 'irreverent.' I recall being given a transcript of his song 'No Man's Land' at school with a number of pivotal words missing that we had to attempt to guess. I think we were too young to appreciate it, but it's a great anti-war song, with the song's character pondering by the grave of a young man cut down in his prime in World War I. 'If wishes were fishes we'd all cast nets in the sea' is a nice metaphor too. Eric provides us with another anti-war anthem to close the album, 'And The Band Played Waltzing Matilda.' But just in case it all gets a bit gut-wrenching, there's 'Somebody's Moggy,' 'Silly Slang Song' and 'Santa Bloody Claus' – he's getting close to 'Kevin Bloody Wilson' territory at times! One glaring omission is 'Do You Sing Any Dylan?' which is always amusing to hear.

5.105) A Festival Of Folk – Various Artists (1996)

This Emporio compilation was lent to me by a lady who sung traditional folk music from my village, but the fare here gives even the oldest material a modern twist. The two Billy Bragg songs are brilliant, with the political song 'A World Turned Upside Down' recounting a historical event relating to issues of inequality that have sadly never gone away. He also performs the song he gave to Kirsty MacColl, 'New England.' Rory McLeod sounds a bit like Chas & Dave at times 'with the jiggery-pokery' and Michelle Shocked sounds as though she's singing around a campfire. If you're searching for something more traditional there's 'Byker Hill' and 'Geordie.' Ewan MacColl's 'Dirty Old Town' is also very nice. My mother particularly likes the Oyster Band tracks, proving that all in all there's something for everyone here.

5.106) Rave On – Various Artists (1990)

Another fortuitous find from the shed. Music was changing as the nineties began, with the new sound that replaced the pop and synth era of the eighties distilled to perfection in this Rough Trade compilation. The Happy Mondays track 'Step On' opens the album ('You're twisting my melon man'), the Farm do a cover of 'I'm Not Your Stepping Stone,' there's an early hit by the Charlatans, the Shamen feature and for once it's not that 'Es are good' song, plus the inclusion of 'Loaded' and 'Soon' illustrates the crossover point between the dance and indie cultures. Interesting things were happening...

5.107) 25 Years Of Rock N' Roll Volume 2 – 1968 – Various Artists (1992)

It doesn't take a rocket scientist to work out that this was one CD in a series (Connoisseur Collection). I picked out '1968' because the material is just so good. Barry Ryan's 'Eloise' was a song I appreciated as a child with its shifting rhythms and crazed vocal delivery. It was written by Barry's brother and former singing partner Paul. The instrumental 'Classical Gas' by Mason Williams nestles alongside Otis Redding's '(Sittin' On) The Dock Of The Bay,' another song I liked as a child with its lapping waves and whistled coda. Cilla Black intones 'Step Inside Love,' Mama Cass serenades 'Dream A Little Dream Of Me' and the Marbles declare 'Only One Woman.' Seriously, how much quality do you want? If only 'MacArthur Park' by Richard Harris was here as well...

ii) Blue

5.108) Boogie Man – John Lee Hooker (1993)

This was the first disc in the megalithic Orbis partworks series 'The Blues Collection.' John Lee Hooker had a resurgence in popularity in the 1990s, and tracks like 'Boom Boom' and 'Boogie Chillun' will sound familiar to most with its vocal, 'Let that boy boogie-woogie / Because it's in him / And it's got to come out!' His percussive 'boogie' guitar style is distinctive, often maintaining the same chord throughout a song, rather than progressing through the usual twelve-bar sequence. 'One Bourbon, One Scotch And One Beer' is a cover of a song that will be familiar to many, and Hooker's own song 'Dimples' is also classic fare. You do know it!

5.109) The King Of The Blues – B.B. King (1993)

B.B.'s name was indeed 'King,' but he changed his initials from R.B. to B.B. I seriously wonder if I'd sell more books with a name-change, as it seems to be a popular thing for artists of all persuasions to do. There's a great deal of variety here, from the minor key blues soloing of 'The Thrill Is Gone' right through to the jazzy sounding 'Don't Break Your Promise.' King's vocal on 'Outside Help' unflinchingly communicates the frustration of discovering infidelity; he literally roars. These brooding songs like 'The Letter' are what the blues is all about in my opinion and King is clearly a master, even being name-dropped by John Lennon in the Beatles track 'Dig It.'

5.110) Blues Berry – Chuck Berry (1993)

This disc is packed with late fifties and early sixties hits, from 'Memphis Tennessee' to 'Johnny B. Goode' which has become a guitar axeman's staple, partly due its inclusion in a pivotal scene in 'Back To The Future,' but mostly just due to the brilliance of Berry's soloing which has been copied by everyone from the Rolling Stones to the Beatles. 'No Particular Place To Go' illustrates Berry's lyrical humour well and 'You Never Can Tell' gained popularity as a result of its inclusion in Tarantino's film 'Pulp Fiction.' The burning question is, did Chuck Berry influence Marty McFly or was it the other way round?

5.111) Stone Crazy – Buddy Guy (1993)

The music here dates from the sixties and the seven-minute title track encapsulates what Buddy Guy was all about, with his screaming almost falsetto vocals and plenty of guitar fills between the vocal lines. 'Slop Around' is getting into rock and roll territory, and '$100 Bill' is an adaptation of 'Money (That's What I Want).'

This is impassioned stuff.

5.112) Jungle Music – Bo Diddley (1993)

Although Bo Diddley's career started much earlier, it is his late fifties chug-a-lug guitar style with minimal chord changes which is instantly recognisable, not least because of its influence extending well into the sixties and beyond. 'Who Do You Love?' became a 1970 UK hit for Juicy Lucy and 'Bo Diddley' was a posthumous hit for Buddy Holly in 1963, but perhaps Bo Diddley's influence on the Rolling Stones was the most profound. 'Before You Accuse Me' has a more traditional blues style, so he was certainly no 'one trick pony.'

5.113) Red Hot Blues – Robert Johnson (1993)

We're going right back to the thirties with this one. Robert Johnson was the original member of the '27 club,' which is an exclusive group that nobody wants to be a member of. Among others, rock stars Jimi Hendrix, Brian Jones, Jim Morrison, Janis Joplin, Kurt Cobain and Amy Winehouse all died at 27. It was also postulated that Robert Johnson sold his soul to the devil at a crossroads in order to receive his guitar playing skills via an instant Matrix-style download into the brain. Whether you believe in any of this or not, the songs are very good, in spite of being accompanied by nothing more than a lone acoustic guitar. Johnson's picking style is immediately identifiable and several of the songs on this album are blues standards such as 'Sweet Home Chicago' and 'I Believe I'll Dust My Broom.' 'Me And The Devil' added fuel to the fire of rumour no doubt.

5.114) New Bluesbreakers – John Mayall (1993)

John Mayall & The Bluesbreakers were almost like a talent incubator in the sixties, with Eric Clapton being the most famous graduate. This 'Blues Collection' disc gives us live concert performances from the eighties and shows that Mayall was still working with supremely talented musicians even then. If you like electric guitar solos you'll enjoy this. It's all pretty upbeat, for example the harmonica-driven 'It Ain't Right.' 'Room To Move' is the disc's eleven-minute closing track with some 'drum and synth' effects that you wouldn't normally expect in a blues song.

5.115) Nine Below Zero – Sonny Boy Williamson II (1993)

Sonny was a master at wailing on the harmonica and these tracks date from what I view as the most atmospheric era in blues – the late fifties and early sixties. The influence reverberated far and wide here. 'Nine Below Zero' is a plodding classic, (the best subgenre of blues is 'plodding' is my opinion), and the track is referenced in Bob Dylan's 'Outlaw Blues.' Meanwhile 'Bring It On Home' was lifted, complete with its vibrato vocal, to form the opening and closing of Led Zeppelin's track of the same name. No further endorsements required!

5.116) Long Tall Sally – Little Richard (1994)

Little Richard's brand of high energy rock and roll is well represented here, opening with 'Whole Lotta Shakin' Goin' On' which has a surprisingly contemporary sounding guitar solo. Richard's instrument was of course the piano, with his trademark rapid staccato hammering out of piano chords. The material here is pretty much page one in the encyclopedia of rock and roll, with staples such as 'Tutti Frutti,' 'Rip It Up' and 'Long Tall Sally.' His vocal on 'Lucille' is certainly the wildest thing that folk would have experienced at the time. Two of my friends have the unusual claim of having bumped into him in a lift in Nashville. You don't care!

5.117) Eric Clapton And The Yardbirds – Eric Clapton And The Yardbirds (1994)

This is the nearest to pop that 'The Blues Collection' got, and sixties hits like 'For Your Love,' with its shifting rhythm, and 'Evil Hearted You,' with its demonic sounding guitar, nestle alongside straighter twelve-bar material. Their lively cover of Bo Diddley's 'I'm A Man' seems to pre-empt Bowie's 'The Jean Genie' and the Sweet's 'Blockbuster' by the best part of a decade. 'Shapes Of Things' was another top three UK chart hit and has what must have sounded like a futuristic guitar solo at the time. The brooding 'Still I'm Sad' seems to pre-empt the backing vocals on the Specials song 'Stereotype' by fifteen years. Following Clapton's departure from the band, Jeff Beck joined, and later Jimmy Page. The band then morphed into Led Zeppelin and the rest is history.

5.118) Be My Guest – Fats Domino (1994)

This 'Blues Collection' disc is actually a live concert with audience cheers throughout. Fats performs his biggest hits, two of which were favourites of my paternal grandmother, 'Blueberry Hill' and 'Red Sails In The Sunset.' 'Ain't That A Shame' was another big song in Domino's late fifties heyday. The bassline from this track also appears in 'Blueberry Hill.' In fact it is transposed to many of Domino's songs, becoming something of a trademark sound, along with his piano of course.

5.119) Stormy Monday Blues – T-Bone Walker (1994)

This collection opens with a slightly funky vibe, with its fluid basslines and soulful rhythmic piano playing. 'Slit your wrists' blues it ain't, although I still like it when the mood drops for more lethargic tracks like 'Glamour Girl.' 'T-Bone's [That] Way' is a lively instrumental with a jazzy walking bassline and some fluent organ playing. 'When We Were Schoolmates' is a familiar tale of young romance rendered defunct, while 'Don't Go Back To New Orleans' is 'Baby Please Don't Go' in disguise, which you may know as a sixties hit for Van Morrison's band, Them. There's a great guitar sound on these tracks too.

5.120) Dust My Broom – Elmore James (1994)

Elmore James' whooped slide guitar riff, which occurs between each line on the title track, also punctuates 'Talk To Me Baby' and I'm sure it is used elsewhere in Elmore's canon. 'It Hurts Me Too,' originally recorded by Tampa Red, was also adapted by Bob Dylan on his 'Self Portrait' album. 'Elmore's Contribution To Jazz' is a misnomer if ever I heard one, enjoyable though the instrumental jam is. George Harrison name-drops Elmore James in the Beatles track 'For You Blue' by the way.

5.121) I Can't Quit You Baby – Otis Rush (1994)

The title track was covered by Led Zeppelin on their first album. This is my favourite kind of blues – impassioned vocals, tinkling piano, guitar fills between the lines and a relentless plod through the despondency and despair. 'Groaning The Blues' slows the pace even further and amps up the drama in the vocals, with Rush's characteristic roar before every line. He's clearly had a gutful of life! It's not all doom and gloom though; 'She's A Good 'Un' and 'My Baby Is A Good 'Un' are both positive in sentiment. As for me, I love it when he's angry.

5.122) Ain't Nobody's Business – Jimmy Witherspoon (1994)

This album has a jazz tinge to it with plenty of saxophone and some very adept piano tinkling. The feel of this 'Blues Collection' release is superb as Witherspoon and the band whip the audience into a near frenzy at times, with enthusiastic cheers punctuating songs like *When I Been Drinkin'*. 'See See Rider' is another 1920s standard that Jimmy made his own. This is where jazz and blues meet and if you're looking for atmosphere you've come to the right place.

5.123) Who's Been Talkin' – Robert Cray Band (1994)

Like the John Mayall / Bluesbreakers disc, this is a batch of comparatively late recordings for 'The Blues Collection' but it has the essential components of classic blues for sure. 'I'd Rather Be A Wino' presents the familiar blues theme of finding solace in alcohol, a motif also beloved of country performers. 'When The Welfare

Turns Its Back On You' perhaps needs covering in this era when the poor seem to be demonised by the comfortable at the behest of the wealthy. Sorry, I've drifted into ideology there, but the essence of the blues is one of catharsis for the downtrodden, and you can't take that away from it! There's some good harmonica backing ever-present in many of these tracks and 'Too Many Cooks,' which opens the compilation, uses alternating chords rather than the familiar twelve-bar sequence.

5.124) Blues Power – Albert King (1994)

His real name was Albert Nelson, and here we have a compilation of two halves. The first half has quite a funky soul sound that epitomises the seventies, perhaps best exemplified in the bass groove of 'I Got The Blues.' 'Born Under A Bad Sign' is jazzy with female backing vocals and all these tracks have some very fluid guitar solos. Half way through the album we delve back further with 'California' and the sound that conjures up smoky bars, ending up way back in the fifties with the brilliantly passionate track, 'Murder.' There's a also a very nice rendition of the crooner's favourite 'The Very Thought Of You' too.

5.125) Midnight Special – Leadbelly [Lead Belly] (1994)

It's right back to the forties for this one, but the influence reverberated many decades down the line. Just off the top of my head I can think of covers by Nirvana, Michelle Shocked and the Sensational Alex Harvey Band. Huddie Ledbetter used the two-word form 'Lead Belly' himself. The title track is almost a 'rite of passage' for any blues performer, and really this is like a 'greatest hits of the blues' compilation, with tracks like 'Good Morning Blues,' 'Easy Rider' and 'Rock Island Line,' which was taken to number eight in the UK hit parade in the fifties by Lonnie Donegan. Leadbelly's instrument of choice was a twelve-string guitar, and he often made use of backing vocals which sounded like a gospel chant, giving some tracks the feel of working songs. This is hugely entertaining for something so old.

5.126) Just Got Lucky – Clarence 'Gatemouth' Brown (1994)

This is a very crisp sounding set of recordings compared to many of the discs in 'The Blues Collection.' It amused me when on a coach holiday to Munich with my mother and sister, an old man called Tom started chatting to me about a track called 'Ain't Nobody Here But Us Chickens' which appears on this album. The song was originally by Louis Jordan and his Timpani Five, as was 'Ain't That Just Like A Woman,' which tells biblical stories in an entertaining way. Brown was keen on incorporating elements of other music into the blues and 'Pressure Cooker' is a great example with its jazzy bebop feel and its use of saxophone and organ.

5.127) Statesboro Blues – Blind Willie McTell (1995)

Bob Dylan even wrote a song about Blind Willie McTell, who had a very melodic voice and accompanied himself on a twelve-string guitar, with some occasional slide playing. Every song on this album has 'blues' in the title except for 'Mama, 'Tain't Long Fo' Day' and 'Mama Let Me Scoop For You,' which strays from the blues chord sequence with more of a ragtime feel. Here and elsewhere, he's accompanied vocally by Ruby Glaze, who might possibly have been Ruthy Kate Williams who became his wife, but as with so much of the blues, mystery and legend abound. Because these recordings are so old, there is a certain amount of hiss on them, but if you can overlook this, there is much to enjoy.

5.128) Mississippi Blues – Fred McDowell (1995)

It's back to basics here, with just a lone slide guitar and a vocal style that you can imagine emanating from an 'old man on the back porch' (that's a 'PUSA' reference by the way). The acoustic playing is superb though, and the three tracks that break the seven-minute mark have the feel of a guitar workout, often leaving a single slide note to hang on the breeze before the rhythm brings it back down to earth. In spite of coming from Tennessee the artist was known as 'Mississippi Fred McDowell' and it was his version of 'You Gotta Move' (not included here) that was covered by the Rolling Stones on their 'Sticky Fingers' album in 1971.

There were 92 'Blues Collection' discs, of which I have about a third. I've selected the artists that I find particularly distinctive, although I echo the words of a bearded folk-singer that I knew in the nineties when I asked him 'Are there any particular *Blues Collection* CDs that you recommend?' His reply was, 'Any you can get your hands on.' Although some fellow folkies found his style an acquired taste, it was his renditions of both Jimmy Witherspoon's 'Ain't Nobody's Business' and Joni Mitchell's 'The Circle Game' that I heard first. My friend Mark used to come along to his music club with me when we were in our twenties and he was treated to a pat on the head with the line 'And one day we'll get you singing too!' I prefer to think of this as 'encouraging' rather than 'patronising.' My friend just found it funny!

Chapter 6 – Je Suis Un Rock Star

This period begins when a local man named Perry decided to toss a hard drive filled with music at me in the local Duke's Head pub, consequently expanding my knowledge of the erratic legend known as Frank Zappa and introducing me to Leonard Cohen, a glaring omission in my collection until then. Critics of this way of acquiring music should note that since receiving this clutch of freebies I have purchased *bona fide* CD editions of many of those albums. Like listening to an album posted on the YouTube website, experiencing music in this way could be viewed as freeloading, or it could be viewed positively as a shop window for artists. Debate.

I use the title of Bill Wyman's 1981 hit humorously of course. In my early thirties my first generation of friends had moved on to do their bit for expanding the human population (as if it needs any help with that!). My peers at the local pub were now mostly twice my age, so when the landlord of a now-defunct alehouse called the World's Wonder said that two lads were jamming in his shed and that I could join them on guitar I jumped at the chance, and the Soaring Phoenix pub band was born.

But being in a rock band is like a marriage, and it brings with it further challenges. Eventually there were five of us in the band which seemed to double as a social 'pub quiz' group, but suddenly I realised what musicians mean by 'musical differences' and 'interpersonal tensions.' The Soaring Phoenix had become the 'Warring Phoenix.' I hadn't really done 'angst' thoroughly as a teenager, so now was the time for some serious turmoil it seemed. Thus from mixing with pensioners to doing 'teenage trauma' at 32, Bob Dylan's lyric from 'My Back Pages' seemed prophetic; 'I was so much older then / I'm younger than that now.'

The band gigged around the pubs of Southeast Kent throughout the autumn of 2007. It was a peculiar amalgam, with two of us being into classic rock, our drummer being into indie bands, our bass player into punk and our female vocalist into eighties music among other things. We finally threw in the towel in early 2008 (becoming the Boring Phoenix!) and I was left wondering 'what next?'

Disillusionment at work meant a transfer to the town of Ramsgate for a while, and similarly disappointed with rock I set about buying as many CDs as I could from the Orbis partworks series, 'The Classical Collection,' from the charity shops there (see Appendix I). On the plus side, the Phoenix band had introduced me to some of my closest friends. The rhythm guitarist, Cliff, sent a lot of albums my way and I joined him for hedonistic 'rock star' nights drinking tea and playing Scrabble. My job changed to minibus driving for the same company, but I found that having a lot of time between runs meant a lot of space for thought, which was the opposite of what I needed really. I tried living in a bedsit in the town where I worked, but I wouldn't say that I felt happy until I met my future wife in 2011. So these are the albums that guided me through that transitional period, again lighting the way like beacons through the mist.

It was Cliff who persuaded me to purchase an iPod; I sometimes think Apple were giving him a cut! Initially I was just amazed at how literally hundreds of albums could be stored on a device the size of a mobile phone without needing advice from a paranormal investigator. Funnily enough I'd just made a new friend called Simon (yes, another one) who had introduced himself as just that. He was a friend of former Soaring Phoenix drummer Jim and his brother Dan, and the threesome encouraged me to come camping with them, promising no ouija boards or seances, and soon these camps became a habit bordering on addiction. Strangely enough there is a family's crypt in the field next to the private woodland that we use for camping, so perhaps the spirits don't need any encouragement!

Initially we made do with the radio for entertainment, but once we realised that none of us actually liked what was being played we upgraded to an iPod speaker. We were now able to share music and consequently influence each other's tastes, which was of course a good thing. In particular the pair of siblings idolised the Kings Of Leon, and once again I encountered that rarest of things – some current music that I actually enjoyed. Some of the albums we'll encounter later in this chapter (Kings Of Leon, Arctic Monkeys, Pearl Jam, etc.) were works that I might not have discovered otherwise. I would also find a cheap way to explore Southern England during these years, combining cycling and wild camping, eventually releasing a book called 'Stair-Rods & Stars' documenting these travels many years later, so I guess new seeds were being sewn in what seemed like a barren landscape.

This period also saw me complete a collection of every UK number one from 1952-1992, after which I just collected the ones I could listen to without wanting to punch the CD player! This involved buying CDs that I wouldn't have previously considered, in order to fill in the missing number ones, and in spite of the availability of music online I still like to have a CD copy of everything I own, recording a disc of any music that I download to file away in my collection.

With an iPod (or MP3 player) you can still browse through your old albums, revisiting music and memories serendipitously, but to my mind with streaming you will only really hear what your brain (or an online algorithm) tells you to choose, consume it, and then forget it until next time, if there is one. Sadly it seems that arts of all kinds have been reduced to products for consumption in this way, and all creativity seems to be moulded to fit specific markets. You should try selling a book that you haven't written with any particular genre or trope in mind, which is precisely what I wanted to do during this era, launching myself on what folk singer Vin Garbutt described as 'years of successful anonymity.'

I'm going to split the music into three sections, trying to keep the acts we've met already at the beginning as far as possible, with the exception of Leonard Cohen who I think should usher in this particular era. The first section is a bit of a potpourri, while the second section looks at music of a heavier nature, and the third section looks at some female artists that came to my attention during these years. As I said way back in this tome, some overlap is inevitable, and by the time I had some of these albums I had met my future wife, but let's save the romance for the next chapter. Kind of.

i) Bits And Pieces

6.1) The Essential Leonard Cohen – Leonard Cohen (2002)

This was my introduction to the legendary Canadian songwriter who gave us 'Suzanne' and the frequently covered hit 'Hallelujah.' I hate to admit it but I actually prefer Jeff Buckley's version of the latter song which has an added layer of sadness when you realise how his life was cut short at such a young age. Conversely, this collection begins from Cohen's relatively late launch into the music world at 33 and covers his biggest songs all the way up to the 2001 album 'Ten New Songs.' The chronological sequencing means that Cohen's voice starts off deep and ends up somewhere near the earth's core, while the level of cynicism in the lyrics slowly cranks up.

Until experiencing this album the deepest voice I'd heard in rock was of Brad Roberts of the Winnipeg-based band, Crash Test Dummies, whose hit 'Mmm Mmm Mmm Mmm' was always a favourite among my CD singles. Is there something in the water in Canada?

6.2) Songs Of Leonard Cohen – Leonard Cohen (1967)

I'm only going to review a handful of Leonard Cohen's albums, as I feel that the most important tracks of these works are already covered by 'The Essential Leonard Cohen.' This was the songwriter's debut in 1967 and it included 'Suzanne' as well as 'So Long, Marianne,' which sounds like a mental battle between positivity and melancholy. The musical additions to Cohen's guitar are minimal. Think 'gentle tinkling' and the occasional female backing vocal. 'Sisters Of Mercy' and 'Hey, That's No Way To Say Goodbye' are also standout tracks. His next album was called 'Songs From A Room' (1969) and it contained one of my favourite Cohen tracks, 'Bird On A Wire,' which I always think would make a great funeral song.

6.3) Songs Of Love And Hate – Leonard Cohen (1971)

Later in his career Leonard Cohen asked 'You Want It Darker?' Well, this album is pretty dark, opening with the fast picked, yet brooding 'Avalanche,' with its ominous strings and opening line of 'I fell into an avalanche / It swallowed up my soul.' The only light relief is the track 'Diamonds In The Mine' where he taunts a lover who has clearly used up all his patience and energy. His vocal performance in the final chorus sounds genuinely crazed. Then we've 'Dress Rehearsal Rag' in which a blade could be used for a shave or something a lot more sinister, but as it's just a dress rehearsal, the singer lives to tell the tale. Like I said, it's dark!

6.4) Death Of A Ladies' Man – Leonard Cohen (1977)

After the 1974 album 'New Skin For The Old Ceremony,' Cohen teamed up with producer Phil Spector, who had produced pretty much every big name going at some point. He even took over the Beatles' 'Let It Be' project. Critics panned this album, and it is the only one that wasn't represented at all on 'The Essential Leonard Cohen' when the compilation was released. The sound is very different but there really is no need to toss it in the bin. I quite like the bawdy humour of what I shall politely refer to as 'track six,' as it's an angrily raucous side of the man that we don't often see. 'Fingerprints' is similarly cheeky, but the bulk of the album has a very odd feel to it, kind of dark but in a distorted way, as if viewed through a lens of decadence. It seemed to me that Leonard was pretending to be someone he wasn't and that this was coming from a place of inner turmoil. That said, I never met the man, so what do I know? Still, the closing track, which is the title cut, runs for a full nine minutes, so there's plenty of time to ponder such theories.

6.5) I'm Your Man – Leonard Cohen (1988)

After 'Recent Songs' (1979) and 'Various Positions' (1984), which gave us the ubiquitous 'Hallelujah,' this is the first of two superlative albums that marked Leonard Cohen's comeback. It opens with a 'whopper' and never really drops the ball. So we begin with 'First We Take Manhattan,' where Cohen emerges from the doldrums with a new voice declaring, 'They sentenced me to twenty years of boredom / For trying to change the system from within.' I mean, how many albums start with such a bold statement? I love the deranged laughter he injects into some of the lines of this song as though he really has lost his mind; 'You loved me as a loser / But now you're worried that I just might win.' Fantastic! 'Jazz Police' is an interesting curio, not least for paraphrasing the melody from the 'Star Trek' theme. As for 'Everybody Knows' and the world-weary closer, 'Tower Of Song,' surely everybody knows that they are towering songs. See what I did there?

6.6) The Future – Leonard Cohen (1992)

The Cohen renaissance continued and this one might even eclipse 'I'm Your Man.' We begin with a lyrical deluge *a la* Dylan's 'Subterranean Homesick Blues,' with the recurring punchline 'I've seen the future … It is murder.' 'Closing Time' and 'Democracy' are both brilliant lyrically, so much that you don't want either of these lengthy tracks to end. And the nine-minute rendition of an old standard, 'Always,' has a fantastic blues / jazz vibe and perhaps the deepest vocal note of Cohen's entire career. It's near the end if you need a pointer.

The low-energy album 'Ten New Songs' (2001) was next, followed by 'Dear Heather' (2004) which has a wider variety of styles and a live rendition of 'Tennessee Waltz,' a great song which Leonard covered in the days before his voice plunged so dramatically.

6.7) Burnt Weenie Sandwich – Frank Zappa / Mothers Of Invention (1970)

Both this album and 'Weasels Ripped My Flesh' were almost like sweepings from the floor of the Mothers Of Invention's early career, meticulously sequenced. Doo-wop pastiches open and close this album and the filling of the sandwich is avant-garde experimentation, but it seems more accessible than that of 'Weasels.' 'Overture To A Holiday In Berlin' seems pretty comfortable until a demented saxophone cuts in. The second version proves that they could play it properly when they wanted to. There's plenty of percussive messing about and eighteen minutes of 'The Little House I Used To Live In,' with the organ and violin taking centre stage and Frank masterfully declaring 'You'll hurt your throat. Stop it!' at the end when some members of the audience decide to heckle.

6.8) Weasels Ripped My Flesh – Frank Zappa / Mothers Of Invention (1970)

I first bought this album on a holiday to Toronto, but a half a dozen listens wasn't enough to endear it to me and I ended up selling it to a work colleague, along with some unwanted vinyl records that I'd found in the shed. A few years later it was time for a reassessment, and although Zappa later created an album called 'Jazz From Hell' I would say that this offering fits that title much better, with some completely deranged use of wind instruments, let alone human voices. It is interesting how the straightforward blues of Little Richard's 'Directly From My Heart To You' is segued between two absolutely bonkers 'free for alls,' the second of which even finds time for a snippet of Tchaikovsky's sixth symphony with Zappa self-referencing when he says 'Blow your harmonica, son.' It's that 'conceptual continuity' thing again.

'Get A Little' has a funky blues feel, but it's the last four tracks that create a feeling of gradually building energy, beginning with 'My Guitar Wants To Kill Your Mama,' treating us to a lyrical version of 'Oh No' which appears instrumentally on 'Lumpy Gravy,' turning jazzy on 'The Orange County Lumber Truck,' and concluding with a couple of minutes of terror-inducing noise. The fact that I've written two paragraphs would suggest that I've finally learned to appreciate 'Weasels' for more than just its comical cover design.

6.9) Chunga's Revenge - Frank Zappa (1970)

This one is not a 'Mothers' album, although it's often very hard to tell where the 'Mothers' end and 'pure Zappa' begins just from listening. We touch all bases of what the crazy experimenter was up to in the early seventies here, with electric guitar workouts, the jazzy 'Twenty Small Cigars,' and some full blown rock on 'Tell Me You Love Me,' which later became the tune for Zappa's Michael Jackson pastiche on 'Broadway The Hard Way.' There's some innuendo, some percussive 'dossing about' and some comedy lyrics.

Whilst 'Chunga's Revenge' is pretty good, I found some of Zappa's albums from this period a bit undisciplined. For example, '200 Motels' mixes the kind of rock / pastiche material found on this album with Frank's unorthodox orchestral compositions and way too much 'sledgehammer' innuendo, but that's just my opinion - for some, the innuendo is the bait that reels them in. Maybe Frank knew what he was doing after all.

6.10) One Size Fits All – Frank Zappa / Mothers Of Invention (1975)

Like 'Weasels,' this album has been in and out of my collection more times than you've had hot dinners! Zappa albums are like that. When you first hear them it's just too much to take in, then little bits start working on you subconsciously, and before you know it, you're giving it a second try. The problem with 'One Size Fits All' was that I actually found it too straightforward. I was expecting serious guitar shredding, biting satire and eccentricity, and what I got was a fairly restrained rock album. The two 'Sofa' songs are almost easy listening, although the second one has some nutty German vocals. 'Can't Afford No Shoes' and 'San Ber'dino' indicate the more rocky direction Frank would go with the 'Zoot Allures' album. 'Po-Jama People' seems to poke fun at people like me who like to wear something at night, but I can forgive Frank for his cheek as the guitar solo is pretty awesome.

6.11) Zoot Allures – Frank Zappa (1976)

Zappa is an acquired taste that is a bit like Marmite. You either love it or hate it. Most of what the man did was in rebellion to being arrested for an obscene audio tape in 1965. His view was that restricting language and subject matter is just a form of control. Thus, I think this is the approach you have to take to his lyrics, as there is usually a purpose behind what can often seem like adolescent humour. That said, this is the 'go to' Zappa album for me. The guitar playing is phenomenal throughout and the segue going into 'Wino Man' is the album's high point in my opinion. 'Disco Boy' is Frank's Mickey-take of the scene at the time, and the wailing women on 'The Torture Never Stops' are controversial to say the least, but if you put predispositions aside and get used to Zappa's deep almost satirical vocal style you'll find this album very enjoyable. Apologies to hardcore fans but I'm skipping the album 'Zappa In New York.'

6.12) Studio Tan – Frank Zappa (1978)

Right, what's Frank up to now? Ah yes, pretending to be a cartoon pig! The twenty-minute track 'The Adventures Of Greggery Peccary' certainly sounds like music composed for a cartoon to me. It's bonkers, it's fun, and for once it isn't rude. Humour is also evident on 'Lemme Take You To The Beach,' and that leaves two instrumental tracks that you may have to bend your mind around to make any sense of.

6.13) Sleep Dirt – Frank Zappa (1979 / 1991)

This is where it gets confusing. The album was originally released in 1979, but the 1991 CD re-release has additional vocals by Thana Harris which were added in the eighties. It is interesting to hear such wacky lyrics sung in a straight jazz / lounge style, and as this is the version of the album I have always known, it is hard to imagine the three tracks in question without the vocals. Of the instrumental tracks, the opener is a brooding electric guitar workout, while the title track is a sublime piece for two acoustic guitars, with some truly stunning playing. 'The Ocean Is The Only Solution' is also enjoyable in spite of its unwieldy thirteen-minute length, with some frenetic acoustic sounding strumming and bass playing eventually giving way when the electric guitar solo is unleashed just before the seven-minute mark. I'm going to move forward into the eighties now.

6.14) Ship Arriving Too Late To Save A Drowning Witch – Frank Zappa (1982)

Although there are only six tracks on this album, the first three are pretty straight rock compositions albeit with wacky vocals. Of these, the most fun is 'Valley Girl' in which Frank's daughter, Moon Unit (yes, that's her name), satirises a certain kind of young woman in California. I think this is something like what we call a 'Sloane Ranger' in Britain. Whatever it is, it became Zappa's only top forty single in the USA. The album becomes hard work for the duration of tracks four and five, the latter of which segues into 'Teenage Prostitute.' 'Uh oh!' I hear you exclaim. Well, in spite of the frivolous operatic vocal by Lisa Popeil and some aggressively percussive use of the xylophone, I get a sense that the song is actually sympathetic towards its central character, in sending up the sheer absurdity of the position she finds herself in. Well, that's my take on it and I'm sticking with it.

6.15) The Man From Utopia – Frank Zappa (1983)

Zappa's disdain for drug use is well known and it was never expressed so directly as on the opening track, 'Cocaine Decisions,' which lambasts the rich elite who run our economies but think nothing of sticking white powder up their noses. What I refer to as Zappa's 'bonkers narrative voice' appears on three tracks here, which cover subject matter from sci-fi to kitchen appliances. With the vocal tracks laid down, Steve Vai then added a guitar part which exactly replicates the intonations of Zappa's voice, creating a remarkable effect. 'Tink Walks Amok' is a nice instrumental, but some of the tracks on this album take the shades of blue a bit too far for me. It's a sure-fire 'certificate 18' from me.

6.16) Them Or Us – Frank Zappa (1984)

This double album opens with two doo-wop tracks, of which 'In France' perhaps satirises America's stereotypical ignorance of other cultures. Either that or it just plays right into it. 'Ya Hozna' sounds like a track from a horror film with its backwards vocals, and we get the album's first example of Zappa 'mangling' his guitar towards the end of 'Sinister Footwear II.' Whilst the soloing is very clever, there's an awful lot of it on this record, it's not very subtle and it does get a bit much after a while. 'Stevie's Spanking' has a stupid lyric but the guitar duel between Zappa and Vai at the end is really quite something. 'Truck Driver Divorce' is another silly song, but here the guitar mutilation overstays its welcome. However, the finale, 'Whipping Post,' is a cover of an Allman Brothers Band song, with a truly inspirational vocal by Bobby Martin delivering a lyric that feels like the triumphant overcoming of adversity; 'Sometimes I feel / Like I've been tied to the whipping post / Good Lord I feel like I'm dying.' The band could be poignant went they wanted to be, but to be frank (groan), Zappa was mostly a mad genius with no notion of self-censorship.

6.17) Dire Straits – Dire Straits (1978)

One of Britain's biggest selling bands hit the ground running with this eponymous album. Everyone knows 'Sultans Of Swing' which evokes the experience of playing in a pub band and then treats us to one of Mark Knopfler's most memorable guitar solos. They make it all sound so easy, listen to the laid back rhythm of 'In The Gallery' for example. 'Water Of Love' and 'Wild West End' both have nice melodies too. Relax and enjoy!

6.18) Communiqué – Dire Straits (1979)

More top notch stuff from the brothers Knopfler with Illsley (bass) and Withers (drums). 'Lady Writer' was the hit this time around, but 'Angel Of Mercy' gets the gold star for melodiousness, especially with the Spanish feel at around 2.50. 'Once Upon A Time In The West' has a great rhythm and the quality of Mark Knopfler's solos goes without saying. Brother David would leave after this album, consequently missing most of the action.

6.19) On Every Street – Dire Straits (1991)

'Brothers In Arms' was a tough act to follow, but why overlook a classic album like this? 'Calling Elvis' name-drops a lot of songs by 'The King,' just as many other bands created songs which name-dropped Beatles songs. The philosophical track, 'The Bug' has a country feel *a la* 'Walk Of Life' on 'Brothers In Arms.' 'Heavy Fuel' satirises rock lifestyles, but the best tracks are all laid back and dreamy. These are the title track, 'You And Your Friend' and 'Fade To Black' – oh my gosh, that guitar is just succulent!

Unbelievably, the band only produced six studio albums. If you want to experience their fun side you can't go wrong with the four-track 'Extendedance Play' EP (1983), but seriously, why is there no CD release of this? That wish list is getting longer.

6.20) Flowers – Rolling Stones (1967)

This was more of a compilation than a regular album, aiming to fill in the gaps where the publishers had chopped up the USA editions of 'Aftermath' and 'Between The Buttons.' Yet surprisingly this is a 'go to' album for me, almost as much as 'Beggars Banquet' or 'Let It Bleed.' 'Ruby Tuesday' is, in my opinion, perhaps the best song Jagger and Richards have ever written, while 'Let's Spend The Night Together' is a piano-driven rocker which was Ruby's 'flip side' on the double A-sided single. I mean, how the hell did that pairing not get to number one? There's a lot of duplication, with tracks like 'Out Of Time,' 'Mother's Little Helper' and 'Lady Jane' popping up again, but the folky closing track, 'Sitting On A Fence,' is a little known Stones masterpiece as far as I'm concerned.

6.21) Their Satanic Majesties Request – Rolling Stones (1967)

The title is nothing so demonic but a play on the words within British passports ('Her Britannic Majesty ... Requests'). The Stones were considered 'followers' rather than 'leaders' when this was released roughly six months after the Beatles put out 'Sgt. Pepper.' I think this was unfair, as nothing on 'Pepper' was as undisciplined as the eight-minute jam 'Sing This All Together (See What Happens)' or as dark sounding as '2000 Light Years From Home,' which starts with 'Pink Floyd' style tinklings and ends up an eerie mellotron-dominated song about the loneliness of space. A lot of the album is very melodic, in spite of the experimentation, and 'She's A Rainbow' is catchy enough to have been used in TV adverts. The critics need to lighten up. Sadly they managed to put the Stones off of such wild experimentation for good.

6.22) Black And Blue – Rolling Stones (1976)

After the run of classic albums from 'Beggars Banquet' to 'Exile On Main Street,' and what I view as a couple of 'run of the mill' albums, 'Goats Head Soup' (1973) and 'It's Only Rock 'N Roll' (1974), the Stones put out this eclectic little package. 'Hot Stuff' is pure funk and 'Cherry Oh Baby' is pure reggae. 'Fool To Cry' is one of their finest ballads, and the chord change at 3.50 packs a punch, as though the band were changing up a gear. It turns out that this was just a warm up for the next album.

6.23) Some Girls – Rolling Stones (1978)

'Miss You' opens this seminal album with a blues-disco vibe (have I invented a genre?). If you bought the single and flipped it over you were treated to 'Far Away Eyes,' a tongue-in-cheek country song that among other things lambasts the blind devotion to wealthy evangelists with a comical metaphor of driving through red lights. 'Respectable' rocks, and indeed several tracks here may have been the band's attempt to keep up with punk. 'Beast Of Burden' is a classic ballad and 'Shattered' is a fun closer.

For those wishing to explore the band's later catalogue you can't go far wrong with 'Bridges To Babylon' (1997) or 'A Bigger Bang' (2005).

6.24) Sunshine Superman – Donovan (1966)

The title track reached number two in the UK singles chart in 1966, the closest Mr. Leitch ever got to the top spot. In the USA it made number one and the American album of this name is the 'proper' one. 'Legend Of A Girl Child Linda' runs to almost seven minutes and is a folky ditty with sparse strings, a sound Donovan would come back to with 'Laléna.' There is Indian instrumentation on 'Ferris Wheel,' and 'The Trip' is evocative of the swinging London of the sixties (no illegal substances were taken I'm sure!). 'The Fat Angel' is yet another psychedelic gem, while 'Celeste' is a dreamy closer. And I haven't even mentioned the best track, 'Season Of The Witch.'

6.25) The Great Escape – Blur (1995)

Critics panned this album and declared Oasis the winners of the Britpop war at the time, but in hindsight this was unfair, especially knowing now that Blur went headlong into avant-garde territory with their next two albums. As you may have noticed, I finally got my hands on this Blur album much later than the others, and I'm sure it was those poxy critics who put me off it. This one has a similar structure to 'Parklife' with some anthems like 'The Universal,' which sees the band emulating the gang of thugs in 'A Clockwork Orange' in the video. There's also the odd punk blast, as well as the 'National Lottery' themed anthem 'It Could Be You.' However, in spite of the jolly melodies and harmonies, there is a darker feel to this album than 'Parklife,' from the jaded guest vocal from Ken Livingstone on 'Ernold Same' to the resigned sadness of 'Best Days.' If your mood needs picking up again at the end, simply replay the openers, 'Stereotypes' and 'Country House.'

6.26) Dig Out Your Soul – Oasis (2008)

This was the swansong of Britpop's biggest band. Perhaps they made a conscious decision to quit at the top and remain legends because the writing was on the wall for guitar bands, with even Coldplay adopting a more 'poppy' sound to survive.

Well, the Mancunians certainly went out with a collection that touring drummer Zac Starkey's father Ringo would have been proud of, for the sixties vibe emanates throughout. 'Bag It Up' is epic sounding Oasis at its best, 'Waiting For The Rapture' seems to borrow the guitar riff from 'Five To One' by the Doors, and 'The Shock Of The Lightning' pays homage to their Liverpudlian idols in its lyric about 'a magical mystery.' They boys get the sitars out for 'To Be Where There's Life.' Remarkably this was the band's first album since 'Definitely Maybe' not to contain any number one hits, which is insane when the quality was so good. I can only think of one way they could have improved it and that would be by closing the album with the B-side 'Those Swollen Hand Blues,' leaving Noel's vocal reverberating through time like a ghostly echo of the sixties channelled through the noughties.

6.27) Green – R.E.M. (1988)

It's called 'Green' but the cover is yellow. As they say in R.E.M.'s home country 'Go figure!' The band were just over two years away from superstardom when they released this and there are plenty of hints as to why they made it big here. There's a grungy guitar sound on 'Pop Song 89' and Michael Stipe's menacing vocal on 'Turn You Inside-Out' is most enjoyable. The drums sound great on this track too. There are a few folky tracks indicating where the band would go next, but my favourite is 'Get Up' which has a brilliant melody and a surprise tinkly bit as we go off into the world of dreams.

6.28) Stereopathetic Soulmanure – Beck (1994)

Such a lovely title! This pre-fame album of Beck's reminds me of searching for a diamond ring in a rubbish tip. There are some country-tinted gems here, such as 'Rowboat,' which is adorned with steel guitar and was even covered by the legend that was Johnny Cash. 'Crystal Clear (Beer)' is an earnest folky number, and 'Satan Gave Me A Taco' is a good natured 'shaggy dog story' in a similar vein to 'Bob Dylan's 115th Dream.' The bit about the water from a hose shooting right up his nose always raises a smile with me. A very pleasant EP could have been created by combining these tracks with 'The Spirit Moves Me,' 'Puttin It Down' [sic] and 'Modesto,' but Beck also set out to assault our senses, and much of the rest of this album seems to wander between 'noise' and 'poor taste.' For example, are the audience laughing *at* Beck or *with* him during his performance of 'Ozzy?' As with a lot of Frank Zappa's albums, a little bit of restraint could have allowed the obvious talent to shine more clearly. The editing seems to deliberately evoke the feeling of a teenager messing around with tapes.

6.29) Sea Change – Beck (2002)

It's back to the downbeat 'relationship break up' theme so beloved of Leonard

Cohen, with another *volte-face* by Beck, who leaves the 'Prince' affectations of 'Midnite Vultures' behind for this soul-baring collection which leans towards country music at times, but being Beck he still has his feet in multiple genres. My favourite here is 'Lost Cause,' which seems to encapsulate the devastating feelings that everybody has experienced at least once. 'The Golden Age' starts as a country ballad before the ambient wash of sound literally engulfs him. Are you still in there, Beck? He also sounds absolutely broken at the start of 'Paper Tiger.'

I didn't continue much further with Beck's work after this, although I can tell you that the 2005 album 'Guero' is an enjoyable mix of many of the styles he'd covered on previous albums, with a slightly Spanish twist.

6.30) Incantations – Mike Oldfield (1978)

This one is a challenge, being a double album of just four tracks that continually repeats its themes, sometimes cycling through the same series of chords for many minutes at a time. 'Part One' opens with strings evoking images of the launching of a ship. Female vocalists recite the names of the Roman goddesses, Diana, Luna and Lucina. In 'Part Two' Maddy Prior sings part of Longfellow's poem 'Ode To Hiawatha.' Mike unleashes the electric guitar on 'Part Three' and in 'Part Four' Maddy returns to sing 'Ode To Cynthia' by Ben Johnson.

If you wish to bulk up your Mike Oldfield collection further, 'The Complete Mike Oldfield' (1985) is a double album that covers all bases, from his short instrumentals to poppier hits, of which 'Moonlight Shadow' featuring vocalist Maggie Reilly is perhaps the best known, as well as extracts from the kind of albums I've reviewed in this book.

6.31) Talking Book – Stevie Wonder (1972)

With 'Songs In The Key Of Life' a now firm favourite of mine, it was time for a trawl through the multi-instrumentalist's back catalogue. This album seemed to mark his transition from a Motown singles artist into a creative force in the Beatles / Stones league. Yet, he still managed to turn out the hits too. 'You Are The Sunshine Of My Life' and 'Superstition' are the biggies here. 'I Believe (When I Fall in Love)' is now a standard, having been covered by everyone from Art Garfunkel onwards, but nobody broke it down with the funky finish the way Stevie did. The high point is 'You And I' where Stevie turns out a vocal performance that is epic in its emotional quality. Today's vocalists who have the technical ability for extended melismas still can't seem to grab that vital quality that flows in abundance here.

6.32) Innervisions – Stevie Wonder (1973)

Yet more quality from Mr. Stevland Morris. 'Living For The City' expresses the frustrations of urban life with edgy voices illustrating the point towards the end. 'Visions' is dreamily blissful, and you all know 'Higher Ground,' which is similar to 'Superstition' with its guitar-like synthesiser sound. 'He's Misstra Know-It-All' completes the set, with Stevie giving us a completely different vocal sound, imitating the bombast of the song's central character.

6.33) Stevie Wonder's Journey Through "The Secret Life Of Plants" – Stevie Wonder (1979)

An ambitious double album, but you couldn't get more different to 'Songs In The Key Of Life.' This is loosely an attempt at new age music but it does contain some more traditional songs like 'Same Old Story.' 'Race Babbling' is a lengthy disco-style instrumental, and 'Venus' Flytrap And The Bug' [sic] features some bizarre processed vocals, but all in all there a sense that we should appreciate nature more than we do – a musician ahead of his time, once again. Put this in the 'eclectic' pigeonhole next to George Harrison's 'Wonderwall Music.'

6.34) The Invisible Band – Travis (2001)

Travis's third album was initially a disappointment to me as they dispensed with the 'rock' aspect of their music altogether. Songs like 'Sing' and the philosophical 'Side' are quality cuts. 'Flowers In The Window' has a great melody, and 'Dear Diary' communicates a haunting sadness, but you do wish they'd amp up the guitars occasionally for a bit of contrast.

The album that followed, '12 Memories' (2003), is a frustrating affair, although I recommend the three CD singles that were released from that album, which contain some great B-sides including 'Definition Of Wrong' and the anti-war sing-along, 'I Don't Mean To Get High.' I've no idea why they didn't pep up the album by including these tracks.

6.35) XTRMNTR – Primal Scream (2000)

Keeping it Scottish we return to Primal Scream, who changed styles pretty much as often as they changed their socks. After the sixties-tinted psychedelia of 'Vanishing Point,' they gave us a full on rave album. 'Swastika Eyes' is the standout track with its pounding drums grinding on relentlessly for seven minutes. 'Blood Money' is a similar affair, incorporating saxophone and a sound that wouldn't be out of place in a spy film. If you're missing guitars, these are turned up to eleven on the cacophonous 'Accelerator' and then almost obliterated by electronics. The lyrics are politically charged, describing society with lines like 'A military industrial illusion of democracy' while 'Pills' eventually simplifies its message into pure swearing!

6.36) This Is Hardcore – Pulp (1998)

This Britpop band's follow up to 'Different Class' had a bleaker feel and a heavier sound. The title track starts with an orchestral sample and builds up into power rock done 'Pulp style.' 'Help The Aged' is a touching song asking for a bit more respect for the elderly who once lived it up as much as today's youngsters do. I also like 'I'm A Man,' in which singer Jarvis Cocker rejects the emptiness of macho behaviour with a memorable melody. The last track leaves its final note hanging for a full ten minutes, which isn't interesting enough to qualify as ambient music and isn't obvious enough to qualify as a statement. Sorry Jarvis.

6.37) The Essential Billy Joel 3.0 – Billy Joel (2008)

I'm going to insert Billy Joel at this point. I had acquired 'Greatest Hits Volume I & II' on vinyl courtesy of the instant record collection that I found in the shed when moving house. However, it was during my time trawling the charity shops of Ramsgate in my lunch breaks that I purchased all three volumes on CD, which I later replaced with the '3.0' collection that I'm reviewing here.

It all starts with 'Piano Man,' a Dylan-esque classic reflecting on performing for lonely people in bars. A favourite of mine is 'Scenes From An Italian Restaurant,' a story song in multiple parts which looks back at youth with rose-tinted glasses. 'Uptown Girl' brings to mind many a school disco for me, while its antithesis, 'We Didn't Start The Fire,' combines two of my favourite subgenres, the 'lyrical deluge' song and the 'list' song, rapid-firing pivotal news events from post-war history at us. It's impossible to list all the brilliant hits. There are even a couple of Joel's classical pieces, which remind me of Chopin, but the show stopper for me is 'Leningrad.' If you feel nothing when listening to this anti-prejudice song then you can get your coat!

6.38) Ring Of Fire: The Legend Of Johnny Cash – Johnny Cash (2005)

Johnny Cash was a true legend in country music who later performed rock songs in his own unique style. Both aspects are represented here and always delivered with a world-weariness. You all know hits like the title track and 'I Walk The Line,' but listen to the desperation in tracks like 'Cry, Cry, Cry' and 'Guess Things Happen That Way.' Meanwhile 'A Thing Called Love' was a favourite of mine that I used to hum while doing my paper round as a teenager. From the later period, the cover of Depeche Mode's 'Personal Jesus' is fantastic, and 'I've Been Everywhere' is another one of those 'list' songs, this time consisting of American towns, and Johnny sounds old enough to have actually seen them all. The pinnacle though, is the cover of 'Hurt' by Nine Inch Nails, which sounds like he is literally staring death in the face to see who cracks first. If you feel nothing when listening to this... Hang on, I've said this before somewhere.

6.39) Chronicles (1968-1984) – Dave Edmunds (1994)

When an album opens with Dave's bombastic guitar workout of Khachaturian's 'Sabre Dance' with Love Sculpture it almost doesn't matter what happens after that. Fortunately, Dave didn't let the quality drop. 'I Hear You Knocking' provided him with a UK number one single in 1970. Then we are into Spector-style 'wall of sound' territory with 'Baby, I Love You' and 'Born To Be With You.' Dave's next peak seemed to be riding the wave of artists like Nick Lowe (whose 'Jesus Of Cool' album is great), with hits like 'Girls Talk,' 'Queen Of Hearts' and the uplifting 'Crawling From The Wreckage.' Later tracks have a country feel, and my only criticism was that DE's other early classical guitar adaptation 'Farandole' isn't included. It's fantastic, but you'll have to buy another compilation such as 'The Collection' on the Disky label for this one. Don't miss out...

6.40) Asylum Years – Tom Waits (1986)

This is a compilation of what I would call Tom's 'jazz years,' although in truth his music is hard to pigeonhole. 'The Ghosts Of Saturday Night' is an atmospheric piece that brings to mind a dimly lit jazz bar.'Tom Traubert's Blues' was a hit for Rod Stewart in the early nineties and not the only poignant song to utilise the chorus of 'Waltzing Matilda' (see Eric Bogle). In truth, Tom's gravelly vocal here makes Rod's voice sound like silk. He's bordering on 'Louis Armstrong' territory with 'Potter's Field,' and if you want to explore his more avant-garde style I recommend the 1983 album 'Swordfishtrombones.'

6.41) The Very Best Of The Four Seasons – The Four Seasons (1995)

This was Music Club release that I bought purely to get my hands on 'December '63 (Oh What A Night)' in order to complete my set of UK number one hits from 1976. The Four Seasons had some great harmonies with striking falsetto vocals from Frankie Valli, but they weren't smooth like the Beach Boys, to the point where some music fans in the USA thought the brash English Beatles were trying to copy them. The early sixties hits like 'Sherry' and 'Walk Like A Man' are very enjoyable, and 'Let's Hang On' has a great intro, beginning so smoothly that when the guitar and drum motif kicks in it seems almost irreverent. The band had a second wind in the seventies, with a more disco-oriented sound. The bridge / riff section on 'Who Loves You' is great by the way.

6.42) Robert Post – Robert Post (2005)

Occasionally you get an artist from mainland Europe who sounds more British than most true Brits do. A good example is Nina Persson of the Cardigans, who we'll get to later. Another example is Norway's Robert Post (the name rhymes with 'frost'), and it seems remarkable that he produced such a good debut and then became almost unknown again. 'There's One Thing' has a touch of Bob Dylan about it, while 'Got None' is more akin to Ray Davies stylistically. The lyrics often deal with the transition of moods and phases in life; 'It hasn't always been like this,' 'A better set of days will come,' etc. The album sounds more like the work of a band than a solo artist, although 'Everything Is Fine' is a wistful acoustic track with a great melody. The brief harp sound near the start of 'Ocean And A Tear' is a nice touch. It would be nice if more singer-songwriters incorporated the said instrument, but I don't want to harp on...

6.43) Costello Music – The Fratellis (2006)

The opening track, 'Henrietta,' sounds like Britpop-era Blur, although be warned, there's a C-word almost as soon as it gets going and it's not 'Costello.' The Scottish band seemed to have a perfect blend of melody and punk attitude. 'Chelsea Dagger' was the big hit but 'Whistle For The Choir' shows just how melodic and gentle these boys could be. 'Baby Fratelli' is also memorable for its alternating rhythms.

6.44) Youth And Young Manhood – Kings Of Leon (2003)

The Kings Of Leon mythology is second only to the Beatles in my opinion, being four country boys from Nashville who played retro sounding music and somehow made it massive. The group of three brothers and one cousin initially gained a larger following in the UK than in their homeland, so they always have plenty of time for the British fans. I remember at the time my soon-to-be camping buddy suggested that we play the track 'Trani' in our pub band. In hindsight I'm not sure we could have pulled it off. It builds to a frenzy and Caleb Followill's vocal is nothing short of crazed.

Other highlights include 'Molly's Chambers,' a title referencing a line from 'Whiskey In The Jar,' a hit for Thin Lizzy. 'Joe's Head' perhaps unintentionally demonstrates why the wide availability of guns isn't a good idea, and 'Dusty' has a great bluesy feel with encouraging shouts from the band's musicians. Don't turn off after the final track – the hidden track 'Talihina Sky' is an atmospheric country song and well worth waiting for.

6.45) Aha Shake Heartbreak – Kings Of Leon (2004)

Before the pub band I was in imploded our drummer's sister Tracy gave me a CD of this, the second Kings Of Leon album. One evening while waiting for the train home from work I thought I'd give it a spin on my generic 'Discman,' and by about a minute into the first track I knew I was going to like this band. We already covered 'Four Kicks' in our band and much of the album has the feel of being composed through a 'post drinking binge' haze! 'Day Old Blues' and 'Rememo' are some of the album's more laid back moments.

6.46) Because Of The Times – Kings Of Leon (2007)

Musically I think this was the band's most accomplished album. Just listen to
Nathan Followill's drums which excel on 'McFearless' for example. Opening with
'Knocked Up,' which is the longest track the band have ever produced at over
seven minutes, the album never drops the baton, all the way to 'Arizona' which is
one of their best songs. There were some great B-sides from the early singles too,
of which 'My Third House' encapsulates the creative surge of this album despite
not being on it. 'Wicker Chair' and 'Head To Toe' are worth seeking out too. It's
amazing that a 'B-sides and rarities' album has never been compiled. That wish list
is growing.

6.47) Only By The Night – Kings Of Leon (2008)

This is when the Kings made it big and finally got the attention they deserved in
their homeland too. 'Sex On Fire' was a UK number one and consequently became
a song that the band became tired of playing, to the best of my knowledge. 'Use
Somebody' was almost as big. This album had a more polished sound than the first
three, although personally I preferred the rawness. 'Revelry' is a mellow moment,
'17' sounds like it should have been a Christmas hit, 'Crawl' really rocks and 'Cold
Desert' is a brooding finale evoking images of the lead singer wandering alone in
the desert. However, my favourite track is 'Be Somebody,' with its pounding
rhythm and a feel that recaptures the energy of the first three albums. Caleb's
vocals have a greater clarity on this album, perhaps enhancing accessibility for the
masses.

6.48) Come Around Sundown – Kings Of Leon (2010)

I always had an opinion of this as being a more mellow, almost country album, but
really it isn't that at all. Only 'Back Down South' truly goes in the country direction
with its pleasant violin accompaniment. 'The End' is a dark sounding opener and
'Radioactive' was the lead single. 'Mary' and 'No Money' are both great rockers. I
think the fact that the Kings seemed to have had their chips when it came to the
singles chart represented a change in the kind of singles that became hits rather
than a loss of popularity for the band. The KOL still shift albums by the ton and
even Oasis didn't make number one with any singles from their final album in
2008.

6.49) The Seldom Seen Kid – Elbow (2008)

We now come to a band that I first heard playing over the speakers at our local

Woolpack Inn. As I sat quaffing my ale it was clear that this was a break from the norm, The landlord lent me the CD and the rest is history. The opening track, 'Starlings,' sets the scene with its unusual downbeat style occasionally punctuated by blasts from a brass section. 'Grounds For Divorce' is a great bluesy rock song which has the feel of a gospel chant, and 'The Loneliness Of A Tower Crane Driver' creates something evocative from an unusual observation that you're closer to a deity at the top of a crane. From my deliveries to Southampton Docks I can confirm this to be true. Also, just wait for the awesome chord change before Guy Garvey sings 'They say I'm on top of my game.' 'The Fix' is a song about horse racing and features Richard Hawley who was in the nineties band, the Longpigs. The big hit was 'One Day Like This,' and the jazzy closing track clearly aims to create a warm feeling after so much angst; 'World do your worst / She and I have closed our eyes.'

And if the Richard Hawley track has made you curious, the Longpigs CD singles 'Lost Myself' and 'She Said' are superb, with some fabulous B-sides too.

6.50) Asleep In The Back – Elbow (2001)

Having got thoroughly acquainted with the Bury band's monster album, I decided to explore the back catalogue. The melancholy tone seemed to suit my mood as I spent nights alone in a flat in the seaside town of Folkestone, and the opening lyrics of the first track seemed to sum it up, 'Got a lot of free time / Some of my youth / And all of my senses on overtime.' 'Bitten By The Tailfly' has a brooding feel and some aggressive guitar playing. 'Newborn' builds from an acoustic ballad into something mesmerising, and the band sounds like a northern version of Blur on 'Coming Second.'

6.51) Cast Of Thousands – Elbow (2003)

I always found this the weak link in the Elbow discography. It didn't have the majestic lugubriousness of the first album or the melodic anger of the third, so what did it have? The opening track eventually evolves into a gospel-style chorus. 'Buttons And Zips' has a nice rhythmic sound, while 'I've Got Your Number' represents the opposite end of the romantic spectrum, being an angry 'end of love' song with the memorable line 'Grow a f***ing heart!' The album takes its name from 'Grace Under Pressure,' which features an entire festival crowd singing the hook-line. A selection of the participants had their names enshrined on the album artwork. Talking of names, the band's moniker comes from a line in the TV drama 'The Singing Detective,' where 'elbow' is declared the 'loveliest word in the English language.'

6.52) Leaders Of The Free World – Elbow (2005)

This was the nearest Elbow got to sounding like an indie rock band. 'Station Approach' celebrates returning to one's home town. In lead singer Guy Garvey's case this was Bury. The title track encapsulates my thoughts on modern hate-based politics with the line 'I think we dropped the baton / Like the sixties didn't happen.' It also has a great chord sequence. 'Mexican Standoff' is a full blown tongue-in-cheek rocker, wishing death on a love rival. The effect this has is probably not what the band desired, as you just wish the energy stayed at this level for the rest of the album. Or is that just me?

6.53) Build A Rocket Boys – Elbow (2011)

Quite where Elbow would go after their monster album 'The Seldom Seen Kid' was a matter for conjecture. The eight-minute opener is this album's high point, doing that classic 'Elbow' thing of building a track up from next to nothing into high drama. There's a great moment when the keyboard kicks in preceding the refrain 'What are we gonna do with you? / Same tale every time.' In an interesting 'curveball' move, it is a piano tuner who sings the lead vocal on the reprise of the song. Initially I wondered if Guy had drafted in his dad or something. While 'With Love' mixes up the sound with an Eastern feel, I must admit to finding this CD generally a bit too stripped back and I almost gave *them* the elbow after this point. However, I can confirm that 'The Take Off And Landing Of Everything' (2014) and 'Little Fictions' (2017) are well worth investing a bit of time in to appreciate.

6.54) It's... Madness / It's... Madness Too – Madness (1990 and 1991)

Lead singer Suggs was one of the finest things to come out of Hastings, unless you count the A259 and the A21, that is! You will know most of the hits inside out and it's surprising that 'House Of Fun,' a song about buying condoms, was the band's only number one hit. 'Baggy Trousers' is tremendous fun in looking back on school days, but it's the B-sides that surprise and intrigue, such as the shoplifting tale 'Deceives The Eye.' The second volume gives us the ska instrumentals 'Night Boat To Cairo' and 'One Step Beyond' and more 'house music' with 'Our House.'

6.55) Legend – Bob Marley And The Wailers (1984)

Surely, this is *the* definitive reggae album. You will know virtually every track; 'No Woman No Cry,' 'Three Little Birds,' etc. are 'bread and butter' stuff. Later on we get Marley with a lone acoustic guitar on 'Redemption Song,' while 'Exodus' has a bit of a voodoo feel. My favourite is 'Waiting In Vain' which has a sleepy vibe which is great for sitting round a campfire staring into the lapping flames. It's so laid back it's all too easy to overlook the obvious skill of the musicians.

And while we're on the subject of reggae, check out the Easy Star All-Stars albums 'Dub Side Of The Moon' (2003) and 'Easy Stars Lonely Hearts Dub Band' (2009). Both are reggae / dub versions of the complete albums they are named after. They've done a version of Radiohead's 'OK Computer' too.

6.56) Rumours – Fleetwood Mac (1977)

This was a massive album which was on the UK chart for something like a million weeks! The blues era of Peter Green is long gone and the rock is smooth with plenty of radio hits that you know like 'Don't Stop' and 'Go Your Own Way.' I once played 'Songbird' at a wedding and at the time I didn't know the song or the album. Hard to believe really. And you've still got the moody track 'The Chain' to go, which develops into what became the Grand Prix theme music for many years.

6.57) Tango In The Night – Fleetwood Mac (1987)

This is a poppy affair for the British / American band, opening with acoustic sounding guitar juxtaposed with crisp drums in 'Big Love.' 'Little Lies' and 'Everywhere' are the hits everybody knows and loves, and you'll recognise the catchy synth melody of 'You And I, Part II.' Best of all is the 'Welcome To The Room' version of 'Sara,' with its haunting vocal by Stevie Nicks, whose voice is one of the most easily identifiable of all time.

6.58) The Chain [Disc 4] – Fleetwood Mac (1992)

This disc from the four-disc box set is a comprehensive and roughly chronological journey from the band's blues days with Peter Green, to the smoother style of the seventies when Stevie Nicks, Christine McVie and Lindsay Buckingham were added to the Fleetwood and the Mac. 'Oh Well, Part 1' is a fab song with a great lyric; 'Don't ask me what I think of you / I might not give the answer that you want me to.' 'Albatross' is an instrumental hit, evoking a sense of being on a desert island. It was the band's only UK number one single. 'Man Of The World' has the feel of the sun breaking through the clouds, in spite of its truly bleak lyric proclaiming 'I just wish I'd never been born' six years before Freddie Mercury expressed the same sentiment in 'Bohemian Rhapsody.' From the seventies I like the melodic 'Heroes Are Hard To Find' which comes from an album with truly dreadful cover art!

6.59) Procol Harum – Procol Harum (1967)

In the UK in the sixties it was generally assumed that if your album included singles that fans had already bought it was something of a rip off, so the larger pieces of vinyl rarely contained the big hits. Procol Harum's debut album was a prime example, with 'A Whiter Shade Of Pale' omitted in the UK but included in the USA. The Germans got 'Homburg' instead, and everybody got confused. Either way, I would recommend getting a remixed edition from 2009 or later, as this will enhance your enjoyment massively. Matthew Fisher's organ playing is pivotal to the sound, although vocalist Gary Brooker is pretty adept on the keys too, adding plenty of piano. Some tracks are circus-like, such as 'Mabel' and 'Good Captain Clack,' but for me the whole album is really just a build up for 'Repent Walpurgis,' which is my favourite rock instrumental of all time, combining Bach, ominous chords and a splendid guitar solo. Allow me to indulge myself. It's epiiiiiiiiiiiiiiiic!!!

6.60) Whatever You Say I Am That's What I'm Not – Arctic Monkeys (2006)

The Arctic Monkeys were big news when they launched their ship onto the turbulent waves of popular music. The band's name seems to be taking the insult 'northern monkey' to comedic lengths, and their debut album presents lots of snapshots of working class life in a northern city. This album contains two UK number one singles, 'I Bet You Look Good On The Dancefloor' and 'When The Sun Goes Down,' which points the guilt for prostitution squarely at the kerb crawlers while referencing the Police in the line 'He told Roxanne to put on her red light.' 'Mardy Bum' is a great slice of domestic life from the 'it's not all bliss' school of thought. The musicianship is punchy and slick from beginning to end.

6.61) Favourite Worst Nightmare – Arctic Monkeys (2007)

With a similar feel to their first album, FWN is another confident collection from Alex Turner and pals. 'Teddy Picker' has a very catchy riff, 'This House Is A Circus' ends up absolutely frenetic and the band finally show a gentler side with the closing track, '505,' which is adorned with a dreamy organ.

6.62) Humbug – Arctic Monkeys (2009)

This one begins moodily with 'My Propeller,' and 'Pretty Visitors' has an amusing take on the 'chicken and egg' conundrum along with some virtuoso drumming from Matt Helders. The sound of this album is not as raw as the first two although 'Dangerous Animals' has a great riff. The jangly guitar notes on tracks like 'The Jeweller's Hands' could almost be from a sixties spy movie.

6.63) Suck It And See – Arctic Monkeys (2011)

This was the first Arctic Monkeys album that I really took notice of, courtesy of my two camping buddies who put the album on one afternoon in our hallowed glade in a private woodland in Kent. The beers were going down well, and it was the group's lyrics that struck me initially, being full of puns and creative turns of phrase. 'Don't Sit Down 'Cause I've Moved Your Chair' is a good example. I also like 'Brick By Brick,' and the line 'Lately I've been seeing things / Belly-button piercings' in 'Black Treacle' always strikes me as amusing. While the band lost some of their initial fans with their new approach to both music and lyrics, this was exactly where I picked them up...

6.64) Elephant – White Stripes (2003)

We used to play 'Seven Nation Army' in our pub band, although I don't think this one ever made it out of the garage where we used to practise, not least because nobody was singing it. It has a great riff and is quintessential stuff from Jack and Meg White, a married couple who adopted Meg's surname and then pretended to be brother and sister. Er...right! The whole album really rocks with tracks like 'Girl, You Have No Faith In Modern Medicine,' and there's even a cover of the Bacharach and David song 'I Just Don't Know What To Do With Myself,' which you may know as a Dusty Springfield hit. The quirky final track flirts with the brother / sister pretence, country style.

If you enjoy this album I recommend the track 'Death By Diamonds And Pearls' by Band Of Skulls which has a similar sound.

6.65) Meet The Eels: Essential Eels Volume 1, 1996-2006 – Eels (2008)

'Novocaine For The Soul' is both a great concept and a great song, delivered with a downbeat vocal, setting the tone for the album. 'Susan's House' is similarly enjoyable with spoken-word verses. If your mood needs a lift 'Mr. E's Beautiful Blues' should fit the bill. There's a wacky cover of 'Get Your Freak On' which was a hit for Missy Elliot, and as the tracks are arranged chronologically, things get less angsty as the album goes on, although 'Hey Man (Now You're Really Living)' shows that it was still there beneath the surface in 2005, as they declare that both the good and the bad are essential components of life's rich tapestry. 'Do you know what it's like to fall on the floor? / Cry your guts out till you've got no more?' Well, do you?

6.66) Urban Hymns – The Verve (1997)

This was an album I that originally had on tape. 'Bitter Sweet Symphony' declares that 'You're a slave to the money, then you die,' which was something the band found out the hard way with a plagiarism charge for using a string motif from an orchestral version of 'The Last Time' by the Rolling Stones. 'The Drugs Don't Work' was the band's only number one, but 'Sonnet' and 'Lucky Man' were also nice hits from this album, as is the melodic track 'Velvet Morning.' To sum up this album in a word I would say 'moody,' and the front man, Richard Ashcroft, finally erupts cathartically on 'Come On,' before 'Deep Freeze' calms us back down, ambient style, complete with the obligatory crying baby.

6.67) New Boots And Panties!! - Ian Dury & The Blockheads (1977)

Yes, two exclamation marks. How indulgent is that? There was a poster of this stereotypical Essex boy on the wall at my primary school, presumably because of his example of achieving success in spite of having polio. I doubt the teachers had listened to a lot of his lyrics, and the expletive-intensive opening to 'Plaistow Patricia' would have got that poster ripped down in seconds I'm sure. This is one of the three punk-style tracks at the end of the album, of which 'Blackmail Man' has the most deranged sounding vocal. The rest of the album is more subtle, with tracks like 'My Old Man,' a genuinely sad song Ian wrote in tribute to his father, and 'Sweet Gene Vincent.' There are characters like 'Billericay Dickie' and 'Clever Trevor' and I find the whole album very enjoyable, although the two friends that I go camping with are not convinced when I put it on as a campfire classic. Naturally this makes me play it all the more!

6.68) The Studio Albums Collection CD 9 - Ian Dury & The Blockheads (2014)

I'm including this disc from a box set here as I had most of the tracks from it as bonus tracks on 'New Boots...' and 'Do It Yourself' (1979), which I never really rated as an album, as it seemed to lack the rawness and accessibility of the band's debut. In addition to those bonus tracks there's 'You'll See Glimpses,' but not 'Superman's Big Sister' as this melodic hit was included on their third album. You'll hear the disco influenced hits like 'Hit Me With Your Rhythm Stick' and 'Reasons To Be Cheerful (Part 3)' which seems to satirise the trend at the time for rock bands to record songs in multiple parts. 'What A Waste' and 'Sex And Drugs And Rock And Roll' are both essential, and 'England's Glory' seemed to predict Chas & Dave's 'That's What I Like' with its list of things that Ian regards as quintessentially English.

6.69) The Very Best Of Supertramp – Supertramp (1990)

You'll come for the hits and stay for the extras. I don't need to say much about tracks like 'The Logical Song,' 'Breakfast In America,' 'Dreamer' and 'It's Raining Again,' but it's not just about the electric piano – the band could really rock too, as demonstrated on tracks like 'Bloody Well Right' and 'Ain't Nobody But Me.' The longer coda to 'Goodbye Stranger' lets the guitar solo take the song to another level compared to what you hear on the radio. The best song of all is 'Rudy,' with an energised 'question and answer' session between the two vocalists and some sadness as the central character's train journey ultimately leads nowhere. Just listen to the desperation in that final vocal note.

6.70) The Very Best Of 10cc – 10cc (1997)

Another top notch British band creating finely crafted pop hits in the seventies. The order is chronological (yay!) so you can hear their progression from glam rock into the etherealism of 'I'm Not In Love' and the middle section of 'Art For Art's Sake' to the reggae of 'Dreadlock Holiday.' 'I'm Mandy Fly Me' reminds me of 'Band On The Run' by Wings with its distinctive segments, while 'Life Is A Minestrone' with its 'chain of thought' lyrics seems to convey something about the bittersweet nature of life. I particularly like the line 'I'm like a gourmet in a skid row diner.' 'Silly Love' is also great fun and the lyrics are consistently clever and amusing. Also included are some later tracks from Godley & Crème, and 'Neanderthal Man,' which was released in the Neanderthal days of several of the band's members when they went under the name 'Hotlegs.'

6.71) Ken Burns Jazz: Miles Davis – Miles Davis (2000)

Miles Davis would be an artist who I would appreciate much more ten years after buying this compilation, which provides a great overview of the legendary trumpeter's varied career from the late forties all the way to the eighties. The thirteen-minute track *Walkin'* rolls along like a runaway train, while 'Générique' is all atmosphere, bringing to mind the disconsolate wandering of city streets at night. 'So What' from 'Kind Of Blue' is of course included, and on 'My Funny Valentine' you can hear the band's mood switch from despair to joy at around the three-minute mark. There's a representative sample of the fusion of 'Bitches Brew,' which combined jazz improvisation with rock instruments, and to finish 'Tutu' is a sample of what the man was up to in the eighties.

6.72) The Best Of BBC TV's Themes – Various Artists (1987)

When I was a child I often used to tape the theme tunes to television programmes. It made a change from recording the music from the test card, and if you listen to this BBC collection you'll see that they weren't half bad either, for example, the dramatic opening of 'Mastermind' which is known as 'Approaching Menace' and still in use today, and the semi-psychedelic 'Doctor Who' theme. A lot of the tunes have sections that you never got to hear on TV. Did you know that the music to 'Eastenders' has a honky-tonk pub piano section? Or that the sparse strings on the 'Fawlty Towers' music play the tune at a variety of tempos? George Fenton was a big name in TV and film music at the time, and his 'Bergerac' music stands alone even without the lens of nostalgia. 'Peg Of My Heart' reworks a 1940s hit evocatively on accordion and harmonica for the surreal drama series 'The Singing Detective,' while Bach is reimagined for 'Ski Sunday.' Forgotten gems for sure.

6.73) Hard To Find 45s On CD Volume II – Various Artists (1996)

When I was a child I used love the music of the sixties so much that I wondered why things ever moved on. I guess this album answers my question. It's entertaining, it's very enjoyable and it's melodic, but I suppose if it was all there ever was things would soon get boring. This collection covers the years 1961-1964 and I bought it to complete my number ones of 1964 with 'Diane' by the Irish group, the Bachelors. This was still a popular request on the radio when I was a child in the eighties, as was 'The Wedding Song' by Julie Rogers. 'Dominique' by the Singing Nun is a track I remember from my father's reel to reel tapes as a child. The Caravelles hit 'You Don't Have To Be A Baby To Cry' has some nice female harmonies, and Diane Renay's 'Navy Blue' is very pleasant too.

ii) Heavy Fuel

6.74) Red Hot Chili Peppers - Red Hot Chili Peppers (1984)

It was a long time before I appreciated the early Chili Peppers albums for the musical dexterity contained within. The band's penchant in the early days for wearing the minimum clothing required to prevent arrest meant a delay of nigh on twenty years for me to try them out, just proving that one person's idea of 'cool' is another person's idea of 'idiotic.'

So this was the Californian group's first album. The funk influence is clear right from the start. Anthony Kiedis raps in his own distinctive style. There are some more sobering moments occasionally, with 'Green Heaven' expressing frustration at issues which sadly haven't gone away and a minor / major alternation that seems to contrast the hell of how things are with the heaven that a more ethical approach could bring about. 'Mommy, Where's Daddy?' is a quirky number with some acoustic funk guitar and even some saxophone, and the album concludes with a moody instrumental called 'Grand Pappy Du Plenty.' 'You Always Sing The Same' is eighteen seconds of insanity by the way.

6.75) Freaky Styley - Red Hot Chili Peppers (1985)

The foursome upped the funk on this their second album, drafting in renowned producer, George Clinton. We get some brass adornments to a few of the tracks, although the title track is a psychedelic instrumental with an expletive filled chant fading in as though the band are marching towards you and it's probably best to run! There are controversial lyrics elsewhere too, particularly on 'Sex Rap,' which shows an adolescent side of the Chilis that I never really appreciated. 'Thirty Dirty Birds' replicates the inclusion of a microscopic track *a la* their first album and 'Yertle The Turtle' is both funny and funky.

6.76) The Uplift Mo-Fo Party Plan - Red Hot Chili Peppers (1987)

Adolescent tastes are catered for with the 'special secret track' and to a certain extent by 'Love Trilogy.' The titular 'plan' is mentioned in several of the tracks so there's a kind of party theme going on. It is enjoyable overall, being very funky and sometimes punky. 'Behind The Sun' is a rare mellow moment where you can hear some actual singing. Imagine that! There's a cover of Dylan's 'Subterranean Homesick Blues,' and 'Skinny Sweaty Man' is as crazy as Zappa. 'Walking Down The Road' has a great rhythm and the musicianship is remarkable throughout.

6.77) Mother's Milk - Red Hot Chili Peppers (1989)

The band were on the verge of hitting the big time with this album, which contains a cover of 'Fire' by the Jimi Hendrix Experience which seems to be played at double speed. 'Good Time Boys' includes snippets of other people's songs, perhaps satirising the trend for sampling which was *de rigueur* at the time. The speed of Flea's bass playing on 'Nobody Weird Like Me' is not of this world and the track has a psychedelic feel which is repeated on 'Johnny, Kick A Hole In The Sky.' Not bad for the young yobbo who goads Marty in the 'Back To The Future' films, hey? 'Pretty Little Ditty' is the instrumental track this time and it is exactly what the title suggests, providing a break in the unhinged energy found elsewhere.

The line up changed on this album with Chad Smith taking over from Jack Irons on drums and John Frusciante filling the void created when guitarist Hillel Slovak passed on. There were other members on the first two albums but let's move on before we get bogged down.

6.78) Blood Sugar Sex Magik - Red Hot Chili Peppers (1991)

Behind all the antics the Chilis had a moral indignation at society's norms which bands like Rage Against The Machine would take to the nth degree. So we open with 'Power Of Equality.' The band have matured with acoustic introspective tracks like 'Breaking The Girl' and the sublime 'Under The Bridge,' a song expressing loneliness. Some folk viewed it as sacrilege when the girl band All Saints covered the song, taking it to number one in the UK in 1998, though I doubt the Chilis had any objection to the royalties. 'Suck My Kiss' and 'Give It Away' combine funk and rock to perfection, and 'Sir Psycho Sexy' opens as a lyrically backward step towards adolescence but develops into a mellotron-driven psychedelic instrumental. 'They're Red Hot' updates a Robert Johnson song with respect and humour in equal measure, and the title track has a blistering guitar solo going on beneath the vocals towards the end.

6.79) One Hot Minute - Red Hot Chili Peppers (1995)

This was a dark album for a band that had mostly looked on the bright side of life until this point. Guitarist John Frusciante left and was replaced by Dave Navarro who gave the band a brief heavier sound. 'Warped' has a furious energy and phased vocal, while 'Aeroplane' drafts in a children's chorus in spite of the colourful lyrics sung by Kiedis. The value of friendship within the band is a common theme illustrated in the semi-acoustic 'My Friends.' Funk fans are catered for with the philosophical ditty 'Walkabout,' and the final track feels like being trapped inside a pressure cooker until sheer fury bursts out with a rage which is only matched by another Californian band with 'rage' in their name. It's a bold statement but this might just be the band's best album.

6.80) Californication - Red Hot Chili Peppers (1999)

John Frusciante was back, and this was the transitional album that pointed the way to the more laid back sound of later years. The title track is now a rock classic with its weary take on the California dream. 'Parallel Universe' has a pulsating bassline and it whips itself into a frenzy with effects reminiscent of Hawkwind. Meanwhile 'Porcelain' is a quieter offering which sounds stylistically similar to Blur's 'Miss America.' There's a little bit of funk and a mellow final track too.

6.81) By The Way – Red Hot Chili Peppers (2002)

I initially bought all the singles rather than the album, but as the B-sides included some of the album tracks it gets a listing at this point. With guitarist John Frusciante's influence the Chilis were drifting towards easy listening at times, with the fire, funk and fury now mostly departed. The boys had also discovered the joys of wearing clothes. It was a good move; fabric is cool, whereas *not* wearing it is flipping freezing! The songs here are melodic and enjoyable and there's a glimpse of the old Chilis in the title track, with Anthony Kiedis rapping the verses over a fast bassline from the ever-fluent Flea and pounding drums from Chad Smith, but it is just a glimpse. I recall going to a masked ball (no, not like the one in 'Eyes Wide Shut') and a local chap known as 'Geordie Bill' jumped up on the stage and performed a robotic dance to this track, casually sitting down as though nothing had ever happened at the end. I guess when the Chilis were on fire they had this effect on people.

'Can't Stop' also reprises the funkier style of vocal, while 'Universally Speaking' has a great melody. 'The Zephyr Song' was also a big hit, but my money is on the plodding 'Don't Forget Me,' which has some great guitar effects. Harmonies are to the fore, and savouring this like a fine wine, later tracks such as 'Venice Queen' give me notes of the Beatles and just a hint of Pink Floyd. However, if you listen to an album like 'One Hot Minute' immediately afterwards you'll realise that the emotional kick is absent, and just to illustrate how 'easy listening' the Chilis had become, one of the B-sides was a straightforward cover of 'A Teenager In Love' by Dion & The Belmonts.

6.82) American Idiot – Green Day (2004)

I was never big into Green Day but we did cover three of their songs in our Soaring Phoenix pub band – 'Basket Case,' 'Good Riddance (Time Of Your Life)' and 'Holiday' which is on this album. I liked the political overtones here, which seem pointedly directed at George W. Bush and his controversial 'War on Terror.' No one even imagined that the USA would vote itself even further into controversy two presidents later. The title track sets the tone with lines like 'One nation controlled by the media.' 'Wake Me Up When September Ends' is an epic ballad and there are two nine-minute tracks on the album with contrasting sections.

The band seemed to come of age here, although it lost them a few of their older fans.

6.83) Black Sabbath – Black Sabbath (1970)

The invention of heavy metal was a pure accident. Tony Iommi lost the tips of two of his fingers in an industrial accident which resulted in the playing style that we know and love. The ominous rain and tolling bell which opens the album launches Ozzy Osbourne onto the world stage, with his tortured shout of 'Oh no no, please God help me!' being an iconic moment. This titular track changes gear towards the end – something that would be a trademark of the band. The evidence that the group emerged from the British blues boom of the late sixties can be heard with the use of harmonica on 'The Wizard' which has a fantastic riff. The ten-minute track 'The Warning' further demonstrates the musical ability of Messrs Iommi, Ward and Butler. As if you needed proof!

6.84) Paranoid – Black Sabbath (1970)

Imagine a singles chart where it is possible for Black Sabbath to have a number four hit. Well, that was the world in 1970 and 'Paranoid' was actually a last minute addition to the album. For all the furore about the band being in league with the dark one, 'War Pigs' expresses anti-war sentiments which only somebody with a sense of human empathy would be able to write. Those war pigs are still manipulating, and people are still voting for them. 'Planet Caravan' provides a quiet breathing space, with Ozzy's voice processed for ambience. This is all pretty essential stuff from 'Iron Man' to 'Fairies Wear Boots,' another multi-rhythm affair.

6.85) Master Of Reality – Black Sabbath (1971)

It's pretty obvious that Ozzy is singing about something you're not legally allowed to smoke in 'Sweet Leaf,' but what a riff! Two short instrumentals and the track 'Solitude' provide the quieter moments this time around. The latter even has a flute. Meanwhile tracks like 'After Forever' and 'Lord Of This World' demonstrate that the band's perceived fixation with Beelzebub was perhaps more about the struggle between good and evil. It's a shame, as these knee-jerk reactions prevent a lot of people from experiencing a lot of very good music. I was one such specimen for many years. I recall a boy at my secondary school lending me a Black Sabbath album and being very reluctant to play it for fear of consigning my soul to eternal damnation by instant lightning bolt! To quote Pearl Jam (coming soon), 'I'm still alive.' More to the point, so is Ozzy!

6.86) Nevermind – Nirvana (1991)

I recall hearing 'Smells Like Teen Spirit' in the boss's van when I was window cleaning as a teenager and thinking 'What a bleeding racket!' It would take fifteen years and the near-total demise of guitar bands for me to realise what a classic it was. But no sooner has Kurt Cobain yelled his lungs out by repeating 'a denial,' than the excellent riff of 'In Bloom' comes crashing in. Behind the overdriven sound, these songs are actually very melodic. Dave Grohl's drumming is superlative throughout and Krist Novoselic's bass, which is seldom mentioned, holds it all together. 'Just because you're paranoid / Don't mean they're not after you' is one of the best lines of all time in my opinion, and the album closes sombrely with Kurt recounting his experience of homelessness in 'Something In The Way.' There are great harmonies too and just listen to the defiance in the 'I'm not gonna crack' refrain of 'Lithium.' Sadly Kurt eventually did crack and the world lost a lot of potentially great music.

6.87) In Utero – Nirvana (1993)

Kurt's vocal on the opening track, 'Serve The Servants,' perhaps sums up his feelings about performing, while sounding a bit like Liam Gallagher before anyone knew who the Manchester boy was. The most well known tracks are 'Heart Shaped Box' and the blissful 'All Apologies' with its mesmerising harmonic coda. 'Dumb' is a more laid back moment, although a few of the tracks like 'Tourette's' are a bit too extreme for my own taste. Was this the final gasp of the demon trying to get out of Cobain's mind before it consumed him. Who knows?

6.88) Incesticide – Nirvana (1992)

This is a collection of B-sides and other archival material from the Seattle band and it starts off very well, with a collection of punky grunge tracks which still retain distinctive melodies. Not all of them are written by Cobain / Nirvana, such as 'Turnaround' which looks at the ugliness of human behaviour at all levels of society. As Kurt intones, 'It's pretty scary.' 'Sliver' is an unusual tale of childhood, but the second half of the album seems to go a bit off the rails for me. I prefer to listen to the EPs Nirvana released ('Blew,' 'Hormoaning' and 'Sliver') which contain the best tracks from this album.

6.89) MTV Unplugged In New York – Nirvana (1994)

The 'MTV Unplugged' series was a great innovation as it enabled us to see what bands like Nirvana could achieve acoustically. Their choice of cover songs is interesting, with David Bowie's 'The Man Who Sold The World' occupying the same disc as Leadbelly's 'Where Did You Sleep Last Night,' which has a vocal delivery that seemed to reveal Kurt's desperate state of mind. The cover of 'Plateau' by the Meat Puppets is also very nice. Don't forget your illustrated book about birds, Kurt.

I'm afraid I can't really review Nirvana's debut album 'Bleach' (1989). Whilst 'About A Girl' stands out as a good song, the rest of the album is on the 'tried it once' pile for me. Sorry gents.

6.90) Ten – Pearl Jam (1991)

Pearl Jam were the other big rock band to emerge from Seattle at the beginning of the 1990s and their first album was so good that subsequent work has been somewhat overlooked. Eddie Vedder's vocals were more growly at this stage, and all the songs feel like little stories, 'Jeremy' being a prime example. 'Alive' is one of the highlights with its triumphant repeated statement of 'I'm still alive' and a blistering guitar solo from Mike McCready. In fact I wish he'd done more solos, as he can play the guitar like he was ringing a bell to paraphrase Chuck Berry. 'Black' is another great song, and 'Release,' which closes the album, is 'two tracks in one,' providing a kind of wind-down after the experience, so to speak.

6.91) Vs – Pearl Jam (1993)

Another confident set from the Seattle rockers. I like the pounding toms and indignant vocals of 'W.M.A.' and the introspective closing track, 'Indifference,' which sounds like they've borrowed the organ from Dire Straits while intoning 'How much difference does it make?' Before we get to this we have the first of Pearl Jam's intense tracks in the form of 'Blood,' or should that be 'Blooooooood?' 'Rats' has an odd lyric in my opinion, with a bizarre metaphor concerning rodents defecating, while 'Leash' is a cry for freedom from control without any reference to critters or faeces!

6.92) Vitalogy – Pearl Jam (1994)

PJ began to experiment with this, their third album. They repeat the intensity of 'Blood' with 'Spin The Black Circle,' which is not really anything angsty but a homage to playing vinyl records. 'Not For You' has an ominous feel to it, while 'Nothingman' and 'Better Man' are both pensive numbers which have become live concert favourites. 'Bugs' is particularly strange with its clearly novice use of an accordion, but really it's just a warm up for 'Hey Foxymophandlemama, That's Me' which is a bonkers way to spend almost eight minutes listening to feedback and a clearly disturbed child talking about being attracted to mops. I'll leave it there...

6.93) No Code – Pearl Jam (1996)

The title of this album gives a clue to the varied content, but it feels more restrained than 'Vitalogy.' There's another all out aural assault *a la* 'Blood' and 'Spin The Black Circle' in the form of 'Lukin.' Answers on a postcard if you can understand a word of it. 'Present Tense' has a good message for humanity with its philosophy that life is better lived in the present. 'Smile' rocks nicely and introduces some harmonica, and best of all is the final track 'Around The Bend,' which is a country love song that summons up a similar feeling to the subsequent Kings Of Leon track 'Talihina Sky.'

6.94) Yield – Pearl Jam (1998)

I think by now you're used to what Pearl Jam do. My favourite song here is 'Do The Evolution' which satirises the macho 'F the environment' attitude which seems sadly quite prevalent in the USA. 'Untitled' is the wackiest song ever to include a steel drum, while 'Push Me, Pull Me' sounds like a psychedelic sonic experiment. Don't forget to hang on at the end of the album for the Eastern sounding hidden track. I hate to say it but Pearl Jam's albums seemed to get slightly less essential each time, although they all have their glorious moments, so I'm going to skip to a compilation to finish their section now.

6.95) Lost Dogs – Pearl Jam (2003)

So this is a double album of rarities and they certainly don't skimp when it comes to value for money, even giving us a hidden track at the end. I like the effect of the harmonies against the driving rhythm of the opening track, and Mike McCready is given a chance to shine unfettered on the guitar with the instrumental track 'Brother.' 'Dirty Frank' ends up a parody of Isaac Hayes' 'Theme From Shaft' if you hang on long enough, and 'Last Kiss' is a cover of a song about losing one's girlfriend in a car accident, which must have seemed pretty dark when initially released by Wayne Cochran in 1961. 'Gremmie Out Of Control' is a cover of a surf tune by the Silly Surfers (does what it says on the tin). However, the crown goes to 'Yellow Ledbetter,' which has a sobering feel, an unforgettable acoustic sounding riff and a succulent solo from good old Mike McCready. If you develop a taste for Mr. Vedder's more acoustic side, you can't go far wrong with the folky soundtrack to 'Into The Wild' (2007).

6.96) Greatest Hits – Guns N' Roses (2004)

Another band that I thought were noisy *so and sos* at the time of their peak popularity that I now view as legendary. This was no doubt helped by the fact that the band eventually made it onto the BBC Radio 2 playlist, so I grew to appreciate Slash's virtuoso guitar conclusion to 'Paradise City' and the epic 'end of love' song 'November Rain,' which dies down only to surprise you with yet another iconic solo. Vocalist Axl Rose blasts his way through covers of Dylan's 'Knockin' On Heaven's Door' and Wings' 'Live And Let Die,' as well as a less well known cover of the Rolling Stones track 'Sympathy For The Devil.' 'Patience' is a nice acoustic moment, and 'Civil War' is an epic which sums things up in the line 'It feeds the rich and it buries the poor.' You see, all these rockers had hearts of gold really.

6.97) The Best Of Extreme: An Accidental Collocation Of Atoms? – Extreme (1998)

My first experience of Extreme was hearing 'Get The Funk Out' on BBC TV's 'Top Of The Pops,' and I thought 'What a flaming row!' Then soon afterwards they released 'More Than Words,' an acoustic ballad with harmonies that sounded like the Everly Brothers. It bemused me that this was the same band. When my sister and her husband chose the track for the first dance at their wedding in 2008 I thought I'd give Extreme another chance. I'm glad I did. The heavy funk tracks are infectious, but it is indeed the gentler material like 'Tragic Comic' and 'Hole Hearted' that stick in the mind. These American boys certainly had a good ear for melody as well as the furious energy they employ on the heavier tracks.

6.98) Rage Against The Machine – Rage Against The Machine (1992)

When a friend who I nicknamed 'Death Metal Dan' lent me this album in the nineties I could tell it was different to his usual fare, but it took a Christmas number one in 2009 for me to properly check it out. This was when the band's track 'Killing In The Name' was bought *en masse* in protest at the festive chart domination by 'X Factor' contestants. I also remember the expletive-ridden song being played unedited, no doubt by mistake, on the top forty chart rundown on the radio in early 1993, and the presenter didn't even bat an eyelid.

So what of the content? Well, this is not so much heavy metal as heavy funk. Zac de la Rocha's vocals are more akin to the early Red Hot Chili Peppers than Pantera and pals, and the indignation at society's norms just builds and builds, with a venom not seen since John Lennon's 'Plastic Ono Band' album in 1970. 'Wake Up' even closed the blockbuster film 'The Matrix.' It's a shame society didn't wake up, as people misdirected their anger at each other rather than at the greedy and powerful, which of course was what they were supposed to do. Other opinions are available, but certainly not on this album (or in this book!).

6.99) Renegades – Rage Against The Machine (2000)

This is an interesting oddity, being an album of covers done in RATM's inimitable style, and the choices are pretty varied to say the least. The best of the bunch for me are Bruce Springsteen's 'The Ghost Of Tom Joad' (what a riff) and Cypress Hill's 'How I Could Just Kill A Man.' The Rolling Stones and Bob Dylan are duly honoured here and Zac de la Rocha gives Devo's 'Beautiful World' the full 'pathos' of a broken man. Conversely, the cover of Minor Threat's 'In My Eyes' possesses a level of anger few have reached. Ever.

This kind of heavy riffing has become more commercial of late and bands like Brighton's 'Royal Blood' are well worth a listen.

6.100) How To Make Friends And Influence People – Terrorvision (1994)

My old friend 'Death Metal Dan' had a tape copy of this album, and although I borrowed it from him in '94, I wasn't yet able to fully appreciate it, but believe me, it's really quite melodic. Listen to the doo-wop backing vocals on 'Oblivion' or the tuneful ballad 'Middleman.' 'Pretend Best Friend' is also good fun with its frenetic rapped vocals, and there's still 'Alice, What's The Matter' to go.

Although this was the only Terrorvision album I really got to know, the singles 'Tequila' (the original 'album' version is a B-side) and 'Perseverance' are both great songs. Terrorvision were ahead of their time really.

6.101) Origin Of Symmetry – Muse (2001)

Overlap alert: Muse was a band I got into in the early days of knowing my future wife, but let's keep all the noisy boys together in this chapter.

I made one of those schoolboy errors with Muse, dismissing them as a 'Radiohead copy' band purely because lead singer Matt Bellamy's falsetto vocal style has some similarities to that of Thom Yorke. It was when I heard the melodic riff of 'Plug In Baby' being performed by a local band containing my camping buddies Jim and Dan that I thought perhaps I should check them out. The vocal is typical of the high drama Matt Bellamy infuses into the material, and virtually every track on this, the second album from the Devon band, sounds like it could have been a hit single. My favourite is the laid back 'Screenager,' with its blissful picked guitar run bringing things back down to earth after each falsetto chorus. And finally, don't forget to unleash the church organ on the final track, boys. Leave a coin in the plate on your way out!

6.102) Absolution – Muse (2003)

Bellamy declares 'This is the end of the world' on 'Apocalypse Please.' Well, you might as well open with a bold statement after all. It's always nice when there's a bit of contrast on a Muse album though, and the quiet sections of 'Time Is Running Out' provide this, along with a great melody. In contrast, 'Stockholm Syndrome' is pretty much heavy metal. It's clear which end of the political spectrum the band's sympathies lie and I wonder if they were hinting that people have developed an unhealthy sympathy for the elite who yank their strings. And just in case the sound isn't big enough, why not throw in an orchestra on 'Butterflies & Hurricanes' as well as some brilliant piano playing that sounds like Chopin has joined the band?

6.103) Black Holes & Revelations – Muse (2006)

This time around the album opens with Matt gleefully declaring 'You'll burn in Hell for your sins,' seemingly at the world's leaders. Did they predict the economic collapse that was to follow with lines like 'Our freedom's consuming itself?' Who knows? We then plunge into the more radio friendly rhythm of 'Starlight,' and the bluesy 'Supermassive Black Hole.' The pivotal moment of 'Knights Of Cydonia' is when the descending guitar line leads from the intro into the pulsating rhythm of the song itself. A segue within a song – now that's the kind of thing I like!

6.104) The Resistance – Muse (2009)

With Muse's anti-establishment songs selling by the proverbial ton all around the world, how was it possible that global society has become ever more right wing and insular? Maybe people are too busy tapping their toes and humming the melodies to spot the message. Seriously, listen to 'The Uprising' and take it from there. This album contains some different instrumental techniques, such as the plucked strings on 'Undisclosed Desires.' 'United States Of Eurasia' expresses a desire for unity across the continent while managing to sound like Queen before collapsing into a lonely piano recital of Chopin's 'Nocturne In E Flat Major' which is bliss in itself. 'I Belong To You' sounds like a long lost 10cc track, or is it just the French lyrics that remind me of *Une Nuit A Paris*?'

6.105) The 2nd Law – Muse (2012)

This seemed to be the peak of the Devon band's boundary-pushing before reverting to the 'safer' rock style that they master so well. 'Supremacy' sounds like the band were aiming for inclusion in a Bond film with the spy theme being referenced by the strings. 'Madness' has a lo-fi feel and an economic guitar solo, reminding me of U2. Some of this album sounds like Queen, and while the guitar and synth sounds are more varied, there is a definite melodic structure that says 'Muse' all over it. After the half way point there is less bombast, until the ending takes us into 'dubstep' territory whilst delivering the message that an economy based on endless growth is unsustainable. It took our leaders forty years to realise that global warming needs dealing with, so I wonder how long it will take them to realise that this pearl of wisdom is not a joke either. As ever, our rock stars are ahead of the curve.

iii) Girls Aloud

6.106) Back To Black – Amy Winehouse (2006)

In 2008 I began a new hobby of cycling around different areas of Southern England, camping in woods, which enabled me to be completely free to go wherever I jolly well liked. And save money on hotel rooms! Back on that first trip I heard this album playing in a pub on Hayling Island, Hampshire, and I was duly impressed with the sixties style vocals and instrumentation. Prior to this I'd heard 'Rehab' on the radio and I had initially thought that it was a song from the sixties that I'd never heard before. As if such a thing existed!

Let's just say that Amy doesn't hold back, singing about drugs and peppering her lyrics with the vernacular, yet in spite of this, there is a desperate sadness here which is reminiscent of artists like Billie Holiday. If you don't believe me, the title track should confirm this straight away. 'Love Is A Losing Game' is also melancholy in feel. The deluxe edition has a second CD of cover songs, also very enjoyable. My favourite cover of Amy's wasn't released until after her death however, this being 'Our Time Will Come,' which prompts fond memories for me of the early days of knowing my future wife, in spite of the sadness that Amy had already left this mortal plane.

6.107) Alright, Still – Lily Allen (2006)

'Smile' was a UK number one single, and at the time it was something of a novelty to hear Lily's down to earth London accent on a pop song. Her debut album incorporates a ska style. 'LDN' is lyrically interesting and notably rhymes 'Tesco' with 'al fresco,' while 'Alfie' is a song about her little brother which starts off sounding like Sandy Shaw's 1967 Eurovision winning hit 'Puppet On A String.' Like Amy Winehouse, Lily doesn't mince her words. Her style changed dramatically as time went on, and although Lily's next two albums netted her a number one single each, her third album 'Sheezus' (2014) is not to my taste and the title reviews itself for me. 'Alright, Still' on the other hand was a refreshingly different debut. Her cover of 'Oh My God' by the Kaiser Chiefs is also worth seeking out.

6.108) Born To Die – Lana Del Rey (2012)

Lana's stripped back piano ballad 'Video Games' received regular airplay at the time of its release and has a haunting quality to it, perhaps partly due to its unusual chord sequence. My initial reaction to the album was that it all sounded quite similar with its big production and atmosphere of decadence. I hoped for a simple song with an acoustic guitar to break up the denseness. In hindsight, it remains an enigmatic debut, with a fixation on death, which can also be said of Bob Dylan's first album, and some very memorable songs like 'Diet Mountain Dew.' Her deep voice sounds like it is emanating from a much older person, with occasional breaks into a higher register. 'Off To The Races' demonstrates both.

6.109) The Whole Story – Kate Bush (1986)

There used to be a rumour going round that Kate Bush grew up in my home village in Kent which I do not believe to be true, although it's a great story. She actually grew up in Welling which is firmly within Greater London, although it would have been in Kent in centuries past. For this compilation Kate re-recorded her number one hit 'Wuthering Heights.' 'Army Dreamers' is a great anti-war song, which perhaps needs greater airplay in this era when war seems to be increasingly glorified. 'Babooshka' is an interesting story adorned with breaking glass, which is always good (well, Nick Lowe thought so, didn't he?). 'The Man With The Child In His Eyes' is another great song from Kate's teenage songbook. The only glaring omissions from the era that this compilation covers seem to be 'Them Heavy People' and 'Hammer Horror,' both firm favourites of mine. If you seek out the EPs, 'On Stage' and the second '4 Successos' release, you'll have these tunes, but it's cheaper just to buy the albums they're on.

6.110) Tapestry – Carole King (1971)

Carole King and Don McLean both released completely different albums called 'Tapestry,' although Mr. McLean got in first, releasing his in 1970. Carole had written many well known hits of the early 1960s including 'Will You Love Me Tomorrow' with her first husband Gerry Goffin, a song she performs herself on this album. The double A-sided single of 'It's Too Late' and 'I Feel The Earth Move' combined two of her best ever songs and it may come as a surprise to learn that King also penned 'You've Got A Friend' which was made famous by James Taylor. '(You Make Me Feel Like) A Natural Woman' was another big hit from Carole's pen, also included here.

6.111) The Very Best Of Nina Simone – Nina Simone (2006)

'My Baby Just Cares For Me,' with its famous descending piano motif was a surprise UK number five hit almost thirty years after its initial release. There are two versions of 'Ain't Got No, I Got Life' here, the latter version being a remix similar in style to the JXL remix of Elvis Presley's 'A Little Less Conversation.' 'Mr. Bojangles' has a nice harmony and then there's the ten-minute epic 'Sinner Man' which famously closes David Lynch's bewildering film 'Inland Empire.'

6.112) All-Time Greatest Hits, Volume 1 – Peggy Lee (1990)

Peggy Lee's biggest songs used to be regularly requested on BBC Radio Kent when I was a child, and although 'The Folks Who Live On The Hill' isn't on this album, most of the biggies are, including of course 'Fever.' 'Mañana' is good fun and a track that I play whenever I go anywhere remotely Spanish. 'I'm A Woman' has a bluesy feel, and best of all 'Is That All There Is?' expresses a deep disillusionment rarely heard in popular songs as she ticks off everything from the circus to love as being profound disappointments. These last two songs were written by Leiber and Stoller, who wrote many of the hits of the late fifties and early sixties, but Peggy Lee certainly made them her own.

6.113) Your Mamma Won't Like Me – Suzi Quatro (1975)

This album marked a change in style from the earlier rock and roll influenced tracks that netted Suzi her two UK number ones in the early seventies ('Can The Can' and 'Devil Gate Drive'). I was given this album on vinyl as a 'hand me down' as a child and decided to revisit it some thirty plus years later. I wasn't disappointed. Both the title track and 'I Bit Off More That I Can Chew' have a jazz / funk feel, 'Paralysed' seems slightly punky, there's a cover of 'Fever' (see Peggy Lee above), and 'Michael' has a country feel. My favourite track always was, and still is, 'Prisoner Of Your Imagination,' with its interesting structure and lightly psychological subject matter. I purchased this album as a double reissue with 'Aggro-Phobia' (1976).

6.114) Aggro-Phobia – Suzi Quatro (1976)

The playing on the cover of 'Heartbreak Hotel' sounds like a hybrid of 'Framed' by the Sensational Alex Harvey Band and 'Ain't Nobody But Me' by Supertramp. And that's a very good thing indeed. There's a fairly straight cover of 'Make Me Smile (Come Up And See Me)' by Steve Harley & Cockney Rebel and generally this album is a more rocky affair than 'Your Mamma Won't Like Me,' with tracks like 'Tear Me Apart' leading the way. Suzi's vocals, as always, are distinctively raw and slightly husky.

Chapter 7 – The Wedding Present

In this chapter I will look at albums that I discovered both before and after my wedding at the age of forty in 2015. I had met my other 'nought point five' at a barbecue in London, and a brief chat revealed that there was at last somebody who liked the Beatles as much as I did. I didn't think such a thing was scientifically or statistically possible, and from here on we began visiting Liverpool on a regular basis, with the Mecca of the Cavern Club drawing us back time and time again. In one year, we actually visited the city four times. Not a big deal if you live in Chester; quite a big deal if you live in deepest darkest Kent. Or Russia.

As Katrina lived in Moscow it wasn't practical to continue this distance relationship *ad infinitum* with the amount of travel involved so we decided to bite the bullet and get married, and we managed to put together an entire playlist of music that we both liked for the wedding reception. With nine syllables less to her name, she then moved to England and we attempted all that settling down 'cosy home' stuff. Music was always important though, with us attending stage shows like 'Let It Be' and 'We Will Rock You,' as well the odd Tchaikovsky ballet, giving us myriad excuses to travel to London and feast our ears.

This period in my musical odyssey will include a lot of albums that both Katrina and my future father-in-law, Vladimir, sent my way, especially from Paul McCartney and Queen. I also filled in some of the gaps within my collection, topping up my Bob Dylan, ELO, Lou Reed, King Crimson and David Bowie, almost to the brim. But of all of these it is perhaps the early post-Beatles albums of Paul McCartney that will be forever associated with that time of courting for me, as we often listened to these while sitting contentedly together on a tube train travelling to the Travelodge hotel at Heathrow, a frequent stop-over before the sad farewell after each visit.

We marked my fortieth birthday with a musical pilgrimage to the now-derelict London pub pictured on the Kinks' 'Muswell Hillbillies' album, and following David Bowie's death in early 2016 we visited his childhood home in Brixton, as well as Heddon Street, the location of his 'Ziggy Stardust' album cover. Of course we'd already done the Beatles Mecca of Abbey Road, and Berwick Street which appears on the '(What's The Story) Morning Glory?' cover by Oasis. We'd also popped into Cambridge for a look at Grantchester Meadows, which provided the title of a Pink Floyd song. Anyway, this is a book of album reviews, not a tourism guide, so let's crack on...

7.1) The Very Best Of Prince – Prince (2001)

Prince gets the honour of opening this section for reasons I shall explain. As regular visitors to Liverpool, Katrina and I got to see a band of superb musicians in the Cavern Pub (opposite the Cavern Club) many times. I was even more amazed when after several visits it was pointed out that the lead guitarist was playing his impressive solos with a hook. One track that I'd never really appreciated until then was the Prince classic 'Purple Rain,' which now always reminds me of those blissful early days. Naturally, a 'greatest hits of Prince' album seemed in order, although there are a few glaring omissions on this one, such as the potty-mouthed 'Sexy MF' and his only UK number one, 'The Most Beautiful Girl In The World.'

Prince was a bit like Bob Dylan in that other artists often had bigger hits with his compositions, so we have Prince's crazed vocal instead of 'smoothie' Tom Jones on 'Kiss,' It's a shame that we don't get a Prince rendition of 'Nothing Compares 2 U' which gave Sinéad O'Connor her only UK number one. 'Sign Of The Times' is a song with a social conscience, 'Alphabet Street' is very catchy, and it all gets very funky towards the end of the disc. However, 'Purple Rain' definitely towers over all for me, and here it is presented as it should be - in its full-length splendour.

7.2) McCartney – Paul McCartney (1970)

This is quite possibly my favourite album of McCartney's solo material. Bizarrely, it wasn't appreciated at the time of its release in spite of the fact that Paul plays every instrument on the album, pretty much inventing the genre of lo-fi DIY production. The songs are extremely melodic and seem to reflect the fact that Paul was dealing with depression following the break up of the Beatles, seeking solace in a quiet life with his first wife, Linda. The romantic vibes were in perfect sync with my own life at the time I discovered this album; 'Man We Was Lonely,' 'That Would Be Something' and 'Every Night' encapsulate the feel perfectly. The most well known song here is probably 'Maybe I'm Amazed,' a rousing piano ballad that was later released as a live single by Wings. The album contains a few Beatles leftovers like 'Teddy Boy' and 'Junk' and personally I think the critics of the time needed to open their ears a bit.

7.3) Ram – Paul And Linda McCartney (1971)

More early gold from McCartney's epic solo career, this time with Linda in tow, and without being mean I would say that her vocals are less of an acquired taste than Yoko Ono's. The romantic vibes continue with 'Long Haired Lady' and 'The Back Seat Of My Car.' I have no idea why 'Uncle Albert / Admiral Halsey' is sometimes slated, as I find it a very evocative song, and it was even used in an episode of the classic BBC comedy 'Only Fools And Horses.' 'Too Many People' was perceived as a dig at John Lennon at the time and 'Ram On' has a bittersweet feel. It seems that Paul was struggling with his emotions in this era, and if he *was* letting off steam it was pretty heavily veiled in my opinion. Personally I can't really imagine him taking potshots like today's celebrities often do, so three cheers for our greatest living British composer!

7.4) Wild Life – Paul McCartney / Wings (1971)

This was the first Wings album and it was a very low-key start. This isn't helped by the fact that the first two tracks have nonsense lyrics and the third is a cover of 'Love Is Strange,' which had been recorded by Buddy Holly and provided a minor hit for the Everly Brothers. Paul finally steps up to the hotplate when we get to the title track which is an impassioned plea to respect nature. Sadly it's fifty years later and we still haven't listened. 'Dear Friend' seems like an attempt at reconciliation with John Lennon after their recent musical slanging match which culminated with Lennon's truly vicious track, 'How Do You Sleep?' If you get the version with the bonus tracks this album is improved further with McCartney's banned single, 'Give Ireland Back To The Irish,' and his Mickey-taking follow up, 'Mary Had A Little Lamb,' the joke being that these were lyrics that were suitable for airplay on BBC radio.

7.5) Red Rose Speedway – Paul McCartney / Wings (1973)

Another inconspicuous early Wings release that didn't really set the world on fire. 'My Love' is a sumptuous ballad with lush strings, perhaps the McCartney that most people know and love, but the rest of the album sounds like he's just having fun. 'Single Pigeon' brings to mind sitting on a bench disconsolately watching a bird pecking around on the ground. Surely you've done that at least once in your life? I have! 'Loup (First Indian On The Moon)' is an instrumental in a similar vein to 'Kreen-Akrore' on McCartney's first solo album. The eleven-minute medley that concludes the album hinted that Paul still hadn't lost the knack, with the 'Hands Of Love' section being particularly melodic with a nice harmony from his wife, Linda.

7.6) New – Paul McCartney (2013)

Paul returned to a Beatles-esque composing style for this album, which includes the rocking 'Queenie Eye,' a track reprising the 'O-U-T spells out' lyric from the Beatles' 'Christmas Time (Is Here Again).' 'New' opens with a harpsichord sound and is a tuneful celebration of new relationships. The mention of a girl in a magazine from the West Sussex city of Chichester in 'On My Way To Work' always amuses me, but then I suppose Paul had given Scarborough and Walthamstow a moment in the limelight in his 1979 hit 'Old Siam, Sir,' so why not?

7.7) George Harrison – Wonderwall Music (1968)

George Harrison had contributed three songs to the Beatles catalogue with all-Indian instrumentation, and he was also the first Beatle to release a solo album, which was the rather unappetising 'Electronic Sounds.' This album, the follow up, is very listenable however. We are treated to a range of Indian instrumentals, broken up with some quirky tunes like 'Drilling A Home,' which sounds suspiciously as if one of the mellotron demos has been used. If you just wish he'd play some guitar, there's a track called 'Ski-ing.' 'Dream Scene' is a surreal mash up which will appeal to fans of 'Revolution 9.' There are some, I'm sure. None of the tracks outstays its welcome and there are nineteen of them. However, looking at the average price of this album online, one would still struggle to use the phrase 'value for money.' Darn those capitalist Western ways!

7.8) Queen – Queen (1973)

One of the most versatile rock bands ever produced on Earth began very much in the style of Led Zeppelin. The Brian May-penned 'Keep Yourself Alive' opens one of the most distinguished careers in history and was the group's first single. 'Modern Times Rock 'N' Roll' sounds like a lost Black Sabbath track, with drummer Roger Taylor handling his own composition vocally. Similarly Sabbath-esque is the grungy 'Son And Daughter.' There's a tantalising minute-long instrumental version of 'Seven Seas Of Rhye' to close the album.

7.9) Queen II – Queen (1974)

Ah cool, some Roman numerals again. Now that's how you name an album! 'Father To Son' ends with an early example of the kind of singalong chorus that the band would become known for. 'The Loser In The End' has a great rhythmic feel to it, and it is another song penned and sung by Roger Taylor. I never really got what the 'white side' and 'black side' concept was all about, but it's a good album and we get the 'proper' version of 'Seven Seas Of Rhye' at the end, complete with its 'Oh I do like to be beside the seaside' finish. Great things were coming...

7.10) Sheer Heart Attack – Queen (1974)

Uh-oh, what happened to 'Queen III?' Just as I was expecting a good run of Roman numerals as well! It seems that Chicago will forever hold the crown in this department, having eventually reached 'Chicago XXXVI' in 2014. That is serious dedication to numerals. Either that or a lack of imagination when it comes to titles.

Anyway, 'Sheer Heart Attack.' If you need a few hits to hang on to like a lamppost in a storm there's 'Killer Queen' and 'Now I'm Here,' but more importantly this is the album where the band demonstrated that they were masters of pretty much any musical style they attempted. 'Brighton Rock' sees Brian May left alone to doodle on the guitar for a considerable length of time, which is no bad thing. The harmonies on the coda of 'In The Lap Of The Gods' are blissful, and the boys go all 'twenties' on us with 'Bring Back That Leroy Brown' (clue: I'm not talking about the 2020s). However the standout tracks for me are the last two, 'She Makes Me' and 'In The Lap Of The Gods... Revisited.' The latter song is melodic to the core and the endlessly circling coda can only end one way – by exploding in a crack of thunder. It seems that God answered back.

7.11) News Of The World – Queen (1977)

After the twin albums of 'A Night At The Opera' and 'A Day At The Races,' there was a new kid in town – punk. Queen collectively decided 'if you can't beat 'em, join 'em' and stripped down their sound, opening with one of the most famous rhythms of all time. They would have had no idea that eventually an entire musical dedicated to their work would be named after this song. It is of course 'We Will Rock You.' Released as a double A-side with 'We Are The Champions' you would have expected a UK number one, but the charts and the public are funny. 'Sheer Heart Attack' is a full blown punk parody. The band also pre-empt the disco flavour of some of their later hits with the cheeky 'Get Down, Make Love.' Brian May gets to perform a bluesy vocal on 'Sleeping On The Sidewalk' and Freddie tries his hand at jazz with 'My Melancholy Blues.' Is there nothing this band couldn't do? That's rhetorical by the way.

7.12) Jazz – Queen (1978)

Don't be deceived by the title, this ain't jazz! 'Fat Bottomed Girls' and 'Bicycle Race' formed another double A-side, both containing lyrics that reference the flip side. 'Fun It' is a disco-oriented prototype of 'Another One Bites The Dust,' and the perennial favourite 'Don't Stop Me Now' is here too. 'More Of That Jazz' serves as a résumé of 'Jazz,' with clips of a lot of the album's songs included, which is great for reviewers like me wishing to quickly remind themselves of the contents.

7.13) The Game – Queen (1980)

A lot of the bands from the sixties and seventies didn't adapt well to the sounds and styles of the eighties, whereas Queen not only lapped it up but pretty much led the way. 'Dragon Attack' sets the scene for bassist John Deacon's anti-war hit 'Another One Bites The Dust,' with the rhythm section of Taylor and Deacon to the fore. 'Play The Game' and 'Save Me' are archetypal Queen hits, while 'Crazy Little Thing Called Love' is a fifties pastiche, located somewhere between Showaddywaddy and Shakin' Stevens. 'Don't Try Suicide' is the catchiest song you'll ever hear about this topic, as well as good advice. If you shuffle off this mortal coil you'll miss out on a load more great Queen albums for a start. I'm not sure 'Nobody gives a damn' has quite the required level of empathy to save a life mind you!

7.14) Hot Space – Queen (1982)

Glossing over the 'Flash Gordon' soundtrack, the band's next regular album was this, with a new 'eighties' poppy sound presenting a challenge to listeners and causing some disagreement within the band. That said, Brian May still gets some superlative guitar work onto the album, for example on 'Dancer.' 'Life Is Real (Song For Lennon)' has a more traditional Queen sound and was a nice tribute to the recently deceased Beatle with a chord sequence that could have been written by John himself. File this one alongside Paul Simon's 'The Late Great Johnny Ace' and Bob Dylan's 'Roll On John.' The album finishes with 'Under Pressure,' the group's collaboration with David Bowie that scored them their second UK number one in 1981.

7.15) The Works – Queen (1984)

This was the comeback album that set Queen on a trajectory to become national treasures. Here they combined the pop and rock aesthetics perfectly for hits like 'Radio Ga Ga,' a song written by Roger Taylor, which laments the demise of radio in a similar vein to the Buggles song 'Video Killed The Radio Star.' Thankfully, this didn't really happen and radio laments the loss of Queen instead. 'I Want To Break Free' follows a twelve-bar pattern in spite of its slick production, and the fact that it was written by bassist John Deacon sometimes surprises even more than the video of Freddie in a skirt pushing a Hoover. 'Man On The Prowl' is getting into 'Shakin' Stevens' territory, while 'Hammer To Fall' really rocks. My favourite track here is the extremely melodic 'It's A Hard Life,' which begins dramatically and reminds me of those aforementioned train journeys down to Heathrow Airport, although lyrically it was perhaps a warning that living together has its challenges. There's even enough sobriety for a thoughtful acoustic moment to conclude the album.

7.16) A Kind Of Magic – Queen (1986)

Queen were riding the second wave of success, reinvigorated by their legendary performance at Live Aid. The contribution of drummer Roger Taylor to the band's discography shouldn't be underestimated; the title track was another one of his. Meanwhile 'One Vision' furthers the band's idealism lyrically, until one reaches the line about fried chicken at least! I remember on the day that the Berlin Wall came down in 1989 we were called into a small theatre room at school and shown images from the news with this track playing. It's such a shame we are back in another cold war now. 'Friends Will Be Friends' is a melodic rock song similar to 'It's A Hard Life,' and 'Who Wants To Live Forever' is extra poignant now considering Freddie's early death, even though it was written by Brian May. The band also rock out more than ever on 'Princes Of The Universe' and 'Gimme The Prize,' which must have the most self-congratulatory lyric since Don McLean's 'Everybody Loves Me, Baby.'

7.17) The Miracle – Queen (1989)

This is an album loaded with singles, of which the plucked string sound and dramatic melody of the title track stand out. Freddie dreams of 'Peace on earth / An end to war' but admits 'It's a miracle we need.' We still need it in the 2020s. The rhythm-change three minutes of the way through 'I Want It All' is reminiscent of Black Sabbath, while 'Khashoggi's Ship' has a touch of Led Zeppelin about it. Best of all is the final track, 'Was It All Worth It,' which has a fantastic guitar riff while Freddie weighs up the pros and cons of the rock star life, concluding 'It was a worthwhile experience.' Brian May excels with his guitar solo as usual, and it all ends up very symphonic, even shoehorning a musical reference to 'Death On Two Legs' into the mix.

7.18) Innuendo – Queen (1991)

The title track was a multiple-rhythm affair, similar to 'Bohemian Rhapsody,' with a flamenco middle section bookended by two slabs of mighty rock. The band were rewarded with their third UK number one. 'These Are The Days Of Our Lives' is a sublime ballad which ended up as a double A-side with 'Bohemian Rhapsody,' which topped the charts again after Freddie's death. Some of the songs on the second half of the album seem fairly lightweight, but they rock it right up with 'The Hitman' and they were clearly mustering up for the finale which is one of the best songs of all time - 'The Show Must Go On.' It's even more surprising to learn that it was mostly Brian May and not Freddie Mercury who wrote it.

7.19) Made In Heaven – Queen (1995)

This was Freddie Mercury's parting gift to the world, having recorded as many vocals as possible before he died with the hope of the band completing the tracks. This was perhaps the most pertinent 'goodbye' album, at least until David Bowie's 'Blackstar' (2016). The title track here is a very positive reflection upon life in the 'what will be will be' vein, while the Taylor-penned 'Heaven For Everyone' laments the fact that the world falls far short of most people's idea of what it could be. I have often wondered as to whether this is because narcissists and psychopaths, whose desires are purely selfish, are more attracted to positions of power than the other 95%. Feel free to discuss after class! 'Too Much Love Will Kill You' is another 'Queen hit by numbers,' but at the end, the band's shortest track (a four-second exclamation of 'yeah') precedes the band's longest track – 22 minutes of ambience called '13.' Unlike the final track on Pulp's 1998 album, 'This Is Hardcore,' which attempts something similar, this actually seems to work.

Freddie has left the building.

7.20) Muswell Hillbillies – The Kinks (1971)

The Kinks' 'Arthur' album of 1969 has never been far from my CD player, but just a couple of years later came this little-known classic. The songs are something of a catalogue of disorders, dealing with alcoholism, anorexia and anxiety (and we haven't even got to 'B' yet), but the subjects are always dealt with humorously, and Ray Davies even recommends a good old fashioned cure for all – 'have a cup of tea!' A folky feel pervades, and sadly the pub that appears on the album cover is now in a state of disrepair. The opening track sums it up; it starts quietly, when Mick Avory's drums kick in they never sounded better, and then it builds to Ray's deranged shout of 'I'm a 20th century man but I don't wanna be here.' Brilliant!

7.21) Everybody's In Show-Biz – The Kinks (1972)

This is a double album a bit like Pink Floyd's 'Ummagumma,' in that the first CD is a studio album and the second CD is a live album. CD1 deals with fame and life in a band. 'Celluloid Heroes' reflects on the loneliness of Hollywood legends in spite of all the glitz and glamour, and the theme of eating crops up a lot with 'Motorway Food' and 'Hot Potatoes.' 'Supersonic Rocket Ship' was even a minor chart hit and quintessential Kinks. The live album is tremendous fun, with Ray just letting the audience get on with it when it comes to 'Lola' and a fair bit of goofing around between the classics. Their previous album 'Muswell Hillbillies' is well represented and this was actually the first time I heard absolute rippers like 'Alcohol,' 'Skin And Bone' and 'Acute Paranoia Schizophrenia Blues.'

Ray Davies really was a songwriting legend, and with the advent of the Kinks-themed musical 'Sunny Afternoon,' which my wife and I watched at the Marlowe Theatre in Canterbury, he may at last be getting some of the recognition he deserves. Have no doubt, Johnny Rogan's biography of the man ('Ray Davies: A Complicated Life') is not pretty reading, but I think Ray has redeemed himself in song for sure.

7.22) Soap Opera – The Kinks (1975)

Sorry folks, I'm not going to review the Leviathan that is 'Preservation Act Parts 1-3,' simply because parts two and three left me cold. Maybe it's too much to take in, maybe I'll eat my words when I'm 57, who knows? So, we move on to Ray Davies' next theatrical project, 'Soap Opera,' which depicts an ordinary man swapping lives with a rock star. The conundrum as to whether or not the life of fame and fortune was something Ray Davies actually wanted had no doubt entered his mind at this stage. As Bob Dylan once sang 'It's either fortune or fame / You can pick one or the other, though neither of them are to be what they claim.' 'Soap Opera' presents a range of styles from the raucous 'Ducks On The Wall' to the vaudevillian 'Holiday Romance' which is actually kind of sad. 'You Can't Stop The Music' is a fitting conclusion.

7.23) Schoolboys In Disgrace – The Kinks (1975)

This was yet another one of Ray Davies' concept projects but one that appealed to his younger brother Dave no doubt, as the tale of teenage pregnancy was something he could relate to and he was allowed to let rip with the guitar solos too. The Kinks rock out in the most obvious way since their early hits like 'You Really Got Me.' 'I'm In Disgrace' is a prime example of this. The album seems to give us not just one but two endings, with 'The Last Assembly' concluding the tale of school life and then 'No More Looking Back' seeming as though Ray is shaking himself out of his reverie and declaring that he has to move on. 'Jack The Idiot Dunce' is also very funny with its collection of childhood insults.

7.24) The Electric Light Orchestra – Electric Light Orchestra (1971)

This was the genesis of a legendary band which had a dual career as the Move at the time. '10538 Overture' is a track you will recognise, with its drop-bass guitar pattern and scratchy cellos. The band had two main composers at the time, Roy Wood and Jeff Lynne. 'Look At Me Now' is typically 'Roy Wood' and has no rock instruments at all, while 'Mr. Radio' is typical of the symphonic Mr. Lynne. '1st Movement' is a nice ditty combining picked acoustic guitar and strings, in a similar vein to the Mason Williams hit 'Classical Gas.' This album has sometimes been compared to chamber music and I wonder what ELO's career would have been like if Roy Wood had stayed longer.

7.25) ELO 2 – Electric Light Orchestra (1973)

With Roy Wood off to have a 'Wizzard' time elsewhere, Jeff Lynne steered the Brummie band into the waters of prog rock with plenty of guitar riffing in the opening track. 'Momma / Mama' is a gentler moment, well, a gentler seven minutes in fact. With no track significantly under seven minutes, you only get five songs this time around, and the full eight minutes of 'Roll Over Beethoven' is a rocking romp which even incorporates a bit of Beethoven's fifth symphony into Chuck Berry's classic song.

7.26) On The Third Day – Electric Light Orchestra (1973)

The title was almost 'ELO 3' I guess – it has a reference to the number at least. This time you may recognise the rocking 'Ma-Ma-Ma-Belle,' and 'Showdown' which has a strong rhythm and some nice harmonies on the 'It's raining all over the world' lines. The composer Grieg gets the ELO treatment with the closing track, 'In The Hall Of The Mountain King,' which was also covered by The Who and the Wombles. It's just a great tune and I even shoe-horned it into my own composition, 'Parallel Universe' – as Jack Nicholson says in 'The Shining,' 'Go, check it out!' 'Oh No Not Susan' is typical of the later melodic style of ELO and it is the only instance I can think of where Jeff Lynne used an expletive in song. I guess he tried it once and decided he didn't like it!

This album was followed by 'Eldorado' (1974) and 'Face The Music' (1975) but it was on the next release that things really stepped up a gear.

7.27) A New World Record – Electric Light Orchestra (1976)

I remember receiving ELO's back catalogue from my father-in-law and trying this one out in the car while driving to the little town of Heathfield in Sussex to cycle a disused railway line. With its epic orchestral opening to 'Tightrope' it felt like I was off for a trek round the Amazon rainforest! Indeed, this was the first of four regular albums that set the bar so high that the critics of the eighties dismissed ELO altogether (see the ELO reviews in Chapter 5 for the other three 'whoppers'). Sadly I think it will only be when Jeff Lynne shuffles off this mortal coil that the masses will realise just how good his compositions were. Classic follows classic - 'Telephone Line.' 'Rockaria,' 'Livin' Thing,' you know these songs! 'Mission (A World Record)' is a futuristic song with a melancholy tone; 'Who are you and who am I? / How's life on earth?' Meanwhile 'Shangri-La,' which closes the album, repeats the emotional punch and name-drops the band's heroes in creating the idiom 'Fading like the Beatles on *Hey Jude.*' I might start using that myself!

7.28) Xanadu (Soundtrack) – Olivia Newton-John And The Electric Light Orchestra [Various Artists] (1980)

I've never seen the film and I probably won't bother judging by the reviews, but the soundtrack album is great. ELO provide contrasting moods. 'Don't Walk Away' encapsulates their 'lonely' style and 'All Over The World' is a melodic rock / disco crossover. The title track, which features both ELO and ONJ, was a UK number one single, but it wasn't the first song with 'Xanadu' in its title to top the charts. That honour went to Dave Dee, Dozy, Beaky, Mick & Tich in 1968. It's clearly a good strategy to get the X-word in somewhere anyway. Newton-John's tracks are pretty varied too, with the rock / forties jazz pastiche of 'Dancin',' which features the Tubes, standing out among the mellower tracks which sound perfect for couples who fancy a slow dance at the end of the night. She also performs with both Cliff Richard and Gene Kelly. You'd never guess that Olivia was in between getting 'greasy' with John Travolta and getting 'physical' in the eighties.

7.29) Secret Messages – Electric Light Orchestra (1983)

This offering can seem a bit weak after the previous album, 'Time,' but once you get used to the crisp 'eighties' sound there is much to enjoy. The title track opens in an upbeat style, before 'Loser Gone Wild' gives us alternating verse and chorus rhythms as well as a wandering trumpet sound. Some of the tracks are quite strange, such as 'Letter From Spain,' but there are two top notch rockers in the form of 'Four Little Diamonds' and 'Rock And Roll Is King.' After two more albums it would be a long wait for Jeff Lynne's next 'ELO' release, but as you're reading a book, you only have to cast your eyes on to the next paragraph.

7.30) Alone In The Universe – Jeff Lynne's ELO (2015)

This album brings to mind an eventful trip my wife and I made to Bath, as we listened to it on the long drive home. 'When I Was A Boy' has a characteristic drop-bass sequence while expressing nostalgia for a time when radio was king and 'there was no money.' The album is a very melodic affair from beginning to end, and a few tracks remind me of Roy Orbison, which is praise indeed. The harmonies are perhaps the best sign that this is at least connected with ELO in some way. 'All My Life' is another great song, as is the title track. If you get the Japanese edition you get three good bonus tracks too but do you really want to travel 'all over the world?' Boom boom.

7.31) Everything At Once – Travis (2016)

Travis singles were always pretty reliable, but I tended to lose interest in their albums after 'The Invisible Band,' so for me this seemed like a kind of a comeback album. The singles received plenty of airplay on BBC Radio 2, and according to Wikipedia there were eight of them (sorry about the pun, but is this a record?). Anyway, I duly bought the album and was well pleased. 'Magnificent Time' even sounds like a comeback song. The title '3 Miles High' sounds like a respectful nod to the Byrds who preferred a loftier altitude, but for me the best song is 'Idlewild' where front-man Fran Healy sings the fast-paced lyrics in perfect sync with Josephine Oniyama.

7.32) All Summer Long – Beach Boys (1964)

An album that starts with 'I Get Around' and 'All Summer Long' can't really go wrong, can it? With the band's fascination with cars now abundantly clear, it's not surprising that there's a song about a motorbike on here in the form of 'Little Honda' (was that a product placement?). 'Girls On The Beach' sees the boys return nostalgically to their original seaside subject matter, which for me always evokes memories of camping at Fairlight Cliffs in Sussex as a teenager. I guess I was the target age group and quite close to a beach at that time. 'Don't Back Down' has an unusual chord pattern, and there was an early sign of their experimentation with 'Our Favourite Recording Sessions' which shows them stuffing up and clowning around while recording the album. They'd already included a track like this on 'Shut Down Volume 2' (1964) called *"Cassius" Love Vs "Sonny" Wilson.*

Historians may want to dig back further, as the first four albums, 'Surfin' Safari' (1962), 'Surfin' U.S.A.' (1963), 'Surfer Girl' (1963), and 'Little Deuce Coupe' (1963), are all pleasant and show the development of the band, although the constant theme of cars on the last of these does get a bit much. If you're wondering what happened to 'Shut Down Volume 1' this was a 'various artists' compilation of car songs.

7.33) The Beach Boys Today! – Beach Boys (1965)

I always enjoyed 'When I Grow Up To Be A Man,' although it's not so comfortable to be right off the scale when they count off the years into early adulthood at the end. 'Don't Hurt My Little Sister' is a nice song with a nice sentiment, and rockers will be satiated with 'Do You Wanna Dance?' and 'Dance, Dance, Dance.' It's the second half of the album that showed the direction that the band were to head to on 'Pet Sounds,' with succulent harmonies elucidating innocent dreams on 'I'm So Young.' It is with some surprise that one encounters the slightly dissonant ending to the brilliant 'In The Back Of My Mind.' Just like the Beatles five months later, they didn't want to end on a 'weepie,' but whereas the Beatles followed 'Yesterday' with the rocker 'Dizzy Miss Lizzy,' the Beach Boys included a track of themselves chatting and munching junk food, the third of their 'fly on the wall' tracks. For this brief moment the California boys were even ahead of people like Frank Zappa whose whole career would pretty much adopt this approach.

7.34) Summer Days (And Summer Nights!!) – Beach Boys (1965)

The double exclamation mark is not a sign of me getting excited, it's part of the title. Some reviewers cite this album as a backward step before the 'two steps forward' of 'Pet Sounds.' I just think it's an enjoyable album. The boys celebrate the American dream of being young with tracks like 'Amusement Parks U.S.A.' and 'Salt Lake City.' 'You're So Good To Me' is a stomper with added passion, and 'Girl Don't Tell Me' comes across like a conscious effort to sound like the Beatles. There's humour too, and 'I'm Bugged At My Old Man' is Brian Wilson's poke at his father who had a lot of control over the group. And then there's those succulent harmonies on 'And Your Dream Comes True.'

If you get this album as a 'two for one' CD with 'Today!' you'll be treated to some bonus tracks too, of which 'The Little Girl I Once Knew' evocatively recalls the changes of growing up.

7.35) Beach Boys' Party! – Beach Boys (1965)

This should be viewed as a bit of fun rather than a serious marker of the band's progression. The group fake a party atmosphere for the entire album – imagine them strumming acoustic guitars at a barbecue. They cover no less than three Beatles songs as well as Dylan's *The Times They Are A-Changin'*. In a self-deprecating move they play their own hits 'I Get Around' and 'Little Deuce Coupe' in a comedic style. The 'almost nonsense' songs of 'Hully Gully' and 'Alley Oop' are high points and the closing track is the full-length version of 'Barbara Ann,' with the all-important messing around after the radio edit fades. In spite of the fun, the 'acoustic jam' album was yet another concept seemingly invented by Brian Wilson's ingenious group.

7.36) Friends – Beach Boys (1968)

After 'Pet Sounds' and Brian Wilson's creative burnout with the 'Smile' project, the group went to India, along with the Beatles and Donovan, to learn transcendental meditation. This was the album that resulted and it certainly has a very relaxed feel to it, although the songs are often staggeringly short. 'Friends' itself is an innocent teenage tale ('Let's be friends') with nice harmonies, while 'Anna Lee, The Healer' is also very nice and pronounced 'Ahna Lee.' 'Diamond Head' is an instrumental with a Hawaiian feel and is perhaps the album's high point with its overdubbed lapping waves. The album closes with 'Transcendental Meditation,' just in case you didn't know what they'd been up to.

7.37) 20/20 – Beach Boys (1969)

The Beach Boys' popularity waned as the sixties closed, with a barbed comment from Jimi Hendrix, and the Beatles song 'Back In The USSR' being a thinly-veiled Mickey-take of the group. However, fashion is flippant and this album demonstrates that they were still churning out quality, with no less than four UK top ten hits (five if you include the bonus track, 'Break Away'). Admittedly the single version of 'Cotton Fields' was overdubbed with steel guitar. 'Do It Again' gave the group their second UK number one hit (after 'Good Vibrations') and the electric guitar solo on 'Bluebirds Over The Mountain' is phenomenal. 'All I Want To Do' really rocks, and the instrumental 'The Nearest Faraway Place' sounds like a long lost 'Pet Sounds' track. The album ends with two leftovers from the 'Smile' project, which it goes without saying are fabulous.

7.38) Singles As & Bs... Plus - Small Faces (1990)

For many years I was content with 'The Immediate Record Collection' box set which contained a compilation album called 'The Autumn Stone' containing all the greatest hits and more. However, the two albums I am going to review here expand upon this collection comprehensively. This 'See For Miles' disc contains all the A-sides first and then all the B-sides, so we start off with guitar-based rhythm and blues / mod rock and venture twice into psychedelia. I remember hearing 'Itchycoo Park' from those Marble Arch compilations of sixties hits as a child and thinking 'What is he doing with his voice?' when the phasing kicks in. The early heavy rock of 'All Or Nothing' (1966) was the band's only UK number one single, and tracks like 'Sha La La La Lee' are very catchy. 'The Universal' was recorded as a demo, complete with a barking dog in the background, but it was turned into a melodic single which seems to reject the counterculture of the time. 'I Feel Much Better' is one of the best B-sides, although it does have one of those annoying 'fade out and back in' endings which were popular at the time.

As an aside I recall waking early one morning when wild-camping in a small woodland next to the canal at Market Harborough (*a la* my book 'Stair-Rods & Stars'). I was listening to this collection on my iPod and drifting back to sleep, only to wake up again to find a man with a rifle scouting the wood with a small child. I laid very still and tucked my head into the sleeping bag, using the bizarre logic that if I couldn't see him he couldn't see me. It worked thankfully, and I'm still here to write this review.

7.39) In Memoriam – Small Faces (1969)

This was a 'bits and pieces' album with a live side and a studio side, released when vocalist Steve Marriott had moved on to cook up some Humble Pie. The screams of the audience on the live half are pretty intense and when things die down for an impassioned rendition of 'Every Little Bit Hurts' it is with some sense of relief. The studio tracks were intended for an album that never was. 'The Autumn Stone' is a nice mellow song adorned with a flute and 'Red Balloon' is not to be confused with the Dave Clark Five song of the same name.

7.40) Grrr! CD2 – Rolling Stones (2012)

I'm not going to review CD1 as if you have all the sixties albums and 'The Singles Collection: The London Years' you will already possess all the necessary hits – you know, 'Satisfaction,' 'The Last Time,' 'Paint It Black,' etc. For many years I had the 'Jump Back' compilation for the best of the seventies and eighties but this 2012 release updates the selection further. I don't really need to justify the merit of seventies classics like 'It's Only Rock 'N' Roll' and 'Angie,' but the eighties were a strange period where perhaps the most memorable single after 'Start Me Up' was a cover of Bob & Earl's 'Harlem Shuffle.' However, the 'new' track, 'Doom And Gloom,' takes the prize for me. It's one of those 'lyrical deluge' songs which pretty much summed up the news in 2012 with lines like 'Lost all the treasure in an overseas war / It just goes to show you don't get what you paid for.' The song even mentions the controversial 'fracking' method of fuel extraction. Whoever said that the Stones were dinosaurs clearly got it wrong.

7.41) I Was Made To Love Her: The Collection – Stevie Wonder (2011)

If you want an overview of Stevie's sixties output, look no further than this Spectrum Music compilation. 'I Was Made To Love Her' and 'For Once In my Life' are Motown classics, and his harmonica hit 'Fingertips, Part 2' topped the USA chart when he was just thirteen. The standout tracks for me are the succulent ballads, 'My Cherie Amour' and 'Yester-Me, Yester-You, Yester-Day.'

7.42) In The Wake Of Poseidon – King Crimson (1970)

This was the follow-up to 'In The Court Of The Crimson King,' following the same format, albeit with added links all called 'Peace.' The opening track is pretty much 'Twentieth Century Schizoid Man' by numbers, with its 'sax and guitar' riff loosely based on the twelve-bar sequence. 'Cadence And Cascade' fills in for 'I Talk To The Trees,' and the mellotron wash of the title track has echoes of 'The Court Of The Crimson King.' 'Cat Food' has some nice jazz piano chords and 'The Devil's Triangle' is an attempt to simulate the feel of Holst's 'Jupiter' from 'The Planets' without copying the melody, or *any* melody! It sounds like I'm being critical, so just to clarify, the album is brilliant.

7.43) Lizard – King Crimson (1970)

This was the nearest King Crimson got to fusion, that fascinating mix of rock and jazz that united musicians from both genres in the early seventies. 'Indoor Games' is catchy, with a deranged laugh to conclude the affair. There's an interesting synth effect on 'Happy Family,' and 'Lady Of The Dancing Water' is a sweetly-sung melodic love song with plenty of flute. The second half of the album is a suite in four parts with oodles of trumpet, mellotron, major / minor key switches, and the odd bit of discordance – all the things we love about King Crimson.

7.44) Islands – King Crimson (1971)

I used to regularly get three-hour paid breaks at work, and while this may sound like heaven, I couldn't go home and consequently I had a lot of time to fill. A good strategy was to put my earphones in and stroll some of the local paths, and that's precisely what this album reminds me of, as I stomped off up the track-bed of the former Elham Valley railway line trying to make sense of this transitional work. You see, it doesn't really sound like the group's first three albums, and neither does it sound like the three that followed. 'Sailor's Tale' has some aggressively jangly guitar which seems to use chords as a method of soloing, before building up to one almighty racket. 'Ladies Of The Road' is the nearest you'll get to straight up rock here, and it covers a topic that Frank Zappa often mused about. The eleven-minute title track which closes the album is very laid back and relaxed, peculiarly ending with the orchestral instruments tuning up and a count-in, almost implying that this should lead back into the first track, 'Formentera Lady,' making the album a continuous loop.

7.45) Starless And Bible Black – King Crimson (1974)

The title is a quote from 'Under Milk Wood' by Dylan Thomas, which is a great thing to reference. The music is trickier however and I find this the most difficult of King Crimson's first seven albums, as it's a bit of a hotch-potch of live recordings bolstered up with some studio tracks. 'The Great Deceiver' is a bit Zappa-esque in its frenetic execution, uncompromising lyrics and rhythm changes. The evidence of additional percussive effects on top of Bill Bruford's drumkit can be heard here, as well as on 'Larks' Tongues In Aspic' (where Jamie Muir provided the additions) and 'Red.' 'Trio' is a sweet instrumental and 'The Mincer' ends abruptly. Apparently the tape ran out and the band just liked the effect. Robert Fripp also plays some fiendish guitar in 'Fracture.'

7.46) Red – King Crimson (1974)

I completed my King Crimson collection up to the album 'Discipline' around this time, and 'Red' seems to be a standout release. The overdriven guitar sound dominates this work, which was a favourite of Nirvana's Kurt Cobain. The title track is an instrumental which uses the rising chord sequence beloved of KC. 'Providence' is the least melodic offering here and 'Red' is one of the best songs ever written, opening as a gentle mellotron-adorned ballad before breaking down for Robert Fripp to build a stunning guitar solo from just a handful of notes, until the frenetic drums crash all around him. Epic stuff.

7.47) Discipline – King Crimson (1981)

After a hiatus, King Crimson returned with a new sound and an American vocalist, Adrian Belew. The album seems to be more in the style of 'Talking Heads' and the opening track sees Belew listing different types of talk alphabetically. 'Thela Hun Ginjeet' ends up more like a monologue, repeatedly declaring 'This is a dangerous place.' The sound is complex and frenetic throughout. Listen to the speed of the playing at the start of 'Frame By Frame' if you need evidence.

7.48) The Endless River – Pink Floyd (2015)

And so, we finally reach a stage where Pink Floyd's latest release can be filed under 'ambient.' This album was collated from instrumental tracks which were recorded at the time of 1994's 'The Division Bell' and the feel is very different to what we thought had been the band's swansong. In part, I think David Gilmour deliberately kept his guitar playing more subtle to allow bandmate Richard Wright to shine on the keys. The tracks take us through some of the sounds from previous albums, most notably the 'Saucerful Of Secrets' sounding track 'Skins.' There's a more pulsating rhythm on 'Allons-y' and you finally get some singing on the last track which amuses me in using the nineties expression to 'diss' someone, meaning 'disrespect.' All in all, it's just a bit too laid back to be the Floyd that *I* know and love. The cynical lyrics of Roger Waters are much missed, and I always wish Mr. Gilmour would really let rip on the guitar. The bonus track, 'Nervana,' partly satisfies this wish.

7.49) The Early Years – Pink Floyd (2016)

This is a monster of a box set which retailed at somewhere between £200 and £300 upon its release. Twenty years after the Beatles had given us the 'warts and all' experience of their 'Anthology' project, the band who were recording their first album at Abbey Road while said foursome were recording 'Sgt. Pepper' decided to follow suit, and like 'Anthology,' this is very much a 'curate's egg' experience.

The highlight is the concert of 'The Man & The Journey' from 1969, which I'd previously had as a bootleg album. The audience reactions create a great atmosphere as the band re-employ what were recent songs, especially from their 'More' album, to illustrate 'a day in the life' so to speak. The band sound like they're sawing up wood on stage in the 'Work' section, and the eccentric 'Teabreak,' where the band have a cup of tea on stage, is understandably edited here. It is great to hear tracks like 'Cymbaline' played in a more rocky style and this leads into the 'Nightmare' section which is abruptly terminated by an alarm bell heralding dawn. This really is good stuff, and the second half ('The Journey') is almost as good.

The John Peel session from 1970, which includes extended proggy versions of 'Fat Old Sun' and 'Embryo,' is also superlative, as is the first CD which takes us from their first tracks from 1965, recorded in a similar blues vein to early Rolling Stones material, up to previously unreleased psychedelia like 'Vegetable Man' and 'Scream Thy Last Scream,' teasing us with us a brief look at Syd Barrett's brain before it imploded.

Curious in its absence is 'Biding My Time,' presumably because they still want us to buy the 'Relics' compilation. Meanwhile 'Seabirds' is not the track you can hear in the background during a party sequence in the film 'More' – the title is actually erroneous. The studio version of 'Embryo' is nothing short of brilliant, making you almost nostalgic for a time none of us can remember. You will still need to buy 'Zabriskie Point' (coming later in this book), as the tracks in the box set are in addition to those on the 1970 soundtrack album. Great they are nevertheless.

Disappointing are the tuneless 'John Latham Versions 1-9' and the bonus disc which is of bootleg quality. If you're expecting a cleaned up version of 'Moonhead' or the pieces used in 'The Committee,' you're not going to get them. There is also a LOT of repetition. The capitals ARE justified.

7.50) Is It The Fifth? – Roger Waters (2010)

More to the point, is it even legal? The official 'greatest hits' package 'Flickering Flame' had a great title but was quite frankly bizarre in its selections. 'Is It The Fifth?' augments the studio albums much better, by gathering together all the excellent material that you'll struggle to find elsewhere. 'Get Back To Radio' is an atmospheric track that was missed off of 'Radio K.A.O.S.' and 'Hello (I Love You)' is nothing to do with the Doors song of the same name but a clear attempt to recall the glories of the past by referencing 'Comfortably Numb' with its line 'Is there anybody in there?' 'Leaving Beirut' is a twelve-minute monologue promoting tolerance, and also included is the entire 24 minute piece that Waters contributed to the soundtrack of Raymond Briggs' animated film 'When The Wind Blows.' Roger's crusade against war and brutality is undiluted, and the version of 'Lost Boys Calling' here is way better than the one on 'Flickering Flame.'

Pulling out my wish list, I would have added Roger's covers of 'We Shall Overcome' and 'Knockin' On Heaven's Door,' as well as the 'Live In Berlin' version of 'The Tide Is Turning' which is pretty awesome.

7.51) Is This The Life We Really Want? – Roger Waters (2017)

This was Waters' first proper rock album since 'Amused To Death' in 1992. The colourful language is more prominent this time around, but then I suppose he is exorcising fifteen more years of frustration at this unjust world. The title track opens with some speech from Donald Trump and really hammers home its sobering message about modern society with its brooding atmosphere and drooping strings. It's powerful stuff, *and* it contains the word 'nincompoop.' I think you can guess who he's referring to. The next track, 'Bird In A Gale,' compounds the feeling, and the tension briefly drops with 'The Most Beautiful Girl' before 'Smell The Roses,' which sounds like a long lost Pink Floyd track. The world needs more people like Rog to speak out against its power-crazed narcissists and psychopaths.

7.52) Knocked Out Loaded – Bob Dylan (1986)

When I first heard Bob's fourth eleven-minuter, 'Brownsville Girl,' on 'Greatest Hits Volume 3' (1994) I found it a bit dull compared to his first three songs that exceeded this duration. However, when experienced in the context of the album, it seems to shine, being stylistically different to the other material here. I actually like 'You Wanna Ramble' which seems to be getting into 'Shakin' Stevens' territory. 'They Killed Him' is a song about peaceful game-changers like Gandhi, Martin Luther King and Christ meeting tragic fates. However, 'Driftin' Too Far From The Shore' is a bit too 'eighties' sounding for me. I just don't think this kind of production is conducive to artists whose appeal is predominantly lyrical. That said the proof of the pudding is in the listening, and I tend to put this album on more often than 'Down In The Groove' (1988) or even 'Oh Mercy' (1989).

7.53) Tempest – Bob Dylan (2012)

For the latter part of Dylan's career I am just reviewing what I think are his masterworks. 'Duquesne Whistle,' which opens the album, seems to have a 1940s chord pattern and it's all very pleasant. He rocks a bit, he swears a bit, but then he scales things up for the trilogy of long songs that close the album. 'Tin Angel' reminds me of the traditional folk song 'Matty Groves' where an extra-marital affair results in the death of all three characters. 'Tempest,' Bob's third longest ever studio track, recounts the drama of James Cameron's film 'Titanic,' and 'Roll On John' is perhaps the most stirring tribute to John Lennon ever written.

7.54) Orchestral Favourites – Frank Zappa (1979)

Apologies to hardcore fans, but I'm not reviewing 'Sheik Yerbouti,' also from 1979, which contains one of Zappa's most famous but most puerile songs. 'Orchestral Favourites' is far more enjoyable in my opinion, and unlike Zappa's compositions on '200 Motels' (1971), most of the pieces here have actual melodies. Imagine that! 'Strictly Genteel' is the closing track on '200 Motels,' but it is the opener here, and more enjoyable without the operatic vocals about 'terrible English food,' etc. 'Duke Of Prunes' rearranges a track from the 1967 Mothers Of Invention album 'Absolutely Free' and contains a much welcome electric guitar solo. 'Bogus Pomp' is also enjoyable, sounding like an upgrade of 'Pedro's Dowry' from the 'Sleep Dirt' album. The other two tracks are hard work, but thankfully they don't run on too long.

7.55) Frank Zappa Meets The Mothers Of Prevention – Frank Zappa (1985)

It's back to the land of confusion for this one, as different versions were released in the USA and Europe. Fortunately the CD release combines both versions and it's an interesting mix. 'I Don't Even Care' is a genuinely funny song which seems to satirise the fashion for not giving a flying whatsit, while 'We're Turning Again' lambasts the hippie phenomenon in the spirit of 'We're Only In It For The Money,' although I do ask 'Was this really relevant in the 1980s?' What *was* relevant was Zappa's hearing with the Parents Music Resource Center [sic] who lobbied to restrict his controversial lyrics, and in typical 'Frank' style he chose to satirise snippets from the hearing in his track 'Porn Wars.' Freedom of speech was always a massive issue to Zappa and his boundary-pushing was a political act of defiance.

There are some instrumental pieces composed on the Synclavier too, an instrument which dominated the man's mid-eighties albums, including 'Francesco Zappa,' which sounds like a collection of electronic arrangements of Bach, and 'Jazz From Hell,' which takes the same approach but pretty much abandons the concept of melody. If you're longing for an impassioned guitar solo, stick with this album and wait for the second half of 'What's New In Baltimore.'

7.56) David Bowie / Space Oddity – David Bowie (1969)

This album spawned a monster single that eventually hit the top of the UK singles chart in 1975. Did it really take that long for most people to catch up with Bowie? The space theme ends there. 'Unwashed And Slightly Dazed' is long and bluesy, and 'Memory Of A Free Festival' seems to be inspired by the Beatles' 'Hey Jude,' with its lengthy repeated coda even replicating the same chord progression. The best song here is the nine-minute epic, 'Cygnet Committee,' which for me seems to postulate that the maxims of the hippie era were created by a committee, with lines like 'We can force you to be free.' Bowie gives the first awe inspiring vocal of his career, sounding like a possessed man delivering a broadcast. 'Cygnet Committee' is one of my three favourite Bowie songs along with 'Time' and 'All The Madmen.'

7.57) Diamond Dogs – David Bowie (1973)

After 'Aladdin Sane' came 'Pin Ups' (1973) which was an album of covers. 'Diamond Dogs' was a kind of concept album which took its inspiration from George Orwell's '1984,' although it was Bowie's version of dystopia. The rocking title track is a favourite of mine, and along with 'Rebel Rebel,' it's one of his final concessions to glam rock. The track '1984' seems to indicate the direction he was going, with a more rhythmic soul sound, and 'Rock And Roll With Me' is enjoyably melodic. There's plenty of saxophone on this album too.

7.58) Young Americans – David Bowie (1975)

To misquote Dylan 'something was happening and Mr. Jones *did* know what it was.' Bowie aka David Jones's next move was to embrace American soul styles, but the Beatles were clearly on his mind, with a cover of 'Across The Universe' and a reference to 'A Day In The Life' at the end of the title track ('I read the news today, oh boy'). There's even a duet with John Lennon on the funky ditty, 'Fame.' Tracks like 'Fascination' ditch the melodic approach, being almost entirely rhythmic. The version of the album with three bonus tracks is well worth getting for 'John, I'm Only Dancing (Again),' a reboot of one of his 'oldies' as a seven-minute disco track. I think it would have been interesting if Bowie had re-recorded the song every time he embraced a new style, but I guess John would have got tired and stopped dancing first.

7.59) Station To Station – David Bowie (1976)

Given Bowie's tendency to lose himself in his characters, the Thin White Duke was always a bit of a dodgy persona, being a slick-looking character with a bent towards fascism. However, the music from this era is top notch. The ten-minute opening track begins with the sound of a train and is the nearest clue to the Germanic sound David would embrace on 'Low.' 'Golden Years' and 'TVC15' were both hits and 'Word On A Wing' seems to be about prayer. 'Stay' uses the same chord pattern as 'John, I'm Only Dancing (Again),' and finally we have 'Wild Is The Wind' which I don't think counts as 'plastic soul' as it seems to be one of Bowie's most impassioned love songs.

7.60) Low – David Bowie (1977)

A highly acclaimed album and yet another new sound. This was the first of Bowie's 'Berlin trilogy' of albums ('Heroes' and 'Lodger' followed). The drums were often played faster and slowed down to create the crashing snare sound. 'Breaking Glass' was surely the inspiration for Nick Lowe's 'I Love The Sound Of Breaking Glass' on his excellent album 'Jesus Of Cool' (1978). 'Sound And Vision' was a hit single and structurally it reminds me of a lot of songs from the 1940s, running through the melody entirely as an instrumental before any vocals come in. The second side / half of the album is more challenging with Bowie hanging up his microphone and giving us lots of synthesiser ambience. You just have to let it lap over you. The tide is high but the album is...

7.61) Lodger – David Bowie (1979)

Observant listeners will immediately notice that the melodies of 'Fantastic Voyage' and 'Boys Keep Swinging' are identical. In fact, Bowie considered creating an entire album from this one melody. The former of these seems to be trying to say something deep, with lines like 'We're learning to live with somebody's depression' and 'I'll never say anything nice again / How could I?' Meanwhile, the latter could be filed next to the Spice Girls as 'boy power,' but are the lyrics ironic? The song 'DJ' declares 'I am what I play.' Perhaps Bowie was acknowledging his tendency to confuse himself and the characters he created. 'Look Back In Anger' implores us to do the opposite of what Noel Gallagher would encourage over fifteen years later, and domestic violence is touched upon in 'Repetition.' Not one of Bowie's most arresting albums, but OK.

7.62) Tonight - David Bowie (1984)

This is certainly not an album that springs to mind as classic Bowie, in fact initially I thought 'What on earth has happened to him?' However repeated listens make it more palatable and you can even overlook the eighties production. 'Loving The Alien' is actually a very good song, and it's quite novel to hear him having a go at reggae as well as covering a Beach Boys classic, a feat few would attempt. Most of the songs were written by Iggy Pop, but eventually you do appreciate this as much as Let's Dance, although 'Ziggy Stardust' it ain't!

As a footnote, there is a version of this album with three bonus tracks including 'Absolute Beginners.' However, stylistically these tracks don't seem to gel with the album. Personally I'd download the single of 'Absolute Beginners.' The full-length version is a tour de force *a la* Lets Dance, and there are two interesting B-sides too.

7.63) Tin Machine / Tin Machine II – Tin Machine [David Bowie] (1989 and 1991)

'Never Let Me Down' (1987) is an album I just can't listen to, so quite why the critics slammed Bowie's rock band, Tin Machine, I have no idea. Both of their albums are tremendously furious rock, which seemed to pre-empt the burgeoning grunge style. Listen to Reeves Gabrels' flamboyant guitar solo at the end of 'Heaven's In Here.' And that's just the opening track. Then there's Bowie's desperate sounding vocal at the end of 'I Can't Read,' which rivals Ozzy Osbourne's terrified 'Oh no no, please God help me!' in the song 'Black Sabbath' and indeed Bowie's own vocal on 'It's No Game' from 'Scary Monsters...' The second volume is less of a sonic assault, and it even contained a minor hit, 'You Belong In Rock 'N' Roll.' Two songs are sung by the drummer, Hunt Sales, and the bass player is his brother Tony Sales. Ah, how nice! But seriously, the cover to the second album is awful. Cover those statues for goodness sake!

7.64) Black Tie White Noise – David Bowie (1993)

'The Wedding' begins with church bells heralding in the next phase in this man's chameleon-like career. This album sounds very 'nineties' with its ever-present 'dancy' drumbeats. The cover of Cream's 'I Feel Free' is unexpected, and both the title track and 'Jump They Say' are memorable. 'Miracle Goodnight' is a catchy track too and there's a fair bit of saxophone on this album, which is always a plus point. After the sprawling epic '1. Outside' (1995) he'd go all 'drum and bass' with 'Earthling.' Jungle was massive.

7.65) Hours – David Bowie (1999)

The later albums of David Bowie were 'all over the place' in terms of sound to the point that some even left *me* behind, which is remarkable when even Lou Reed's 'Metal Machine Music' once made it into my collection! Fortunately 'Hours' has plenty of guitar, both acoustic and electric, so it's a thumbs up from me. The solo on 'What's Really Happening?' is reminiscent of Mick Ronson's work from the 'Ziggy' era. 'The Pretty Things Are Going To Hell' is full-on rock and surely a reference to Bowie's own 'Oh! You Pretty Things.' Is he saying that humanity is going to Hell? We're certainly working on it, it would seem. The Eastern-flavoured instrumental 'Brilliant Adventure' perhaps doffs a titular cap to 'Fantastic Voyage' while sounding nothing like it. The crunchy guitar stabs in the final track are very nice too.

7.66) Reality – David Bowie (2003)

'Heathen' (2002), which spawned the single 'Everyone Says Hi,' always seemed a bit bland to me, although the critics loved it, whereas 'Reality' seems to pick up where 'Hours' left off. We open with the pulsating rhythm of 'New Killer Star,' and the cover of 'Pablo Picasso' by the Modern Lovers is entertaining. 'Never Get Old' was not just a statement but pretty much how Bowie lived, and on 'The Loneliest Guy' he sounds like he really feels this way while denying it by singing 'I'm the luckiest guy.' There's a George Harrison cover and a nice jazzy / lounge finish to things. An underrated album.

7.67) The Next Day – David Bowie (2013)

I remember checking out this album on my iPod during a stress-busting day trip to walk around Arlington Reservoir in East Sussex, which was particularly nice as the winter sun set over the water. The cover art is a reference to Bowie's own 'Heroes' – something to do with subverting the image I think. The music itself is a slow-burn, which finds its stride during the second half in my opinion. 'I'd Rather Be High' is a catchy anti-war song; 'I'd rather be dead or out of my head / Than training these guns on those men in the sand.' Then there's 'Boss Of Me' which makes great use of saxophone.

7.68) Blackstar – David Bowie (2016)

I was too young to remember the death of John Lennon, but when David Bowie departed in January 2016 the impact was huge. There were Bowie hits playing all day in the shopping centre where my wife worked at the time, and we even made our own pilgrimage to his childhood home in Brixton. There was a mural on a wall nearby which was strewn with flowers.

Bowie knew the grim reaper was coming and the evidence is here in this album. At just under ten minutes, the title track was one of his longest ever, with the pivotal line 'Something happened on the day he died.' Just wait for that chord change at 5.22. 'Lazarus' is another high point, with its hypnotic feel, saxophones and plodding rhythm. The line 'Look up here / I'm in danger' again indicates that he knew he was on his way to the great beyond. *'Tis A Pity She Was A Whore* is a drum-led exposition of er... something! 'Girl Loves Me' was lyrically inspired by the teen language of 'A Clockwork Orange' before developing into a swearathon. Bob Geldof didn't like Mondays, while Bowie wondered 'Where the f*** did Monday go?' He was cutting and edgy (cutting edgy?) right to the end.

7.69) New Sensations – Lou Reed (1984)

Lou released four 'OK' albums after 1978's 'Street Hassle,' but 'New Sensations' seems to be a cut above the rest. With his lifestyle cleaned up and a relatively new marriage, he sounds refreshed, with a crisp 'eighties' sound and his most positive set of lyrics ever. 'Turn To Me' has a great rhythm, bassline and melody, while the prominent bassline of the title track drives the song along as he eulogises about taking off on his motorbike and drinking a Coke. Was he ever really this clean living? 'Fly Into The Sun' resurfaced again on the 'Magic And Loss' album (1992), and Lou also seemed to be keeping up with eighties gaming trends with 'My Red Joystick' and 'Down At The Arcade.' This is a very enjoyable album and Fernando Saunders (bass) and Peter Wood (drums) were certainly pivotal to its sound.

For later albums, apart from the obvious 'New York' and 'Magic And Loss,' I recommend 'Songs For Drella' (1990) where Lou reunited with his Velvet Underground bandmate John Cale for a tribute to the artist Andy Warhol, and I would urge people not to be put off of 'Set The Twilight Reeling' (1996) by the shocking title of track six which is really just a pun aimed at hypocritical politicians. So it's fair game, right?

7.70) Chelsea Girl – Nico (1967)

You may recall that Nico was a German songstress who added a touch of diversity to the Velvet Underground's first album. This solo release could be filed under both 'folk' and 'baroque pop' as the guitars and vocals are often overdubbed with cold sounding strings. Nico's former bandmates from the VU provide a lot of the material, but she also covers three Jackson Browne songs (he who penned 'Take It Easy' for the Eagles) as well as 'I'll Keep It With Mine,' a Bob Dylan song that he didn't release himself until 1991's 'The Bootleg Series Volumes 1-3.' The best track, without a doubt, is 'Chelsea Girls' with its sparse wintry arrangement and downbeat vocal. It's nothing to do with London however; it concerns the famous hotel in New York.

7.71) 5 Album Set – Hawkwind (2013)

Here were get the band's first four albums, 'Hawkwind' (1970), 'In Search Of Space' (1971), 'Doremi Fasol Latido' (1972) and 'Hall Of The Mountain Grill' (1974). You'll no longer need disc one of the 'Epocheclispe' box set as all the tracks are here. Some of the bonus tracks are merely edits of the album tracks, and the final disc is actually 'Masters Of The Universe,' presumably tossed in just in case you don't buy the excellent live album 'The Space Ritual Alive' (1973) for 'Orgone Accumulator' and 'Sonic Attack.' The set begins with the mix of sonic experimentation and acoustic folky material of the first album, with interesting bonus tracks including a cover of Pink Floyd's 'Cymbaline.' On 'Doremi Fasol Latido' Lemmy seems to be playing power chords on his bass towards the end of

'Lord Of Light.' I also like the quiet alien warning to humanity in 'The Watcher.' They've got a point; we really do need to sort our act out.

7.72) Levitation – Hawkwind (1980)

This album shows Hawkwind at a junction point, returning to a certain extent to the space rock and psychedelia of their early years. The rock anthems like 'Motorway City,' 'Levitation' and 'Who's Gonna Win The War' are broken up with ethereal instrumental music. The bonus tracks go much deeper into experimental territory, particularly the completely bonkers 'Douglas In The Jungle.' 'Valium 10' is also good fun (not taking it, listening to it, I hasten to add), and the live rendition of 'Brainstorm' gives an oldie of theirs a twist, opening with a jazzy drum solo. (This review refers to disc one of the three-CD set.)

7.73) Mechanical Bull – Kings Of Leon (2013)

Although Caleb Followill no longer lacerates his vocal chords in quite the same way that he did on the group's early albums, 'Supersoaker' does have a certain rawness in its vocal delivery. 'Don't Matter' is a full on rock track, but then they bring it down with the introspective 'Beautiful War' which postulates that couples fight because they matter to each other. The song also contains the lyric 'Doing my head in,' this being a phrase the Nashville boys had heard from their English fans. 'Family Tree' has a funkier feel, but the deluxe version of the album is a must for 'Last Mile Home.' There is an even nicer, more mellow version available if you search around. The top track for me is 'On The Chin,' which professes the value of friendship. A friend of mine who I go camping with seems to like it for its alcohol related lyrics, '...Said make yourself at home so I started day drinking.' My friend has never stopped.

When compiling the playlist for my wedding reception I ran the song 'Don't Matter' past my mum to check the suitability of the lyrics. As she didn't even notice the use of the F-word the song went in and no one batted an eyelid. Phew!

7.74) WALLS – Kings Of Leon (2016)

Up till this point all KOL album titles had conformed to five syllables, but what's going on here? Well, just for fans 'WALLS' stands for 'We Are Like Love Songs' which is five syllables. 'Waste A Moment' opens the album and pays lyrical homage to Bruce Springsteen. There is a triple whammy mid-album in my opinion, with the majestic 'Over,' the laid back 'Muchacho' with its electric piano sound, and 'Conversation Piece' which reminds me of slightly off-key tracks like Blur's 'Miss America' and the Red Hot Chili Peppers' 'Porcelain.' This is a good thing by the way. 'WALLS' itself is a stripped back ballad on piano and acoustic guitar.

7.75) AM – Arctic Monkeys (2013)

In 2013 the Arctics threw us a curveball – an album incorporating influences from R&B, and I don't mean the original 'rhythm and blues' kind. 'Do I Wanna Know?' introduces us to falsetto vocals and has an infectious riff. 'No.1 Party Anthem' is a piano-led song with shades of John Lennon about it. The R&B influences get stronger on tracks like 'Mad Sounds' and 'Why Do You Only Call Me When You're High?' In hindsight, I guess this is what makes a band good – they challenge their fans with styles that we might not have considered before. Bowie did it. And funnily enough their next album would have a lot of influence from the original 'Starman.'

7.76) Tranquility Base Hotel & Casino – Arctic Monkeys (2018)

David Bowie departed Planet Earth in early 2016 and his influence is everywhere here. For a start this is a concept album about a hotel on the moon – the perfect place for rock stars to do their thing. 'Four Stars Out Of Five' received regular radio airplay at the time. 'Science Fiction' sounds as if they've been listening to Abba's 'Money, Money, Money,' and 'The Ultracheese' is a rousing piano ballad which echoes Bowie's 'Five Years' and perhaps Lennon's 'Mother' to a certain extent. The whole album is very enjoyable. Don't listen to the whiners; it's a classic Arctic Monkeys style-shift.

7.77) Madman Across The Water – Elton John (1971)

A number of Elton John's seventies albums have been in and out of my collection over the years, and most people opt for 1973's 'Goodbye Yellow Brick Road.' However, I'm nailing my colours to the mast with this set which opens with the classic, 'Tiny Dancer,' a track that takes some time to build up via its verses and pre-chorus for added impact. Bernie Taupin's lyrics are at their creative story-telling peak and most of the songs have a confident anthemic quality, without the decadence that Elton would embrace a year or two down the line. 'Razor Face' and 'Rotten Peaches' are great examples of this, while 'Levon' made it onto the second of his many greatest hits packages. This album's title was a reference to Richard Nixon apparently. We've had a few madmen across the water since then, and a few closer to home too, but oh dear, such a plain looking album cover!

'Honky Château,' which followed this album, is also superb. It contains two of my all-time favourites by the piano-tinkler (the approximated title track and 'Rocket Man'), as well as 'I Think I'm Going To Kill Myself' which plays light and fast with the serious subject of teenage suicide ideation. Different times I guess.

7.78) The Road To Hell – Chris Rea (1989)

Chris Rea always sounded more 'Middle America' than 'Middlesbrough,' but it has been said that this album's title track was inspired by travelling on London's orbital motorway, the M25. Indeed, you can imagine him stuck in a jam, mesmerised by the red brake lights thinking 'What has become of us?' To really appreciate this track you need 'Part 1' and 'Part 2' which you'll only get here on this album for that delicious segue. 'You Must Be Evil' reflects on the corrupting influence of TV, which may seem rather dated now that we are far more worried about what youngsters view on the Internet. However, this was the eighties, the era of the *video nasty*; nowadays, all TV is nasty! It goes without saying that Chris is a master of the guitar and occasionally he plays slide guitar. I do wish he'd pronounce the 'th' in 'I Just Wanna Be With You' however. The track's closer 'Tell Me There's A Heaven' lulls us with piano and strings while dealing with the paradox of the existence of evil within Christian belief.

7.79) Hozier – Hozier (2014)

When my wife and I were compiling a playlist for our wedding reception she suggested Hozier's hit 'Take Me To Church.' At first I thought 'Really?' having dismissed it as a sycophantic love song, but upon taking another listen I realised that Hozier had produced something dark, passionate and different, with a gospel feel. The rest of the album follows suit, with a few rockier tracks like 'Jackie And Wilson' providing a bit of light relief. 'Like Some People Do' is a highlight for me and some of the themes are relentlessly dark, such as 'In A Week,' which attempts to find romance in the fate of a murdered couple, literally 'together forever.' And finally, the most disturbing track of all is 'Cherry Wine,' where the narrator romanticises being the victim of a violent relationship. Uneasy listening for sure and the darkest 'new artist' since Lana Del Rey.

7.80) The Best Of Abba: The Millennium Edition – Abba (2000)

The Swedish giants Abba have been in and out of fashion so many times that no one has any idea if they are cool or not any more. Who cares? The music here is top quality, superbly crafted and always melodic. My favourites are not the big hits, with the exception of the harrowingly bleak 'The Winner Takes It All,' but some of the less often played tracks, such as the diary-like hit 'The Day Before You Came,' which is my favourite Abba track of all, plodding along relentlessly as its major / minor key shifts manipulate the emotions, feeling like clouds drifting across the sky or moods drifting across the mind. 'Happy New Year' is also great, being a breaking up song for the party season; 'No more champagne / And the fireworks are through.' 'One Of Us' is another weepy classic, and 'Thank You For The Music' is nostalgic for me, having often been requested on those radio shows I used to listen to as a child. This is a seriously good collection.

7.81) Parachutes – Coldplay (2000)

Whereas most bands like to explode with fire and fury on their first album, Coldplay's Chris Martin started out with the low energy vocals of a broken man, occasionally making use of falsetto. I got into Coldplay a long time after most, although I always liked the songs 'Yellow' and 'Trouble.' I think the absence of any significant solos, be they on guitar or keyboard, was a hurdle for me. The minimalist guitar riff on 'Yellow' is simple but effective however. The other single from this set was the spikier sounding track 'Shiver.' The opener, 'Don't Panic,' is pleasant with its hook line of 'We live in a beautiful world,' and the general feel is 'easy listening.' The track 'Help Is Around The Corner' is my favourite song of theirs from this era, delivering its hopeful message acoustically. However it is not on the album, being a 'hidden treasure' B-side.

7.82) A Rush Of Blood To The Head – Coldplay (2002)

In my opinion this was the finest hour of Chris Martin and pals. The pulsing rhythm of 'Politik' is reminiscent of the Velvet Underground's 'Waiting For The Man' and it just takes off from there. Several songs open with just a strummed acoustic guitar and build to something epic. 'God Put A Smile On Your Face' is a case in point. 'In My Place,' 'Clocks' and 'The Scientist' were big hits, but the crown goes to the majestic title track, which is great for staring into the flames, sitting round a campfire. 'Green Eyes' is also a poignant moment, particularly when I'd just married someone whose eyes were...

7.83) X&Y – Coldplay (2005)

I didn't like the song 'Fix You' when it first came out, finding the sentiment a bit twee, but the song has been a 'grower' over time, with production reminiscent of Simon & Garfunkel's 'Bridge Over Troubled Water' in holding back and then throwing everything but the kitchen sink in at the end when 'tears stream down your face' to quote the lyrics. There's certainly more of a 'band' sound to this album than 'Parachutes' as it has more of a 'plugged in' feel. 'What If' and 'Speed Of Sound' are tracks you know, while the title track has some nice chords and an epic feel.

7.84) Viva La Vida Or Death And All His Friends – Coldplay (2008)

This one divided the fans, but I didn't fall off the Coldplay wagon just yet. That would come with the next album, 2011's 'Xylo Myloto.' 'Life In Technicolor' has an Eastern feel, even if it does sound like they've copied the acoustic guitar riff from Fairground Attraction's 'Find My Love.' The styles are varied and 'Viva La Vida' gave the band their first UK number one single, while 'Violet Hill' sounds like something Oasis could have written, which as you know, is good thing.

7.85) Ghost Stories – Coldplay (2014)

Around about the late-noughties Coldplay's sound changed to a much more poppy style, ensuring continued chart success, whereas other indie rock groups became purely album artists, no doubt due to the average age of the singles market being about five! Previous fans like me stuck doggedly to the 'tried and tested' early albums, although I did find 'Ghost Stories' sufficiently interesting, being a downbeat, almost ambient affair, seemingly inspired by lead singer Chris Martin's split from the actress Gwyneth Paltrow. 'Magic' is a low-energy love song, and the tempo only increases for one track, the rave-like 'Sky Full Of Stars.' There's even some acoustic guitar strumming on 'Oceans.' It seems to me that most artists produce their best work when they're unhappy. Pile on the misery, boys!

7.86) Employment – Kaiser Chiefs (2005)

Quite what the fascination with pivotal figures from the First World War was all about in the mid-noughties, I have no idea. The other band to go down this route was Franz Ferdinand, whose hit 'Take Me Out' was omnipresent in 2004. I was late to the party with 'Employment,' purchasing this album in 2021, but as I already had the four singles that were released from it I am placing it here. The Kaisers certainly knew how to vocally whip up a frenzy before their choruses which was something of a trademark on hits like 'Oh My God' and 'I Predict A Riot,' which we used to cover in our pub band. Their lyrics are consistently interesting dollops of working class life, for example, 'Time Honoured Tradition' is a darkly humorous skit about health, lifestyle and death.

'Yours Truly, Angry Mob' (2007) is also well worth a listen, containing the band's only UK number one single, 'Ruby,' as well as the scathing title track aimed at those who unquestioningly follow the mantra of tabloid newspapers. To paraphrase Pete Seeger, 'When will they ever learn?'

7.87) Moseley Shoals – Ocean Colour Scene (1996)

The nineties were hailed as the 'new sixties,' and with music like this it's easy to see why. 'The Riverboat Song' has a Hendrix-style riff, while 'The Day We Caught The Train' resembles later Beatles songs such as 'Hey Bulldog.' 'The Circle' and 'You've Got It Bad' were also big radio hits, but there are more pensive moments such as 'Lining Your Pockets,' while the final track,' Get Away,' has plenty of psychedelic effects and runs to almost eight minutes. Chris Evans' use of 'The Riverboat Song' when guests walked in on 'TFI Friday' pretty much epitomised the nineties.

7.88) Supergrass Is 10 – Supergrass (2004)

This is a bumper collection of 21 tracks, and where I normally prefer twelve-track compilations which concentrate on the 'whoppers,' with nineties acts like Supergrass the quality doesn't really drop at all. The album opens with the biggies, such as 'Alright,' which I always muse has a remarkably similar chord pattern to 'Doctor Robert' by the Beatles. 'Moving' is an atmospheric track and 'Grace' was a really catchy hit from the less fruitful noughties. It's nice that 'Time' is included too – a quieter moment on a rocking album.

7.89) Sixteen Stone – Bush (1994)

Named after Shepherd's Bush in West London, the band frequently sounded more like they came from Seattle, specifically like Nirvana. Witness Gavin Rossdale's demented vocal at the end of 'Swim.' Every track is an anthem, and that's no exaggeration. 'Testosterone' satirises the macho obsession with guns and showing off, and I used to sing the conclusion to 'Little Things' whenever my wife and I went shopping; 'Lidl, Lidl, Lidl.' 'Glycerine' employs strings, adding some contrast, and after 'Alien' burns out there's a quirky stab at punk called 'X-Girlfriend.' The group's second album 'Razorblade Suitcase' (1996) is almost as good and contains the hit 'Swallowed.'

7.90) Everything Must Go – Manic Street Preachers (1996)

The Welsh rockers produced one of the classic albums of the decade here, with 'A Design For Life' still receiving regular radio airplay today. The addition of strings gives this song and the title track extra weight. 'Australia' is another memorable track, and when the album was released there was a boy called Kevin Carter living down the road from us, so my sister and I found the song of that name rather amusing. The album's closing track has a hypnotic quality to its gentle guitar motif being performed over 'epic rock.' For me, this album will forever remind me of my friend Dan sitting in the porch of his tent on one of our legendary camps. The album seemed to have the effect of turning him somewhat smarmy, remarking on how much more beer he'd drunk than myself or his brother, as though it was some sort of competition. Perhaps the lyric 'I wish I had a bottle / Right here in my pretty face' had worked its magic on him. As for the Manics, also worth a try is 1998's 'This Is My Truth Tell Me Yours,' a title which sums up this book really!

7.91) Just Enough Education to Perform – Stereophonics (2001 / 2002)

I finally decided to purchase this album in 2021, but it is placed here because I bought the five singles that were released from the 2002 edition of the CD ('Handbags And Gladrags' didn't appear on the original 2001 release). It's also fashionable to be late, although twenty years might be stretching it.

'Handbags And Gladrags' is a crusade against superficiality which was written by Manfred Mann's Mike d'Abo. When I first heard this on the radio I thought 'That's a nice new song from Rod Stewart,' and indeed Kelly Jones's vocals do sound like Rod's. Either that or he is permanently hung over. 'Step On My Old Size Nines' has some nice harmonica, and my favourite track is 'Mr. Writer,' which has a hypnotic chorus combining anger and pity at a journalist who described the Stereophonics as having 'Just enough edu...' OK, OK, you've got it. It's certainly the most visceral song to be fired at a journalist since 'Mr. Reporter' by the Kinks. 'Vegas Two Times' is the rockiest offering, and you won't forget the line about canning processed fish in 'Have A Nice Day.' My favourite 'deeper' album cut is 'Caravan Holiday' which discusses the phenomenon of tourism to locations of atrocities. When you think about it, this paradox could relate to music too, as we get pleasure and interest from songs that are often about unpleasant things that we wish had never happened.

7.92) Rings Around The World – Super Furry Animals (2001)

This album almost seems like a calculated demonstration of versatility by another Welsh band. It also sounds a lot like '13' era Blur at times, with songs plastered in effects. 'Juxtapozed With U' is a soul-flavoured offering, which has something of a 'Marvin Gaye' vibe about it, in spite of the heavily processed vocal. 'Receptacle For The Respectable' ends up with a death metal style vocal. Yes, seriously! '(Drawing) Rings Around The World' sounds like the Beach Boys singing over backing by Hawkwind, and my favourite track is 'Run! Christian, Run!' which seems to be about the phenomenon of suicide cults, combining a rousing melody and genuine empathy for the victims.

7.93) All Change – Cast (1995)

At the time I was something of an 'Oasis purist' and a colleague called Greg used to repeatedly sing this Liverpool band's hit 'Sandstorm' at me, as though this would somehow make me appreciate it. The camping thing went through a similar phase of three friends singing in each other's faces. Jim and I never did manage to get Dan to appreciate Queen though, so my scientific verdict is that this method of conversion doesn't work. Anyway, I'll admit it now, 'Sandstorm' is a great rock song. 'Walkaway' is a quieter affair but equally enjoyable, and my favourite Cast cut has always been 'Four Walls,' with its repeated line 'Will I ever get out of here?' echoing the fact that we all want to get out of our own minds and away from troublesome thoughts at times.

7.94) Kollected: The Best Of – Kula Shaker (2002)

'K' (1996) was another one of those albums that was always around in the nineties, with cover artwork that was reminiscent of 'Sgt. Pepper,' except that all the names to the faces had to be associated with the letter 'K.' The album contained some great singles which are all on this compilation. These included 'Hey Dude,' and

'Govinda' which had Indian lyrics. The interests and instrumentation of the late sixties prevail here, and the cover of Deep Purple's 'Hush' possibly outstrips the original, but hush, I didn't say that! 'Sound Of Drums' was one of the group's later hits, and don't forget '303,' a track dedicated to the A303 because this road heads towards Glastonbury and its famous festival. Yes, seriously – it's not just me who tries to get road numbers into everything!

7.95) Do It Yourself – Seahorses (1997)

Ex-Stone Roses man, John Squire's brilliant guitar playing is to the fore throughout this album, with its typically down to earth lyrics like 'Look at Auntie George and Uncle Mabel.' The melodic sound says 'nineties' all over it and the work is completely dominated by the lengthy track 'Love Is The Law' with an awesome guitar solo that just builds and builds. If only Mr. Squire would let rip like this on some of the other tracks. 'Blinded By The Sun' was the group's only other UK top ten hit, with its catchy staccato guitar lead-in to the verses no doubt playing a part.

7.96) Singles – The Smiths (1995)

In the eighties I found Morrissey's voice whiny and depressing, but a few sessions with the Smiths playing while sitting around a campfire allowed these songs to work their magic. 'This Charming Man,' 'Heaven Knows I'm Miserable Now' and 'William, It Was Really Nothing' are all memorable, and 'Panic' seems to utilise the same melody as 'Metal Guru' by T. Rex. Johnny Marr's jangly guitar is pivotal to the sound, while the opening to 'How Soon Is Now?' has been frequently sampled over the years. For a solo Morrissey hit, 'First Of The Gang To Die' (2004) is great and it has a typically downbeat B-side which seems to muse about lost friendships, intoning 'My life is an endless succession / Of people saying goodbye / And what's left for me?' Always the party animal, hey?

7.97) The Early Years – T. Rex (1991)

Opening with the catchy semi-electric hit, 'Ride A White Swan,' this album illustrates the transitional years of Marc Bolan's band from psychedelic folk to glam rock. The band started out as Tyrannosaurus Rex, and 'One Inch Rock' exemplifies the kind of thing they did. 'Hot Love,' with its 'chant-along' coda was a sure-fire number one, as was 'Get It On.' The group would top the UK chart twice more. 'Mambo Sun' sounds like it was influential when the Black Keys recorded their album 'Brothers' almost forty years later, and 'Rip Off' is an aggressive but fun rocker.

7.98) Free Bird: The Very Best – Lynryd Skynyrd (1994)

This is a Nectar compilation and first of all everyone is going to know 'Sweet Home Alabama' which has a poke at Neil Young for his generalisations in the song 'Southern Man.' Most people will also know 'Free Bird' which is a solid candidate for the best guitar solo of all time, even if it isn't a solo but a duet. This whole compilation is very enjoyable; 'That Smell' rocks, 'Gimme Three Steps' has a catchy melody and 'Tuesday's Gone' is a great ballad that has the same feel as the first half of 'Free Bird,' which can only be a good thing, right?

7.99) Lizzy Killers – Thin Lizzy (1981)

Thin Lizzy came from Dublin, so I always wondered if the band's name is a pronunciation joke referencing the Ford Model T car, which was known as the 'tin Lizzie.' Anyway, this is 'bread and butter' classic rock from the band led by Phil Lynott. Everybody knows 'The Boys Are Back In Town,' but my money is on 'Jailbreak' for sheer riffability. There's a nod to folk with their version of the traditional Irish song 'Whiskey In The Jar.' 'Dancing In The Moonlight' and 'Sarah' are lighter tracks, while 'Do Anything You Want To Do' has a great pounding rhythm. For a brilliant track that isn't included here, try 'Renegade.' It is also worth noting that the guitar hero, Gary Moore, had a brief stint with the band. Yes, he of 'Parisienne Walkways' fame. No more questions your honour.

7.100) S.F. Sorrow - The Pretty Things (1968)

This was arguably the first rock opera, pipping 'Tommy' by The Who at the post. The story is bonkers but the music is excellent and the 'cut and paste' edits and segues work brilliantly. A prime example is 'Private Sorrow,' with its 'war memorial' epilogue crashing into 'Balloon Burning.' There's plenty of mellotron and acoustic guitar soloing. 'She Says Good Morning' has a great rhythm, and 'Baron Saturday' has a frenetic psychedelic drum solo before the pulsing rhythm of the chorus returns. This particular '1-1 2' rhythm (with the emphasis on the '2') was popular at the time. Other examples are 'Foxy Lady' by Jimi Hendrix and 'Corporal Clegg ' by Pink Floyd. The lyrics are actually pretty dark, concluding with 'The Loneliest Person In The World.' The raw edge to Phil May's vocals is always enjoyable. It's just a shame the bonus tracks are only in mono, so you can add a stereo remix of 'Defecting Grey' to my wish list. A 'grey' meant a 'square' person by the way. You can't beat a bit of sixties slang.

7.101) Parachute – The Pretty Things (1970)

Another fabulous effort from this band, with the guitars plugged in more firmly than on the previous album. I first listened to 'Parachute' online after purchasing 'S.F. Sorrow' on CD. There are great melodies throughout, and the creativity seems to step up a gear when we get to 'Cries From The Midnight Circus' with its dramatic chords that kick in after the four-minute mark. 'Sickle Clowns' is also a high point with its jazzy alternating chords. The title track at the end has an atmospheric chord pattern with some succulent harmonies. Why were this band not bigger?

7.102) Music In A Doll's House – Family (1968)

Roger Chapman's vibrato-laden vocal is distinctive and this is very much a period piece from the late sixties, with plenty of guitar, organ and additions of brass and strings. 'Winter' is a highlight, opening with the statement 'Winter time / It brings me down,' long before people really knew about Seasonal Affective Disorder. Typical sixties lyrical themes abound, with tracks like 'Hey Mr. Policeman' and 'Mellowing Grey' – back to that sixties terminology again! There are several short 'variations' of songs contained elsewhere on the album, a great technique for giving a collection of tracks the feel of a concept piece, as does concluding with 'God Save The Queen,' something Queen (the band, not the monarch) would do seven years later on 'A Night At The Opera.'

7.103) The Best Of Focus: Hocus Pocus – Focus (1993)

Focus were a Dutch prog rock band who occasionally used to yodel. Their hit 'Hocus Pocus' was seemingly conceived as a joke, with full blown rock interspersed with wacky whistled and yodelled sections. It was something my old friend Mark and I used to listen to on the way to the pub, along with that other eccentric seventies instrumental hit, 'Mouldy Old Dough' by Lieutenant Pigeon. I had a vinyl single of 'Hocus Pocus,' and the B-side 'Janis' was a much more laid back affair, where a flute leads the melody. The rocky 'Sylvia' occasionally receives radio airplay even today, as does the catchy flute hit 'House Of The King.' This is a chronologically arranged compilation, and I find the earlier material from the dawn of the seventies to be the most enjoyable. The nine-minute track 'Focus' is a high point. Oh yes, and the band love their Roman numerals as you'll see from the track listing.

7.104) A Tab In The Ocean – Nektar (1972)

This is pure prog rock from a British band that formed in Germany, which I stumbled across on YouTube. I recall listening to this on my iPod while my wife was waiting to have an operation at a hospital in Herne Bay on the Kent coast. The skill of the musicians is certainly clinical, with shifting rhythms throughout. It always amazes me how bands could remember the structure of pieces like the sixteen-minute title track, let alone play it. It begins ethereally, sounding like a long lost Pink Floyd track, and whips itself up into a frenzy, dominated by guitar and drums. Although 'progressive' was more a description of the evolution of music at the time, the word could often be used to describe the song structures too. I also like the way 'Desolation Valley / Waves' builds up to a frenetic syncopated rhythm.

While we're talking about prog rock, I've owned the album 'Selling England By The Pound' (1973) by Genesis for many years, but with the exception of 'I Know What I Like (In Your Wardrobe)' I've always struggled to get into it, finding obscure bands like 'Nektar' more accessible. Music is such a subjective thing, so I offer my apologies to Peter, Phil and the boys for the lack of a review.

7.105) Pussy Cats – Harry Nilsson (1974)

The tracks 'Without You' and *Everybody's Talkin'* were already staples in my collection but neither of these were written by Harry himself, so I had an oblique introduction to the legend purely because three tracks on a bootleg Beatles CD called 'Sweetest Apples' were actually Harry Nilsson recordings on an album produced by John Lennon, namely 'Pussy Cats.' This was in between wild bouts of excessive drinking for both of them. By this time, it was regarded that Harry's best work was behind him, so I'm going to review his albums in reverse chronology.

There are some great covers including Jimmy Cliff's 'Many Rivers To Cross' and Bob Dylan's 'Subterranean Homesick Blues,' as well as a frenetic version of 'Rock Around The Clock' with no less than three drummers. Harry lacerates his voice at times; listen to how it cracks on 'Old Forgotten Soldier' and compare this to the smooth version he does as a bonus track on 'Nilsson Schmilsson.' 'Loop De Loop' is a fun song which will always remind me of an afternoon dancing around the campfire with my two camping buddies! 'Don't Forget Me' sounds a bit like 'Without You' but it has a dark reference to cancer, and 'Black Sails' has a punchline satirising Carly Simon's 'You're So Vain,' as he intones 'You're so veiny!' The bonus tracks are great too and I actually prefer these early versions of 'Down By The Sea' and 'The Flying Saucer Song' to the 'proper' versions that followed. It's also quite remarkable that this album followed a collection where Harry crooned the standards of the past, namely 'A Little Touch Of Schmilsson In The Night' (1973).

7.106) Son Of Schmilsson – Harry Nilsson (1972)

Harry showed his irascible side with this release which followed the album containing 'Without You.' No doubt the studio wanted more big ballads, but instead Harry gave us satire in droves. 'Remember (Christmas)' is the only token to earnestness, and he even parodies this with the beginning of the track 'At My Front Door.' 'Spaceman' is a great song that should be mentioned in the same breath as Bowie's 'Space Oddity' and Elton John's 'Rocket Man.' 'I'd Rather Be Dead' is a song about senility with a chorus of elderly singers who seem to be having a whale of a time, and 'The Most Beautiful World In The World' combines poignancy and humour. The whole album is incredibly melodic, perhaps in a way that only Paul McCartney can match, and I'd give it a '15' certificate because of 'Take 54' and 'You're Breaking My Heart' which no doubt released some therapeutic rage at Harry's own marriage break up. And just when you think he's played all his aces he displays a staggering vocal range on 'Campo De Encino' and then hides it away as a mere bonus track! An awesome album.

7.107) Nilsson Schmilsson – Harry Nilsson (1970)

This was Harry's monster album. It contains 'Without You,' penned by Beatles protégés 'Badfinger,' as well as 'Coconut,' a humorous and eccentric song where Harry does funny voices and demonstrates his vocal range. The song ended up as the play-out track to the film 'Reservoir Dogs' 21 years later. 'The Moonbeam Song' is the most sublime composition with the word 'crap' in it that I've ever encountered, and the whole album has a feel of Harry trying to drag himself up mentally after his marriage imploded. 'Jump Into The Fire' rocks, but even when he's having fun there seems to be a sadness lurking just beneath the surface.

7.108) The Point! – Harry Nilsson (1970)

Here's yet another little known masterwork from Mr. Nilsson. This one is a children's story recited by Harry himself, with great timing, including the bit where you can hear him turn the page. The melodies are incredibly catchy and most of the piano-driven songs have a similar rhythm to the Beatles' 'Mean Mr. Mustard.' The story is actually quite dark in places, perhaps being a metaphor for depression, but it's also a great morality tale about inclusion, a message that certainly needs a rerun in this era of division and scapegoating. There is also sadness beneath the delivery of songs such as 'Are You Sleeping?' and 'Life Line,' as well as a circular 'nursery rhyme' structure to the song 'Think About Your Troubles.' This album is just so good. 'Then the rain starts to fall / Making fools of them all...'

7.109) Pandemonium Shadow Show – Harry Nilsson (1967)

We now rewind to Mr. Nilsson's first proper album. 'Ten Little Indians' reminds me of the nursery rhyme 'Ten Green Bottles,' and in '1941' Harry gets almost uncomfortably autobiographical. 'Cuddly Toy' was even a hit for the Monkees, and Harry professes his undying love for the Beatles with two covers, one of which set the trend for shoehorning as many Beatles song titles as possible into a lyric, a tactic later employed by everyone from Barclay James Harvest to Oasis. The instrumentation is very 'sixties' and he even has a crack at Tina Turner's anthem 'River Deep Mountain High.' Remarkably, he pulls it off.

7.110) Harry Styles – Harry Styles (2017)

From Harry Nilsson to Harry Styles – slick or what? Well, I've never been a fan of boy bands, but just as Robbie Williams turned out some excellent post-Take That hits, of which 'No Regrets' should send a shiver down even the hardest spine, Harry Styles emerged from One Direction with some very good solo material. 'Sign Of The Times' runs to almost six minutes, including a mellotron, with shades of Bowie and Lennon. 'Two Ghosts' was another hit, which reminds me of Beck's low-key 'Sea Change' album. Harry rocks out on 'Kiwi,' while 'Woman' sounds like he's been listening to Elton John's 'Bennie And The Jets.' Keep listening to the classics, Harry, and an obscure writer from Kent may just review you again!

7.111) As You Were – Liam Gallagher (2017)

The Oasis frontman's first solo album prompted many of us to wonder 'Where did *that* come from?' Nobody really imagined that the former hell-raiser could turn out such a crisply majestic collection of songs. From the opening harmonica wail that begins the album, this is melodic and confident, almost seeming to pick up where the final Oasis album, 'Dig Out Your Soul,' left off in 2008. The top track for me is the semi-acoustic 'Paper Crown' which has a great melody and harmonies. Liam's Beatles influence is never far away. Fifty years after they did it all he's keeping the dream alive. I'm glad somebody is.

7.112) Superorganism – Superorganism (2018)

This is the most poppy album in this chapter, and perhaps in this whole book, assembled in separate countries by a group of young technologically-minded musicians. It was introduced to me by the older of my two camping buddies and best man at my wedding, who strategically waited until his brother and myself had consumed plenty of wine before sticking it on. This tactic worked wonders, at least for me. Vocalist Orono Noguchi actually sounds remarkably similar to the Velvet Underground's Maureen Tucker in her downbeat delivery. I love the 'kerching' sound of the ringing till in 'Everybody Wants To Be Famous' and the distorted guitar sound on 'Nobody Cares.' Orona allows some severe manipulation of her voice on 'Something For Your M.I.N.D.,' another top tune. This is easily the most original thing I've heard in the teenies, or whatever they decided to call the decade from 2010-2019.

7.113) Easy Rider Soundtrack – Various Artists (1969)

This is another album that seemed to suit the laid back mood of my camping trips. The film starring Peter Fonda and Dennis Hopper, as well as a young Jack Nicholson, pretty much invented the road movie, and like Stanley Kubrick's '2001: A Space Odyssey,' it was more of an 'experience' than a traditional plot-driven film. A major part of the film's success is the choice of music, so the soundtrack album was an inevitable winner. Steppenwolf contribute two tracks, one of which is the legendary 'Born To Be Wild.' Be warned, the album is littered with drug references, especially the country song 'Don't Bogart Me' by the Fraternity Of Man, and 'If You Want To Be A Bird' by the Holy Modal Rounders will make you feel like you are on something even though you're not! The whole thing is very American and very atmospheric, with a couple of folky finishers from Roger McGuinn from the legendary Byrds.

7.114) Zabriskie Point Soundtrack – Various Artists / Pink Floyd (1970 / 1997)

Michelangelo Antonioni's 1970 film featured an iconic scene of a luxury pad blowing up in slow motion to Pink Floyd's 'Come In Number 51, Your Time Is Up,' itself a variation on 'Careful With That Axe, Eugene.' Here the mighty Floyd give us a sound collage with 'Heartbeat, Pigmeat' and they go slightly country on us with 'Crumbling Land.' The genuine 'country' tracks on this album are a marked contrast but seem to fit in regardless, with fiddles to the fore on Kaleidoscope's 'Brother Mary,' picked banjo on 'I Wish I Was A Single Girl Again' by Roscoe Holcomb, and an all-time great from way back in 1950 – Patti Page's rendition of 'The Tennessee Waltz.' Pink Floyd return on the second disc and all the tracks are interesting, showcasing Gilmour's bluesy soloing and an almost classical piece improvised by Richard Wright. Jerry Garcia of the Grateful Dead was the successful candidate who actually got his music used for the love scene (basically rolling around in the desert with not a lot of clothes on). However, the four alternate takes of his lone guitar doodling are somewhat excessive.

7.115) 2001: A Space Odyssey Soundtrack – Various Artists (1968)

Stanley Kubrick's 'art film' has long been a favourite of mine, and whilst this is really a classical album, its place in popular culture is assured. Johann Strauss's 'The Blue Danube' is split in two, just as it is in the film, and Richard Strauss's 'Also Sprach Zarathustra' appears twice, just as it does in the film. Khachaturian's 'Gayane Ballet Suite' is actually quite eerie, but it's the composer György Ligeti who steals the show with three of his surreal works, of which my favourite is 'Atmospheres,' which leads nicely into our next section on more esoteric music. Kubrick's soundtrack choices for his films were never short of inspirational.

Chapter 8 – Further To Fly

My marriage operated according to the traditional template as laid down by almighty man for around three years before morphing into something different. I often muse how the period prior to marriage is perhaps like the golden years of psychedelic and progressive music of the late sixties and early seventies, when guitar pop developed into rock. It was a fascinating transitional period that I always wish had lasted longer, at least into my own lifetime, but once any transition has been made you can't really recreate that time of change authentically. People take a similar view to the years of growing up, but personally I didn't find those years so enjoyable!

As we near the end of this book, I take the optimistic view that I am roughly half way through my life. This means that I could theoretically discover as much music as is contained in these pages again, and who knows what genres might become more accessible given time? With no disrespect to fans of the following musical styles, the only genres that I have generally found too challenging are opera, rap, and death / doom / thrash metal (and variants). Conversely, music I have found not challenging enough would include most pop music since the millennium. Of course, I do realise that my reviews are subjective and that everybody has different points at which attention is held and attention is lost. So please don't throw this book or your digital reading device across the room just yet. My opinions are merely food for thought rather than something carved into tablets of stone like commandments.

I think my interest in genres that were previously alien to me began shortly before I got married. I had stumbled across Chris Morris's controversial ambient comedy sketches which were more like a series of twisted and disturbing dreams. There was always ambient music in the background which seemed to evoke a feeling of detachment and disbelief at the material. I decided to investigate what this music was and found that this opened up an entire new avenue of electronic and often surreal music by artists such as Aphex Twin and DJ Shadow. The first section explores this genre.

A few years later I was browsing through a book that partly inspired me to write this one, namely Colin Larkin's 'The All-Time Top 1000 Albums' (Virgin). I noticed the high placing that many jazz albums had in the book, particularly those of the trumpeter Miles Davis, and curiosity finally got the better of me. This opened up another vista, that of free-form instrumental jazz and fusion which will form the second section here.

Finally, we will look at a mixture of albums that have kept me entertained from 2019, on into the coronavirus 'lockdowns' of 2020 / 2021, when we were all forced to stay indoors to prevent something akin to the Black Death. This section is suitably named after the Radiohead track 'Climbing Up The Walls.' The usual format will apply, with artists we have encountered before coming first. I shudder to think how dull the lockdowns would have been without music, and the worst fate that I can imagine in later life would be being unable to ever hear it again. To quote Frank Zappa's lyrics from his *shock opera* 'Joe's Garage,' which is based around a society where music is illegal, one would surely become 'sullen and withdrawn, [and] dwindle off into the twilight realm of [one's] own secret thoughts, in a semi-catatonic state.'

Who knows what the future will bring, but I can't see myself putting my metaphorical record deck in the metaphorical attic anytime soon. Keep spinning those wheels of steel...

i) Technotronic

8.1) Kraftwerk – Kraftwerk (1970)

Before the German group Kraftwerk became the synthesiser gurus we all know, they were an experimental outfit and you can't get more experimental than this offering with a single orange traffic cone on the cover and much weirdness within. 'Ruckzuck,' meaning 'rucksack,' is a flute dominated track, but played rhythmically and not melodically. 'Stratovarius' is grating while 'Megaherz' is soothing, and 'Von Himmel Hock' is an anti-war piece with the sound of bombs dropping created electronically and a surprisingly funky conclusion which sounds as though it is made from little more than frequency generating devices and drums. Just don't expect any vocals.

8.2) Kraftwerk 2 – Kraftwerk (1972)

This time a green traffic cone graces the cover and the avant-garde pieces sound less synthesised. 'Klingklang' is a kind of precursor to 'Autobahn,' gently chugging along relentlessly, albeit with occasional tweaks to the playback speed. 'Atem' means 'breath' and it is the nearest thing to Ron Geesin's 'Body Transport' that I've heard elsewhere. 'Harmonica' sounds nothing like the said instrument, being a series of keyboard notes. The whole album is very soothing. Just don't expect any melodies.

8.3) Ralf Und Florian – Kraftwerk (1973)

The final album before Kraftwerk got the show on the road with 'Autobahn' is a more melodic affair than the previous two, although still very much in the experimental camp. 'Kristallo' has a pulsating synth effect adorned doodles that sound like a harpsichord, and the vocals in 'Tanzmuzik' give a track that is similar to 'Klingkang' an ethereal feel, and whereas the former had one chord, this one has two. Double bubble! The finale, 'Ananas Symphonie', is the album's key track, being thirteen minutes in length and demonstrating a variety of effects including a steel guitar sound, with a hypnotic organ omnipresent. Just don't expect. Full stop.

That said, the first four Kraftwerk albums (we've already looked at 'Autobahn') appeal to me much more than their later work, but as is often the case, I seem to be in the minority.

8.4) Tone Float – Organisation (1970)

This was released just before band members 'Ralf und Florian' formed Kraftwerk, and at the time they were firmly in the prog rock genre. The twenty-minute title track begins with tinkles and rattles, finally establishing a rhythm after nearly five minutes. The organist wakes up round about the eight-minute mark and the bass player finally picks up his instrument at around ten minutes. It's a marked contrast to today's music which is aimed at those with pitifully low concentration spans. Apparently if there isn't a vocal within the first seven seconds modern listeners just switch off. 'Milk Rock' sounds like a gargling flute over a prominent bass riff. Be warned, it's interesting and entertaining but not exactly hummable!

8.5) Hystery – Ron Geesin (1994)

Ron Geesin famously provided the orchestrations for Pink Floyd's epic track 'Atom Heart Mother.' He also collaborated with Floyd's bassist Roger Waters to produce a soundtrack to an educational film called 'The Body.' In his own right he has provided music for television and has put together an impressive, albeit eccentric, body of work (the pun is deliberate). This album is a great overview, and if there's one thing I like even more than a chronological overview, it's one in reverse chronology. I wrote a whole book this way once. You don't care!

After 'Parallel Bar,' from Ron's album 'Bluefuse' (1993), which provides a twelve-bar instrumental in every conceivable key, we get a track made entirely from coughs. There are synthesiser tunes and vocal experiments galore, as well as the odd bit of poetry recited in Ron's distinctive Scottish accent. As we delve back further we get more banjo and piano, some ambience and increasingly bizarre vocalisations, ending with the doolally 'No. 8 Scalpel Incision Foxtrot.'

8.6) As He Stands – Ron Geesin (1973)

This can be purchased as a double CD with Ron's first album, 1967's 'A Raise Of The Eyebrows.' By this time Ron had perfected what he does and the opening track is a microcosm of this in three parts. I view Mr. Geesin as a kind of 1970s 'Aphex Twin.' Listen to 'A Cymbal And Much Electronics' to see what I mean. Occasionally he recites some of his quirky prose, and 'Upon Composition' is like a mini-sampler of his old work for adverts and the like. 'Can't You Stop That Thing' provides a lively finish on banjo and guitar. And remember Ron played everything himself in the days when perhaps Paul McCartney was the only well-known artist who had produced an album this way. 'To Roger Waters Wherever You Are' is a wacky simulation of the Scottish Highlands in winter, complete with synthesised bagpipes. It seems that Rog didn't answer. His loss.

8.7) Right Through – Ron Geesin (1977)

This is a totally bonkers affair from start to finish. The chanting of prepositions sounds like the Smurfs have been at the wacky baccy, and there seems to be some kind of concept about a revolving door taking off and landing us in varying musical terrain. 'Throb Thencewards Thrill' is a synthesiser piece which finishes with a sound illusion of notes getting ever-higher. This effect is reversed on 'Gong Of Gong Goes Right Through' which builds up an ominous atmosphere before seeming to fall into the earth's core. There is one recitation on the album and a track made entirely of vocal moans and groans. If you get the CD reissue, 'Right Through – And Beyond,' you'll be treated to some short pieces that were put together for a BBC New Year programme. For my wish list, I would like to see Ron's piano album, 'Patruns' (1975), made available on CD too. Is anyone writing all these down?

8.8) Funny Frown – Ron Geesin (1991)

This is a collection of later ditties put together by the enigmatic Mr. Geesin. Some tunes are very melodic like 'Piano Prance' and 'Mad Kite.' He plays a remarkably straight version of 'Vivaldi's Largo In D' and there's still a healthy dose of his scat singing style with 'Throat Poise.' Expect plenty of creative synthesiser use too. There is another compilation called 'Land Of Mist' (1995) which collates Ron's more ambient sounding tracks. It's rare as rocking horse ejectamenta and does contain a fair few tracks that are also on 'Hystery.' I never quite got Ron's later album 'Roncycle 1' (2011), but if you fancy some more avant-garde synthesiser work you may wish to try it. The collage of weather presenters is most amusing; 'And Monday's a write-off!'

8.9) Electronic Meditation - Tangerine Dream (1970)

When I downloaded TD's 'Pink Years' compilation I had no idea how much of their music would infiltrate my collection. Well, let's deal with the albums I view as 'essential' in order. Before discovering synthesisers, this German band were creating textures from a regular 'rock' set up with guitars and drums. They were named after a line in the Beatles song 'Lucy In The Sky With Diamonds' and heavily influenced by Pink Floyd at this stage. This is an album for anyone who loves the Floyd track 'A Saucerful Of Secrets.' 'Journey Through A Burning Brain' builds to a frenzy; just wait for that electric guitar drone to kick in. 'Cold Smoke' does the same, using a panning effect dramatically. And don't panic, the backwards vocal in 'Resurrection' is perfectly innocuous, being nothing more than the blurb on a cross-Channel ferry ticket.

8.10) Alpha Centauri - Tangerine Dream (1971)

These were the days when you could create an album from just three tracks if they were long enough. The opener has a church organ sound, whilst 'Fly And Collision Of Comas Sola' begins with electronic squishing noises and builds to a dense wall of reverberating tom-tom sounds cut across by flowery flute lines. And then the drums kick in! Then there's the title track which suffers production-wise to the extent that even the 2018 remastered version still sounds overloaded at points. There's more flute, more organ and a choral ending introduced by what sounds like an intergalactic radio broadcast in German. If you think you'll need waking up after this, the older four-track version includes the rocking 'Ultima Thule, Part 1' as a finisher.

8.11) Zeit - Tangerine Dream (1972)

Just when you thought Tangerine Dream couldn't get any more experimental they up the ante even further, with four movements that are each just shy of twenty minutes. They open the album with looping cellos improvising around a single note for seven minutes before the electronics take over. The second movement sounds like metal debris clanging around in space. There's even a recognisable guitar sound at the start of the third movement before bubbling space volcanoes take over. 'Zeit' means 'time' by the way. You'll need a lot of it to really appreciate this one.

8.12) Atem - Tangerine Dream (1973)

BBC radio DJ John Peel took a shine to this album and thus the Germanic experimenters became known in Blighty. The twenty-minute title track sounds like a frenetic ritual in space with thumping toms building to a crescendo where crazed organ chords burst through until the whole thing explodes into crepuscular ambience. Woohoo! I try to get that C-word into every book I write so that's ticked another box. 'Fauni-Gena' sounds like a night in an aviary with a mellotron player, while we are treated to some animalistic vocal noises on 'Wahn.' 'Atem' still means 'breath' by the way.

8.13) Phaedra - Tangerine Dream (1974)

And on the seventh day Tangerine Dream discovered sequencers. This is the album that introduced what would become their trademark sound. The sequencer enabled musicians to pre-program a series of notes and these could be repeated at speeds faster than they would naturally be played, eventually becoming the 'backing of choice' on eighties pop records. However, in 1974 its use was far more experimental.

A lot happens during the seventeen minutes of the title track and much of this is very spacey and hard to describe. The sequencer tended to destabilise, but the band liked the effect of it rising in pitch and left this on the track. I think that's what you call 'serendipity.' The atmospheric 'string section' sound of the mellotron takes over towards the end of the track and it ends with what sounds like a recording from a school playground. 'Mysterious Semblance At The Strand Of Nightmares' provides another hypnotic mellotron wash. 'Phaedra' is a Greek name meaning 'bright' by the way.

8.14) Rubycon - Tangerine Dream (1975)

There are just two tracks on this album, each a side long. Remember what a 'side' was? Good! After six minutes of ambient synth doodling it's time to fire up the sequencer. This builds dramatically and the backwards notes followed by what sounds like a processed guitar twang is the spine-tingling *pièce de résistance*. 'Part 1' dies away with jangly processed piano sounds, before the choral synth effect and sequencing get another airing in 'Part 2.'

8.15) Stratosfear - Tangerine Dream (1976)

I was never a fan of 'Ricochet' which was partly a live recording. I'm not sure if it's the brassy synthesised trumpet effect that I don't like or what. Either way, lets skip to 'Stratosfear,' and it's hard to believe it but this one even has musical notes in it. How's that for a concept? Opening with some actual guitar, the sequencer and synthesiser soon take over, building steadily until an all-too-brief electric guitar solo from Edgar Froese breaks through. The harpsichord and flute effect that bookends 'The Big Sleep In Search Of Hades' sounds like it could have been made by Pink Floyd in their 'Julia Dream' era. There's a lonely harmonica on the third track, and the piano at the end of the final track sounds inspired by Beethoven's 'Moonlight Sonata.' TD were getting awfully eclectic.

8.16) Cyclone - Tangerine Dream (1978)

'Encore' (1977) is another live album, and like 'Ricochet' it seems to lack something to me. Anyway, how's this for a curveball? 'Cyclone' even has singing on the first two tracks, and I mean actual singing, not just reading from a ferry ticket. As far as I'm aware, the last time anyone from TD had sung any lyrics was on a mid-sixties single released under the name 'The Ones.' The keyboard on 'Rising Runner Missed By Endless Sender' sounds like a guitar, another new sound in the group's arsenal. Meanwhile 'Madrigal Meridian' runs for twenty minutes, and once the sequencer has established itself Mr. Froese lets rip on the electric guitar. He was a seriously underrated soloist. Things then die down for some 'Middle Eastern' sounding violin and a return of the synth-guitar effect with added flute to conclude matters.

8.17) Force Majeure - Tangerine Dream (1979)

This is the final TD album I'm going to review. The eighties saw the band try a more commercial sound, although 'Hyperborea' (1983) and 'Green Desert' (1986) are worth a listen; the latter has another satisfying guitar solo in its title track. For a much later album check out 'Oedipus Tyrannus' (2019) which hones an abandoned 1974 project into something quite remarkable. Anyway, 'Force Majeure' is the nearest the band ever got to 'rock.' There's even proper drums on this album. The title track has a creepy opening reminiscent of Tangerine Dream's early sound before it gets going. 'Cloudburst Flight' opens with acoustic guitar and lets the sequencer and synth do their thing before Edgar Froese again demonstrates that he is not just a master of the keyboard but that he can give any rock guitarist a run for their money. 'Thru Metamorphic Rocks' builds hypnotically until the werewolves begin to howl and an ominous repeated dissonant note pulses the track to its natural conclusion. Phew!

8.18) Selected Ambient Works 1985-1991- Aphex Twin (1992)

In the nineties there was a genre of music along the lines of 'young men mixing up tapes in their bedrooms.' This was perhaps the best example, although in truth I have no idea where Richard D. James blended his samples. It could have been in the kitchen for all I know. 'Xtal' sets the scene, while 'Tha' is a nine-minute relaxation epic. 'Green Calx' is the first of the Twin's 'coloured calx' tracks. 'Calx' means 'calculations' as far as I'm aware, so the mix of colours, mathematics and music hints at Richard's synaesthesia. Clearly he's a man after my own heart as we will see later.

8.19) Selected Ambient Works Volume II - Aphex Twin (1994)

Aphex Twin was the principal alias of Richard D. James, who is known to be a synaesthete. There is an appendix about this subject as it provides an interesting starting point to discussing how individuals perceive music in different ways. The tracks on 'SAW2,' which isn't to be confused with a gruesome horror film, are apparently inspired by lucid dreaming, a phenomenon where the dreamer realises that he or she is asleep and can take control of the dream. I often experience this myself and maybe that's why I like the surreal feeling of this music. The tracks are rarely short, very few of them have any kind of beat, and none of them were named on the album cover. Instead Richard provides a pie chart and a series of corresponding images so you can deduce which image goes with which track from the lengths. How thoughtful!

Some like 'Grass,' 'Tree' and 'Curtains' are very creepy, while if you listen to 'Lichen' in a 'half asleep half awake' state it feels positively celestial. Various versions of the album were produced with different numbers of tracks. The download version is a complete set with a creepy bonus called 'Th1 [Evnslower].'

Catchy title, hey? Oh yes, and this time the calculations (calx) were blue.

8.20) ...I Care Because You Do- Aphex Twin (1995)

This was the crossover album between the Twin's ambient experiments and his more dance-oriented material. The drum beat on 'Acrid Avid Jam Shred' is hypnotic, and 'Icct Hedral' has a dark orchestral feel, with its high point being the bridge in the middle. The piece would later be arranged for orchestra by Philip Glass and would turn up on the 'Donkey Rhubarb' EP. The middle section of this album is not easy listening. 'Ventolin' assaults the eardrums with its screech, which is supposed to mimic a side effect from taking the asthma reliever of its title, while 'Come On You Slags!' samples some innocent dialogue from a pornographic film. Classy, hey? Towards the end of the album things mellow out again. 'Next Heap With' has a similar feel to 'Icct Hedral,' but the standout track is 'Alberto Balsalm' which feels like walking on air. Just in case you're wondering where the wacky track titles come from, many of them are anagrams of 'Aphex Twin' or 'The Aphex Twin,' so if they ever come up in a cryptic crossword you'll know what to do!

8.21) The Richard D. James Album - Aphex Twin (1996)

This is the last of the Twin's albums I am going to review, and it marks his shift from analogue to digital techniques. Unless you want to buy the separate 'Girl/Boy Song' EP I'd recommend getting the fifteen-track version, as you'll actually hear Richard sing a couple of times. 'Beetles' is innocent fun and nothing to do with Lennon, McCartney and all that lot, while 'Milkman' is extremely naughty. '4' (which is confusingly track one) and 'Girl/Boy Song' both mix an orchestral feel with rapid drumbeats, which occasionally jar for added effect. 'Logon Rock Witch' could even be a long lost Beach Boys track from the 'Smile' era, as could 'Goon Gumpas.' The calculations were yellow this time.

After this Aphex Twin had a brief dalliance with the singles charts with 'Come To Daddy,' which had a genuinely scary video, as well as 'Windowlicker.' If you are going to venture beyond these I recommend the five-track 'Drukqs' promo disc, as the full double album is pretty unwieldy. The EP 'Computer Controlled Acoustic Instruments Pt 2' is also worth a listen. ('Pt 1' was 'Drukqs' itself apparently, now is everybody clear?).

8.22) Halfway Between The Gutter And The Stars – Fatboy Slim (2000)

I liked the four singles Norman Cook, alias the 'Fatboy,' released from the album 'You've Come A Long Way, Baby,' and their B-sides are also interesting. However, I couldn't stomach a whole album by the bloke until this, his third release, which has more contrast and a couple of guest vocals from Macy Gray, of which 'Love Life' is both cheeky and funky. 'Weapon Of Choice' has a similar feel to those early singles, and some of the tracks are pretty full on, but the ambient eleven-minute closing track is the clincher for me. Good things were coming out of Brighton, and I don't mean just the A23 and the A259. Yes, I know I've done that one; we all replay our favourite songs, so why can't we repeat our favourite jokes?

8.23) The KLF – The White Room (1991)

When the KLF were big in the early nineties I dismissed them as a 'bunch of nutters.' They burnt a million pounds for art after all, which simultaneously makes me think 'what a statement' and 'what a waste.' They'd already had a novelty chart-topper as the Timelords, but what of *The White Room*?

If you get the USA version, the album is of a similar format to Primal Scream's 'Screamadelica,' being half rave music and half 'chill out / wind down' material. The UK version winds down sooner, as the version of 'Last Train To Trancentral' is more laid back than the single version. 'Trancentral' was the studio where the mixing was done apparently. The vocals continually self-promote, with impassioned vocal lines like 'Take me to the church of the KLF' and constant reference to the 'Justified Ancients Of Mu Mu,' an alternative moniker the band used. Regardless, it's all very enjoyable, and American country singer, Tammy Wynette, was clearly impressed enough to re-record 'Justified And Ancient' with them. It's the original version that graces this album.

Jimmy Cauty was also one half of the Orb (where his partner in crime was Alex Paterson as opposed to Bill Drummond), so the ambient direction the album hints at shouldn't be surprising. Ditto for the KLF's album 'Chill Out' (1990) which pays homage to the album art from Pink Floyd's 'Atom Heart Mother.'

8.24) The Orb's Adventures Beyond The Underworld – The Orb (1991)

This is a lavish double CD opening with 'Little Fluffy Clouds,' which samples an interview with Ricky Lee Jones, the singer of 'Chuck E's In Love.' The Orb's tune reached the UK top ten in 1993. The second most commercial track is the reggae-influenced 'Perpetual Dawn' with its ridiculous 'gibberish' vocal sample. The tracks flow together seamlessly into a dreamy collage of vocal sounds and planes streaking across the sky (or are they rockets?). And just in case you're not chilled out enough, there's the eighteen-minute ambient wash of the final track to close things. There's even a sample of Minnie Riperton's 1975 hit 'Lovin' You' in there somewhere. Sweet dreams.

8.25) Endtroducing – DJ Shadow (1996)

Credited as the first album where not a single musical note was played by the creator, this is 'cut and paste' music at its best. The whole affair has a dark ambience to it. 'What Does Your Soul Look Like (Part 1)' is particularly nice with its jazzy feel aided by the saxophone sample. 'Part 4' also appears here. Samples often turn up on multiple tracks in different contexts, such as the one used on 'Transmission 2' and 'Midnight In A Perfect World.' There's even a sample from 'The Body' by Roger Waters and Ron Geesin. I mean how many people have *that* in their collection to start with? There's also a weird narrative about beaming things directly into your consciousness. It sounds like one of my fiction plots, but as you can see from the release date Mr. Shadow got there first!

And just in case you're wondering what happened to parts two and three of 'What Does Your Soul Look Like,' you'll need an album called 'Preemptive Strike' for these.

8.26) The Campfire Headphase – Boards Of Canada (2005)

Boards Of Canada are not from Canada but the UK. Now we've got that cleared up I can tell you that this was introduced to me by my camping buddy Dan, who happens to be the world's biggest Kings Of Leon fan. Fact! It was uncanny that the three of us each discovered ambient styles of music independently around the mid-teenies (I still don't like that term). Anyway in 'Campfire Headphase' you will regularly hear eerie sounding acoustic guitar, such as on the tracks 'Chromakey Dreamcoat' and 'Satellite Anthem Icarus.' Some of it is very dark sounding, for example 'Slow This Bird Down,' which is like music filtering in from a distant planet, distorted by space and time. If you do choose to put it on round a campfire, I'd advise doing this in the daytime. Falling asleep next to fire can be dangerous.

8.27) Clear – Bomb The Bass (1995)

I've never been hugely into dance music, and with the full-on rap opener I wasn't expecting to like this album. However, I bought it for the ambient track, 'Somewhere,' and consequently grew to like the experimental fare elsewhere on the album. Author, Will Self, does a bizarre monologue, which may have inspired comedian Chris Morris with his own disturbing monologues, and Sinéad O'Connor likens England to a vampire in the final offering (!) which even has an acoustic guitar strumming away. There's even a sound like Tibetan bells in one of the tracks, and it's fun to try to spot all the classic rock references in 'Brain Dead.' Anyone ever fallen in a bowl of Rubber Soul? No, I didn't think so.

8.28) Dummy – Portishead (1994)

Portishead is a pleasant little seaside town near Bristol, and Beth Gibbons provides the melancholic vocals on this trio's remarkable debut album. There were hits in the form of 'Numb,' 'Glory Box' and the brilliant 'Sour Times,' which has a cold Russian feel to it. All of it sounds like it has been put together for a dark espionage thriller. 'Strangers' has a remarkably deep bassy effect. With its liberal use of samples, this is all darkly exquisite stuff.

8.29) Frédéric Galliano – Espaces Baroques (1999)

Was this my gateway to jazz? Who knows, but the jazzy samples flow with abundance on this album by the French musician. Anything with numbers appeals to me and 'Pils Infinis Nos. 1-4' each have a different flavour. Bits of saxophone, piano and woodwind mingle around the beats and there's an amusing vocal sample on 'No.4.' The jazz vibe gets stronger still on the 23-minute 'Nomades Monades,' resplendent with slamming doors. And finally, 'Multiples Un' is about as minimalist as it gets, with a laid back piano motif repeated *ad infinitum* adorned with simple bass doodles and the incessant crackling of vinyl almost acting as an instrument in itself.

ii) All That Jazz

8.30) Kind Of Blue – Miles Davis (1959)

Jazz is a genre I got into relatively late compared to many, with the first *bona fide* jazz album (as opposed to a compilation) entering my collection at the age of 43. 'Kind Of Blue' by Miles Davis featured highly in Colin Larkin's book of 'The All-Time Top 1000 Albums' so I thought I'd give it a bash. If I had to explain the appeal of jazz to my younger self I'd say something like, 'You know you like guitar solos? Well, these solos are not on guitars and the solo is the song itself,' at which point I'd have probably reached for the nearest Beatles album.

The blues pervades on 'Kind Of Blue,' which is an exercise in modal jazz. The feeling is ultimately one of deep relaxation, as Miles' trumpet, Cannonball Adderley's alto sax, John Coltrane's saxophone and Bill Evans' piano all take turns in the limelight. Wynton Kelly takes over piano duties on one track, but John Coltrane almost steals the show from all in my opinion.

8.31) Sketches Of Spain – Miles Davis (1960)

This was one of three Miles Davis albums with orchestrations by Gil Evans. When I first heard it I found the trumpet lines rather incessant, but now I view it as an atmospheric masterpiece. The sixteen-minute treatment of Rodrigo's 'Concierto De Aranjuez' seems to pre-empt what the rock band Emerson, Lake & Palmer did with Aaron Copland's 'Fanfare For The Common Man,' in taking the basic melody of a classical piece and making it your own with lengthy improvisation. Bells tinkle and the whole album brings to mind the feel of a dusty square in a hilltop village.

8.32) In A Silent Way – Miles Davis (1969)

This was the first full blown fusion album from Miles Davis. I must admit that I like the 'cool jazz' sound of the late fifties, but tend to get lost in the abstractions when it comes to the post-bop era of the mid-sixties. If this all seems a foreign language to you, it was to me too for most of my life. With post-bop done and dusted, we got the warm sound of electric piano, and rock influences merging with the improvisational ethos of jazz. Miles' albums of the period were often carefully constructed from recordings of jams, and it is most obvious on this album, as the beginnings of both lengthy tracks are repeated at the end of them. When I first realised this I felt a little cheated, but the music was relaxed and almost ambient in feel, so such materialistic notions can soon be soothed away by playing it again.

8.33) Miles In The Sky – Miles Davis (1968)

The title was inspired by the Beatles song 'Lucy In The Sky With Diamonds' and the psychedelic colour-burst cover image was very much of its era too, but if you're expecting something that sounds like 'Sgt. Pepper' think again. This was the first album where Miles Davis included electric instruments, albeit very gently. Herbie Hancock's electric piano on 'Stuff' is very pleasant indeed and George Benson provides the subtle electric guitar accompaniment on 'Paraphernalia.' The second half of the album is acoustic jazz, but with 'In A Silent Way' not far off, the times they were a-changing.

8.34) Jack Johnson – Miles Davis (1971)

I never really got 'Bitches Brew' (1970) which is often cited as the pinnacle of fusion. Perhaps I find the sheer length of this double album daunting; in truth I find the album that followed it, 'Jack Johnson,' to be much more accessible. There are just two tracks and John McLaughlin's rock guitar playing is excellent. Miles even includes a section torn out of 'In A Silent Way,' appearing like an eerie ghost from the not-so-distant past. Soon after this Herbie Hancock strolls into the studio, yes, he of 1980s 'Rockit' fame, and puts in some initially jarring blasts on the organ. This is jazz at its best – edgy, but ultimately enjoyable. There is a short section of inspiring speech at the end and you may recall that Bob Dylan wrote a song about the boxer Jack Johnson at the same time.

My next move was to try the mix of studio and live recordings entitled 'Live-Evil.' Personally, I think the first disc completely eclipses the second, with its two short ambient pieces, one full blown rocker (with McLaughlin's guitar dominating again), and two lengthy jams, one of which ('What I Say') includes one hell of a drum solo!

8.35) On The Corner – Miles Davis (1972)

This album takes a bit of work to appreciate, as repetition is key. This album takes a bit of work to appreciate, as repetition is key. Sorry, I couldn't resist that. OK, so what we have here is some serious dabbling with Indian instrumentation, and Miles' trumpet is perhaps more distorted and ambient than on any other album. You have to really concentrate to follow the trumpet lines as there's just so much going on. Occasionally the rhythm dies down and the lengthy pieces take on a psychedelic feel, but the main bass-led rhythm is pretty incessant and unvarying across multiple tracks. Once you accept that, it's easier to enjoy.

8.36) Big Fun – Miles Davis (1974)

The title is a strange choice for an album that has such a crepuscular feel to it. Yay, I got it in again! But seriously, there is definitely something of the twilight about this album. For a start, with four tracks representing the four sides of the original double album, it's a formidable listen. The highlight is perhaps 'Go Ahead John' where, thanks to the marvels of the cutting room, we hear Miles' trumpet dueting with itself, the lines weaving around each other in a playful dance. The drum track is also mercilessly chopped from channel to channel, creating a bizarre effect, especially if you're using headphones. The opening track on this album uses repetition in a similar way to the much older tune, 'Nefertiti,' and the whole album seems to be a hybrid of 'In A Silent Way' and 'Bitches Brew' in terms of its overall sound.

8.37) Get Up With It – Miles Davis (1974)

Miles Davis was suffering from depression at the time this album was put together and I think it comes across in the dark feel of the music. Two tracks are over half an hour in length, these being the brooding 'I Loved Him So Well,' which was Miles' tribute to the jazz pianist Duke Ellington, and 'Calypso Frelimo' which is far removed from the light hearted feel of a calypso. The funk groove of 'Billy Preston' is a veritable earworm, and 'Rated X' is like an early drum and bass experiment with 'Halloween' organ. That said, 'Red China Blues' could have been released as a single with its conventional structure and wailing harmonica.

Like many, I think that the inventiveness of the fusion era has tended to overshadow Miles' later work, but if you need recommendations for a couple of eighties albums try the bluesy 'Star People' (1983) and 'Aura' (1989), which is an intriguing mixture of the 'ambient' and 'lounge' styles.

8.38) Round About Midnight – Miles Davis (1957)

Delving back into Miles' earlier period, this album opens with the atmospheric title track where his muted trumpet brings to mind wandering empty city streets in a film noir. 'All Of You' is nice and melodic, and 'Bye Bye Blackbird' is an easy high point for me, as I already knew the tune from which the improvisations stem. John Coltrane excels on the sax as always, and Red Garland's stabby style on the piano is very enjoyable on this album.

For more melodic jazz from this era, you can hear Miles on a twelve-inch single of 'Alison's Uncle' and 'Autumn Leaves' (1958) which was released under the name of Cannonball Adderley. The other version that I have of the latter tune is an ambient track by Coldcut which would belong in the last chapter if I was reviewing it. Chalk and cheese I guess. And finally if you want to hear a Disney tune transformed, 'Someday My Prince Will Come' (1961) is available as a single-track download if you're not ready for the whole album.

8.39) My Favourite Things – John Coltrane (1961)

This is an album for those who like to hear tunes they recognise played in an improvisational way. Coltrane's saxophone playing is superb and occasionally bordering on frenzied, while the piano breaks from McCoy Tyner are also pretty amazing. 'Every Time We Say Goodbye' evokes the feel of a smoky jazz bar, while the version of 'Summertime' reminds me of several Pink Floyd tracks, such as 'Echoes,' because of its alternating major and minor chords between the verses.

8.40) Time Out – The Dave Brubeck Quartet (1959)

Pianist Dave Brubeck's most famous album explores unusual time signatures, but this is not difficult listening like some of Frank Zappa's experiments were. 'Take Five' is perhaps the most famous jazz piece ever and it was even used as the theme tune to a TV comedy when I was a child. 'Blue Rondo A La Turk' also succeeds in sandwiching a blues sequence in between two slices of traditional Turkish rhythm. 'Three To Get Ready' is a nice laid back piece, which was used in the David Lynch film 'Inland Empire' before it all got horrific. Brubeck's piano comfortably shares the limelight with the alto sax playing of Paul Desmond.

8.41) Ken Burns Jazz: Herbie Hancock – Herbie Hancock (2000)

This is a representative collection of the key-tinkler's esteemed work, beginning with 'Watermelon Man,' with its typically 'sixties' vibe and bluesy structure. It's as much Freddie Hubbard and Dexter Gordon's tune as Herbie's, with their pivotal contributions being on trumpet and alto sax respectively. Miles Davis had made the transition to fusion a few years before, but the fifteen-minute 'Chameleon' from 1973's 'Head Hunters' album was a bold move nevertheless. Whereas the music of Miles Davis tended to become darker, Hancock's sound was perhaps closer in feel to Stevie Wonder's work at the time, and after the electric piano workout of 'Actual Proof' and the typically 'eighties' pop hit 'Rockit' which reached number eight in the UK singles chart, he does indeed give us a barely recognisable rendition of one of Stevie's songs.

That's all the jazz for now, but I can imagine this section expanding in years to come.

iii) Climbing Up The Walls

8.42) Mellow Yellow – Donovan (1967)

Oddly, the USA version of this Scotsman's album is the 'proper' one. After the jazzy title track, we have 'Writer In The Sun' which perhaps reflects Donovan's thoughts on retiring from the music scene. 'House Of Jansch' and 'Young Girl Blues' are performed on acoustic guitar and wouldn't have sounded out of place on Donovan's 'Fairytale' album. Mr. Leitch references numerous places in London in his songs of this period. He had thrown himself completely into the swinging sixties scene for sure. He swings right into jazz on 'Bleak City Woman.'

8.43) Wear Your Love Like Heaven – Donovan (1967)

This was the first record from a double release called 'A Gift From A Flower To A Garden.' The second record is an acoustic disc called 'For Little Ones' – he's pretty much reviewed it himself with the title there, saving me time and effort, so thanks Donovan. The title track on 'WYLLH' seems to be virtually a list of colours sung with unusual intonations. In truth, the disc is not as eclectic as 'Sunshine Superman' or 'Mellow Yellow,' and the ever-present organ clearly dates the album. 'Sun' is nice and melodic, but the overall feel is that it's all a bit 'hello trees, hello flowers.' 'Mad John's Escape' is amusing in many ways however.

8.44) Hurdy Gurdy Man – Donovan (1968)

The opening track is full blown rock with some searing electric guitar most likely from a 'pre-Led Zeppelin' Jimmy Page. I like the line about 'Damp through all eternity / The crying of humanity' – fifty years later and we're still no better at improving our lot it seems. Indian influences can frequently be heard on this album, with particular use of a drone style (basically improvising around a chord for the whole of a song). 'Hi, It's Been A Long Time' perhaps acknowledges the dark side of the hippy life and its negative effect on the body. It also has some great drum fills which were *de rigueur* on late sixties hits. 'The River Song' is a nice acoustic ditty and Donovan also tries his hand at French in 'Jennifer Juniper.' There's not much he *couldn't* do really.

8.45) Barabajagal – Donovan (1969)

This was the album after which most people stopped exploring Donovan's music. More fool them. The Jeff Beck Band gave the title track a rocky 'voodoo' feel, while 'Where Is She' is a hauntingly sad 'soft jazz' ballad. 'Happiness Runs' is like a children's song being sung as a round, but it begins with a philosophical verse about the transience of human life compared to that of a stone. 'I Love My Shirt' is a jolly comedy song (is it comedy?) and the last track sounds like a Cockney sing-along. You would have thought the finale would have been 'Atlantis' to be honest.

8.46) Open Road – Donovan (1970)

The opening track, 'Changes,' has nothing to do with David Bowie, but to a certain extent Donovan was almost as chameleon-like as Bowie, morphing from 'protest folk' to 'hippie psychedelia,' and in this incarnation forming a rock band. The song also contains a great couplet; 'The absurdity of greed / How much can one man possibly need?' It's such a shame that the spirit of Mammon won the West and that views against the 'greed is good' brigade seem increasingly marginal. 'Song For John' has a country flavour and 'Riki Tiki Tavi' has some great cowbell action. This track, along with 'Poke At The Pope,' demonstrates that Donovan could be almost as direct as John Lennon when it came to questioning society's norms. 'Clara Clairvoyant' has a funky rock sound and 'People Used To' is a melodic nod to his folkier past.

8.47) Cosmic Wheels – Donovan (1973)

Donovan's next album, 'H.M.S. Donovan' (1971) is a double acoustic album for children, although it does contain the atmospheric song 'Lord Of The Reedy River.' He plugs back in for 'Cosmic Wheels' which has a title track alluding to astrology, a subject that was probably still on Donovan's mind when he wrote 'Earth Sign Man.' 'Wild Witch Lady' is not as satisfying as 'Season Of The Witch' (1966) and it has some peculiar vocals which are a cross between a falsetto and screaming. 'I Like You' contains the interesting line 'You're such a good friend / I'd hate to have you as an enemy,' while 'The Intergalactic Laxative' is far less poetic, concerning the toilet habits of astronauts with details that I never expected to hear in song. Was he just taking the...

1973 was a productive year for the 'Scottish Dylan,' with a second album appearing in the form of 'Essence To Essence.' This contained 'There Is An Ocean,' a brilliant acoustic track musing on good and evil which seems to be in the spirit of yin and yang.

8.48) The Hurting – Tears For Fears (1983)

When I was a child in the eighties I was not a fan of the 'current' bands, despising what I viewed as excessive use of synthesisers and much preferring the 'real instruments' of the sixties. However, with the passing of forty years, the bands of the era seem worth reappraising and this album is a gem. Like U2's 'The Joshua Tree,' the first half of the album is so strong that the second half tends to get passed over. 'Mad World' is a classic, even if you only know the Gary Jules

'Christmas number one' version, but there are plenty of other angst-ridden atmospheric pieces here including 'The Hurting,' 'Pale Shelter' and 'Ideas As Opiates' which could be an anthem for our age – 'Lies spread on lies / We don't care.' Trump, anybody?

We've already looked at 'Songs From The Big Chair' so I will just add that their 1989 single, 'Sowing The Seeds Of Love,' is something of a masterpiece, combining its political message with as many musical references to the Beatles as possible. Bits sound like 'Penny lane,' bits sound like 'I Am The Walrus,' what's not to like? That said, I still prefer my misheard lyric of '*Balls* to the rules!'

8.49) SAHB Stories - The Sensational Alex Harvey Band (1976)

Ah yes, back to the legendary Scottish band SAHB. 'Jungle Rub Out' incorporates a bit of funk into the usual rock and 'Boston Tea Party' gave the band a UK hit single. 'Dogs Of War' is nothing like the Pink Floyd track of the same name, in spite of expressing the same sentiment about the futility of war. Alex Harvey's deranged staccato vocal on this rocker is the album's high point.

8.50) Rock Drill – The Sensational Alex Harvey Band (1977) [UK: 1978]

This was Alex's final album with the titular band, named after a 1913 sculpture. Here Alex raises awareness of environmental issues with tracks like 'The Dolphins.' 'Who Murdered Sex?' is bordering on comedy but has a great guitar riff. 'Water Beastie' has a reggae feel in spite of being about the Loch Ness Monster, and the album ends with 'Mrs. Blackhouse,' a parody on Mary Whitehouse's attempts to censor the 'mind destroying filth' on UK television at the time.

I recommend getting the box set of SAHB for the fantastic track 'No Complaints Department' which Alex withdrew from 'Rock Drill' because he feared that the mention of his brother's death would have upset his parents. The song is a great philosophical statement about life delivered in the manner of somebody at the end of a heavy night's drinking. 'Engine Room Boogie' is pretty good as an extra track too. The band were on a high and it's such a shame they didn't continue to work together.

8.51) Rough And Rowdy Ways – Bob Dylan (2020)

This was Bob Dylan's first album since receiving a Nobel Prize for literature on grounds of the poetic and prolific nature of his work. Just as you thought he'd turned into a 1940s cover artist, he releases an album of all-new material and his longest ever track, so let's start with the seventeen-minute 'Murder Most Foul.' The song begins by expressing sadness about the assassination of John F. Kennedy in 1963 and moves on to Bob listing artists and songs that he admires, perhaps hinting that music itself is bigger than death. Some of the references are surprising, such as Queen for example, but then again he name-dropped Alicia Keys a few albums back, didn't he? 'I Contain Multitudes' perhaps expresses the idea that everybody is an amalgam of different personalities and influences. 'Goodbye Jimmy Reed' has a feel reminiscent of 'Leopard Skin Pill Box Hat' from way back in 1966, and he uses the melody of Offenbach's 'Barcarolle' for 'I've Made Up My Mind To Give Myself To You.' This album is good. Correction - it's very good.

8.52) Back To The Egg – Paul McCartney / Wings (1979)

We've reviewed the excellent 'Band On The Run' album already, which was when Wings showed that they truly were a force to be reckoned with. 'Venus And Mars' (1975) is merely 'pleasant,' with the melodic 'Listen To What The Man Said' being a highlight, while 'Wings At The Speed Of Sound' (1976) has two great songs ('Let 'Em In' and 'Silly Love Songs') but doesn't really engage much beyond these. We've already reviewed 'London Town' (1978), so now we arrive at 'Back To The Egg,' and here the band embrace the musical changes of the times, with punky tracks like 'Spin It On,' while 'Arrow Through Me' dips a toe into 'Stevie Wonder' waters. 'Rockestra Theme' is not an ELO pastiche but a lively rock instrumental and if you get the version with the bonus tracks there are a couple of festive favourites to finish. No big hits, but a satisfying album.

8.53) Off The Ground – Paul McCartney (1993)

The 1980s were a difficult period for sixties musicians, with everyone from Bob Dylan to the Rolling Stones attempting to update their sound and often neglecting what they do best. The single 'Once Upon A Long Ago' was one of Paul's better moments in the eighties, and 'Flowers In The Dirt,' the 1989 album which featured collaborative work with Elvis Costello, is good nonetheless, but it was Paul's first album of the nineties where he seemed to reconnect with his melodic past.

'Hope Of Deliverance' could almost be a lost Beatles song and the title track has a nice percussive drive to it. 'C'mon People' starts with Paul and a lone piano and builds into an epic, with an orchestra thrown in for good measure. There's a snippet of a ditty called 'Cosmically Conscious' at the end, and if you get the two-disc version called 'The Complete Works' you'll be able to hear the full track, which is simple with a great 'retro' Beatles feel. You'll also get the folky anti-greed anthem, 'Big Boys Bickering,' where McCartney lets out a few rare expletives. Even national treasures get angry sometimes.

8.54) Driving Rain – Paul McCartney (2001)

After the excellent 'Flaming Pie,' Paul teamed up with David Gilmour for an album of rock and roll covers called 'Run Devil Run' (1999). In 2001 we were treated to more underappreciated quality from Mr. PM, and he certainly delivers value for money here when it comes to both length and diversity. It's towards the end of the album that things get very good indeed. 'Heather' is not the track that he demos on some bootleg Beatles albums, but a melodic piano ditty, clearly dedicated to his second wife, Heather Mills. His feelings were genuine, that's for sure. 'Riding Into Jaipur' is an Eastern-flavoured piece, and 'Rinse The Raindrops' exceeds ten minutes and was the boldest thing he'd done in years, with some deliciously crunchy guitar chords that remind me of 'I Want You (She's So Heavy)' by the Beatles. And to top it off, the vocal almost reaches the frenzied levels of the coda of 'Hey Jude.' Absolutely superb!

8.55) McCartney III – Paul McCartney (2020)

While locked down as part of Britain's attempt to control the spread of coronavirus, Mr. McCartney was forced to work alone, in the same way that he produced his albums 'McCartney' (1970) and 'McCartney II' (1980). The results are interesting. Just wait for the drumbeat to drop in on 'Long Tailed Winter Bird.' 'Deep Deep Feeling' is getting into ambient territory, while expressing the paradox that you can both love and hate feelings simultaneously. He puts an acoustic coda on the end of this track just to demonstrate the inherent melody, and I can even imagine it being performed this way by a cover artist in Liverpool's Cavern Club. 'Lavatory Lil' harks back to Lennon's character songs, 'Mean Mr. Mustard' and 'Polythene Pam' on 'Abbey Road.' Sometimes Paul rocks, sometimes he keeps it acoustic, and it all just proves that he is not creatively finished yet. Hopefully we'll get 'McCartney IV' in time for his hundredth birthday.

8.56) Then Play On – Fleetwood Mac (1969)

This was Peter Green's last album with Fleetwood Mac and pretty much the end of the band's blues era. The two 'Madge' tracks are jams, of which 'Searching For Madge' has some surprising cuts. 'When You Say' is a bittersweet acoustic track and 'My Dream' is a succulent instrumental. Getting the version with bonus tracks is imperative, with parts one and two of 'Oh Well' seeming to segue even though 'Part 1' fades. This is simply one of the best songs the group ever produced with simple but brilliant lyrics. 'Green Manalishi' was psychedelic blues rock at its best, and don't forget the sublime 'World In Harmony.' It's a goodun for sure!

8.57) Vol. 4 – Black Sabbath (1972)

The 'catchy' title was dreamed up by the record company. They must have thought long and hard to come up with that. This was the album that contained the piano and mellotron ballad, 'Changes,' which Ozzy re-recorded with his daughter Kelly and took to the top of the UK singles chart in 2003. 'FX' is typical 'seventies' tinkling, whereas 'Laguna Sunrise' is a more satisfying instrumental with a Spanish feel. Tracks like 'Cornucopia' and 'Under The Sun' are supremely heavy for 1972;

on the periodic table of metals think 'tungsten' or 'polonium.' Ozzy's voice is superb as always, and it seems remarkable that he comes across as almost clownlike on TV but can turn out epic vocals like these at the drop of a hat. The orchestra at the end of 'Snowblind' surely set the stage for the myriad 'heavy rock and orchestra' albums that followed in later decades.

8.58) Sabbath Bloody Sabbath – Black Sabbath (1973)

Black Sabbath always provided a bit of breathing space on their albums, and here the acoustic instrumental 'Fluff' and the beginning of 'Spiral Architect' provide this, sounding not dissimilar from the Peter Green era of Fleetwood Mac. The band experiments with a variety of sounds and fans must have had a shock when first encountering a synthesiser on 'Who Are You?' 'Looking For Today' gets close to ELO territory with some nice flutey bits, and the aforementioned 'Spiral Architect' ends up sounding like a hybrid of Hawkwind and the song 'Question' by the Moody Blues. Just in case you think the boys had forgotten how to rock, the finale of the title track and the riff of 'Killing Yourself To Live' were pretty much the heaviest metal apart from uranium in 1973 for sure.

A second wave of heavy metal took place in the eighties and nineties, with bands like Metallica picking up the baton, but with the exception of crossover tracks like 'Enter Sandman' and 'Nothing Else Matters' it was generally a bit too much for me. I prefer my metals lighter. The Beatles would surely be gold...

8.59) Shine On Brightly – Procol Harum (1968)

...Which brings us back to the sixties. It never fails to amaze me how often critics get music wrong. To me, this album sewed the seeds for Barclay James Harvest and myriad others by pretty much inventing prog rock. The critics thought that it wasn't much different to the band's first album. What?! There's a seventeen-minute track for a start (now split into five parts on the CD edition). Apart from shamelessly name-dropping their record company in the title of 'Magdalene (My Regal Zonophone)' the band don't put a foot wrong here in my opinion. The lengthy track is called 'In Held 'Twas In I,' a title comprising the first words of various lines throughout the sprawling piece which opens with a spoken word intro. Apart from the short section called *'Twas Teatime At The Circus* the lyrics seem to be groping around for the meaning of life. The guitar has a great sound throughout and the ending is hymn-like. King Crimson and others got the credit, but Procol Harum were first. Sadly modern generations may have them marked down as a 'one hit wonder.' I did too for many years, until I saw the light. Shine on brightly!

8.60) Showbiz – Muse (1999)

Devon's biggest musical export actually emerged as though they'd been doing it for years on their debut album, although I didn't own it until a box of free CDs was flung my way. The alternating quiet piano and rock sections of the opening track, 'Sunburn,' show the band's classical approach to rock music from the outset. It's actually quite refreshing when Muse adopt a simple chord structure such as on the bluesy 'Falling Down' and 'Unintended' with its gently picked Spanish guitar. Don't worry, there's plenty of Muse's trademark bombast too!

8.61) Standing On The Shoulder Of Giants – Oasis (2000)

This is often viewed as the album where the legend imploded and I was formerly of that opinion. However, a listen twenty years later reveals that we were all wrong. Admittedly, the expletively-titled opening track leaves you wondering what kind of ride you're in for, but the content is actually surprisingly good. 'Go Let It Out' perhaps sums up our feelings about authority at times; 'Is it any wonder that princes and kings / Are clowns that caper in the sawdust rings?' The album has a darker, more brooding feel than most Oasis albums and the final track, 'Roll It Over,' is sublime, but for me the high point is when Noel launches into the guitar solo on 'Sunday Morning Call.'

8.62) Chasing Yesterday – Noel Gallagher's High Flying Birds (2015)

With Oasis disbanded Noel Gallagher formed a new band, and the first album produced the enjoyable single 'AKA...What A Life!' His younger brother Liam formed Beady Eye, which was basically 'Oasis without Noel,' but with 'Chasing Yesterday' it did seem that the older sibling had won the war. It's all very anthemic and slightly hypnotic at times. 'Riverman' opens the album with shades of Travis about it and 'Ballad Of The Mighty I' closes it with a solid drumbeat as its anchor. There is much to be enjoyed between these two tracks as well. I always enjoy a bit of cowbell action, and 'The Mexican' provides this, being a Rolling Stones style rocker.

8.63) White Ladder – David Gray (1998)

My camping buddy, Jim, who had been best man at my wedding, had nailed his colours to the mast in giving me his entire CD collection, relying on streaming services for music thenceforth. His brother Dan followed suit around eighteen months later, again proving the adage that one man's trash is another man's treasure. In truth there were a lot of albums that I already had and a lot that went straight to the local 'bring and share' box in a 'do not pass go, do not collect £200' style, but there were also some nuggets that I'd previously missed. 'White Ladder' was one such album. I think at the time of its release I was disappointed that the blow and bluster of the nineties was fizzling out with a whimper and that all this new 'girlie' music had taken over the charts.

David's acoustic guitar is accompanied by subtle beats, it's all very laid back and gentle, and you will all know 'Babylon' and 'This Year's Love.' It sounds like there's even a theremin on 'We're Not Right.' David's voice has a slightly Dylan-esque quality about it; listen to the unusual emphasis when he sings 'I used to be so definite.' That said, the nine-minute cover of Soft Cell's 'Say Hello Wave Goodbye' trumps the lot, providing a hypnotically sad conclusion.

8.64) Inside In / Inside Out – The Kooks (2006)

A number of guitar-based bands became popular in the second half of the noughties in the wake of the Arctic Monkeys, and to be honest I didn't take a lot of notice until that batch of freebies came my way over a decade later. Vocalist Luke Pritchard has a very distinctive voice with very English intonations. 'Ooh La' was a popular radio hit at the time, as was 'Naïve' and the melodic 'She Moves In Her Own Way,' with its positive message, 'I'm a better man / Moving on to better things.' All three hits have an acoustic / light guitar sound, but the band do have a more heavily amplified aspect too, as demonstrated on tracks like 'See The World.' 'Seaside' seems an appropriate opening track for a band from Brighton.

8.65) Razorlight – Razorlight (2006)

Another album from Jim's box of delights. Razorlight's UK number one single, 'America,' reminds me of when I was doing deliveries to the cruise terminal in Southampton as this was a big hit on the radio at the time. The jangly guitar opening was atmospheric as the sun was coming up on those early morning runs, and the line 'All my life / Watching America' sums up how we often feel in the UK, where a culture that is really quite different to ours still seems to be all around us. The singer acknowledges 'Nothing on the TV / Nothing on the radio / That means that much to me.' The album's opening track, 'In The Morning,' is extremely catchy and demonstrates a more punchy sound, as does 'Who Needs Love?' with the addition of rhythmic piano chords.

8.66) Tellin' Stories – The Charlatans (1997)

Tim Burgess 'out-Liams' Mr. Gallagher with his sneering vocals, but in truth this West Midlands band were around before Oasis existed, although the popularity of the Manchester band probably helped keep the Charlatans riding high as the nineties went on. 'North Country Boy' was another one of those hits that my colleague Greg used to sing at me in the nineties when I was at work, presumably because I was the only person there who came from a place of under 2,000 inhabitants, although 'north' was severely stretching it – any further south and you'd be in France! 'One To Another' is a good rock track with a pounding guitar riff and piano rhythm. The keyboard playing of Rob Collins is a major factor in the band's sound, with the settings clearly fixed on 'Hammond organ' mode. 'Area 51' demonstrates the band's prowess, being all instrumental, and 'How High' seems to borrow a melodic line from 'Street Fighting Man' by the Rolling Stones, but don't tell Sir Mick.

8.67) Greatest Hits – The Police (1992)

This is an album with five UK number one singles and yes, it's arranged chronologically. Hurrah! 'Every Breath You Take' is often mistaken for a love song, but is actually quite menacing. 'Don't Stand So Close To Me' is the only song I know to reference the Russian author, Nabokov, and angst abounds in spite of the terrific melodies. Just listen to the lyrics of 'So Lonely' or the suicide contemplation of my favourite song by the band, 'Can't Stand Losing You.' Occasionally there are hints of the 'dub' production style too. It may be poor taste but 'Don't Stand So Close To Me' is surely the perfect title if you're listening during a pandemic.

8.68) Singles - 45's And Under [Sic] – Squeeze (1982)

There are longer collections which include all these tracks and continue further into the eighties, but this is the solid gold era of the band that introduced us to the songwriting partnership of Difford and Tilbrook, as well as Jools Holland, now a national treasure. Perhaps the only indication of the direction he would go is his tinkling electric piano solo on 'Cool For Cats,' a song with a vocal that is encroaching on 'Chas & Dave' territory. 'Take Me I'm Yours' is very much of its era with its synths dominating the sound, pre-empting bands like Depeche Mode, but who would have imagined that they'd go all country on 'Labelled With Love?' 'Up The Junction' and 'Pulling Muscles (From The Shell)' are of course superb, but did you need me to tell you that?

8.69) The Singles – The Clash (1991)

I'd had the album 'Combat Rock' (1982) for many years, bought purely for the track 'Should I Stay Or Should I Go,' which topped the UK singles chart in 1991. The chronological arrangement here shows the band's journey from the pure punk of early hits into more diverse styles which even include a bit of reggae. 'London Calling' is a radio favourite, but for me 'Bankrobber' tops the list, with its tongue in cheek lyric and a style that is approaching the sound of the Specials. 'Know Your Rights' is described as a 'public service announcement with guitars' and it highlights the hypocrisy of our beloved institutions. Nothing ever changes, ho hum.

8.70) The Best Of Van Morrison – Van Morrison (1990)

It took many years for me to appreciate this prolific composer from Northern Ireland. I could always hear the classic sixties hits he recorded with Them, like 'Brown Eyed Girl, the bluesy 'Baby Please Don't Go' and 'Here Comes The Night,' on the radio, so I just didn't get round to exploring Van's work very deeply. Some of his later output could be categorised as 'easy listening' and there is only one track from his acclaimed album 'Astral Weeks' here. Two high points melodically are 'And It Stoned Me' and 'Wonderful Remark.' There's also the original version of 'Jackie Wilson Said' which Dexys Midnight Runners famously covered on BBC TV's 'Top Of The Pops' by playing in front of a giant picture of darts player Jockey Wilson. Sack that props man!

8.71) Astral Weeks – Van Morrison (1968)

When I first bought this critically acclaimed album in my late twenties I couldn't see what the fuss was about. There were just eight long tracks that all sounded quite similar. I decided to give it another try in my early forties and found it easier to appreciate in the same way that I viewed Marvin Gaye's 'What's Going On.' Both are albums that aim to create a certain vibe with repeated ideas and themes. 'Sweet Thing' graces the 'Best Of' album so this is a good gateway to the style which consists of acoustic guitar, double bass, 'stream of consciousness' lyrics and subtle use of orchestral instruments. 'Cypress Avenue' follows a twelve-bar pattern and has a nice harpsichord effect. It's worth the effort to appreciate this album, even if does take nigh on twenty years.

8.72) Saint Dominic's Preview – Van Morrison (1972)

Opening with 'Jackie Wilson Said,' this album has a jazzier vibe than 'Astral Weeks.' 'I Will Be There' has the feel of an old standard, and the title track has an uplifting feel and some nice steel guitar. There are two tracks that break the ten-minute mark and on one of them Mr. Morrison seems to metamorphose into a growling lion. Well, why not?

8.73) Days Of Future Passed – Moody Blues (1967)

This was a perhaps rare example of a record company and a band in symbiosis. Decca suggested recording an album that combined orchestral sections with the band's songs, and the Moody Blues jumped at the chance. Although the Beatles' 'Sgt. Pepper' had been released over five months earlier, this was a bolder attempt at a concept album, representing a day in an ordinary life, a theme Pink Floyd replicated with their suite 'The Man' (available in 'The Early Years' box set). Anybody used to the Denny Laine era of the Moodies (which provided them with the UK number one single 'Go Now' in early 1965) would have been perplexed as the first track is entirely orchestral, although there are shades of rhythm and blues on 'Lunch Break: Peak Hour' and 'Twilight Time.' 'Nights In White Satin' is the most well known track with its haunting mellotron. Was this the first prog rock album, or was it symphonic pop? Who knows? The poem at the end is reminiscent of 'Under Milk Wood' by Dylan Thomas, neatly concluding this truly ambitious work.

8.74) Safe As Milk – Captain Beefheart And His Magic Band (1967)

At least twenty years after I tried in vain to appreciate an artist that many regard as a genius, I can at last give myself a pat on back and say 'I *get* Beefheart.' Well, sort of. My schoolboy error was jumping straight in with 'Trout Mask Replica,' which would be like trying 'Stereopathetic Soulmanure' as your first Beck album. In truth both albums are remarkably similar in structure. However, 'Safe As Milk,' as its name implies, is the less challenging end of Don Van Vilet's work, which is not to say that it isn't pretty adventurous for a debut album.

The band's sound is very much of the same ilk as Jefferson Airplane and other San Francisco guitar bands of the era, but Beefheart's vocals have been compared to the bluesman Howlin' Wolf. This is demonstrated best on the opening track. Hardly any of the songs are simple though, for example, 'Yellow Brick Road' sounds quite quirky until the shouted refrain kicks in, and then there's the surprising middle section of 'Dropout Boogie.' 'I'm Glad' is a rare sad moment from Mr. Beefheart, with a similar feel to Frank Zappa's doo-wop songs. You won't be surprised to learn that the pair went to the same high school, which may prompt you to ask 'What the hell kind of lessons did they teach there?'

8.75) Mirror Man – Captain Beefheart And His Magic Band (1971)

Although not released until four years later, this seems like the proper successor to 'Safe As Milk,' with the bluesy tracks now extended into lengthy jams where anything goes, meaning that you only get four of them. 'Tarotplane' is a reference to Robert Johnson's 'Terraplane Blues' although it is more directly an improvisation upon 'You're Gonna Need Somebody On Your Bond' by Blind Willie Johnson, which was also covered by Donovan. As well as harmonica, Beefheart plays the oboe in a style that reminds me of some of the jagged improvisations on the Miles Davis album 'On The Corner' (1972). If you're not used to the Captain's wheezy whoops at the end of each line you will be after nineteen minutes of this track. 'Kandy Korn' presents a sound more akin to sixties pop than the other tracks, with John French really shining on the drums. The title track is catchy and sounds like the Captain has got some kind of electronic equipment lodged in his voice box, and I don't mean like Cher's digitised vocal on her 1998 hit 'Believe.'

8.76) Lick My Decals Off, Baby – Captain Beefheart And His Magic Band (1970)

And the prize for the most ridiculous album title goes to... Yes, glossing over 'Strictly Personal' (1968) and 'Trout Mask Replica' (1969) we come to this, the band's highest charting album in the UK. We love eccentricity here, and the music provides that in droves, if you can call it music. I can imagine if an alien had heard various human forms of late sixties music and tried to replicate them, this is what you'd get. The musicians are clearly playing exactly what they're supposed to play but the rhythms clash, the sound is frenetic, the lyrics are insane and melody is a non-starter. Yet it works. It's hard not to enjoy Beefheart's devilish laugh on 'I Love You, You Big Dummy,' and a couple of instrumental tracks demonstrate that the band can still dish out the arrhythmic madness semi-acoustically. As the Captain says, 'This song ain't no sing-song.'

As a footnote, this album also reassured me that I haven't lost the ability to form synaesthetic associations (see Appendix III) as I instantly thought 'This album is yellow.'

8.77) Muddy Waters – Chicago Blues (1994)

It's back to 'The Blues Collection' for this one. Those Orbis partworks discs are still out there if you search hard enough, and this is a good one, recorded from a concert in 1976, by which time McKinley Morganfield (less memorable than Muddy Waters, hey?) had been singing the blues for several decades. He blasts his way through standards like 'Corinne Corinna' [sic] and 'Baby Please Don't Go.' The criminally glaring omission seems to be 'Mannish Boy' which Muddy wrote himself. The version from the 1977 'Hard Again' album is about as good as you can possibly get. However, this disc does contain a cover of Willie Dixon's 'I'm Your Hoochie Coochie Man' which contains almost the same guitar and harmonica riff. There are quite a few instrumental tracks, allowing each musician in the band to display their skills, although the bass riff at the start of 'Floyd's Guitar Blues' sounds as though the player has mixed up his minor and major scales. Or is this jazz-blues?

8.78) Big Bill Broonzy – Whisky And Good Time Blues (1994)

We are going right back to the late thirties and just into the forties for this melodic country-tinted disc from 'The Blues Collection,' so you'll understand that some of the tracks are a little crackly. This is a supremely enjoyable collection in spite of this. Some of the tracks incorporate trumpet and fiddle, and the political sentiments of tracks like 'Stuff They Call Money' and 'Unemployment Blues' demonstrate how slow human progress has been since then. The piano is often the dominant instrument, giving the whole CD an authentic pre-war feel, although Broonzy didn't tinkle the ivories himself.

8.79) Life – The Cardigans (1995)

The Cardigans were a band from Sweden and amazingly two of the members were formerly heavy metal musicians. This was the album they released before they made it big. The band went for a harder image as time went on, but on these early recordings Nina Persson's voice has an enchanting quality about it that I can only sum up as 'fresh sounding.' The version of this album released in Sweden was different to what we got in the UK. Our version is a kind of hybrid, selecting tracks from their first album (1994's 'Emmerdale') and omitting three from the Swedish version of 'Life.' Got that? Now, this was good as we got to hear the full-length version of 'Celia Inside' which is my personal favourite, complete with a jazz-inspired guitar solo, but it was also annoying as the three omitted tracks are also very good. Why no deluxe version? Another item for the wish list.

The music here ticks all the boxes; crunchy guitar, great melodies, sixties instrumentation, quirky flute bits, nice harmonies – in hindsight it seems bizarre that I took so little notice of this band in the nineties. 'Hey! Get Out Of My Way' has a motif reminiscent of Johnny & The Hurricanes and there's even a laid back cover of Black Sabbath's 'Sabbath Bloody Sabbath.' What's not to like?

8.80) First Band On The Moon – The Cardigans (1996)

It's no secret that I love a good segue and on this album the Swedish band employed that approach right the way through. The melodies are still superb and Nina Persson's voice still has the quirky quality that she would ditch either consciously or unconsciously later on. The single 'Lovefool' is a song that seemed to encapsulate the naïve optimism of the mid-nineties. It still gets regular airplay today. The end of 'Been It' gives a hint of the band's penchant for heavier styles and there's another Black Sabbath cover in the form of a jazzy rendition of 'Iron Man.' In spite of the Beatles-esque melody, 'Step On Me' takes the 'damsel in distress' motif of 'Lovefool' a somewhat disturbing stage further, while 'Choke' has a Black Sabbath-esque riff which is augmented by flute. There's some seriously good drumming from Bengt Lagerberg too, but the band were about to dump the quirkiness, making these two albums seem like youthful innocence frozen in time.

8.81) The Other Side Of The Moon – The Cardigans (1997)

Just in case you needed any more proof that the Cardigans were a supremely talented outfit, this selection of B-sides and rarities should seal the deal. There's an alternate 'male vocal' version of 'Carnival' and it's interesting to consider that Nina wasn't the band's original lead singer. There are two interesting covers; Thin Lizzy's 'The Boys Are Back In Town' and an *a capella* version of Ozzy Osbourne's 'Mr. Crowley.' 'Laika' is a very nice instrumental (the name is a type of dog). The lengthy closing track, 'Cocktail Party Bloody Cocktail Party,' is a titular reference to their heroes Black Sabbath again, but actually this is band member

Lars-Olof Johansson playing snippets of the entire 'Life' album (Swedish edition) in the style of a jazz pianist while the rest of the band presumably drink cocktails! This collection is another hour thoroughly well spent, but criminally it has never had a UK release. Translation: you can either put on your eye-patch and take up piracy or pay through the nose online.

8.82) Gran Turismo – The Cardigans (1998)

Gone are the woodwind adornments, sublime melodies and the feel of a band you can imagine practising in a garage, and in comes an almost clinical sound utilising electronics which is more in the vein of bands like Portishead. Nina's voice is still nice, but minus the aura of innocence as she sings about losing her 'Favourite Game' and 'changing her mind' ('Erase / Rewind'). It's still great work and an enjoyable album. If you're missing the strum of an acoustic guitar 'The Junk Of The Heart' has more of a traditional 'band' feel, while the final track, 'Nil,' is an exercise in ambience. Some of the album really rocks, and from here on there was no going back; the band were huge and all grown up.

8.83) Emmerdale – The Cardigans (1994)

Who wants to rewind? Oh, you don't. Well, we're doing it anyway. Rather than move on to the band's slightly country-tinted final albums I'm going back to the Cardigans' debut album. In spite of the group's youth here, you'll find some of the songs less quirky / melodic and more languorous than on 1995's 'Life.' Nina sings about being bored, tired and 'scaring close to insanity' among other things, so lyrically it's very '2021.' I do wonder how a new band got access to the varied orchestrations here. These days they just mutilate your songs with computers. There's even some dissonance in the brassy conclusion to 'It's Hard.' The cheerful flute motif of 'Over The Water' gives a hint of the direction the band were headed, while 'Last Song' expresses dark sentiments over a serious sounding string section. And yes, the album is named after the British TV soap opera.

8.84) Stoosh – Skunk Anansie (1996)

I never appreciated this band in the nineties, finding them somewhat scary, not least because of the shaved head of lead singer, Skin (real name: Deborah Anne Dyer, which sounds much less scary). The rageful opening track lays the band's cards on the table with zero subtlety, addressing the way the media tend to criticise political lyrics. The subject matter is unrelenting, including violent relationships and racism, although the swearword count doesn't increase dramatically between the first and last tracks. 'Everyday Hurts,' 'She's My Heroine' and 'Hedonism (Just Because You Feel Good)' are all great rock songs and I love the harmonics on the acoustic guitar of 'Pickin' On Me.' 'We Love Your Apathy' sums up my thoughts on politics; the fact that people don't want to vote or don't want to think just offers the elite a field day which they grab heartily with both hands. The band have even added some semi-ambient doodles between some of the songs just in case you need a moment to cool off! And by the way, the 'Cake Mix' of 'Everyday Hurts' (single release) is nothing short of awesome.

8.85) The Best Of Steely Dan: Then And Now – Steely Dan (1993)

Let's calm things down with some American 'jazz rock.' Until I bought this album I mistakenly thought that Steely Dan's Donald Fagen was the singer on the theme music to the British TV comedy 'Auf Wiedersehen, Pet.' How silly – that was Joe Fagin! No, Steely Dan were smooth operators who surprisingly hardly touched the British singles chart even during their seventies heyday. In spite of that, many of the songs are unquestionably classics. Check out that guitar solo on 'Reelin' In The Years,' savour the voodoo vibe of 'Do It Again,' enjoy more guitar on the reggae inflected 'Haitian Divorce' and savour that sax on 'FM (No Static At All).' Walter Becker was the other mover / shaker in this group. One of the tracks here inspired a Scottish band to call themselves 'Deacon Blue.' No more questions your honour.

8.86) The Great British Psychedelic Trip Vol 2 1966-1969 – Various Artists (1986)

At least twenty years after I bought volume one I finally got my hands on volume two. In truth tracks like 'Kites' by Simon Dupree And The Big Sound and 'Excerpt From A Teenage Opera' by Keith West have always been 'bread and butter' classics for me, the latter being a heart jangling morality tale about appreciation. 'My White Bicycle' by Idle Race is quintessential late sixties fare, there are two Beatles covers and a couple of pivotal tracks from the album 'S.F. Sorrow' by the Pretty Things. This review refers to the cassette version which has a different track listing to the CD. Why do record companies do that? I'm quitting!

STOP PRESS:

I can hear you now, 'This author is like *the boy who cried wolf.* He said he was quitting and now he's back for more.' Well, here are just a handful of albums that I've got into in between releasing this book and sending my file copy off to the British Library. They seemed to be crying out for inclusion, so I got my crowbar out and forced open a crack in the manuscript just wide enough to usher them in. Enjoy...

8.87) When You See Yourself – Kings Of Leon (2021)

The eighth five-syllable album from the Nashville boys presents a different sound, with some almost ambient keyboard work reminiscent of the Radiohead track 'A Wolf At The Door' (2003), although the crisp rhythm section provided by Jared on bass and Nathan on drums gives the collection a feel not dissimilar to the Mumford & Sons album 'Wilder Mind' (2015). In short it's comfortingly familiar and refreshingly different too.

'When You See Yourself, Are You Far Away?' is one of several songs which gains impact by using one particular chord in its melody that you didn't expect. It also seems to present an interesting comment on self-perception without being too specific. Meanwhile, 'Supermarket' seems to reflect the enforced isolation of the coronavirus epidemic without actually being about it, as Caleb intones 'I'm going nowhere if you've got the time.' 'Golden Restless Age' encapsulates the new sound perfectly, with gentle keyboard work punctuated by Matt's recurring guitar lick, while the slidey guitar on 'Stormy Weather' reminds me of the Stereophonics song 'Step On My Old Size Nines,' which is of course a good thing. I think by now we've got the idea - if you want the rawness of 'Youth And Young Manhood' play 'Youth And Young Manhood!'

8.88) A Moon Shaped Pool – Radiohead (2016)

I haven't reviewed 'In Rainbows' (2007) or 'The King Of Limbs' (2011), although neither should be overlooked. A glance at the track listing of this album reveals something new – the tracks are arranged in alphabetical order, so it's like one of those 'chicken and egg' questions as to whether the band had a rough order in mind and named the tracks to fit the concept or literally just banged them out and hoped it worked. Either way, we open with the band accompanied by an orchestra on 'Burn The Witch,' which begins with staccato playing and ends with droopy strings reminiscent of 'How To Disappear Completely.' Whereas the vocals of Caleb Followill (Kings Of Leon) seem to have got clearer with time, you have to really listen to pick out Thom Yorke's words, which seem to have got increasingly opaque over the years. I think there's a message about the environment in there somewhere, 'You really messed up everything,' to quote.

'Daydreaming' has a really spooky sounding ending, but what's the most radical thing Radiohead could do after all these years? Yes, throw in a guitar solo on 'Identikit' and some acoustic guitar on 'Desert Island Disks.' Great work boys, and I think by now we've got the idea - if you want the guitar anthems of 'The Bends' play 'The Bends!'

8.89) The Dreaming – Kate Bush (1982)

I haven't heard all of Kate's albums, but of the clutch of early works that I know this is my favourite for the sheer experimentation. There's a lot of synthesiser, but there's a lot of other stuff too. Vocally she plays with her voice in a way that perhaps only David Bowie had done before, fluctuating between the three styles of singing in a deep, almost satirical register, singing in a coy, very English way and screaming out cathartically. 'Sat In Your Lap,' which opens the album, is a perfect example. The subject matter is very varied too. 'There Goes A Tenner' is an amusing tale of a heist, 'Get Out Of My House' is inspired by 'The Shining,' reflecting upon the idea of emotions leaving a residue in a residence, and 'Suspended In Gaffa' seems to take the metaphor of tying oneself up in knots to the max, as the 'Gaffa' refers to 'gaffer tape.' Tribal rhythms abound, not least on the title track, which is about the Western disregard for indigenous cultures such as the Aborigines in Australia. However, my favourite here is the sobering 'All My Love,' which reflects upon how people only seem to fully appreciate one another when they are gone forever. The glib answerphone messages that conclude the song seem to illustrate this chillingly.

8.90) The Kick Inside – Kate Bush (1978)

This was the first album by the youthful Miss Bush, and it's astonishing how young she was when she wrote this set of remarkably adult songs. 'Wuthering Heights' will always be a classic, and 'The Man With The Child In His Eyes' was written when she was just thirteen. Seriously, compare that with today's 'I love you, you love me' pop princesses and think about it! The title track is far from an innocent celebration of pregnancy, being a tale of incest which resulted in the expectant mother committing suicide to save her family from shame. It's not all piano balladry either, with reggae-inflected tracks such as 'Them Heavy People' (yay!) and 'Kites.'

The follow up album, 'Lionheart' (1979), is similarly enjoyable, with 'Hammer Horror' (yippee!) and Kate rocking out on 'Don't Put Your Foot On The Heartbrake.' Sometimes it's necessary to do a bit of research on the inspiration for her songs to appreciate the depth involved.

8.91) Hair Of The Dog – Nazareth (1975)

My father-in-law introduced me to the title track of this Scottish rock band's album when I was visiting Moscow ('Hello, Mr. Title Track, how do you do?'). I was impressed by the combination of an infectious riff and incessant cowbell, while being amused by the repeated refrain of 'Now you're messing with a son of a bitch.' The pun in the title substitutes 'heir' (hair) for 'son' and 'dog' for... The whole album is a brilliant example of seventies rock. 'Miss Misery' grinds out another top notch riff, while 'Guilty' and a cover of 'Love Hurts' show the band's gentler side. 'Whiskey Drinking Woman' has a very Black Sabbath-esque melody while being a nod to blues music, and 'Changin' Times' sounds as though they've been listening to Led Zeppelin's 'Black Dog' a lot. Supremely enjoyable. Put it on after you have a couple of beers and you'll get it straight away.

Chapter 9 – It's My Party

It's probably ill-advised to review your own albums but no one else is going to do it, and as it's my book I'm going to do precisely that, figuratively detaching my brain so that I can review them reasonably objectively. The following albums by Adam Colton & Teresa Colton are available on iTunes, Amazon, YouTube and myriad other streaming sites. We are a mother and son act who appreciate any chance to get our songs heard; think acoustic guitars, harmonica and vocals. Although we used to play in folk clubs around Kent, we mostly concentrate on recording our own material these days, and as we've just had a pandemic, it seems that we are not the only musical act that has gone in this direction.

9.1) Fat Cats With A Death Wish On The M25 – Adam Colton & Teresa Colton (2012)

It was something of a coup for us that the legendary DJ Dave Cash took a liking to the title track and played it regularly on his BBC Radio Kent programme. Sadly Dave Cash is no longer with us. This album is a compilation of what we viewed as our best songs from 2003-2012. Teresa's 'Customs Man' is a folky tale of smuggling times in Dover, while my own 'Leaves On The Line' was the first song I'd written that I actually recorded, a humorous catalogue of genuine excuses I'd encountered for late trains – yes, one of those 'list songs' I keep talking about. My favourite is Teresa's song, 'Train To Nowhere' – great lyrics and a succulent acoustic guitar solo, even though I played it myself.

9.2) Mixed Messages – Adam Colton & Teresa Colton (2014)

The radio listeners seemed to respond best to comedy songs, so we decided to include several on our next album. Teresa's 'Press Button One' reflects on frustrating customer service phone lines, while my own 'Make A Fat Cat Fatter This Christmas' was a natural sequel to the M25 song, poking fun at Christmas commercialism. Some classical influences come through too in 'Beethoven Rock' and 'Parallel Universe.' No prizes for spotting the Pink Floyd influence in my song about old age, 'God's Waiting Room.'

9.3) Landscape: An Anthology 2003-2012 – Adam Colton & Teresa Colton (2019)

This collection features self-penned tracks from 2003-2012 that aren't featured on the 'M25' compilation. These are arranged the way I like my albums - chronologically, beginning with folky material and songs that we recorded to promote the book 'England And Wales In A Flash,' with mentions of places and particularly lighthouses that my father and I visited while researching the tome. We move on via my own song 'Hot Air,' which expressed frustration at George W. Bush's obfuscation of the climate change issue, opening the floodgates for more protest material towards the end, often composed in response to the global financial crash. If the lyrics aren't for you, just enjoy the harmonies and harmonica solos. Some of Teresa's songs were inspired by holidays, such as 'Arctic Waters' and 'Arizona Sunrise,' while the wintry images of the title track provide a soothing finish.

9.4) Silicon Country – Adam Colton & Teresa Colton With Anna Vaughan (2021)

Our latest album is a game of two halves. I was hoping to follow the model of the Beatles' 'Abbey Road' to a certain extent. The first half comprises Teresa's country songs, augmented by my sister Anna on bass and supplying additional vocals. My favourites are the ballads, 'Broken Toy' and 'Running With Vampires.' The second half is my attempt to single-handedly bring back the segue, being a medley in two eleven-minute tracks, loosely telling the story of my latest novel, 'The Nightshade Project.' In short, a girl receives a silicon chip brain implant from the government and an influence from outside hacks into the chip to give her important messages about humanity's future. Yeah, I know, it's not going to appeal to fans of Justin Bieber or Little Mix!

With just the appendices and the index to go, in the words of the onion seller 'That's shallot!'

Appendix I – Classical Gas

Just as one's dreams can often seem like a parallel life to the one lived in reality, classical music has been a parallel musical interest to the albums that form the bulk of this book for me. My father used to have a vinyl record of Gershwin's symphonic pieces being played by Daniel Blumenthal and during my late teens, I often used to listen to this when everyone else was either at work (or at school in the case of my sister).

A few years later I was drawn to the first movement of Beethoven's third symphony. I had an unusual hobby at the time of videoing local road journeys as I drove them, using a video camera fixed to a tripod mounted in the footwell in front of the passenger seat. The idea was that I would record journeys through the local area for posterity, before the proposed massive expansion of Ashford obliterated the countryside with overpriced little boxes. The videos of course needed some music, and what better choice could there be to overdub a rural ride through the Kent countryside than the opening to 'Eroica?'

Having lent the video that I produced to a security guard called John at my place of work, he declared that this reminded hm of Stanley Kubrick's film, 'A Clockwork Orange,' which uses Beethoven and Rossini to dramatic effect while the central characters carry out all manner of criminal acts. For educational reasons he then lent me an illegal copy of the film, which was banned in the UK at the time, and perhaps it was this that encouraged me to explore the dramatic music of Beethoven further. Every now and again I would purchase a classical tape instead of the usual sixties and seventies fare from that hallowed second hand shop in Folkestone. Later on when the pub rock band I performed in imploded, I bought up every CD of the Orbis partworks series, 'The Classical Collection,' that I could find in the second hand shops of Ramsgate, in order to divert my musical attention.

I am going to refrain from reviewing every classical album I own, as this would merit another book, but here is a 'top twelve' of my favourite pieces just to whet your appetite. And please don't get irksome that it's not a 'top ten' – if humans had six fingers on each hand 'top twelves' would be the norm.

12) Tchaikovsky - Sleeping Beauty, Act 1: Pas D'Action

We begin with a bit of drama. Tchaikovsky couldn't help but be melodic even at his most dramatic. This was a kind of a shoo-in because eleven was a weird number to have in a list, although if humans had eleven fingers... Upon listening again it seems criminal to place it right down at number twelve, especially when it reaches its awesome crescendo. Spine tingles all round.

11) Wagner - Prelude To Tristan And Isolde

I first encountered this piece when watching Lars Von Trier's film 'Melancholia.' It has a romantic feel that builds interminably (similar to Ravel's 'Bolero' which would probably be my 'number 13'), but perhaps like my number one choice, there is a sense of impending darkness beneath the romance. In Von Trier's film it was the complete destruction of the earth!

10) Mascagni - Intermezzo From Cavalleria Rusticana

We begin our top ten with a short three-and-a-half-minute piece which has a bitter-sweet quality about it - a kind of peacefulness coupled with resigned sadness. I always imagine this as a great funeral piece, with the final notes drifting away as the curtain closes on somebody's life. Less dramatic types will remember it as the music from an advert that I can't quite recall!

9) Holst - The Planets

Yes, it's commercial, but who cares? The most famous movements are the dramatic war theme of 'Mars' and the 'jollity' of 'Jupiter,' which should bring to mind a little bit of pride (in an inclusive way of course) to all British folk. As the suite progresses and we reach the mysterious distant planets the pieces become more surreal. As an aside, for a true sense of the distance we are dealing with, the scale model of the solar system at Otford in Kent is well worth a visit. If you enjoy walking a mile to look at a dot on a plinth you'll love it!

8) Bach -Tocata And Fugue In D Minor

Possibly originally composed for a harpsichord, this piece is much better known as an organ piece, routinely heard at Halloween. From the dramatic opening to the virtuoso gymnastics (IMO) on the keys, the piece regularly returns to the epic long chords that we know and love. Bach's 'Air On The G String' is a close second from this composer for me, as well as for those with a penchant for cigars!

7) Beethoven - Symphony No 3 (Eroica)

This one opens with the famous melodic first movement (I favour the full 17-minute version), which I once dubbed over a video that I made of a country drive through Kent, thus it will forever bring to mind the glorious B2067 for me! This is followed by a dramatic funeral march, a light third movement and a rousing finale. Initially composed to honour Napoleon, Beethoven changed his mind as the leader's lust for power became apparent. His 5th, 6th and 9th symphonies are also pretty essential – Fate, Pastoral and Choral.

6) Mozart - Piano Concerto No. 21 In C

This whole piece is very pleasant with contrasting moods, but it is the middle movement that steals the show with its sense of contentment and just a touch of decadence. I first took notice of this piece when I heard it at a friend's wedding, previously having only known it as 'the music from the Yardley advert.' These days it almost makes my top five.

5) Rossini - The Thieving Magpie Overture

It is hard for me to disentangle this piece from the scenes of 'ultra-violence' in Stanley Kubrick's 'A Clockwork Orange,' or failing that the graphic scenes of tarmac in 'A28 – The Movie!' Either way, this only adds to the drama when hearing it. Following the opening drum roll, this is predominantly a cheerful melodic piece which repeatedly builds to a crescendo of dramatic full-orchestra chords, each time dying away, until the finale whips up the pace into a fitting conclusion. Ten minutes of good fun!

4) Beethoven - Piano Sonata No 14 (Moonlight)

The piece begins with the famous moody section during which it is easy to imagine moonlight reflecting on a lake with all its drama kept safely beneath the surface. The middle section is a cheerful little ditty, before the finale adapts the melody of the first movement but this time at speed, with a sense of triumph but always with the brooding feel trying to break through.

3) Rossini - William Tell Overture

I am not familiar with the legend of William Tell beyond 'arrows and apples,' but this is not necessary to appreciate this twelve-minute piece which seems to take us through the entire gamut of human emotions. It begins with resigned sadness and builds to a storm-like passage of anger and turmoil which then gives way to a relaxed section, a bit like the sun coming out after the rain has passed. Then comes the triumphant finale which everybody will recognise, containing what seems like one of the longest and most dramatic conclusions you'll encounter - you can hear the end coming about a minute before it does!

2) Gershwin - Piano Concerto In F

The version I have features Daniel Blumenthal on piano, and with 'Rhapsody In Blue' and 'An American In Paris,' this may have even been the first classical album I appreciated, having plenty of time on my hands to listen to vinyl during short days at college and long days of unemployment. 'Piano Concerto In F' always returns fatalistically to the same dramatic orchestral chord, with variations that include the bluesy second movement and a high-speed summary of all that went before in the third movement. A sense of the bustling positivity of the 1920s is evoked several times throughout the piece. This was the pop music of its day and much more besides.

1) Tchaikovsky - Romeo And Juliet

Sit back and enjoy twenty minutes of dramatic bliss. The piece begins slowly with a fatalistic feel, presaging the story's ultimate destiny – death. The romantic theme has graced many a film and TV programme, perhaps to the point of becoming a cliché, but heard in its context with the turmoil of the feuding Capulets and Montagues seeming to butt in on the romantic vibes, the piece becomes much more interesting. The love theme reasserts itself only to collapse into a funereal finale with a sense of resigned defeat. You'll struggle to find a more impassioned piece of music. For more Tchaikovsky, I'm assuming you know the ballets inside out, so have a bash at symphonies number 4 and 6 for a glimpse into the man's tumultuous mind!

Appendix II – Don't Let The Bells End

No book on rock and pop music should ignore the phenomenon of the Christmas song. These are often kitsch and riddled with clichés, but they are the biggest earner for many a musician, with guaranteed airplay for a whole month of every year until kingdom come. Or at least until Christmas come.

I think my main issue with Christmas is the way it suddenly ends on Boxing Day. I mean, you've waited for interminable months through all that build up and when it *is* actually Christmas you turn on the radio and you won't hear a single Christmas song for love nor money. It's a bit like turning eighteen really. You get all that nurturing and build up for eighteen years and then suddenly the advice is all gone, you've got no plans and you become a window cleaner. Or was that just me?

Anyway, next time the airwaves are awash with Slade, Wizzard, etc., have no fear. Much as many of these seasonal tracks give you a warm feeling inside, a bit like sherry, this is a chapter for those who fancy a change from the norm, like a mince pie with real mince. Scouring my music collection I've tried to find all the Christmas songs that you won't hear played on the radio. Let's begin, as all music lists should, with the Beatles.

The Beatles – Christmas Time (Is Here Again) (1967 / 1995)

This was just a recurring jingle on one of the group's annual Christmas discs for fans, but it was nicely edited into a full-length track as a B-side on the 'Free As A Bird' single released in 1995. The lyrics are somewhat minimalist and Paul McCartney would revive the 'O-U-T spells out' motif on his 2013 track 'Queenie Eye.' I wonder if there was a wry comment on the furore concerning Lennon's 'bigger than Jesus' comment in the line 'Been around since you know when...' as though it's better not to name him. Who knows. The track ends with John putting on his best Scottish accent for an atmospheric little bit of nonsense.

The Sensational Alex Harvey Band – There's No Lights On The Christmas Tree, Mother... (1972)

...They're Burning Big Louie Tonight. That's the punchline, folks. Yes, this is a Christmassy tale about a man being arrested and sentenced to death by electric chair, consequently shorting out the electricity and prompting the singer to observe that the Christmas tree lights are off. Alex Harvey was a distinctive performer from Scotland with a superb bunch of musicians, often employing risqué lyrics, but occasionally there was a moral message, such as regarding protecting the environment. Any DJ willing to play this gets a Victoria Cross for bravery however.

Wings – Rudolph The Red-Nosed Reggae (1979)

This one's safe as milk. It's a quirky instrumental rendition of the traditional favourite, which appears as a bonus track on the album 'Back To The Egg.' Harmless fun which started off as the B-side to the much more often played 'Wonderful Christmastime.'

Paul Simon – Getting Ready For Christmas Day (2011)

This was the opening tune on Paul Simon's album 'So Beautiful Or So What?' It's an unusual rhythmic track with something resembling gospel chanting in the background. Paul Simon was no stranger to Christmas songs, especially when teamed up with Art Garfunkel. Guess who's next...

Simon & Garfunkel – 7 O'Clock News / Silent Night (1966)

The transatlantic harmony duo sing the traditional favourite with just a piano for accompaniment as reality breaks in in the form of a particularly nasty edition of the seven o'clock news. The juxtaposition seems to say something about the essentially fantastical nature of believing in peace on earth for a single day of the year. It's the only Christmas song I know with brutal murders in it. Simon & Garfunkel *did* record the odd Christmas song straight however, such as 'Star Carol,' 'God Rest Ye Merry Gentlemen' and 'Go, Tell It On The Mountain.' All are worth checking out.

The Who – Christmas (1969)

Another dark Christmas song. This one was part of The Who's rock opera, 'Tommy,' contrasting the Christmas that most children have with the severely limited experience that the deaf, dumb and blind central character has. 'How can he be saved / From the eternal grave?' Harsh stuff, hey?

Chas & Dave - Long, Long Ago (1986)

Just when you're thinking 'Where's the warm Christmassy glow in this lot?' along come Chas & Dave to fill the void. I remember my sister coming home from primary school having learned this as a carol. The teachers must have been pretty quick off the mark to have snapped this yuletide classic up at the time. The

Cockney lads eulogise 'Winds through the olive trees softly did blow' while accompanied by a brass band. The B-side of Silent Night is also very nice and there's no seven o'clock news this time! It just goes to show that the pair of Londoners *could* be serious, although this is as rare as Christmas in February, talking of which...

Lou Reed – Xmas In February (1989)

Venturing across to the dark side again, this one from Lou Reed's album 'New York' is essentially about the lack of work prospects making army life seem appealing, and the consequent rescheduling of Christmas when you're busy with the 'kill or be killed' stuff on December 25th.

Roy Orbison – Pretty Paper (1963)

Roy Orbison is in 'country' mode while exploring the often visited theme of being lonely at Christmas. The song, which was penned by Willie Nelson, seems to reference homelessness in the second verse, so it could even be a socially conscious Christmas song. Right, wipe that tear away, we're going 'punk' next.

Eels – Everything's Gonna Be Cool This Christmas (1998)

The Los Angeles rock band led by 'E' ('Es are good?') gave us this as the B-side to the wonderfully festive 'Cancer For The Cure.' It's actually a fairly straight Christmas song in a slightly 'punk' style. 'Baby Jesus / Born to rock.' Er... quite!

Monty Python – Christmas In Heaven (1983)

Of course it's not serious! This was the musical finale to the comedy group's film 'The Meaning Of Life.' Really it seems to be satirising the stereotypical 'American' idea of what both Christmas and Heaven should be like; 'The Sound Of Music twice an hour / And Jaws I, II and III.' Have TV schedulers had any new ideas yet?

Joni Mitchell - River (1971)

This occasionally gets a play on BBC Radio 2 but I'm including it anyway as it isn't as well known as it should be. It opens with the notes of 'Jingle Bells' played on the piano in an uncharacteristically melancholy fashion before Joni begins the sad tale which has a similar theme to 'Pretty Paper,' being that of the bustle of Christmas going on around a lonely person who wants it all to just go away.

Eric Bogle – Santa Bloody Claus (1993)

Another satirical one. Eric Bogle is a writer of poignant folk songs, but he occasionally lets his hair down with a number like this. It's a little bit rude and I'm not sure if he was trying to compete with Kevin Bloody Wilson here, in which case Mr. Bogle's song will seem positively tame.

Bob Dylan – Must Be Santa (2009)

This is a bit of a cheat as it actually does get regular airplay at Christmas on BBC Radio 2, but the sheer brilliance of Bob Dylan doing a traditional Christmas album with a voice that has been completely ravaged has to be lauded. This is perhaps the standout track on 'Christmas In The Heart,' but in this house the entire CD gets a spin every Christmas. Bob makes this Christmas favourite his own by listing the names of recent USA presidents among the reindeer. Was he being subversive? Oh, I do hope so!

Pink Floyd – Roger's Boogie (1968 / 2016)

A track that lay in the vault until the release of the band's megalithic box set, 'The Early Years.' This is clearly an attempt at a Christmas song with a lyric about Gabriel coming to the stable, and even in the 'anything goes' psychedelic era that it was recorded, I would still say that it's something of an oddity in the Floydian catalogue. It sounds more like funeral music than a boogie.

Bob Dylan – Winterlude (1970)

Not a Christmas song *per se,* but every bit as seasonal as 'Baby, It's Cold Outside,' 'The Power Of Love' and 'Stay Another Day.' Here the legend that is Robert Allen Zimmerman uses the good old fashioned theme of engaging in romantic pursuits while the weather outside is frightful. If he came to the UK he'd merely need a brolly.

Adam Colton & Teresa Colton - Make A Fat Cat Fatter This Christmas (2014)

'Who?' Come on, this should be a Christmas number one! We're a mother and son folk duo and this is a satirical song about Christmas commercialisation. Legendary DJ Dave Cash gave it a spin on BBC Radio Kent and so should you. And just in case you think we're being too irreverent, my mother's two self-penned carols, 'Shepherd Boy Carol' and 'Whisper In The Wind,' should prove otherwise. All are on the download album 'Mixed Messages.'

Appendix III – Music Of My Mind

No, this isn't a Stevie Wonder album that I've decided to bung in at the end; I'm going to talk about the psychological phenomenon of synaesthesia, as this has a very significant effect on the way music is perceived. I do not view this phenomenon as something negative, but as something that enhances perceptions, like an additional dimension to the standard listening experience. Please bear with me while I talk about numbers...

Ever since being a child I have always viewed numbers as positions on curving lines, and it was during my early thirties that I realised that most people don't actually do this. To me, the numbers one to twelve are represented by positions on a clock face (seems logical, right?) and then the numbers 13 to 20 run vertically from the 12. Then each set of ten is a circle, loosely based on the clock face with the 6 at the bottom, but with the zero at the top. Each set of ten (21-30, 31-40, etc.) moves progressively to the left and then curves upwards from 60 to 100. The hundreds, thousands, hundred thousands, millions, billions and powers of ten all follow the same pattern, except that the 1-6 on the clock face are upside down, so 600, 6000, 6 million, etc. occupy the central point of an 'S' shape. I fear I could be losing my readers now, so I'll move on.

The practical implication of this is that I view every event in my life as a position, either located at the number which was my age at the time, or the number of the year at the time. If I think about my time at primary school in terms of my age, it occupies the clock face from 5 to 11; if I think of primary school in terms of the years (81-86), it occupies the right-hand side of the '80s' circle, from zero to six. It may seem a bind to view things in this way, but it does make it very easy to remember such things as the years that songs were released, as naturally the songs have their positions too. Thus, I always relish the music round in a pub quiz, however I will caveat that with the possibility of error just in case any of the pesky things have crept into this book!

It isn't just numbers that work this way for me. Days of the week, months of the year and letters of the alphabet are the same. Saturday is always at the bottom of a circle and Tuesday is at the top, with the days running anti-clockwise. With the months (also anti-clockwise), the circle is a bit distorted - January is at the top right, then there is a long slope running left and then down to August at the bottom left. Then the autumn months stack up vertically on the right hand side – well, it always feels uphill to Christmas, doesn't it?

Even the alphabet brings to mind a curve like an oxbow in a river. A-D occupy the first curve on the left-hand side, E-R occupy the bulging middle curve and S-Z take up the final curve on the right. As you can see, the letters aren't evenly spaced - there is both logic and no logic to this way of thinking!

Thanks to the Internet, I discovered that this mode of thought is called 'spatial synaesthesia' (sometimes spelled 'synesthesia'). It is thought that as babies, our senses are a mishmash of inputs, where sounds can be perceived as colours, words as smells, etc. Most people lose these cross-associations entirely, but the theory is that those who don't lose all of them are 'synaesthetes' (yes, that's a real word!). Thus some people associate certain numbers with colours. If you put a triangle of twos in a grid of fives, most people will struggle to see the pattern, but somebody with 'grapheme-colour synaesthesia' will see the triangle straight away, as it will appear a different colour to them. Some people even associate personalities with different numbers. As a child, I can remember thinking of the number five as very mischievous (along with the colour yellow) and the number seven as very respectable, but for me, these associations no longer exist.

I have never had the 'seeing sounds as colours' experience myself (although I believe some folk try to induce such phenomena illegally), but some of my favourite music albums do always bring to mind a shade. Sorry, my references are very old, but Pink Floyd's 'Ummagumma' album and the Beatles' 'Abbey Road,' both from 1969, each bring to mind a dark green shade to me. But if you think about it, do we not all associate certain colours with certain moods, and therefore the music that evokes such moods? There is a whole genre called 'blues' after all.

Some synaesthetes see all kinds of patterns when they hear music, which isn't anything vastly different from the kind of graphics you can get your computer to generate to accompany music. Indeed, certain songs do bring to mind a kind of illustration to me, such as the guitar noises in the creepy middle section of Pink Floyd's 'Echoes' evoking thoughts of strange spiky lines springing up from the ground (another 'Stone Age' music reference for you). The musician Richard D. James (aka Aphex Twin) is known to have been inspired by his synaesthesia as well as lucid dreams in creating soundscapes such as those in his 1994 album, 'Selected Ambient Works Volume II.' The Russian author Vladimir Nabokov was also a known synaesthete, but I am not aware that Sting is, in spite of name-checking him in a Police song!

Back to the curving lines again, the songs on albums that I've had a long time always seem to be arranged down one side and back up the other, like a loop, or alternatively as two parallel sides joined across the middle like a backwards letter N. I guess younger synaesthetes would not have these perceptions, as modern music formats don't have two sides in the way that vinyl records or cassettes did.

This may all seem very odd to somebody without such neural connections, but to a certain extent, I think everybody experiences a kind of synaesthesia when they dream. The brain is filing away information during dreams, but in a way where everything is jumbled up. People from different eras of your life can intermingle for example, and places never seem quite the same as in reality. An experience I sometimes get is one of waking up laughing at some words that were said in a dream, but when I recall the words, there is nothing remotely funny about them. It's as though they have different associations to the subconscious, and therefore their own code of humour.

Dreams have always fascinated me, so it is no surprise that dreaming forms a core element of most of my psychological fiction works. And with that 'product placement' there is just the index of artists left to go. Happy browsing...

Index Of Artists

Further Suggested Reading

The following books cover albums and artists featured in this book in much greater depth. Fact checking for this book has come from online sources. For further info I heartily recommend the following books:

The Virgin All-Time 1000 Greatest Albums (Virgin) – Colin Larkin

Revolution in the Head (Pimlico) – Ian MacDonald

Ray Davies: A Complicated Life (Bodley Head) – Johnny Rogan

Bob Dylan: Recording Artist (Omnibus Press) – Paul Williams

The Complete Beatles Recording Sessions (Hamlyn) – Mark Lewisohn

Why We Love Music (John Murray Publishers) – John Powell

About Adam Colton

Born in 1975, Adam Colton is a writer of humorous travelogues and short stories from Kent, UK. His first paperback documented an attempt to visit every lighthouse on the mainland coast of England and Wales undertaken with his father, Roger Colton, who published and contributed to the book which was featured on the BBC news to mark National Lighthouse Day and became the subject of a question on the quiz show, University Challenge.

Since then, Adam has straddled the line between documenting his lightly philosophical UK travel escapades and mind-blowing fiction. One of his stories was short-listed for the HG Wells festival's short story competition. He is also a writer of topical songs, performing as one half of the duo Adam and Teresa, whose song 'Fat Cats with a Death Wish on the M25' received airplay on BBC Radio Kent.

If you have enjoyed this book please review it on your favourite online bookstore. Details of other books by Adam Colton are listed below.

NON-FICTION:

England and Wales in a Flash (father and son jaunt around the mainland coast in search of every lighthouse)

Mud, Sweat and Beers (two friends hike across Southern England from Kent to Somerset between two villages of the same name documenting their adventure)

Bordering on Lunacy (father and son explore the lighthouses of Southern Scotland and trace the route of the border with England)

Stair-Rods and Stars (enjoy the positive vibes as our roaming cyclist relishes the rail trails, ale trails, ridgeways and waterways of Southern England)

FICTION:

Codename: Narcissus (in Adam Colton's first novel, Tim is a cold controller, his wife is slowly losing it and his new best friend is you!)

The Dream Machine (Labyrinth of Dreams) (there's no escape from technology – even while you're sleeping. The 'Conundrum' stories about a dream recording machine form the basis of a novella)

The Nightshade Project (Donna is an ordinary teenager, but with a silicon chip brain implant as her eighteenth birthday present, is it Donna who is coming of age or the entire world?)

Conundrum - 'Seven Dreams of Reality' and 'The Kent-erbury Tales' (surreal short stories, often set at iconic Kentish locations, with dark twists and dystopian undertones)

Printed in Great Britain
by Amazon

67272436R00160